Securing Android Apps

In an era where mobile devices are extensions of our personal and professional lives, securing Android applications is no longer optional but imperative. Cyberattacks on mobile platforms surge yearly, with vulnerabilities in banking, healthcare, and social apps exposing sensitive data, eroding user trust, and costing enterprises millions. Yet, many developers and organizations remain trapped in reactive cycles, treating security as an afterthought rather than the foundation of innovation. This book is your antidote to complacency.

Securing Android Apps bridges the gap between mobile technology and cybersecurity, offering industry best practices and the latest research. By examining the Android ecosystem in detail and navigating its complex threat landscape, readers are equipped with robust strategies to integrate security into every stage of the application development lifecycle. Whether you are pioneering innovative mobile solutions or ensuring the safety of existing applications, this book provides the insights necessary for a secure and resilient mobile experience.

Key Features:

- A comprehensive understanding of mobile application security within the Android environment, including its unique challenges and threats.
- Analysis of factors contributing to insecure code empowers you to effectively identify and address potential weaknesses.
- Methods to seamlessly integrate robust security measures throughout the development lifecycle, thereby minimizing vulnerabilities and enhancing your overall security posture.
- Exploration of advanced defensive techniques, offering a deeper look at the inner workings of popular security systems and mechanisms beyond conventional automated tools.

Securing Android Apps

A Practical Approach for Secure Development

Sumit Kalaria

CRC Press
Taylor & Francis Group
Boca Raton London New York

CRC Press is an imprint of the
Taylor & Francis Group, an **informa** business

Designed cover image: Shutterstock ID: 1361135657

First edition published 2026
by CRC Press
2385 NW Executive Center Drive, Suite 320, Boca Raton FL 33431

and by CRC Press
4 Park Square, Milton Park, Abingdon, Oxon, OX14 4RN

CRC Press is an imprint of Taylor & Francis Group, LLC

© 2026 Sumit Kalaria

ISBN: 978-1-041-07044-3 (hbk)
ISBN: 978-1-041-07401-4 (pbk)
ISBN: 978-1-003-64033-2 (ebk)

DOI: 10.1201/9781003640332

Typeset in Sabon
by Deanta Global Publishing Services, Chennai, India

To my beloved wife, Harikrishna, and my extraordinary child, Pinank:

This book is a testament to the unwavering support and encouragement I have received from my wife. Her selflessness in granting me precious moments of solitude over the past six months allowed me to pour my heart into these pages. Without her, this endeavour would not have been possible.

And to my curious and spirited son: Your boundless enthusiasm for unravelling the mysteries of our world ignited a spark within me. It pushed me to explore beyond my perceived limits and to dive into uncharted territories of creativity and imagination.

May this book serve as a tribute to the love, inspiration, and resilience that family provides – a beacon guiding us to reach heights we never thought possible. Who knew parenting would be a crash course!

With heartfelt gratitude,

Sumit Kalaria

Contents

Acknowledgements

I express my deepest gratitude to CRC Press, part of the Taylor & Francis Group, for believing in this vision and providing me with the opportunity to share my work with a broader audience. Your support has been instrumental in bringing this book to life.

To my colleagues and mentors in the field of cybersecurity, thank you for your guidance and encouragement throughout this journey. Your insights have enriched my understanding and inspired the content of this book.

I would like to acknowledge the OWASP Foundation and the contributors to the Mobile Application Security Verification Standard (MASVS) and Mobile Security Testing Guide (MSTG). The organizational framework and security categories outlined in these resources inspired the structure of Chapter 8 in this book. However, all explanations and details are unique and varied.

A special thank you to my family and friends for their unwavering support and patience during the countless hours dedicated to this endeavour. Your belief in me has been a constant source of motivation.

Finally, to all the readers who embark on this journey with me, I hope this book serves as a valuable resource and ignites further exploration and innovation in the Android Application Security domain. Your quest for knowledge and dedication to securing mobile applications drive progress and excellence in this ever-evolving field.

Coverage

Chapter 5: Integrating Security in App Development Process

This chapter outlines strategies for integrating security into every phase of the application development lifecycle. It emphasizes the importance of adopting a proactive and holistic approach to security rather than treating it as an afterthought. Best practices guide developers in implementing a security-focused development process, including real-world scenarios.

Chapter 6: Implementing Secure SDLC for Android Applications

Building upon the principles introduced in the previous chapters, this chapter demonstrates how to implement a secure software development lifecycle (SDLC) specifically tailored for Android applications. It provides a comprehensive guide to integrating security practices into each stage of the SDLC, from project initiation to deployment. Practical illustrations cover the benefits of adopting a secure SDLC approach and help developers overcome common development challenges.

PART 3: SECURITY STANDARDS AND EMERGING TRENDS

Chapter 7: Exploring Android Security and OWASP MASVS

This chapter offers an overview of Android application security principles and introduces readers to the OWASP Mobile Application Security Verification Standard (MASVS). It explains the MASVS's objectives and structure and highlights its importance as a framework for assessing and improving the security of mobile applications.

Chapter 8: OWASP MASVS Insights

Taking a deeper dive into the OWASP MASVS, this chapter explores each level in detail. It provides practical guidance on implementing the MASVS requirements in Android application development, including a process for secure architecture design, coding practices, strategies, controls, etc. This chapter illustrates how adherence to the MASVS can enhance the security posture of Android applications.

Chapter 9: Anticipating Future Trends and Challenges

In the final chapter, readers are introduced to emerging trends and challenges in the field of application security. It explores topics such as emerging technologies (e.g., IoT integration, blockchain), new attack vectors (e.g., supply chain attacks, zero-day vulnerabilities), and evolving regulatory requirements (e.g., GDPR, CCPA). By staying informed about these trends and challenges, developers can anticipate future security threats and proactively adapt their security practices to address them.

Precautions

THE EVOLUTION OF ANDROID DEVELOPMENT AND SECURITY

The Android development landscape and cybersecurity practices evolve at a rapid pace. As a result, certain information presented in this book may become outdated as Android technologies, security frameworks, or standards advance. It is strongly recommended to verify that the content, such as security configurations, case scenarios, code examples, recommended controls, etc., remains current with the latest industry developments and best practices.

REAL-WORLD IMPLEMENTATION CONSIDERATIONS

The inclusion of scenarios, configurations, code snippets, etc., is designed for illustrative purposes and is intentionally simplified. Real-world implementation will require more comprehensive and robust security measures tailored to specific needs. It is advisable to consult experienced security professionals when applying these practices to production environments.

OVERLAPPING SECURITY CONCEPTS

Security concepts may overlap across multiple sections or chapters, as they must adapt to unique requirements. The tools, techniques, and frameworks mentioned are not the sole recommendations and should be selected and tailored based on individual requirements.

AI-ENHANCED CONTENT CREATION

Throughout this book, various AI tools, including large language models and generative AI, were utilized to enhance clarity and coherence. These tools offered invaluable assistance in refining the material while respecting the integrity of the author's original ideas, arguments, and content. Complete responsibility is taken for the accuracy and reliability of this work.

The following web-based AI tools have been used: OpenAI o3/GPT-4o, DeepSeek V3/R1, Claude 3/3.5

These AI tools helped polish the content, surface additional ideas, and identify any overlooked angles that I might not have come across or thought of due to human limitations. They served as supportive aids in enhancing and expanding upon my own work.

TECHNICAL SPECIFICATIONS

At the time of writing, the latest version of Android was 15, and the OWASP MASVS stood at version 2.1.0.

Prerequisites

To fully benefit from this book, you are encouraged to know the following:

FOUNDATIONAL UNDERSTANDING OF CYBERSECURITY PRINCIPLES

Familiarize yourself with fundamental cybersecurity concepts, including common terminology and best practices. It will help you contextualize the use of Android applications within the broader security landscape.

PROFICIENCY IN ANDROID PROGRAMMING (JAVA/KOTLIN)

Since Android applications primarily use Java or Kotlin, having a brief understanding of these programming languages is essential. You shall be working with Android-specific APIs and libraries, so familiarity with Android development is crucial.

AWARENESS OF SECURE DEVELOPMENT LIFECYCLE (SDLC)

Consider security throughout the software development lifecycle. Understand how security practices integrate into each phase, from requirements gathering to deployment. This perspective ensures that security is not an afterthought but an integral part of the development process.

FAMILIARITY WITH MULTIPLE TECHNOLOGIES

Several examples in the book involve Android application security and configurations. A basic understanding of different technologies will enhance your comprehension of this book.

Part I

The Android Odyssey

Android's dominance as a mobile operating system stems from its open-source nature, layered architecture, and vast user base. "Chapter 1: Understanding the Android ecosystem" explores:

- **Android's Architecture and Versions** – The importance of application programming interface (API) levels and security updates for compatibility and protection.
- **App Distribution and Security Policies** – The role of Google Play Store and alternative marketplaces in app security.
- **Challenges of Fragmentation and Android Open Source Project (AOSP)** – Managing device diversity and the implications of open-source development.
- **Development Lifecycle and Tools** – Integrating security from inception to deployment.
- **User Demographics and Market Trends** – Aligning app development with real-world usage patterns.

Android's popularity makes it a prime target for malicious actors. "Chapter 2: Navigating the Android threat landscape" examines critical threats, including but not limited to:

- **Malware and Phishing** – How malicious software and deceptive tactics compromise apps and users.
- **Data Leakage and Insecure APIs** – Risks of unintentional data exposure and vulnerable backend integrations.
- **Authentication Flaws and Man-in-the-Middle Attacks** – Exploiting weak identity management and intercepted communications.
- **Code Injection and Device Exploitation** – Manipulating app behaviour and leveraging hardware vulnerabilities.
- **Permission Misuse** – The dangers of excessive or unnecessary app permissions.

A secure app is only as strong as its testing and auditing processes. "Chapter 03: Android App testing essentials" covers:

- **Testing Strategies** – Ensuring performance, compatibility, and security across devices and OS versions.
- **Testing for Long-Term Integrity** – Regular reviews of security, privacy, and compliance to maintain trust.
- **Essential Tools** – Leveraging automation and analysis tools for efficient vulnerability detection.

DOI: 10.1201/9781003640332-1

Chapter 1

Understanding the Android Ecosystem

> Our goal is to make sure Android is the preferred choice for the next billion people to come online.
>
> – Sundar Pichai

This quote from Sundar Pichai underscores Google's vision for the future of Android: a platform that prioritizes accessibility and inclusivity, aiming to be the operating system of choice for a vast, diverse new wave of users entering the digital world.

The core principle of the Android ecosystem is openness and global reach. Its open-source nature enables affordability and customization, making it attractive to a wide range of users across the globe. The vast Android developer community continuously creates applications that cater to diverse needs, languages, and cultures, fostering inclusivity for these new users. By prioritizing accessibility and adaptability, Android positions itself as a key player in bridging the digital divide, helping to bring the next billion people online.

DOI: 10.1201/9781003640332-2

A LAYMAN'S PERSPECTIVE

Discover the Facets of Android

Welcome to the dynamic world of the Android ecosystem, a vast landscape of innovation, collaboration, and opportunity that has revolutionized how technology is interacted with. Developed by Google, Android stands as the cornerstone of mobile computing, powering a diverse range of devices and experiences that shape daily lives. This chapter embarks on a journey to explore the rich tapestry of the Android ecosystem, from its inception to its current status as the world's most popular mobile platform. By the end, readers will have a solid understanding of how Android works and why it is the preferred choice for billions of users worldwide.

Think of Android as the conductor of an orchestra, seamlessly coordinating apps, interfaces, and functionalities. Without Android, your device would be like a silent violin with no melody. Every action, from tapping a button to streaming a video, is meticulously managed by this operating system.

Now, take a peek behind the scenes. Android's architecture is like a multi-layered cake. At the base lies the Linux kernel, the sturdy foundation that handles essential functions like communicating with hardware (think of it as the cake's secret ingredient). On top of that are layers like the application framework (the creamy filling) and the apps themselves (the colourful icing). These layers work together seamlessly to create a delightful user experience.

Consider Android versions as different flavours of ice cream. Each new version brings unique features and improvements. API levels? They are like secret codes that developers use to interact with Android. Think of them as ensuring that apps speak the same language and work harmoniously, much like friends who understand each other perfectly.

Ever wonder where all those amazing apps on your phone come from? Most of them are available on the Google Play Store! Imagine it as a vast mall where you can find a wide variety of things to download. Developers set up their little shops (app listings), and you can explore, trying out different offerings. But remember, not all shops are equally safe; some might sell quirky hats, while others might be offering something more suspicious (malicious apps).

Have you heard of open-source? It is like sharing your toys with everyone so they can play too. That is what the Android Open Source Project (AOSP) is all about: making Android available for anyone to use and improve. AOSP shares the secret sauce, the code that makes Android work. Developers can look at the recipe, tweak it, and even create their own versions (custom ROMs). It is like turning a regular pizza into a pineapple-and-banana pizza (if that is your thing!).

Now, let's talk about Android phones. Have you ever noticed that not all Android phones look the same? That is because there are so many different kinds! Imagine Android as a big family reunion. Everyone brings their unique dishes (devices); some serve spicy curry (high-end phones), while others offer simple sandwiches (budget phones). Developers need to cook for all tastes, which can be challenging, but this variety keeps the party interesting!

If you have ever wondered how those fantastic apps on your phone are made, you are in for a treat! Developers use special tools to create Android magic (apps). Android Studio is their enchanted workshop, where they mix ingredients (code) and test their creations in emulators (virtual devices). Debugging? It is like fixing a wonky broomstick; it is essential to ensure everything works perfectly!

Creating an app is a bit like baking cookies. You plan (recipe), mix ingredients (code), bake (test), and finally, share with friends (release). The development lifecycle ensures that our cookies turn out delicious and bug-free.

Lastly, let's take a look at who is using Android and what they are into. Android has a massive fan club worldwide. People from different backgrounds, ages, and tastes love it. Trends change; today's unicorn-themed apps might become tomorrow's dragon-themed apps. Keeping an eye on user preferences and technological advancements helps developers stay ahead of the curve, ensuring their creations resonate with audiences worldwide.

1.1 Introduction to Android

A Secure and Versatile Platform

Android, an operating system developed by Google, has evolved from its origins as a mobile operating system (OS) into a comprehensive platform powering a vast array of devices. Initially designed for smartphones, Android's adaptability has allowed it to extend its reach into tablets, wearables, smart home appliances, automotive systems, foldables, and beyond. This versatility, combined with its open-source nature, has established Android as a dominant force in the global technology landscape, providing immense opportunities and security challenges for both developers and users.

1.1.1 Origin and Development

From Startup to Market Leader

From Android's visionary founding to becoming a market leader through continuous innovation, Android's journey has been marked by rapid development and significant advancements in mobile technology.

- **Founding Vision:** Android was founded in 2003 by Andy Rubin, Rich Miner, Nick Sears, and Chris White, with a vision to create a more flexible and user-friendly mobile operating system. Their goal was to democratize mobile computing by offering an open platform that could be adapted to a wide range of devices and use cases.
- **Google Acquisition & Accelerated Growth:** Acquired by Google in 2005, Android's development accelerated rapidly. The first commercial Android device, the HTC Dream (T-Mobile G1), launched in 2008, marked the beginning of Android's journey into the consumer market. Since then, Google has released numerous updates and iterations, each enhancing the platform's features, performance, and security. This rapid evolution has been driven by Google's commitment to addressing emerging user needs and security threats.
- **Continuous Evolution:** This continuous evolution reflects Android's commitment to innovation and security, introducing key enhancements such as biometric authentication, encrypted storage, and improved app permission controls, all aimed at safeguarding user data and enhancing user trust.

1.1.2 Platform Versatility

Beyond Smartphones

Android's unparalleled flexibility has enabled its expansion beyond smartphones to a diverse range of devices, each presenting unique security challenges that require tailored solutions.

- **Expansion into Diverse Devices:** What truly sets Android apart is its flexibility. Initially developed for smartphones, Android has proven adaptable to various hardware configurations, enabling it to power an extensive ecosystem of devices. Beyond phones and tablets, Android now runs on smartwatches (Wear OS), smart home devices (Google

Nest), automotive systems (Android Auto), and smart TVs (Android TV). Recent developments include the integration of Android into foldable devices, offering unique user experiences. This adaptability has made Android the operating system of choice for manufacturers seeking to innovate across multiple device categories.

- **Security Challenges in a Fragmented Ecosystem:** This broad compatibility not only drives Android's popularity but also introduces unique security challenges. Each device type requires specific security considerations due to different usage patterns, hardware capabilities, and user expectations. For example, smart home devices may prioritize seamless connectivity, while automotive systems must ensure real-time data security. The fragmentation of the Android ecosystem, with varying hardware specifications and software versions, further complicates the task of maintaining consistent security standards. Understanding these nuances is essential for developing secure applications across the Android ecosystem.

1.1.3 Developer Ecosystem

Empowering Innovation

Android's success is powered by a dynamic developer community bolstered by robust development tools and extensive frameworks, which enable the creation and secure distribution of innovative applications.

- **Software Development Kit (SDK) & Development Tools:** Android's success is deeply rooted in its vibrant developer community, which Google actively supports with a comprehensive suite of tools and resources. The Android Software Development Kit (SDK) provides developers with robust tools to build, test, and deploy applications, ensuring compatibility and security across devices. With the rise of Kotlin Multiplatform Mobile (KMM) and Jetpack Compose, Google is streamlining cross-platform and declarative UI development, reducing reliance on third-party frameworks. These tools are continuously updated to incorporate the latest security features and best practices.
- **Google Play as a Distribution Channel:** The official app store, Google Play, serves as a crucial distribution platform, enabling developers to reach a global audience while adhering to stringent security guidelines. Google Play's security initiatives, such as Google Play Protect, help maintain a safe app ecosystem by scanning and verifying apps for malware. Additionally, Google Play's App Signing feature ensures that apps cannot be tampered with after publication.
- **Innovation through Frameworks & APIs:** Furthermore, Google's extensive frameworks and APIs, such as those for location services, augmented reality (AR), and machine learning (ML), offer developers the ability to create innovative, secure applications. This dynamic ecosystem fosters collaboration and innovation, making it a fertile ground for developing new security solutions and enhancing app robustness. For example, the Biometric API simplifies the integration of fingerprint and facial recognition, ensuring secure authentication across devices.

1.1.4 Customization and Personalization

Balancing Flexibility and Security

Android's open customization empowers users with extensive personalization options, yet it requires a careful balance with security to mitigate the risks associated with third-party modifications.

- **The Power of Open Customization:** One of Android's defining features is its openness and the ability it gives users and developers to customize their experiences. Unlike more restrictive ecosystems, Android allows extensive personalization, from home screen layouts and third-party launchers to a myriad of widgets and themes. Material You, now fully integrated across Android 13 and 14, allows dynamic theming based on user preferences. However, deep customization, especially through third-party launchers and ROMs, remains a double-edged sword, bringing potential security and compatibility issues.
- **Security Risks of Third-party Modifications:** While this flexibility is a key strength, it also poses significant security challenges. Customization can sometimes lead to vulnerabilities if third-party apps or modifications bypass standard security protocols. For instance, custom ROMs or unauthorized app stores may lack the rigorous security checks of official channels, increasing the risk of malware. Thus, developers must ensure that their applications adhere to Android's security best practices, even when offering extensive customization options. Recent efforts, like the introduction of Play Integrity API, help developers maintain app security even in customizable environments.

1.1.5 Security and Privacy

Cornerstones of the Android Experience

Security and privacy are core pillars of the Android experience, with robust mechanisms and vigilant practices designed to safeguard user data and maintain a secure ecosystem.

- **Core Security Mechanisms:** As the world's leading mobile operating system, Android places a strong emphasis on security and privacy to protect its vast user base. Google regularly releases security updates and patches to address emerging threats, ensuring that users are protected against the latest vulnerabilities. Android incorporates robust security mechanisms such as sandboxing, encryption, and a comprehensive permissions model to safeguard user data. Android 14 further restricts background app access to sensors and introduces per-app language preferences, while Android 15 mandates hardware-backed encryption for app data and strengthens OTA update integrity.
- **Google Play Protect:** The sandboxing model ensures that applications run in isolated environments, preventing malicious apps from affecting other parts of the system. Encryption protects user data, while the permission model gives users control over what information apps can access. Google Play Protect, integrated into the Play Store, adds an additional layer of security by continuously scanning apps for malware and other malicious activities, reinforcing Android's commitment to a secure user environment. This proactive approach helps mitigate risks even before they reach the end user.
- **The Role of User & Developer Vigilance:** Despite these measures, the open nature of Android requires continuous vigilance from both users and developers to maintain a secure and trustworthy ecosystem. Developers must stay informed about the latest security practices, while users should regularly update their devices and be cautious about app permissions. Educating users about security best practices is equally important, as human error remains one of the most common causes of security breaches.

1.2 Architecture Overview

A Secure Foundation

The architecture of the Android operating system is a meticulously designed, multi-layered structure that balances performance, functionality, and security. Built upon the robust Linux kernel, Android's architecture comprises distinct layers, each contributing to the system's overall stability and security. Understanding these layers, from the application layer to the Linux kernel, is crucial for developers aiming to build secure and efficient applications. This section provides an in-depth exploration of Android's architectural components, emphasizing their roles in ensuring a secure foundation for app development.

1.2.1 Application Layer

User-Facing Security

The application layer is the topmost layer of the Android architecture and the interface between the user and the device. It is where all user-installed and system applications reside, providing various functionalities from productivity tools and entertainment apps to communication services and utilities.

- **User Interaction and Security:** Applications at this layer interact directly with the user, accessing a range of device features and data. This makes the application layer a primary target for malicious activities. Understanding how to securely develop and configure applications to minimize risks, such as through proper permission management and secure data handling, is critical. For example, apps should request only the permissions they absolutely need, following the principle of least privilege.
- **Sandboxing and Isolation:** Each application runs in its own sandboxed environment, enforced by the underlying Linux kernel. This isolation prevents applications from directly interacting with each other or the system without explicit permission, significantly reducing the risk of malicious behaviour spreading across apps. Recent security enhancements, like Scoped Storage, introduced in Android 10, it is now enforced by default, significantly limiting app access to shared storage and reducing risks of data leakage. Apps must use media-specific permissions or the Storage Access Framework for broader access.

1.2.2 Application Framework

Tools for Secure Development

The Application Framework provides the fundamental building blocks and APIs (application programming interfaces) that developers use to create applications. This layer includes a rich set of services and system components designed to simplify application development while ensuring security and efficiency.

- **Core Components:** Key components of the application framework include:
  - **Activities:** Define the user interface and handle user interactions.
  - **Services:** Manage background processing tasks.

- **Content Providers:** Facilitate data sharing between applications securely.
- **Broadcast Receivers:** Handle system-wide broadcast announcements.
    - These components are designed with security in mind, ensuring that apps can interact with system resources and other apps only in a controlled manner, governed by a strict permission model.
- **Security Features:** The framework enforces security through permissions, which control what system features and data an app can access. Proper permission implementation and the use of secure APIs help prevent unauthorized access and protect user data. Recent features, such as the Data Access Audit API, allow developers to monitor how their apps access user data, ensuring transparency and compliance with privacy regulations. This is particularly important in light of regulations like General Data Protection Regulation (GDPR) and California Consumer Privacy Act (CCPA), which mandate strict data protection standards.

1.2.3 Libraries

Pre-Built Solutions with Security in Mind

Android includes various libraries that provide pre-built functionality for developers, ranging from graphics rendering and database management to networking and multimedia processing.

- **Optimized and Secure:** These libraries are optimized for performance and security, allowing developers to build powerful applications without needing to write complex code from scratch. Leveraging these libraries helps ensure that common functions adhere to best security practices, reducing the likelihood of introducing vulnerabilities. For example, the SQLite library simplifies database management while ensuring data integrity and security.
- **Security Libraries:** Android provides specific libraries focused on security, such as encryption libraries and secure networking protocols. Developers are encouraged to use these libraries to implement secure communication and data storage practices. For instance, the Jetpack Security library simplifies encrypting files and shared preferences, making it easier to protect sensitive user data. This library uses industry-standard encryption algorithms, ensuring robust data protection.

1.2.4 Android Runtime (ART)

Efficient and Secure Execution

The Android Runtime (ART) is the environment in which Android applications execute. ART replaced the older Dalvik Virtual Machine (DVM) and offers improved performance and security features.

- **Managed Code Execution:** ART executes app code within a managed environment, translating the app's bytecode into machine code. This process includes optimizations for faster execution and better memory management, which is critical for maintaining app performance and security. ART's Ahead-Of-Time (AOT) compilation ensures that apps are pre-compiled, reducing runtime overhead and improving security.

- **Memory Management and Security:** ART includes a sophisticated garbage collection process that helps manage memory more efficiently and securely, reducing the risk of memory leaks and other vulnerabilities that could be exploited by malicious software. Additionally, ART supports features like Just-In-Time (JIT) compilation and Ahead-Of-Time (AOT) compilation, which enhance runtime performance and security. These features collectively ensure that apps run smoothly while minimizing security risks.

1.2.5 Linux Kernel

The Core of Security

At the foundation of the Android operating system lies the Linux Kernel, which provides the core system functionality and enforces the platform's security model.

- **Process Isolation and Security:** The kernel is responsible for managing core system services such as process management, memory allocation, and device drivers. It enforces strict process isolation, which is fundamental to Android's security model. This isolation ensures that each application runs in a separate user space, preventing direct access to the kernel or other applications' memory. This isolation is critical for preventing privilege escalation attacks.
- **Hardware Abstraction and Security Mechanisms:** The kernel also abstracts the hardware layer, providing a standardized interface for interacting with hardware components. This abstraction layer is crucial for security, as it shields the system and applications from direct hardware manipulation. The kernel implements various security mechanisms, including Secure Boot, which ensures the integrity of the operating system from the moment the device is powered on. Recent additions like Project Mainline (now Google Play System Updates) and the introduction of modular system components in Android 15 allow Google to update critical OS components directly through the Play Store.
- **Kernel Hardening:** Android 14+ requires Kernel Control Flow Integrity (kCFI) and memory-safe Rust modules (replacing almost 30% of C/C++ code) to mitigate zero-day exploits.

1.3 Android Versions and API Levels

Evolution with Security in Focus

The evolution of the Android operating system is a testament to continuous innovation and an unwavering focus on security. Each new version, identified by unique names and numbers, brings substantial updates that enhance functionality, optimize performance, and address emerging security threats. Understanding these versions and their associated API levels is essential for developers aiming to build secure and innovative applications. This section explores the significant milestones in Android's security journey, the critical importance of API levels in secure development practices, and how the platform's evolution shapes the modern approach to mobile application security.

1.3.1 Innovation, Security, and Compatibility

Evolution of Android

Android's evolution is driven by a delicate balance between cutting-edge innovation, robust security frameworks, and thoughtful backward compatibility. Developers must master this strategic triangle to create applications that are future-proof, secure by design, and accessible across the diverse Android ecosystem.

- **The Journey of Android Versions:** Android's evolution is marked by incremental version releases, each identified by a number and often a playful name (e.g., Android 4.4 KitKat, Android 5.0 Lollipop). These releases represent significant milestones in the platform's development, introducing new functionalities, user interface redesigns, performance optimizations, and security enhancements. With each update, Google addresses emerging trends and threats in the mobile landscape, ensuring that Android remains a cutting-edge operating system. For developers, understanding these changes is crucial. Major updates not only bring exciting opportunities but also present challenges in adapting to new standards while maintaining compatibility with older devices. This balance between innovation and reach is at the heart of Android development.
- **API Levels: The Developer's Toolkit:** Each Android version is paired with a specific API level, which defines the set of application programming interfaces (APIs) available to developers. These APIs act as the bridge between applications and the operating system, enabling developers to interact with core functionalities such as UI components, device sensors, and security features. Knowing the API compatibility of your app is vital for ensuring it functions correctly across different versions of Android. Each API level corresponds to a specific Android version and includes all previous APIs, allowing developers to target a range of devices. By targeting a specific API level, developers can access the latest features while implementing fallback mechanisms to support older devices.
- **Balancing Innovation with Reach:** One of the key challenges for developers is balancing the use of the latest platform enhancements with the need to maintain compatibility with older devices. To address this, developers must adopt a strategic approach when targeting API levels. For example, using libraries like AndroidX enables developers to incorporate modern features while maintaining backward compatibility with earlier versions of Android. By carefully managing compatibility considerations, developers can ensure their applications reach the broadest possible audience. This approach allows apps to provide a rich, modern user experience on newer devices while remaining functional and accessible on older ones.

1.3.2 Enhancements and Optimizations

Building Better Apps

Android's continuous feature enhancements and performance optimizations provide developers with an evolving toolkit for building applications that are both secure and efficient. By leveraging these advancements strategically, developers can create applications that protect user data without compromising the user experience.

- **Unlocking New Possibilities:** With every new Android release, Google introduces APIs that unlock innovative capabilities and improve existing ones. These feature enhancements empower developers to create more robust, engaging, and secure applications. Each version brings advancements in security mechanisms, such as improved encryption standards, more granular permissions, and better data protection tools. For example, Android 11 introduced one-time permissions, giving users greater control over sensitive data access and helping developers comply with evolving privacy regulations.
- **Enhancing User Experience:** Google is committed to optimizing the performance of the Android platform with each release. These optimizations include improvements to system-level processes, resource management, power efficiency, etc., that result in smoother performance, faster app loading times, improved overall responsiveness, etc. By taking advantage of Android's ongoing optimizations, developers can ensure their apps remain competitive and meet user expectations for speed and reliability.

1.3.3 Security Enhancements Over the Years

From Basics to Breakthroughs

The security architecture of Android has evolved from basic protections to a sophisticated, multi-layered defence system. Understanding this evolution is crucial for developers seeking to leverage the full spectrum of available security mechanisms. Below are the transformative security milestones across different Android versions, each representing a significant advancement in the platform's security posture:

- **Android 4.4 (KitKat, API Level 19–20):** Introduced SELinux (Security-Enhanced Linux) to enforce mandatory access control policies, enhancing overall system security by limiting the permissions of processes. This marked a significant shift in Android's security model, providing a robust foundation for future enhancements.
- **Android 5.0 (Lollipop, API Level 21–22):** Implemented full disk encryption to protect user data on lost or stolen devices and introduced the Material Design for a more intuitive user experience. Full disk encryption ensured that all user data was encrypted by default, significantly reducing the risk of data breaches.
- **Android 6.0 (Marshmallow, API Level 23):** Introduced the runtime permissions model, allowing users to grant permissions at runtime rather than during app installation. This provides better control over app access and increases user trust. This model empowered users to make informed decisions about app permissions, setting a new standard for privacy.
- **Android 7.0 (Nougat, API Level 24–25):** Added Direct Boot for faster device startup and improved security, and implemented File-based Encryption to better separate and protect user data. File-based encryption allowed for more granular control over data access, enhancing security for sensitive information.
- **Android 8.0 (Oreo, API Level 26-27):** Enhanced security with Project Treble, modularizing the OS to speed up updates, and introduced Google Play Protect for app security. Project Treble addressed the long-standing issue of slow OS updates, ensuring that devices could receive timely security patches.
- **Android 9.0 (Pie, API Level 28):** Introduced Android Protected Confirmation for secure transactions, improved biometric authentication, and added privacy enhancements like lockdown mode. Lockdown mode allowed users to disable biometric authentication temporarily, providing an additional layer of security in sensitive situations.

- **Android 10 (API Level 29):** Added support for TLS 1.3 for secure internet connections, improved user privacy controls with more granular location permissions, and enforced scoped storage to limit app access to external storage. Scoped storage was a game-changer for privacy, preventing apps from accessing unrelated files on shared storage.
- **Android 11 (API Level 30):** To enhance user privacy, it introduced one-time permissions for sensitive data access, enforced scoped storage more strictly, and added an auto-reset feature for unused app permissions. Auto-reset permissions ensured that apps could not retain access to sensitive data indefinitely, reducing the risk of misuse.
- **Android 12 (API Level 31–32):** A Privacy Dashboard was added to give users a clear view of data access, microphone and camera indicators were introduced, and users could grant apps access to approximate locations instead of precise locations. These features provided users with unprecedented transparency and control over their data.
- **Android 13 (API Level 33):** Required explicit user permission for apps to send notifications, introduced runtime permissions for accessing specific types of media, and enhanced cryptographic key management with improved Keystore and KeyMint. These changes further tightened app permissions, ensuring that users had complete control over their device's functionality.
- **Android 14 (API Level 34):** Introduced predictive back gestures for better navigation security, implemented the Credential Manager API for secure credential handling, and enhanced malware detection through improvements in Google Play Protect. The Credential Manager API simplified secure authentication, making it easier for developers to implement robust security measures.
- **Android 15 (API Level 35):** Enhanced user privacy by implementing encrypted backups, introduced mandatory hardware-backed encryption for all apps, and improved the security of over-the-air (OTA) updates to prevent unauthorized modifications. These advancements ensured that user data remained secure, even during backups and updates.

1.4 Google Play Store

A Secure Gateway to the World of Apps

The Google Play Store stands as the cornerstone of the Android ecosystem, serving as the primary marketplace for Android applications and a critical component for maintaining the platform's security and integrity. For developers, it offers an unparalleled opportunity to showcase their creations to a global audience, while for users, it provides a trusted environment for discovering and downloading applications. This section explores the significance, functionality, and security measures of the Google Play Store with a focus on how developers can leverage its features for secure application distribution.

1.4.1 Market Dominance and Reach

Connecting with a Global Audience

The Google Play Store dominates the Android app market, providing developers with access to billions of active Android users worldwide. Its widespread availability on Android devices ensures that developers can reach a vast and diverse audience without significant barriers.

The Play Store's global reach, combined with its localized support for different languages and payment methods, allows developers to effectively distribute their apps to users across various regions and demographics. For instance, developers can tailor their apps to specific markets by offering localized content and integrating region-specific payment gateways, such as Unified Payments Interface (UPI) in India or PayPal in the United States.

1.4.2 Monetization Opportunities

Transforming Innovation into Revenue

The Google Play Store provides multiple monetization models for developers to generate revenue from their apps. These models cater to different types of apps and user preferences:

- **Freemium:** Apps offer basic functionality for free while charging for premium features or content, allowing users to try before they buy. This model is particularly effective for gaming apps, where users can unlock advanced levels or features through in-app purchases.
- **In-App Purchases:** Developers can sell additional content, features, or virtual goods within their apps, providing a flexible monetization strategy that can enhance user engagement. For example, productivity apps often offer premium templates or tools as in-app purchases.
- **Subscriptions:** Apps can offer access to premium content or services on a recurring basis, creating a steady revenue stream and encouraging ongoing user engagement. Streaming services like Spotify and Netflix leverage this model to provide continuous value to users.
- **Advertising:** Displaying ads within apps can generate revenue while allowing users to access the core functionality for free. However, developers must ensure that ads are not intrusive and comply with Google's ad policies. Google's AdMob platform provides tools to integrate ads seamlessly while maintaining a positive user experience.

1.4.3 App Submission Process

Ensuring Quality and Compliance

To list an app on the Play Store, developers must package it into an Android App Bundle (AAB) or APK (Android Package) file and provide comprehensive metadata, including the app title, description, screenshots, and promotional images. More importantly, developers must adhere to Google's stringent policies and guidelines regarding content, security, and user experience. The submission process includes several key security checkpoints:

- **Compliance with Policies:** Developers must ensure their apps comply with Google's Developer Program Policies, which cover a wide range of topics, from privacy and intellectual property to user data protection and content restrictions. For example, apps must clearly disclose how user data is collected, used, and shared, in compliance with privacy regulations like GDPR.
- **App Review Process:** Before an app is published, it undergoes a review process by Google to ensure compliance with these standards. This review process is designed to maintain quality across the platform and protect users from harmful content or malicious apps. Google's automated and manual review systems work together to detect policy violations, ensuring a safe and trustworthy app ecosystem.

1.4.4 Global Distribution

Making Apps Accessible worldwide

Once approved, an app is published to the Play Store and becomes accessible to users worldwide. Users can discover apps through searches, categories, recommendations, and curated lists.

The Play Store's powerful discovery tools and algorithms help match users with apps that meet their needs and interests, enhancing user satisfaction and increasing the visibility of quality apps. For instance, Google Play's "Editor's Choice" and "Top Charts" sections highlight high-quality apps, driving downloads and engagement.

1.4.5 User Engagement and Feedback

Building a Strong Connection

The Google Play Store facilitates user engagement through ratings, reviews, and feedback mechanisms. Users can rate and review apps, providing valuable insights to both developers and potential users.

Positive reviews and high ratings significantly impact an app's visibility and success on the platform. Apps with higher ratings are more likely to appear in search results and recommendations, driving organic growth. Developers are encouraged to respond to user feedback, address concerns, and implement suggestions to improve their apps and maintain a positive relationship with their user base. For example, addressing user complaints about bugs or usability issues can lead to improved ratings and increased user retention.

1.4.6 Continuous Updates and Maintenance

Keeping Apps Secure and Current

Developers can release updates to their apps on the Play Store to introduce new features, fix bugs, and improve performance. Regular updates are crucial for maintaining app security and enhancing user experience. The Play Store notifies users of available updates, encouraging them to stay current with the latest versions of their installed apps.

Timely security updates are essential for patching vulnerabilities and addressing security issues. Google's guidelines emphasize the importance of regularly updating apps to fix bugs and security flaws, helping protect users from emerging threats.

1.4.7 Security and Trust

Safeguarding the Android Ecosystem

Security and trust are at the heart of the Google Play Store. Google employs various security measures to ensure the safety of apps listed on the Play Store, including:

- **Google Play Protect:** This is a built-in malware protection service that continuously scans apps on the Play Store and on users' devices for malicious activity. It uses machine learning and threat intelligence to detect and prevent malware and other harmful apps. In 2022 alone, Google Play Protect scanned over 125 billion apps for malware, highlighting its critical role in maintaining app security.

- **App Signing:** All apps on the Play Store are required to be signed by their developers. App signing ensures the authenticity of the app and prevents unauthorized modifications. Google's Play App Signing service offers an additional layer of security by securely managing app signing keys. This prevents attackers from tampering with apps and redistributing them with malicious code.
- **Security Policies and Guidelines:** Google enforces strict security policies and guidelines for apps distributed through the Play Store. These policies cover various aspects of app behaviour, including data privacy, user permissions, and advertising practices, helping maintain a secure and trustworthy environment for users. For instance, apps must request only the permissions necessary for their functionality, following the principle of least privilege.
- **Transparency Reports:** Google regularly publishes transparency reports that detail the efforts taken to remove harmful apps and maintain the security of the Play Store. These reports provide insights into the types of threats faced and the actions taken to protect users. For example, in 2021, Google removed over 1.2 million policy-violating apps from the Play Store, demonstrating its commitment to user safety.
- **Improved Malware Detection:** Google's advancements in malware detection, powered by artificial intelligence (AI) models and machine learning algorithms, have significantly strengthened its ability to identify and remove harmful apps proactively. These efforts have minimized the number of malicious apps reaching users, enhancing the overall security of the Play Store.
- **Privacy Sandbox:** It is a fully integrated initiative within Android that redefines advertising privacy. It enhances user privacy by strictly limiting the sharing of user data with third parties and operating without cross-app identifiers. It has fundamentally changed how apps handle user data for advertising, setting a new standard for creating privacy-focused advertising solutions while complying with evolving regulations.

1.5 Alternative App Stores

Exploring the Appverse Beyond the Mainstream

While the Google Play Store remains the primary marketplace for Android applications, developers have the flexibility to distribute their apps through various alternative app stores. These additional channels cater to different user segments, offer unique opportunities, and can significantly impact an app's reach and visibility. However, distributing through alternative app stores also introduces unique security challenges that developers must address to protect both their applications and end users.

Here are some of the most notable alternative app stores:

- **Amazon Appstore:** The Amazon Appstore is accessible on Amazon Fire tablets, Fire TV devices, and Android smartphones through a downloadable app. It provides developers with an opportunity to tap into Amazon's vast user base, particularly those heavily integrated into Amazon's ecosystem. This store is known for its stringent review process, which helps maintain a secure environment for both developers and users.
- **Samsung Galaxy Store:** Pre-installed on Samsung devices such as smartphones and tablets, the Samsung Galaxy Store offers developers direct access to Samsung's extensive user base. This store allows developers to leverage unique Samsung features and integrations, enhancing app functionality on Samsung devices. The Galaxy Store also employs rigorous security checks to ensure app quality and safety.

- **Huawei AppGallery:** With Huawei's significant presence in the global smartphone market, the Huawei AppGallery serves as a key platform for reaching Huawei device users, especially in regions where Google Mobile Services are restricted or unavailable. Despite challenges, Huawei has been actively developing its app ecosystem and offers various incentives for developers. However, developers must consider the security implications and compatibility issues due to the lack of Google Play Services.
- **Xiaomi GetApps:** Pre-installed on Xiaomi devices, GetApps provides access to a large user base in markets where Xiaomi smartphones are popular. It offers developers an additional channel to distribute their apps, especially in regions like China and India.
- **Third-Party Marketplaces:** Numerous third-party marketplaces exist for Android app distribution, often catering to specific regions or niches. These platforms can offer unique features or focus on particular types of apps, providing developers with opportunities to target niche audiences or gain visibility in specific markets. However, the security standards of these stores can vary significantly, requiring careful consideration.
- **Regulatory Developments and DMA Implementation:** The European Union's Digital Markets Act (DMA) became fully enforceable in 2024, requiring major platforms to allow alternative app stores and sideloading. This has led to the emergence of new regional app stores and changed distribution strategies, particularly in European markets. Google has implemented changes to comply with these regulations while maintaining security standards.

1.6 Android Open Source Project (AOSP)

Building Knowledge and Innovation Together

The Android Open Source Project (AOSP) forms the foundation of the Android operating system, providing a comprehensive, open-source framework accessible to developers and device manufacturers worldwide. Governed by Google, AOSP includes the core OS code, security architecture, tools, and documentation needed to build custom versions of Android. This open approach enables transparency, security validation, customization, and community collaboration, which are the essential elements for a secure mobile ecosystem.

1.6.1 Objectives of AOSP

The Vision Behind the Android Open Source Project

The Android Open Source Project is built on principles that promote an open and collaborative development environment:

- **Openness and Transparency:** AOSP encourages a transparent development process where developers can inspect, modify, and contribute to the Android source code. This openness fosters a global community of developers and allows for diverse contributions, ensuring that the platform evolves with the needs of its users. Android 14 continues this tradition by making its source code available upon release, allowing immediate community engagement.
- **Customization:** AOSP enables device manufacturers and developers to create tailored versions of Android that meet specific hardware and software requirements. This flexibility allows for the development of unique user experiences across a wide range of devices, from smartphones and tablets to smart TVs, wearables, and automotive systems like Android Automotive OS.

- **Community Engagement:** By involving a global community of developers, AOSP promotes innovation and rapid advancements in mobile technology. Projects like the Generic Kernel Image (GKI), which addresses kernel fragmentation by unifying the core kernel and moving SoC and board support into loadable vendor modules, exemplify the collaborative spirit of AOSP. Recent enhancements in GKI have improved kernel modularity, making it easier for manufacturers to provide updates and maintain consistency across devices.

1.6.2 Key Components of AOSP

Building Blocks of the Android Ecosystem

AOSP consists of several key components that provide the foundation for Android development and customization:

- **Source Code:** The comprehensive source code for the Android OS is available for download and modification. This includes the Linux kernel, system libraries, and the Android Runtime, all of which are essential for creating custom Android builds or contributing improvements to the project. The open availability of this code allows developers to innovate freely while maintaining the security standards expected of the Android platform.
- **Documentation:** AOSP provides extensive documentation that covers the architecture, APIs, development practices, and guidelines for contributing to the project. This includes regular updates like the Android Security Bulletin, Android Automotive Bulletin, and Pixel Update Bulletin, which offer critical information about security vulnerabilities and updates. Recent efforts have focused on improving documentation for features introduced in Android 14, such as the Predictive Back Gesture, which enhances navigation experiences. Such transparency is vital for maintaining the security and reliability of the Android ecosystem.
- **Build System:** AOSP includes tools for compiling the Android source code into a runnable OS. These tools, which include build scripts, configuration files, and makefiles, automate the build process and ensure consistency across different builds. This build system is integral for developers who wish to create customized versions of Android that meet specific security or functionality requirements. The adoption of Soong, a new build system replacing the older Make-based system, offers better performance and streamlined configuration. Kotlin support is now mandatory for modern AOSP contributions.
- **Compatibility Test Suite (CTS):** The CTS is a suite of tests designed to ensure device compatibility with the Android ecosystem. It validates that custom Android implementations meet Google's compatibility standards, ensuring that apps work consistently across different devices and versions of Android. Compliance with the CTS helps maintain a secure and unified ecosystem, reducing fragmentation and ensuring a stable user experience.
- **Project Treble and Project Mainline:** These initiatives aim to simplify the update process and reduce fragmentation. Project Treble, introduced in Android 8.0, modularizes the Android OS to facilitate faster updates. Project Mainline (now known as Google Play System Updates) allows critical OS components to be updated through the Google Play Store, ensuring users receive important updates promptly, even without a full OS upgrade.

1.6.3 Benefits of AOSP

Why Open-source Matters

AOSP offers numerous benefits that contribute to the widespread adoption and continuous evolution of the Android platform:

- **Innovation:** By providing open access to the operating system, AOSP fosters innovation, allowing developers to experiment and create new features or enhancements. This openness has led to many groundbreaking features and improvements in Android, contributing to its status as a leading mobile OS.
- **Flexibility:** Developers and manufacturers can tailor Android to suit specific needs, whether for smartphones, tablets, wearables, or other devices. This flexibility supports the development of innovative applications that leverage full hardware capabilities, essential for devices like foldable phones, smartwatches, and Internet of Things (IoT) devices.
- **Security:** The open nature of AOSP allows for continuous scrutiny and improvement of the Android codebase. The community-driven approach ensures that vulnerabilities are identified and addressed promptly, contributing to a more secure platform overall. In Android 14, Google has enhanced security features, such as improved credential management, stricter permissions, and the integration of memory-safe languages like Rust to reduce vulnerabilities.
- **Cost Efficiency:** AOSP reduces development costs by offering a free and well-documented foundation for creating new devices and applications. This makes Android an attractive option for device manufacturers and developers alike, enabling them to focus on innovation without the burden of licensing fees.

1.6.4 How to Get Involved

Contributing to the Android Community

There are several ways for developers to engage with the AOSP community and contribute to the project:

- **Downloading the Source:** Developers can download the Android source code from the official AOSP repository. This access allows them to inspect the code, make modifications, and create custom Android builds that suit their specific needs or contribute new features and improvements to the broader community.
- **Contributing Code:** Developers can contribute to AOSP by submitting patches and improvements through Gerrit, the web-based code review system used by AOSP. Google provides detailed guidelines for contributing to the project, ensuring that all contributions are consistent and of high quality. This collaborative approach helps maintain the integrity and security of the Android codebase.
- **Participating in Discussions:** Developers can engage with the Android developer community through forums, mailing lists, and collaborative platforms like the AOSP issue tracker and Android subreddit. These platforms provide a space for developers to share ideas, ask questions, and find solutions to common problems, fostering a vibrant and supportive community.
- **Reporting Issues and Security Vulnerabilities:** Developers can report bugs or security vulnerabilities via the Android Open-Source Project Issue Tracker or participate in the

Android Security Rewards Program. This collaboration helps improve the platform's security and reliability.

- **Joining Developer Programs:** Participate in programs like the Android Beta Program, which allows developers to test pre-release versions of Android and provide feedback. Attend events like the Android Dev Summit and Google I/O to stay updated on the latest developments and network with other professionals.

NOTE: As of 2025, Google has transitioned AOSP development to focus on the android-latest-release manifest system, automatically pointing developers to the most recent stable release with integrated security patches. The introduction of Rust programming language components in AOSP has significantly improved memory safety, with critical system components being gradually rewritten in Rust to eliminate entire classes of vulnerabilities.

1.7 Device Fragmentation

Navigating the OS Odyssey

In the dynamic landscape of mobile technology, device fragmentation remains one of the most significant challenges for developers within the Android ecosystem. This phenomenon refers to the vast diversity in hardware specifications, software versions, and device capabilities across Android devices, creating a complex environment that requires strategic approaches to ensure consistent app functionality, performance, and security.

1.7.1 Understanding Device Fragmentation

Navigating a Diverse Hardware Ecosystem

Understanding device fragmentation is crucial in navigating Android's diverse hardware ecosystem, which encompasses various device types, hardware configurations, and software versions, each introducing unique complexities in app development.

- **Expanding Device Types:** The range of Android devices has expanded beyond smartphones and tablets to include wearables, smart TVs, automotive systems, foldable phones, and IoT devices. The emergence of devices like foldables with variable screen sizes and shapes introduces new complexities in app design and functionality.
- **Hardware Diversity:** Variations in CPU architectures (ARM, ARM64, x86), GPU capabilities, memory, storage, camera systems, biometric sensors, and connectivity options (4G, 5G, Wi-Fi 6) require developers to account for a wide array of hardware capabilities.
- **Software Versions:** While Android 14 has been released, a significant portion of devices still run older Android versions due to delayed updates from manufacturers or carrier restrictions. This results in a fragmented software landscape where devices operate on different API levels with varying features and security updates.

1.7.2 Key Challenges of Device Fragmentation

Overcoming Compatibility and Performance Issues

Device fragmentation in the Android ecosystem presents significant challenges in compatibility, performance, and security, requiring developers to ensure their apps perform optimally across a diverse range of hardware and software configurations.

- **Hardware Diversity:** Android devices come in many forms, with significant variations in screen sizes, resolutions, CPU architectures, RAM sizes, storage capacities, sensor configurations, and device form factors. This diversity requires developers to design apps that can seamlessly adapt to different hardware specifications, ensuring optimal performance and a consistent user experience.
- **Software Versions:** Due to Android's open-source nature and the wide range of device manufacturers, numerous software versions are running on devices at any given time. Each version may introduce new features or deprecate old ones, creating potential compatibility issues. Developers must account for these differences to ensure their apps function correctly across various Android versions.
- **Security Implications:** Fragmentation also impacts security, as devices running older Android versions may not receive timely security updates, leaving them vulnerable to exploitation. This inconsistency in security patch deployment can lead to a fragmented security landscape where some devices are protected against recent threats while others remain exposed.
- **Testing and Optimization:** Ensuring consistent performance, security, and user experience across diverse devices requires extensive testing and optimization. Developers must invest significant resources into testing their apps across a wide range of devices to identify and address compatibility and security issues.

1.7.3 Addressing Device Fragmentation

Strategies for a Seamless Experience

Addressing device fragmentation involves implementing responsive design, adaptive layouts, and feature detection, alongside ensuring backward compatibility and extensive testing, to provide a seamless experience across a diverse range of Android devices.

- **Responsive Design:** Implementing responsive design principles allows apps to dynamically adapt to different screen sizes, resolutions, and orientations. This approach ensures a consistent user experience across devices, regardless of their display characteristics.
- **Adaptive Layouts:** By creating adaptive layouts that adjust based on available screen real estate, developers can optimize their apps for various screen sizes and resolutions. This not only enhances usability but also ensures that the app remains functional and visually appealing on all devices.
- **Feature Detection:** Utilizing feature detection techniques enables apps to adjust their functionality based on the capabilities of the device. This ensures that features are only enabled on supported devices, enhancing compatibility and preventing crashes or performance issues on devices lacking certain capabilities.
- **Backward Compatibility:** Supporting older Android versions is crucial for reaching a broader audience and maintaining functionality across various software iterations. Developers can use compatibility libraries and tools like the Android Support Library and AndroidX to ensure their apps run smoothly on both new and old Android versions, mitigating fragmentation issues.
- **Dynamic Resource Loading:** Employing dynamic resource loading techniques allows apps to fetch resources based on the device's specifications. This approach optimizes performance and reduces compatibility issues by ensuring that the app only loads necessary resources for a particular device configuration.
- **Security Best Practices:** Developers should implement security best practices, such as targeting newer API levels that provide enhanced security features, using encryption,

and regularly updating apps to address vulnerabilities. Ensuring apps are secure across all devices, regardless of their Android version, is crucial for protecting user data and maintaining trust.

- **Extensive Testing Across Devices:** Given the wide range of Android devices, extensive testing is vital. Using tools like Firebase Test Lab or emulators in Android Studio, developers can automate testing across different devices, configurations, and Android versions to identify and resolve compatibility and security issues before release.

1.7.4 Google's Efforts to Mitigate Fragmentation

Streamlining the Android Ecosystem

Google's initiatives, such as Project Treble, Project Mainline, and Android Go Edition, alongside enhanced developer resources, aim to streamline the Android ecosystem, ensuring faster updates, improved security, and optimized performance across diverse devices.

- **Project Treble:** It introduces a modular architecture that separates the Android OS framework from vendor-specific hardware code, simplifying the process for manufacturers to provide OS updates without extensive redevelopment. This innovation has led to faster updates, facilitating quicker deployment of Android updates across various devices and significantly improving the adoption rate of newer Android versions.
- **Project Mainline (Google Play System Updates):** It enables Google to update core OS components directly through the Google Play Store, effectively bypassing OEMs and carriers. This introduction of modular components allows for more streamlined updates. Consequently, it has significantly improved security by ensuring that users receive critical security updates and bug fixes promptly, enhancing the overall reliability of Android devices.
- **Android Enterprise Recommended Program:** This program establishes a framework of standardization by defining specific requirements for devices and services used in enterprise settings. It ensures consistent security updates and performance standards, providing businesses with reliable and secure Android devices for their operations.
- **Android Go Edition:** It is optimized for low-end devices with 2GB of RAM or less, providing a smoother experience on resource-constrained hardware. It encourages the development of lightweight apps that run efficiently on entry-level devices, ensuring that users with these devices still have access to high-quality apps and a reliable Android experience.
- **Android 15 QPR Updates:** Google has introduced Quarterly Platform Releases (QPR) for Android 15, providing more frequent feature updates and security patches between major version releases. This addresses fragmentation by ensuring devices receive consistent updates throughout the Android version lifecycle.
- **App Bundle and Dynamic Delivery:** It optimizes installations by allowing the Play Store to deliver customized APKs to users based on their device configurations through the Android App Bundle (AAB) format. This approach significantly reduces app size, enhancing installation rates and performance on devices with limited storage.
- **Developer Resources and Tooling:** Regular updates to Android Studio provide developers with enhanced tools for testing and optimizing apps across a variety of devices. Additionally, comprehensive documentation and sample code for large screens and foldables help developers optimize their apps for emerging device categories, ensuring a seamless experience for users on these innovative platforms.

1.8 Key Development Tools

From Concept to Code

The journey from conceptualizing an Android application to delivering a secure, production-ready product requires a sophisticated toolkit. This section highlights the essential development tools that Android developers utilize to create, refine, and optimize their applications. These tools form the foundation for building feature-rich and secure Android applications, enhancing both developer productivity and app performance.

1.8.1 Android Studio

The Command Centre for Android Development

Android Studio is the official Integrated Development Environment (IDE) for Android app development, designed to provide developers with a comprehensive suite of tools and functionalities necessary for building, testing, and deploying Android applications. As the cornerstone of Android development, it offers robust features to streamline the entire development lifecycle. Key features are as follows:

- **Intuitive Interface:** Android Studio provides an intuitive user interface that caters to developers of varying skill levels, from beginners to experienced professionals, facilitating an efficient workflow.
- **Intelligent Code Editor:** The IDE includes a powerful code editor equipped with features like code completion, real-time linting, and refactoring tools. These features help developers write clean, efficient code and adhere to best practices, including security guidelines.
- **Compose-first Approach:** Android Studio now defaults to Jetpack Compose for UI development, streamlining declarative UI creation with real-time previews.
- **Comprehensive Debugging Tools:** Android Studio offers advanced debugging tools that enable developers to identify and resolve issues within their applications. The built-in Android Debug Bridge (ADB) allows for detailed app inspection and debugging on both emulators and physical devices, ensuring that applications are secure and performant.
- **Integration with Android SDK and Google Services:** Android Studio seamlessly integrates with the Android Software Development Kit (SDK) and various Google services, simplifying the development process. This integration ensures that developers have access to the latest APIs, tools, and features provided by Google, including those related to security and user privacy.

1.8.2 Android SDK

The Backbone of Android Development

The Android Software Development Kit (SDK) is a collection of tools, libraries, and APIs provided by Google for building Android applications. The SDK serves as the backbone of Android development, offering developers the resources needed to create innovative and secure apps. Key features are as follows:

- **Compilers and Build Tools:** The SDK includes compilers and build tools essential for compiling code and generating executable binaries. These tools ensure that applications are optimized for performance and security.
- **Emulators and System Images:** Developers can test their applications on virtual devices using emulators and system images provided within the SDK. This capability allows for comprehensive testing across different Android versions and device configurations, helping to identify and address compatibility and security issues early in the development process.
- **Platform Libraries and Documentation:** The SDK offers platform-specific libraries and extensive documentation to assist developers in building feature-rich apps. These libraries include security-focused components such as encryption, secure networking protocols, and user authentication mechanisms.
- **Support for Advanced Technologies:** The SDK supports advanced technologies like augmented reality (AR), virtual reality (VR), machine learning (ML), and the Internet of Things (IoT). These capabilities enable developers to create cutting-edge experiences while maintaining high-security standards.

1.8.3 Android NDK

Strategic Native code Implementation

The Android Native Development Kit (NDK) allows developers to incorporate native code written in languages like C and C++ into their Android applications. The NDK is particularly useful for achieving performance optimizations, accessing low-level system features, and integrating with existing native libraries and frameworks. Key benefits are as follows:

- **Performance Optimization:** By using the NDK, developers can optimize performance-critical parts of their applications, such as multimedia processing, game development, cryptographic operations, and hardware interaction. Native code can execute faster than code written in Java or Kotlin, providing a performance boost for resource-intensive tasks.
- **Access to Low-Level Features:** The NDK enables developers to access low-level system features and hardware-specific capabilities, which can be crucial for certain applications. This access allows for more fine-grained control over the device's hardware, enhancing both performance and security.
- **Enhanced Security:** The NDK can also be used to implement security features at the native level, such as encryption and secure communication protocols. By leveraging native code for sensitive operations, developers can create more secure applications that are resistant to common security vulnerabilities.

1.9 Development Lifecycle Overview

From Idea to App

The Android development lifecycle is a comprehensive process that outlines the stages involved in creating and maintaining high-quality Android applications. Embracing agile methodologies and continuous integration/continuous delivery (CI/CD) practices can streamline development, testing, and deployment, ensuring that applications are delivered efficiently and securely. This section explores each stage of the development journey in detail, emphasizing security best practices and defensive coding techniques at every step.

1.9.1 Ideation and Conceptualization

From Vision to Viable Ideas

These are crucial stages where developers brainstorm ideas, conduct market research, and identify opportunities, ensuring the app concept aligns with user needs and stands out in the competitive marketplace.

- **Brainstorming and Market Research:** The development process begins with ideation and conceptualization, where developers brainstorm ideas and conduct market research to define the app's concept, target audience, and unique value proposition. Understanding the needs, pain points, and preferences of users is crucial for identifying opportunities for innovation and differentiation.
- **Identifying Opportunities:** Analysing market trends, competitor offerings, and user feedback allows developers to refine the app concept to align with user expectations. Embracing Design Thinking methodologies and user-centric approaches ensures the app addresses genuine needs and stands out in the marketplace. This stage involves thorough research to ensure that the app addresses a genuine need and has a competitive edge in the marketplace.

1.9.2 Design and Prototyping

Crafting the Blueprint

It shapes the app's user experience and visual identity through wireframes, mockups, and prototypes, emphasizing usability, accessibility, and iterative refinement based on user feedback.

- **Shaping User Experience:** Design plays a pivotal role in shaping the user experience and visual identity of the app. Developers collaborate with designers to create wireframes, mockups, and prototypes that illustrate the app's interface, navigation flow, and interaction patterns. A focus on usability, accessibility, and aesthetics ensures that the app is intuitive, engaging, and visually appealing. Embracing Material Design 3 (also known as Material You), introduced in Android 12 and enhanced in Android 14, allows for personalized and adaptive UI themes that reflect the user's wallpaper and preferences.
- **Implementing Accessibility and Inclusive Design:** A focus on accessibility is crucial. Utilizing Android's accessibility guidelines and tools like the Accessibility Scanner, developers ensure the app is usable by all, including people with disabilities. Features like voice control, enhanced text readability, and support for assistive technologies broaden the app's reach and compliance with legal standards like the Americans with Disabilities Act (ADA) and Web Content Accessibility Guidelines (WCAG).
- **Refining Design with User Feedback:** Prototyping tools facilitate rapid iteration and feedback gathering, allowing developers to refine the design based on user input and stakeholder feedback. This iterative process helps identify potential usability issues early, ensuring that the final design provides a seamless user experience.

1.9.3 Development and Implementation

Bringing Ideas to Life

It brings app concepts to life by translating design into functional code, ensuring quality and security through robust architectures, frameworks, and best practices.

- **Translating Design to Code:** Once the design is finalized, developers move on to implementation, translating design mockups and prototypes into functional code. This stage involves using programming languages like Java, Kotlin, or C++ and frameworks such as Android Jetpack, Flutter, React Native, or Xamarin to build native, hybrid, or cross-platform applications.

  Kotlin has become the preferred programming language for Android development due to its concise syntax, safety features, and full support from Google. Kotlin Multiplatform Mobile (KMM) is increasingly adopted for sharing business logic across Android and iOS, reducing duplication and improving maintainability.
- **Ensuring Code Quality and Security:** Implementing architectures like MVVM (Model-View-ViewModel) and utilizing dependency injection frameworks like Hilt enhance code maintainability. Version control systems like Git, along with platforms like GitHub, GitLab, or Bitbucket, facilitate collaboration and code management. Security measures are paramount; developers should use Jetpack Security libraries for encryption and BiometricPrompt API for biometric authentication and follow the OWASP Mobile Security Guidelines to safeguard user data.

1.9.4 Testing and Quality Assurance

Ensuring Reliability and Performance

It is crucial for validating app performance, functionality, and security, ensuring reliability through extensive techniques and resolving issues to meet user expectations.

- **Importance of Testing:** Testing is a critical phase encompassing various techniques such as unit testing, integration testing, functional testing, usability testing, performance testing, and security testing. Developers employ testing frameworks, tools, and emulators to validate the app's behaviour, functionality, performance, and security across different devices, screen sizes, and operating system versions.
- **Resolving Issues:** Identifying and resolving issues such as bugs, crashes, memory leaks, performance bottlenecks, and security vulnerabilities ensures the app meets quality standards and user expectations. Continuous integration (CI) and continuous delivery (CD) practices streamline testing, enabling automated testing, deployment, and feedback gathering. Security testing tools like OWASP ZAP, MobSF, and dynamic analysis can help identify and mitigate security risks.

1.9.5 Deployment and Distribution

Launching for Maximum Impact

It involves preparing the app for release, showcasing its features through descriptive metadata, and utilizing effective marketing strategies to maximize visibility and user engagement.

- **Preparing for Deployment:** After thorough testing and validation, developers prepare the app for deployment to users. This involves generating a signed APK (Android Package) or AAB (Android App Bundle) file encapsulating the app's code, resources, and metadata and uploading it to distribution channels like the Google Play Store.
- **Showcasing the App:** Descriptive metadata such as app title, description, screenshots, and promotional materials help showcase the app's features and attract users. Developers must also define pricing, distribution regions, and release tracks to control availability and visibility. Monitoring app performance metrics through the Play Console dashboard and leveraging user feedback are essential for iterative improvements.
- **Marketing Strategies:** Effective marketing strategies, including social media promotion, influencer partnerships, and content marketing, play a vital role in driving app downloads and user engagement. App Store Optimization (ASO) techniques enhance visibility and discoverability in the Play Store, increasing the chances of reaching a broader audience.

1.9.6 Maintenance and Support

Sustaining and Enhancing the Product

It involves continuous monitoring, timely updates, and user feedback analysis, ensuring long-term app success and reliability through iterative improvements and security enhancements.

- **Post-Deployment Tasks:** Post-deployment, developers continue to maintain and support the app to ensure long-term success and sustainability. This involves monitoring performance, gathering user feedback, and releasing updates to address bugs, introduce new features, and enhance stability and user experience.
- **Monitoring and Improving:** Maintenance also involves monitoring analytics, responding to user reviews, addressing security vulnerabilities, and staying abreast of platform updates and industry trends. Developers should prioritize timely updates and security patches to protect users from emerging threats and maintain app reliability.
- **User Feedback and Iteration:** Collecting and analysing user feedback through reviews, surveys, and direct interactions helps identify areas for improvement and new feature opportunities. Iterative development cycles, often following Agile methodologies, ensure that the app evolves in response to user needs and market dynamics. Regular updates and responsive support foster user engagement, loyalty, and advocacy, driving continued growth and success for the app.

1.10 User Base and Market Trends

Targeting Tomorrow's Opportunities

The Android user base and market trends are evolving rapidly, offering developers exciting opportunities to target tomorrow's potential. Key trends include the growth of Android in emerging markets, the rise of foldables and wearables, and the increasing importance of AI and machine learning in Android apps. By understanding these trends, developers can build impactful and relevant applications that serve the needs of a diverse and ever-changing user base. Let's explore these trends and how they are shaping the future of Android development.

1.10.1 Global Reach and Diversity

Connecting a Borderless World

Android's extensive user base spans diverse regions, demographics, and cultures, enabling developers to create globally relevant applications that cater to a wide audience while embracing the needs of digital nomads and remote work.

- **User Diversity:** Android has a vast and diverse user base, spanning different regions, demographics, languages, and cultures. This diversity offers developers an expansive canvas to create applications that cater to a wide range of users worldwide. For instance, apps like WhatsApp and TikTok have achieved global success by adapting to local languages and cultural preferences.
- **Broad Appeal:** By acknowledging and accommodating the diverse needs and preferences of users, developers can ensure that their apps have broad appeal and relevance. This approach not only enhances user satisfaction but also expands the reach and impact of applications across various markets and demographics. Developers should consider localization, accessibility, and inclusivity in their designs to cater to this global audience. For example, incorporating support for right-to-left languages or designing for low-literacy users can significantly enhance app accessibility.
- **Emergence of Digital Nomads and Remote Work:** The rise of remote work and digital nomadism has increased the demand for apps that facilitate communication, collaboration, and productivity across borders. Developers can capitalize on this trend by creating applications that support seamless international connectivity and adaptability. Apps like Slack and Zoom have already set benchmarks in this space, but there is still room for innovation in areas like cross-border payments and virtual team-building tools.

1.10.2 Emerging Markets and Next Billion Users

Expanding Access and Opportunities

Android's widespread adoption in emerging markets presents vast growth opportunities for developers, who can craft tailored applications that cater to the unique needs of these regions, driving financial inclusion and expanding access to digital services.

- **Android's Adoption:** Android's affordability and accessibility have led to its widespread adoption in emerging markets such as India, Brazil, Nigeria, Indonesia, and Vietnam. These markets present substantial growth opportunities for developers as millions of users join the digital ecosystem through smartphones for the first time. For example, India alone has over 600 million smartphone users, most of whom rely on Android devices.
- **Tailored Applications:** Developers can tap into these burgeoning markets by crafting applications tailored to the unique requirements of users in emerging economies. These may include lightweight, data-efficient apps with offline capabilities, support for low-end devices, and localization to cater to diverse languages and cultures. Security is also a key concern; apps should be designed to protect user data, especially in regions with less stringent data protection laws. For instance, apps like Gojek have succeeded by optimizing for low-bandwidth environments and offering region-specific features.

- **Financial Inclusion through Mobile Payments:** The proliferation of mobile payment solutions and digital wallets in emerging markets presents opportunities for developers to integrate Mobile Money and Unified Payments Interface (UPI) systems. Facilitating transactions within apps can drive engagement and monetization. For example, apps like Paytm have revolutionized financial inclusion by enabling digital payments for users without access to traditional banking.

1.10.3 Enterprise Adoption and Digital Transformation

Driving Business Evolution

Android's flexibility and customization options have made it a key player in enterprise environments, driving digital transformation through applications that enhance productivity, streamline workflows, and ensure security and compliance.

- **Android in Enterprises:** Android devices are increasingly being integrated into enterprise environments, driving digital transformation across various industries. The flexibility, versatility, and customization options offered by the Android platform make it well-suited for meeting the diverse needs of enterprise users. For instance, Android's support for custom ROMs and enterprise-grade security features has made it a preferred choice for businesses.
- **Enterprise Apps:** Developers targeting enterprise users should focus on building applications that streamline workflows, enhance productivity, facilitate communication, and promote collaboration. For enterprise-grade applications, developers must prioritize security, scalability, and integration to align with corporate IT policies, regulatory standards, and industry requirements. Apps like Microsoft Teams and Salesforce have set high standards for enterprise applications, but there is still room for innovation in areas like AI-driven workflow automation and secure remote access solutions.

1.10.4 Continued Innovation and Emerging Technologies

Shaping the Future

Android's evolution continues to shape the future with advancements in 5G, foldable displays, AR, VR, AI, ML, and IoT, enabling developers to create innovative and secure applications that meet evolving market demands.

- **Android's Evolution:** Android's evolution is marked by rapid advancements in hardware, software, and user expectations. Android is integrating AI/ML natively through the on-device ML stack (e.g., TensorFlow Lite, Pixel Neural Core) and generative AI APIs. With Android 14+, features like Magic Compose and Audio Magic Eraser demonstrate how AI is becoming a core platform capability, requiring developers to consider privacy, bias, and computational efficiency. For example, 5G enables real-time AR experiences, while foldable displays open up new possibilities for multitasking and immersive interfaces.
- **Leveraging Technologies:** Staying abreast of these trends enables developers to anticipate market demands and differentiate their applications by incorporating innovative features and experiences. For instance, leveraging AI for personalized recommendations, employing AR for immersive storytelling, or harnessing IoT for smart home automation can push the boundaries of what is possible on the Android platform.

Developers should also consider the security implications of these technologies, such as protecting user data in AI models or securing IoT communications. For example, apps like Google Lens and IFTTT demonstrate how AI and IoT can be integrated to create seamless user experiences.

1.10.5 Increasing Popularity of Wearables

The Rise of Smart and Connected Devices

The rise of wearables, particularly in health and fitness, marks a significant shift in technology engagement, with Google's Wear OS leading the charge in providing opportunities for developers to create innovative, secure applications for smart and connected devices.

- **Health and Fitness:** The surge in the adoption of wearables, particularly in health and fitness, represents a significant shift in how people engage with technology. Smartwatches and fitness trackers have become ubiquitous, offering health-monitoring and fitness-tracking features that integrate seamlessly into daily life. For instance, wearables like the Fitbit and Samsung Galaxy Watch have popularized features like heart rate monitoring and sleep tracking.
- **Wear OS:** Wear OS platform, co-developed by Google and Samsung, is at the forefront of this wearable revolution, continually evolving to meet the demands of both users and developers. Developers have a unique opportunity to create applications tailored specifically for wearable devices, focusing on health monitoring, fitness tracking, and lifestyle management. Security is paramount in this space; apps must protect sensitive health data and comply with regulations like the Health Insurance Portability and Accountability Act (HIPAA). For example, apps like Strava and MyFitnessPal have successfully integrated with wearables to provide users with actionable health insights.

1.10.6 Influence of Social Media and Content Consumption

Changing the Digital Landscape

The influence of social media on user behaviour and content consumption creates significant opportunities for Android developers to integrate rich media and social features, enhancing user engagement and creating vibrant communities.

- **Integration with Social Media:** The growing influence of social media platforms on user behaviour and content consumption patterns presents significant opportunities for Android developers. Integrating social media features, such as sharing, commenting, and live streaming, can enhance user engagement and virality. For example, apps like Instagram and TikTok have redefined content consumption by prioritizing short-form videos and user-generated content.
- **Content-Driven Applications:** Developers can capitalize on the popularity of content-driven applications by incorporating rich media, interactive content, and user-generated content features into their apps. This approach can increase user retention and create vibrant, engaging user communities. Developers should also consider content moderation, data privacy, and secure user authentication to maintain a safe and trustworthy environment. For instance, apps like Snapchat have introduced AR filters and lenses to enhance user engagement while ensuring data privacy.

1.10.7 Focus on Sustainability and Ethical Development

Building a Responsible Future

Focusing on sustainability and ethical development, developers are creating energy-efficient apps and prioritizing user privacy to build trust, reduce environmental impact, and promote a responsible digital future.

- **Sustainable Practices:** As awareness of environmental issues grows, users and developers are increasingly focusing on sustainability. Developing energy-efficient apps that minimize battery consumption and optimize resource usage aligns with this trend and can reduce the environmental impact of digital technology. For example, apps like Ecosia, which plant trees based on user searches, demonstrate how sustainability can be integrated into app design.
- **Ethical Development:** Ensuring ethical development practices, such as protecting user privacy, avoiding dark patterns, and promoting digital well-being, is crucial for building trust and maintaining a positive reputation in the market. Developers should adhere to privacy-by-design principles, ensure transparency in data usage, and provide users with control over their data to foster trust and long-term engagement. For instance, apps like Signal have gained popularity by prioritizing user privacy and end-to-end encryption.

1.10.8 The Rise of Super Apps

Integrating Services for User Convenience

The emergence of super apps, integrating a multitude of services into all-in-one platforms, offers unparalleled user convenience and retention, though it demands robust development strategies and regulatory compliance.

- **All-in-One Platforms:** The rise of super apps has led to the emergence of all-in-one platforms that integrate a variety of services within a single ecosystem. These platforms combine messaging, payments, e-commerce, ride hailing, and more to create a seamless user experience, offering both convenience and enhanced user retention. However, integrating such diverse services presents challenges, including the need for robust development strategies and compliance with regulatory standards. For example, WeChat has become a one-stop solution for over 1 billion users in China, offering everything from social networking to financial services.
- **Building Ecosystems:** To build these ecosystems, companies are increasingly relying on the API economy. They use APIs to quickly integrate third-party services and form strategic partnerships to expand their offerings without extensive in-house development. For instance, Grab has partnered with various service providers to offer ride-hailing, food delivery, and financial services within a single app.

Looking Ahead

As this chapter draws to a close, it is clear that understanding the Android ecosystem is fundamental to building secure applications. The diverse and dynamic nature of the Android platform presents both opportunities and challenges for developers. Each aspect plays a crucial role in shaping the security posture of an application.

A clear grasp of the development lifecycle and key tools available empowers developers to make informed decisions from the very beginning of a project. Looking forward, the landscape of Android development will continue to evolve, driven by advancements in technology and shifting market trends. Emerging tools and frameworks will provide developers with new capabilities to enhance app security.

Moving forward in this book, the security risks inherent to Android development and practical strategies to mitigate them will be explored. By leveraging best practices and industry standards, developers can proactively address security concerns rather than reacting to vulnerabilities post-release.

A secure Android application is not just a technical achievement; it is a critical component in ensuring user trust and safeguarding sensitive data. Equipped with the foundational knowledge from this chapter, you are now prepared to dive deeper into securing Android applications with a practical, hands-on approach.

Chapter 2

Navigating the Android Threat Landscape

> In the midst of chaos, there is also opportunity.
>
> – Sun Tzu

Sun Tzu, the Chinese military strategist and author of "The Art of War", emphasized the value of adaptability and seizing opportunities even in the face of uncertainty and disorder.

This principle is especially relevant in the Android threat landscape, where new vulnerabilities, malware variants, and attack techniques emerge almost daily. While this chaotic environment poses significant challenges, it also presents opportunities for proactive cybersecurity measures. By staying vigilant and monitoring the threat landscape closely, organizations can identify potential vulnerabilities and weaknesses in Android systems or applications, allowing them to strengthen defences before an attack occurs.

Moreover, periods of chaos often inspire innovation in cybersecurity technologies and strategies, enabling defenders to anticipate and counteract new threats more effectively. Thus, Sun Tzu's wisdom reminds us that even in the dynamic and sometimes tumultuous world of Android security, there are always opportunities to enhance resilience and maintain a robust security posture.

DOI: 10.1201/9781003640332-3

A LAYMAN'S PERSPECTIVE

Your Compass in the Threat Landscape

Navigating the intricate world of security threats in the sphere of Android applications requires vigilance, adaptability, and a proactive mindset. As technology advances, so too does the sophistication of malicious tactics employed by cybercriminals. These adversaries seek to exploit vulnerabilities in applications, aiming to harvest sensitive user data, compromise personal and financial information, and undermine digital security.

In this constantly evolving landscape, awareness and education are fundamental. The threat spectrum has expanded from rudimentary malware to advanced social engineering tactics, zero-day vulnerabilities, and targeted cyberattacks. As these threats grow in complexity, developers and users must stay informed and continuously update their security practices.

To safeguard digital assets effectively, adopting a proactive approach to security is imperative. Developers must integrate security best practices throughout the software development lifecycle (SDLC), ensuring that applications are resilient against emerging threats. This includes implementing robust encryption protocols, enforcing stringent access controls, and conducting regular security audits to identify and remediate vulnerabilities before they can be exploited.

Fostering a culture of security consciousness is equally important in building resilience against emerging threats. Practising good cyber hygiene, such as regularly updating software, using strong passwords, and being cautious of unsolicited communications, is essential. A mindset of scepticism toward requests for sensitive information can prevent many common attacks.

Collaboration is also a cornerstone of effective defence against malicious actors. Fostering partnerships between industry stakeholders, cybersecurity experts, and law enforcement agencies allows for the pooling of resources and expertise to combat threats more effectively. A unified approach enables a stronger, more coordinated response to the challenges posed by cybercriminals.

The pursuit of a secure Android ecosystem demands unwavering dedication and adaptability. As cyber threats continue to evolve, so must our defensive strategies. Remaining vigilant, proactive, and collaborative is key to navigating the ever-changing cybersecurity landscape with confidence. A security-first mindset ensures that technological advancements can be leveraged safely without compromising user privacy and data security.

2.1 Malware

Understanding Malware and Its Evolution

Malware, short for malicious software, refers to any program or application intentionally designed to cause harm to a device, network, or user data. In the Android ecosystem, malware continues to evolve, becoming more sophisticated and harder to detect. In recent years, emerging technologies like artificial intelligence (AI) and machine learning (ML) have been increasingly leveraged by attackers to create more adaptable and elusive malware, presenting ongoing challenges for both developers and users.

To stay ahead of these threats, it is crucial to understand the various types of malware, how they are distributed, and the strategies employed to detect and prevent them.

Engaging Curiosity: A Thought Experiment

- Have you ever wondered what would happen if your phone suddenly became unresponsive or if strange apps appeared without your consent?

  Imagine your phone freezing, crashing, or behaving erratically. What if you noticed unfamiliar apps installed that you never downloaded? How would you determine if your device was compromised? What steps would you take to regain control, and how would you prevent it from happening again?

- Can you imagine the frustration of losing access to your personal data because a seemingly harmless app turned out to be ransomware?

  You download a simple utility app, and suddenly, your photos, messages, and files are encrypted. A ransom note pops up demanding payment in cryptocurrency. How would you react? Would you pay the ransom or try to recover your data another way? What precautions could you have taken to avoid this situation?

- What if a simple click on an enticing ad led to a cascade of unwanted ads and sluggish performance on your device?

  You click on an ad for a great deal, but instead of the expected website, your device is bombarded with pop-ups, and the performance slows to a crawl. How would you identify the source of the problem? What tools or techniques could you use to clean your device and prevent future adware infections?

2.1.1 Types of Malware

Diverse Threats to Android Devices

Several types of malware can target Android devices, each with unique behaviours and objectives. To maintain a robust defence, let's explore these diverse threats that challenge the Android ecosystem:

- **Viruses:** These are malicious programs that attach themselves to legitimate Android applications or system files. Once a virus infects a file, it can replicate and spread to other files or devices, potentially causing significant damage to system functionality and data integrity.
- **Worms:** Unlike viruses, worms do not need to attach themselves to other files to propagate. They are self-replicating and can spread independently over network connections or removable media. Worms can cause widespread disruptions, often slowing down or halting system operations.
- **Trojans:** Named after the mythological Trojan Horse, these malicious programs disguise themselves as legitimate Android apps. Users are tricked into installing them, after which the Trojans execute their malicious payload, such as stealing data, recording keystrokes, or damaging the system.
- **Ransomware:** This particularly malicious type of malware encrypts user data and demands payment (usually in cryptocurrency) for the decryption key. If the ransom is

not paid, it can result in significant data loss, and even if payment does not guarantee data recovery.

- **Spyware:** Operating covertly, spyware monitors user activities without their knowledge or consent. It can track browsing habits, record keystrokes, and intercept communications, often for purposes of espionage or data theft. Some advanced spyware can even bypass security measures and remain undetected.
- **Adware:** While primarily focused on aggressive advertisement delivery, adware frequently incorporates privacy-invasive components that harvest user data, track behaviour across applications, and build detailed profiles for targeted advertising. Modern adware employs advanced techniques to remain resident in memory, resist removal, and bypass Android's background execution limitations.
- **Botnets:** Malware-infected Android devices can be orchestrated into extensive networks controlled through command-and-control (C2) servers. These botnets execute coordinated activities ranging from distributed denial-of-service (DDoS) attacks to cryptomining operations. Mobile botnets often leverage legitimate communication channels like Firebase Cloud Messaging to receive commands, making their traffic difficult to distinguish from normal application behaviour.
- **Rootkits:** These highly privileged malware variants modify core system components to establish persistent access while actively concealing their presence from detection tools. Android rootkits typically exploit privilege escalation vulnerabilities to gain root access, then modify system libraries or the kernel itself. Their deep system integration makes them exceptionally difficult to detect and remove without specialized tools.
- **Fileless Malware:** A growing threat in the Android ecosystem, fileless malware resides solely in device memory without writing files to storage, leveraging legitimate system tools and processes to execute malicious activities. This sophisticated approach significantly reduces detection potential by traditional signature-based scanning mechanisms and has become a favored technique in advanced persistent threats (APTs).
- **Living-off-the-Land (LotL) Techniques:** Advanced malware that exclusively uses legitimate Android system tools, APIs, and processes to carry out malicious activities. By leveraging trusted system components like shell commands, system services, and legitimate applications, these attacks remain virtually invisible to traditional security solutions that focus on detecting malicious files or processes.

2.1.2 Distribution Channels

Pathways for Malware Infiltration

Malware can be distributed through various channels, each exploiting different vulnerabilities in the Android ecosystem:

- **Third-party App Stores:** These marketplaces exist outside of the official Google Play Store and are not regulated by Google. They often lack stringent security checks, making them popular distribution points for malicious apps. Third-party stores remain a primary vector for trojanized apps, especially in regions with limited Google Play access. Some distribute repackaged apps with malicious SDKs or overlay attacks.
- **Malicious Websites:** Some websites are designed to trick users into downloading malware, often disguised as fake updates or apps. These sites can exploit browser vulnerabilities or use social engineering techniques to deceive users. Drive-by download

attacks, where malware is automatically downloaded when a user visits a compromised website, have become more prevalent.

- **Phishing Emails:** These fraudulent emails appear to be from legitimate sources and contain malicious links or attachments. Clicking these links or downloading attachments can install malware on the Android device. Phishing campaigns have become more targeted and sophisticated, often employing personalized messages to increase their success rates.
- **Compromised Advertisements:** Legitimate websites or apps can unknowingly host malicious ads. When users interact with these ads, they may be redirected to download malware. Malvertising campaigns have become more complex, using advanced techniques to bypass ad network security measures.
- **Infected Devices:** Malware can spread through infected devices via Bluetooth, Wi-Fi, or other connectivity methods, often without the user's knowledge. The rise of Internet of Things (IoT) devices has increased the attack surface for malware propagation.

2.1.3 Behavioural Analysis

Uncovering Malicious Activities

Behavioural analysis involves monitoring and analysing the actions of malware within a system to identify patterns indicative of malicious behaviour. This proactive approach helps us stay ahead of evolving threats by revealing how malware operates:

- **Data Theft:** Malware designed for data theft targets sensitive information on the device, such as login credentials, financial data, or personal information. This stolen data can be used for identity theft or financial fraud or sold on the dark web. Advanced techniques like keylogging and screen capturing have made data theft more effective.
- **Device Hijacking:** Certain malware types gain unauthorized access to device resources, such as the camera, microphone, or contacts. These resources can then be exploited to spy on the user, record conversations, or send spam messages. Some malware can also hijack device functionality for crypto-jacking, using the device's resources to mine cryptocurrency.
- **Financial Fraud:** Banking Trojans and other financially motivated malware intercept and manipulate financial transactions, leading to unauthorized transfers or fraudulent activities. Attackers have become more adept at bypassing multi-factor authentication (MFA) and other security measures to carry out financial fraud.
- **Ad Fraud:** Some malware generates fraudulent clicks or impressions on advertisements, causing financial losses for advertisers and publishers. It can also degrade device performance and consume data. Ad fraud tactics have evolved into sophisticated botnets and automated scripts mimicking human behaviour.
- **Espionage:** Beyond theft, malware gathers intelligence for corporate or political gain, often with state-sponsored backing (e.g., Pegasus).

2.1.4 Detection and Prevention

Building a Robust Defence

Detecting and preventing malware infections on Android devices requires a multi-layered approach, combining proactive measures with advanced security solutions:

- **Antivirus Software:** Reputable antivirus apps can scan for and remove malware from Android devices. Many offer real-time protection features that detect and block malware before it can infect the device. Modern antivirus solutions incorporate AI and ML to effectively identify new and emerging threats.
- **App Sandboxing:** Android's app sandboxing isolates apps from each other and the underlying operating system, preventing malware from spreading or accessing sensitive system resources. Enhancements in sandboxing techniques have further strengthened app isolation and security.
- **User Education:** One of the most effective ways to prevent malware infections is to educate users about the risks associated with downloading apps from untrusted sources, clicking suspicious links, or opening unexpected attachments. Cybersecurity awareness campaigns and training programs can help users stay informed about the latest threats and best practices.
- **Security Updates:** Regularly updating devices and installed apps with the latest security patches is crucial, as these updates often contain fixes for known vulnerabilities that malware could exploit. Automatic update mechanisms have improved to ensure timely and seamless security updates.

2.2 Phishing Attacks

Proactive Defence Against Phishing Innovations

Phishing attacks remain one of the most pervasive and evolving threats in the Android ecosystem. Attackers continually refine their tactics, employ sophisticated social engineering techniques, and exploit new communication channels to deceive individuals into divulging sensitive information such as login credentials, personal details, or financial data. With the advent of advanced technologies like artificial intelligence (AI), machine learning (ML), and deepfake technology, phishing campaigns have become more convincing and harder to detect.

As phishing tactics evolve, leveraging not only emails but also SMS (smishing), voice calls (vishing), social media platforms, and even mobile applications, it is imperative for users and developers to stay vigilant. Implementing innovative security awareness programs, utilizing AI-driven threat detection, and strengthening authentication mechanisms are critical steps toward empowering users with the resilience needed to recognize and resist phishing attempts and safeguard their personal information in an ever-shifting digital landscape.

Engaging Curiosity: A Thought Experiment

- **Imagine receiving a voice call from your bank. Would you trust the voice on the other end if it sounded exactly like your bank manager?**

  The caller knows your name, account details, and even recent transactions. They sound exactly like your bank manager and ask you to verify sensitive information. How would you verify the caller's identity? What red flags would you look for to determine if this is a phishing attempt?

- **What would you do if a QR code in your favourite cafe led you to a seemingly legitimate website, only to steal your credentials?**

You scan a QR code on a table at your favourite cafe, and it takes you to a website that looks identical to your bank's login page. You enter your credentials only to realize later that it is a fake site. How would you detect such a scam in the future? What steps could you take to protect yourself from malicious QR codes?

- **Have you ever thought about how a simple SMS from an unknown number could trick you into revealing your most sensitive information?**

You receive a text message claiming to be from a delivery service, asking you to click a link to reschedule a package delivery. The link takes you to a site that asks for personal details. How would you verify the legitimacy of the message? What precautions would you take before clicking on links in SMS messages?

2.2.1 Attack Techniques

Outsmarting the Attackers

Phishing attacks targeting Android users employ a variety of techniques, each tailored to exploit specific vulnerabilities or behaviours:

- **AI-powered Phishing:** Attackers are using AI and ML to craft highly personalized and convincing phishing messages. By analysing public data from social media profiles and other online platforms, they tailor messages that appear legitimate and relevant to the recipient. This personalization increases the likelihood of users engaging with malicious content.
- **AI Voice Synthesis and Real-time Conversion:** Beyond pre-recorded deepfake audio, attackers now employ real-time voice conversion technology during live conversations. This allows immediate mimicry of trusted voices during phone calls, making vishing attacks virtually indistinguishable from legitimate communications. Advanced neural voice cloning can replicate speech patterns, accents, and emotional inflections with minimal audio samples.
- **Multi-channel Phishing:** Phishing campaigns are no longer limited to emails. Attackers exploit multiple channels, such as SMS (smishing), messaging apps like WhatsApp and Telegram, social media platforms, and even dating apps, to spread malicious links and apps. This multi-channel approach increases their reach and effectiveness.
- **Malicious QR Codes (Quishing):** With the increased use of QR codes for contactless transactions and information sharing, attackers embed malicious URLs in QR codes placed in public spaces or sent electronically. Scanning these codes can lead users to phishing websites or trigger downloads of malicious apps.
- **Dynamic QR Code Attacks:** Sophisticated QR codes that employ time-based or scan-count-based logic to change their destination URLs after initial security scanning. These codes present legitimate content to security tools but redirect to malicious sites when scanned by actual users, effectively bypassing QR code security validation systems.
- **Pharming and DNS Hijacking:** Attackers redirect users to fake websites by compromising DNS settings on devices or routers. When users attempt to visit legitimate sites, they are unknowingly directed to fraudulent ones designed to steal credentials or install malware.

- **Malicious Mobile Applications:** Cybercriminals create fake apps that mimic popular applications. These apps may request excessive permissions, allowing attackers to collect personal data or credentials. Some malicious apps bypass Google Play Protect by using delayed payload activation, benign initial behaviour, or abusing legitimate app functionality (e.g., WebView-based phishing).
- **Social Engineering:** This involves manipulating users through psychological tactics, such as urgency, fear, or curiosity, to elicit a desired response. Attackers may exploit these emotions to trick users into clicking on malicious links, downloading harmful apps, or revealing sensitive information.

2.2.2 Phishing Indicators

Spotting the Deception

Identifying phishing attempts is crucial for preventing them from succeeding. Strengthening awareness can greatly improve the ability to detect these deceptive tactics. Some common indicators of phishing include:

- **Suspicious Sender Information:** Phishing emails often use deceptive sender addresses that closely resemble legitimate ones but contain slight differences, such as misspellings or unusual domain names. If an email appears unexpected or requests sensitive information without a clear reason, it should be scrutinized carefully.
- **Unusual URLs:** Phishing often involves directing users to malicious websites that mimic legitimate ones. Users should check URLs carefully for inconsistencies, such as unfamiliar domains, misspellings, or incorrect subdomains. Using URL preview tools before clicking links can also help avoid malicious sites.
- **Urgency or Requests for Sensitive Information:** Phishing attacks often create a false sense of urgency, prompting users to act quickly to avoid some fabricated consequence. Users should be wary of any communication that pressures them to provide sensitive information or take immediate action without proper verification.
- **Spelling and Grammar Errors:** Many phishing messages contain typos, grammatical mistakes, or unusual language that may indicate they were not professionally crafted. Users should be cautious of poorly written communications, especially if they ask for sensitive information.
- **Inconsistent Branding or Design:** Fake emails, websites, and messages often have slight inconsistencies in branding, logos, fonts, or colours that differ from the legitimate company's official communication style.
- **Unexpected Attachments or Links:** Emails or messages with unexpected attachments or links should always be verified before clicking. These could contain malware or redirect users to phishing sites.

2.2.3 Security Awareness

Empowering Defence

Promoting security awareness among Android users is essential for reducing the risk of phishing attacks. Key strategies for enhancing security awareness include:

- **Comprehensive Training Programs:** Organizations and developers should provide users with up-to-date training on the latest phishing techniques, including AI-driven attacks and deepfake scams. Interactive and engaging training materials can improve user retention of key information.
- **Simulated Phishing Exercises:** Conducting realistic phishing simulations allows users to practice identifying and responding to phishing attempts in a controlled environment. These exercises can help highlight common pitfalls and improve overall awareness.
- **Real-time Threat Intelligence:** Implementing systems that provide users with real-time alerts about ongoing phishing campaigns can help them stay vigilant against emerging threats. Sharing information about recent phishing tactics can empower users to recognize and avoid similar attempts.
- **User-friendly Reporting Mechanisms:** Simplifying the process for users to report suspicious activities, whether through in-app features or dedicated support channels, enables quicker responses to emerging threats. Providing feedback to users who report phishing attempts encourages continued engagement.
- **Community Engagement:** Encouraging users to participate in security forums or communities where they can share experiences and stay informed about phishing trends enhances collective awareness and defence capabilities.

2.2.4 Advanced Authentication Mechanisms

Adding an Extra Layer of Security

Incorporating two-factor authentication (2FA) into Android applications is a powerful measure for mitigating the risk of unauthorized access resulting from successful phishing attacks. These advanced mechanisms align with our proactive security mindset:

- **Biometric Authentication:** Leveraging biometric factors like fingerprint scanning, facial recognition, or iris scanning provides robust security that is difficult for attackers to replicate. Android's BiometricPrompt API allows developers to integrate biometric authentication seamlessly.
- **Phishing-Resistant MFA Methods:** Implementing modern multi-factor authentication (MFA) solutions such as hardware security keys (e.g., FIDO U2F keys) or app-based authenticators reduces the risk of credential theft. These methods validate the legitimacy of the site or app during the authentication process, making phishing attempts less effective.
- **Passwordless Authentication:** Adopting passwordless authentication methods, like single-use tokens or magic links, minimizes reliance on traditional passwords, which are vulnerable to phishing attacks. Utilizing device-based authentication (e.g., using device certificates) can enhance security.
- **Adaptive Authentication:** Employ risk-based authentication systems that assess contextual factors, such as login location, device behaviour, and network reputation, to determine the level of authentication required. Suspicious login attempts can trigger additional verification steps, effectively mitigating unauthorized access.
- **Continuous Authentication:** Implementing continuous authentication mechanisms that monitor user behaviour patterns during a session can help detect anomalies indicative of compromised credentials. For example, sudden changes in typing patterns or navigation behaviour may trigger security actions.

- **User Awareness:** Educating users on the importance of not sharing authentication codes, recognizing fraudulent authentication prompts, and using unique passwords enhances the overall security posture.

2.3 Man-in-the-Middle (MITM) Attacks

Fortifying Against Emerging Threats

Man-in-the-Middle (MITM) attacks involve intercepting and possibly altering communications between two parties without their knowledge or consent. In the context of Android devices, MITM attacks have become more sophisticated, exploiting advanced techniques and emerging technologies to target users and applications.

As the Internet of Things (IoT) expands and 5G networks proliferate, the threat of MITM attacks becomes more pronounced. Attackers leverage vulnerabilities in IoT devices connected to Android systems and exploit weaknesses in mobile networks to intercept communications. Implementing advanced encryption protocols, adopting decentralized network architectures, and fostering a culture of security awareness can fortify defences and thwart malicious actors seeking to manipulate network communications.

Engaging Curiosity: A Thought Experiment

- **Have you ever thought about who might be silently eavesdropping on your private conversations over an unsecured Wi-Fi network?**

  You are at a coffee shop, connected to the free Wi-Fi, and sending sensitive emails or messages. Could someone be intercepting your communications? How would you know if your data was being captured? What tools or practices could you use to secure your connection?

- **Can you imagine the chaos if your router were compromised, redirecting your sensitive data to an attacker without your knowledge?**

  Imagine your home router being hacked and all your internet traffic being redirected through an attacker's server. How would you detect such an attack? What steps could you take to secure your router and prevent unauthorized access?

- **What would you do if a harmless-looking QR code triggered a connection to a malicious network, putting your personal information at risk?**

  You scan a QR code at a public event, and your device automatically connects to a network. Later, you notice unusual activity on your accounts. How would you determine if the network was malicious? What precautions could you take to avoid falling victim to such attacks in the future?

2.3.1 Attack Scenarios

Visualizing the Evolving Threats

MITM attacks can occur in various scenarios, each illustrating the need for proactive vigilance:

- **Unsecured Wi-Fi Networks:** When an application communicates over an unsecured Wi-Fi network, attackers can use tools like packet sniffers to capture and analyse network traffic. This can potentially expose sensitive information such as login credentials, personal user data, or even session tokens, leading to unauthorized access or data breaches.
- **Compromised Routers:** If a router is compromised, an attacker can manipulate its settings, such as DNS configurations, to redirect traffic to malicious servers. This type of attack can lead to MITM scenarios where the attacker intercepts and potentially alters the communication between the application and its intended server, effectively impersonating the server or client.
- **Rogue Access Points:** These are malicious Wi-Fi networks set up by attackers to trick users into connecting. When a device connects to such a network, the attacker can monitor and manipulate the network traffic, leading to MITM attacks where sensitive data is intercepted or tampered with.
- **Spoofing Attacks:** Attackers may use techniques like ARP spoofing or DNS spoofing to redirect network traffic through their own devices, allowing them to intercept, modify, or inject malicious content into the data stream between the user and the intended server.
- **Malicious QR Codes and Near Field Communication (NFC) Tags:** With the widespread use of QR codes and near field communication (NFC) for payments and information exchange, attackers embed malicious codes that redirect Android devices to compromised networks or trigger unintended connections, facilitating MITM attacks.
- **5G Network Slicing Vulnerabilities:** Exploitation of 5G network architecture, where attackers compromise network slices to intercept traffic between different network segments. This sophisticated attack vector allows interception of communications across enterprise, IoT, and consumer network slices, creating new opportunities for large-scale MitM attacks.

2.3.2 Encryption Best Practices

Securing Your Data

Implementing strong encryption practices is crucial for mitigating the risk of MITM attacks and protecting sensitive data transmitted between Android devices and remote servers. These best practices embody our commitment to resilience:

- **HTTPS/TLS Encryption:** HTTPS (HTTP Secure) uses TLS (Transport Layer Security) to provide encryption for data transmitted over the internet. Ensuring all communications between an Android application and its backend servers use HTTPS/TLS is fundamental to protecting data from being intercepted and read by attackers.
- **Strong Encryption Algorithms:** Using robust cryptographic algorithms, such as Advanced Encryption Standard (AES) with at least 128-bit keys or Rivest–Shamir–Adleman (RSA) with 2048-bit keys, ensures the confidentiality and integrity of encrypted data. These algorithms make it computationally infeasible for attackers to decrypt the data without the proper key.
- **Perfect Forward Secrecy (PFS):** Employing cryptographic protocols (such as Elliptic Curve Diffie–Hellman Ephemeral (ECDHE)) that provide PFS ensures that each session uses a unique encryption key. Even if an attacker compromises the server's private key, they cannot decrypt past or future sessions, significantly enhancing the security of communications.

- **Certificate Validation:** Ensuring that applications validate Secure Sockets Layer (SSL)/ TLS certificates properly is essential to prevent MITM attacks. Certificate pinning can prevent MitM attacks but is fragile and breaks during legitimate certificate rotation. Prefer using Android's Network Security Configuration with pinning and automatic fallback handling.
- **End-to-End Encryption (E2EE):** This encryption method ensures that data is encrypted on the sender's device and can only be decrypted on the recipient's device, preventing intermediaries from accessing the data in transit.

2.3.3 Certificate Pinning

Locking Down Connections

Certificate pinning is a security mechanism that helps prevent MITM attacks by binding a specific server's digital certificate to its corresponding public key or cryptographic hash. This technique strengthens our proactive defences:

- **Implementing Certificate Pinning:** This involves hardcoding the server's SSL/TLS certificate or public key within the application. This ensures that the app only accepts connections from servers presenting the expected certificate, adding an extra layer of security against MITM attacks.
- **Public Key Pinning:** A specific method of certificate pinning involves hardcoding the public key of the server's SSL/TLS certificate within the app. This approach prevents attackers from using fraudulent certificates to impersonate the server, even if they have control over the network.
- **Certificate Revocation Checks:** Periodically checking for certificate revocation status using Certificate Revocation Lists (CRLs) or the Online Certificate Status Protocol (OCSP) helps detect compromised or revoked certificates and ensures that the application does not communicate with untrusted servers.
- **Certificate Transparency Monitoring:** Implementing monitoring of Certificate Transparency (CT) logs to detect unauthorized certificate issuance for your domains. This proactive approach identifies potential MitM attacks before they occur by alerting administrators when certificates are issued without authorization, complementing traditional certificate pinning strategies.

2.3.4 Network Security Awareness

Building a Culture of Security

Raising awareness about network security risks and best practices is essential for Android users and developers to mitigate the risk of MITM attacks. Key aspects that foster a vigilant and informed community:

- **Educating Users on Emerging Threats:** Provide up-to-date information about sophisticated MITM attack vectors, such as malicious charging stations (juice jacking), fake network providers, and compromised IoT devices. Awareness empowers users to make informed decisions about network connections. Users should be advised to use USB data blocking accessories or 'charge-only' cables when using public charging stations.

- **Promoting Secure Network Practices:** Encourage users to utilize trusted networks, avoid connecting to unknown Wi-Fi hotspots, and disable automatic network connections on their Android devices. Advise users to verify the authenticity of networks before connecting.
- **Recommending the Use of Advanced VPN Solutions:** Advocate for VPN services that offer advanced security features, such as multi-hop connections and obfuscation techniques, to conceal VPN usage, enhancing privacy and protection against MITM attacks.
- **Implementing Zero Trust Principles:** Adopt a Zero Trust security model where every network interaction is authenticated and authorized, minimizing the reliance on network perimeters and reducing the risk of MITM attacks within internal networks.
- **Practicing Security Hygiene:** Promoting good security hygiene practices, such as regularly updating software and applications, using strong and unique passwords, and avoiding clicking on suspicious links or downloading files from untrusted sources, helps minimize the risk of MITM and other types of attacks. Users should be encouraged to keep their devices updated with the latest security patches and to be vigilant about potential security threats.

2.4 Insecure Authentication and Authorization

Empowering Users Through Next-Generation AuthX

Insecure authentication and authorization mechanisms continue to be a significant concern in the Android ecosystem. They can lead to unauthorized access to applications, exposing sensitive data and functionalities to malicious actors. As cyber threats become more sophisticated, attackers exploit weaknesses not just in password policies but also in advanced authentication methods.

As the digital landscape evolves, so must our approach to authentication and authorization. Adopting cutting-edge technologies such as passwordless authentication, advanced biometrics, and adaptive security measures empowers users to protect their digital identities and secure online interactions, ensuring resilience against the ever-evolving threat landscape.

Engaging Curiosity: A Thought Experiment

- **Have you ever thought about the risks of using the same password across multiple apps and how easily hackers could exploit this vulnerability?**

  If one of your accounts is breached, how quickly could attackers access your other accounts using the same password? What would be the potential consequences of such a breach? How can you manage unique passwords for each account without overwhelming yourself?

- **What if a high-quality mask fooled your device's facial recognition, granting an attacker access to your sensitive data?**

  Imagine an attacker using a lifelike mask to bypass your phone's facial recognition. How would you detect such an attack? What additional security measures could you implement to protect your device from biometric spoofing?

- Can you imagine the havoc caused if an attacker intercepted your SMS-based authentication codes through a SIM swap attack?

  You receive a notification that your SIM card has been deactivated, and shortly after, your accounts are compromised. How would you recover from a SIM swap attack? What alternative authentication methods could you use to avoid relying on SMS-based codes?

2.4.1 Authentication Weaknesses

Identifying Risks

Authentication weaknesses can introduce vulnerabilities that attackers may exploit to bypass login controls or impersonate legitimate users. Recognizing these risks is the first step in building proactive defences:

- **Password-based Authentication:** While this is the most common form of authentication, it often suffers from weak password policies that make it vulnerable to attacks. In the context of Android applications, it is crucial to enforce strong password policies to prevent attackers from guessing or cracking user passwords. This includes setting minimum password length and complexity requirements and preventing the use of common or easily guessable passwords.
- **Inadequate Session Management:** Once a user is authenticated, they are typically issued a session token to authenticate subsequent requests. If session tokens are not handled securely, attackers could intercept and use them to impersonate the user. Secure session-handling practices in Android applications include setting appropriate session expiration times, allowing users to manually end sessions, and securely storing session tokens on the device to prevent unauthorized access.
- **Insufficient Credential Management:** Even with strong passwords and secure session management, user credentials could still be at risk if they are not stored securely. Techniques such as salted hashing and key derivation functions (e.g., PBKDF2, bcrypt) can be used to securely store user passwords and authentication tokens in Android applications. It is also important to avoid hard-coding credentials in the application's source code.
- **Biometric Spoofing Attacks:** With the widespread adoption of biometrics like fingerprint and facial recognition on Android devices, attackers are developing methods to spoof these systems using high-quality images, masks, or synthetic fingerprints. Modern Android devices use liveness detection via depth sensors or infrared (e.g., Face Unlock on Pixel). However, 2D photo spoofing remains a risk on lower-end devices. Developers should not treat biometrics as a standalone authenticator.
- **SIM Swap and MFA Bypass:** Attackers are increasingly targeting multi-factor authentication (MFA) methods by hijacking users' phone numbers through SIM swapping, allowing them to intercept SMS-based authentication codes. Encouraging users to utilize more secure MFA methods like authenticator apps or hardware tokens reduces this vulnerability.
- **Insecure OAuth Implementations:** Misconfigured OAuth integrations can inadvertently expose access tokens or allow attackers to impersonate users. Ensuring proper validation of redirect URIs and state parameters and using PKCE (Proof Key for Code Exchange) enhances OAuth security in Android apps.

- **Passkey Vulnerabilities:** Despite representing a significant improvement over passwords, passkeys introduce new attack vectors, including device compromise scenarios, cloud synchronization attacks, and cross-platform vulnerabilities. Attackers may target the underlying cryptographic implementations or exploit weaknesses in passkey management across different platforms and services.
- **Man-in-the-Middle (MITM) Attacks:** Attackers may intercept authentication requests over insecure networks, capturing sensitive information such as passwords or session tokens. Using TLS (Transport Layer Security) with certificate pinning can mitigate such risks.

2.4.2 Multi-Factor Authentication (MFA)

Adding an Extra Layer

Multi-factor authentication (MFA) enhances the security of Android applications by requiring users to provide multiple forms of identification before accessing their accounts. These layers reinforce our commitment to staying ahead of threats:

- **Biometric Authentication:** Android devices often come with built-in biometric sensors such as fingerprint scanners or facial recognition cameras. These can be used as an additional factor of authentication, providing a higher level of security than password-based authentication alone. Biometric data is stored securely in the device's trusted execution environment (TEE) or Secure Enclave, making it difficult for attackers to access or manipulate.
- **Hardware Tokens:** These are physical devices, like USB keys or smart cards, that generate a unique code for authentication. They can be used in conjunction with or as a replacement for password-based authentication, providing a higher level of assurance that the user is who they claim to be. Hardware tokens are particularly effective against phishing and other credential-based attacks.
- **Zero-Trust Continuous Verification:** Evolution beyond traditional context-based authentication to implement continuous risk assessment and adaptive re-authentication. This approach assumes no implicit trust and continuously evaluates user behavior, device state, network conditions, and access patterns to adjust authentication requirements and access privileges throughout the session dynamically.
- **Behavioral Biometrics:** Continuous authentication mechanisms that analyze unique user behavior patterns, including typing rhythm, device interaction patterns, navigation behavior, and application usage sequences. This approach provides ongoing verification throughout a session rather than single-point authentication, detecting account takeover attempts even when traditional credentials are compromised.
- **Passwordless Authentication with Passkeys:** Passkeys represent a shift towards eliminating passwords altogether, using cryptographic keys stored securely on devices. Android's support for FIDO2 and WebAuthn standards enables developers to implement passwordless authentication that is resistant to phishing and credential theft.

2.4.3 Authorization Best Practices

Defining Access Controls

Authorization best practices are essential for ensuring that users have appropriate permissions to access specific resources or perform privileged actions within Android applications. These practices align with our security-first approach:

- **Role-based Access Control (RBAC):** This approach involves defining user roles within the Android application and assigning permissions based on these roles. For example, an admin role might have full access to all features of the application, while a regular user role might have more limited access. RBAC simplifies permission management and helps ensure that users only have access to what they need.
- **Attribute-based Access Control (ABAC):** This is a more flexible and granular approach to access control that takes into account additional attributes of the user, the resource being accessed, and the current context. For example, an Android application might allow access to certain features based on the user's location, the time of day, or the user's behaviour within the application. ABAC enables dynamic access control decisions that can adapt to changing conditions and requirements.
- **Policy Enforcement:** Enforcing authorization policies consistently across the application is crucial for maintaining security. Authorization policies should be adaptable to respond to changing conditions or requirements. For example, an Android application might dynamically adjust access controls in response to a detected security threat, such as a compromised user account or a network breach.
- **Least Privilege Principle:** Granting users the minimum privileges necessary to perform their required tasks or access specific resources helps reduce the risk of privilege escalation or unauthorized access to sensitive data. This principle limits the potential impact of a compromised account or malicious insider and is a fundamental aspect of secure application design.
- **Zero Trust Architecture:** Adopting a Zero-Trust model assumes no implicit trust within the system. Every access request is authenticated and authorized, reducing the risk of internal threats and attackers' lateral movement.

2.4.4 Security Hygiene

Maintaining Strong Defences

Practising good security hygiene is essential for maintaining the integrity and confidentiality of authentication and authorization mechanisms in Android applications. These habits ensure ongoing resilience:

- **Password Management Best Practices:** Users should be educated on the importance of using strong, unique passwords for each of their accounts and encouraged to use multi-factor authentication where available. Regularly updating passwords can also help mitigate the risk of credential-based attacks. Developers can enhance security by implementing password strength meters and providing feedback during password creation.
- **Security Awareness Training:** Users should receive ongoing training to help them understand common security threats, attack vectors, and best practices for safeguarding sensitive information. Educating users about phishing, social engineering, and other common attack techniques can reduce the likelihood of security incidents due to human error.
- **Regular Security Audits and Assessments:** Conducting regular audits and assessments can help identify and remediate security vulnerabilities in applications, ensuring that the application's security posture remains strong in the face of evolving threats. This might involve automated vulnerability scanning, manual code reviews, or even

simulated attacks known as penetration testing. Regular security reviews help maintain a proactive approach to application security and ensure compliance with best practices.

- **Adopting DevSecOps Practices:** Integrating security into the development pipeline fosters a culture of proactive security. Automated code analysis, dependency checks, and compliance scans catch vulnerabilities early in the development process.
- **Security Logging and Monitoring:** Implementing logging mechanisms to detect and respond to authentication anomalies or brute-force attempts enhances security.

2.5 App Permissions Misuse

Balancing Functionality with Privacy and Security

App permissions allow Android applications to access specific device features and data, such as the camera, microphone, contacts, location, and more. While permissions are essential for providing functionality, they also pose significant privacy and security risks if misused. App permissions misuse occurs when applications request or access more permissions than necessary or handle permissions irresponsibly, leading to unauthorized data access, privacy violations, and potential exploitation by malicious actors.

As the Android ecosystem evolves, new permission-related challenges have emerged, requiring developers and users to stay vigilant. Recent enhancements in the Android platform provide more granular control over permissions, but malicious actors continue to find ways to exploit them. To mitigate these risks, developers must adopt a security-first approach when requesting permissions, adhere to the principle of least privilege, and ensure transparency and user control over data access, fostering resilience in this dynamic landscape.

Engaging Curiosity: A Thought Experiment

- **Have you ever wondered why a simple flashlight app requests access to your contacts and location?**

  Why would a flashlight app need access to your contacts or GPS? What could the developers do with this data? How would you decide whether to grant such permissions, and what risks would you be taking?

- **What if an app running in the background was silently collecting and sharing your personal data without your knowledge?**

  How would you detect if an app was secretly collecting your data? What tools or techniques could you use to monitor app behaviour? How would you hold developers accountable for misuse of permissions?

- **Can you imagine the potential privacy violations if an over-privileged app accessed your sensitive information without a legitimate reason?**

  What kind of sensitive information could an app access if granted unnecessary permissions? How could this data be misused? What steps could you take to minimize the risk of over-privileged apps compromising your privacy?

2.5.1 Common Types

Identifying Risks and Exploits

Understanding how permissions can be misused is crucial for safeguarding user data and maintaining app integrity. Recognizing these common types enhances our proactive stance:

- **Over-privileged Permissions:** This occurs when an application requests more permissions than necessary for its intended functionality. Over-privileged apps may access sensitive data, such as contacts, location, or call logs, without a legitimate need. This not only poses a privacy risk but also increases the potential for data leakage and unauthorized data sharing with third parties.
- **Under-explained Permissions:** When apps fail to adequately explain why certain permissions are needed, users may grant access without understanding the implications. Lack of transparency can lead to user mistrust and increase the likelihood of privacy breaches, as users may unknowingly grant access to sensitive data or device functionalities.
- **Persistent Background Access:** Some apps request permissions to run continuously in the background, accessing data or device features without user awareness. Persistent background access can lead to unauthorized data collection, increased battery consumption, and potential exploitation by malicious actors who manipulate background processes for nefarious purposes.
- **Unauthorized Data Sharing:** Apps that misuse permissions may share collected data with third parties without user consent. Unauthorized data sharing can lead to privacy violations and potentially expose sensitive information to external entities, increasing the risk of data breaches and misuse.
- **Covert Permission Escalation:** Some applications exploit indirect methods to gain higher privileges than initially granted. This may include leveraging third-party SDKs or piggybacking on other authorized applications to access sensitive data beyond their declared permissions.

2.5.2 Best Practices

Ensuring Responsible Data Access

To prevent app permission misuse and protect user privacy, developers should adhere to best practices for permissions management:

- **Principle of Least Privilege:** Request only the permissions necessary for the application's core functionality. By adhering to this principle, developers can minimize the risk of unauthorized data access and reduce the attack surface for potential exploits.
- **Runtime Permissions:** Utilize runtime permissions, where users are prompted to grant permissions when the app requires them for the first time. This approach increases transparency and gives users control over what data or device features the app can access, enhancing privacy and security.
- **Clear and Contextual Explanations:** Provide clear and contextual explanations for why each permission is needed. Use Android's Permission Rationale to inform users about the specific reasons for requesting permissions, helping them make informed decisions about whether to grant or deny access.

- **Background Access Minimization:** Do not request background access permissions unless absolutely necessary. When background access is required, ensure that the app behaves transparently and responsibly, informing users of the data being accessed and providing options to control or revoke permissions.
- **Regular Permissions Review:** Periodically review the app's permissions to ensure they are still necessary and aligned with the app's functionality. Remove or modify permissions that are no longer required to minimize potential security and privacy risks.

2.5.3 Mitigating Risks

Protecting User Privacy and Security

Implementing strategies to mitigate the risks associated with app permissions misuse is crucial for protecting user privacy and maintaining a secure app environment:

- **User Education:** Educate users about the importance of permissions and the potential risks of granting excessive access. Provide guidance on how to manage permissions settings and encourage users to regularly review and adjust app permissions based on their preferences and comfort levels.
- **Permission Monitoring Tools:** Use permission monitoring tools and frameworks, such as Android's AppOpsManager, to track app permissions usage and identify potential misuse. These tools can help detect anomalies or unauthorized access attempts, enabling timely intervention and remediation.
- **Compliance with Privacy Regulations:** Ensure compliance with privacy regulations, such as the General Data Protection Regulation (GDPR) or the California Consumer Privacy Act (CCPA), which mandate transparent data-handling practices and user consent for data access. Adhering to these regulations helps protect user privacy and build trust with users.
- **Data Minimization:** Implement data minimization practices by collecting only the data necessary for the app's functionality. Limiting data collection reduces the risk of data breaches and unauthorized access, protecting user privacy.
- **Security Audits and Assessments:** Conduct regular security audits and assessments to identify and address permissions-related vulnerabilities. Use automated tools and manual reviews to evaluate the app's permissions model and ensure it aligns with best practices and security standards.
- **User-controlled Permissions Management:** Encourage users to proactively manage their app permissions by providing intuitive UI options for reviewing and modifying permissions. Offer features like permission dashboards or notifications for permission changes to keep users informed.

2.6 Unsecured APIs

Innovating API Security in a Connected Ecosystem

Unsecured APIs (application programming interfaces) pose significant security risks to Android applications as they can expose sensitive data and functionalities to unauthorized access or manipulation by attackers.

In an era of interconnected applications and microservices, API security is crucial. Adopting emerging API security standards, implementing robust monitoring and rate-limiting mechanisms, and encouraging collaboration across the developer community contribute to building a resilient API ecosystem capable of withstanding the relentless onslaught of cyber threats.

Engaging Curiosity: A Thought Experiment

- **Have you ever wondered how much sensitive data could be exposed if an API endpoint were accidentally left unprotected?**

  Imagine a scenario where a developer forgets to secure an API endpoint, and suddenly, sensitive user data like names, emails, or even payment information is accessible to anyone who knows the URL. How would you detect such a vulnerability? What steps could you take to ensure that all API endpoints are properly secured before deployment?

- **What if a seemingly harmless API request allowed attackers to manipulate your app's data and functionalities without you knowing?**

  Consider an API that allows users to update their profile information. What if an attacker discovers a way to manipulate this API to change data for other users? How would you design your API to prevent such unauthorized access? What monitoring tools could you use to detect and respond to suspicious API activity?

- **Can you imagine the chaos if your API's security was compromised, leading to unauthorized access and potential data breaches?**

  Picture a situation where an attacker gains access to your API and starts extracting sensitive data or injecting malicious code. How would you identify the breach? What steps would you take to contain the damage and prevent future attacks? How would you communicate the breach to your users?

2.6.1 API Security Threats

Fortifying Your APIs

Various security threats can affect APIs and compromise the security of Android applications, demanding vigilant and proactive countermeasures:

- **API Misconfigurations:** Misconfigured APIs can expose endpoints unintentionally, leading to unauthorized access to sensitive data. Common misconfigurations include a lack of authentication, verbose error messages revealing stack traces, or improper CORS (Cross-Origin Resource Sharing) settings. Regular security audits and configuration reviews are essential to mitigate these risks.
- **Injection Attacks in GraphQL and REST APIs:** With the increasing adoption of GraphQL and RESTful APIs for application development, attackers have found new ways to exploit vulnerabilities specific to these technologies. For GraphQL APIs, which have gained significant adoption, specific vulnerabilities such as nested query attacks (leading to DoS) and inadequate input validation require special attention, including depth limiting and query cost analysis.

- **Broken Object Level Authorization (BOLA):** BOLA is a critical vulnerability where an API grants access to sensitive objects without proper authorization checks. Attackers can exploit this to access or manipulate data that they should not have access to. Ensuring that authorization checks are performed at the object level for every API request is crucial.
- **API Abuse and Business Logic Attacks:** Attackers may exploit flaws in the API's business logic to perform unauthorized actions, manipulate data, or overuse resources. Implementing strict access controls, conducting thorough code reviews, and performing security testing, including logic testing, can help identify and fix these vulnerabilities.
- **Server-Side Request Forgery (SSRF):** APIs that accept user input and fetch data from other services can be vulnerable to SSRF attacks. Attackers can manipulate the API to make requests to unintended destinations, potentially accessing internal resources or services. Validating and sanitizing user inputs, implementing network-level controls, and restricting outbound connections can mitigate SSRF risks.
- **GraphQL Introspection Attacks:** Exploitation of GraphQL's built-in introspection feature to map entire API schemas, identify sensitive queries and mutations, and discover attack vectors. Attackers use introspection queries to understand API structure, locate privilege escalation opportunities, and craft targeted injection attacks against GraphQL endpoints.
- **API Shadow Discovery:** Identification and exploitation of undocumented, deprecated, or 'shadow' APIs that exist in production environments without proper security controls. These forgotten or unmonitored endpoints often lack authentication, input validation, and logging, providing attackers with undetected access paths to sensitive data and functionality.

2.6.2 API Security Standards

Building a Secure Foundation

Adhering to established API security standards and best practices is essential for ensuring the robustness and integrity of Android applications. These standards provide the backbone for resilient API defences:

- **OAuth 2.0:** OAuth 2.0 is a protocol that allows applications to obtain limited access to user accounts on an HTTP service. It delegates authentication to the resource owner's authorization server and issues access tokens to third-party clients. In Android apps, OAuth 2.0 can be securely implemented using libraries such as AppAuth-Android, which supports best practices like Proof Key for Code Exchange (PKCE) and secure token handling.
- **OpenID Connect:** OpenID Connect is a simple identity layer built on top of the OAuth 2.0 protocol. It enables clients to verify the identity of users based on authentication performed by an authorization server. It provides standardized mechanisms for user authentication and single sign-on (SSO), improving both security and user experience. When integrated into Android applications via libraries like AppAuth, OpenID Connect ensures secure session management and identity claims validation.
- **JSON Web Tokens (JWT):** JWT is a compact, URL-safe format for representing claims between parties. JWTs are commonly used in API authentication and authorization flows to encode user identity, roles, and permissions. In Android apps, JWTs should be validated on the server side and handled securely on the client (e.g., avoiding long-term

storage in plaintext). Use of signed (JWS) and optionally encrypted (JWE) tokens is recommended to ensure integrity and confidentiality.

- **OAuth 2.0 Scopes:** Scopes define the permissions granted to a client application during authorization, limiting access to only the resources and actions necessary for its function (principle of least privilege). Properly defined and enforced scopes reduce the risk of privilege escalation and unauthorized data access. Android apps should request only the minimum required scopes and avoid overly broad permissions like admin or full_access.
- **OAuth 2.1 and Financial-grade API (FAPI) 2.0:** Evolution of OAuth standards addressing modern security requirements, including stronger cryptographic requirements, mandatory PKCE for all clients, and enhanced security for high-risk applications. FAPI 2.0 specifically addresses financial services security needs with stricter authentication and authorization requirements.

2.6.3 API Monitoring

Maintaining Vigilance

Continuous monitoring of API traffic and activities is essential for detecting and responding to potential security incidents or anomalies. This vigilant oversight ensures proactive threat management:

- **Real-Time Monitoring:** Real-time monitoring involves capturing and analysing API traffic as it happens, enabling immediate detection of anomalies, suspicious activities, and potential security incidents. For Android apps, developers can use dedicated API monitoring solutions or build custom monitoring logic into their apps. Tools like Charles or Wireshark can be used during development and testing to monitor API traffic and identify potential issues.
- **Log Aggregation and Analysis:** Centralizing API logs and analysing them for patterns of malicious behaviour or unauthorized access attempts allows for timely detection and response to security threats. Aggregated logs provide valuable insights into API usage and potential vulnerabilities, helping developers identify and address issues proactively.
- **Threat Intelligence Integration:** Integrating threat intelligence feeds into API monitoring systems enables the correlation of API traffic with known indicators of compromise (IOCs) and emerging threats. This enhances detection capabilities and helps respond to security incidents more effectively.

2.6.4 API Rate Limiting

Controlling the Flow

Implementing API rate-limiting controls is essential for protecting backend servers from abuse, DoS attacks, and unauthorized access attempts. These controls maintain a balanced and secure ecosystem:

- **Advanced Throttling Techniques:** Implementing algorithms like token bucket or leaky bucket for rate limiting provides flexible and fair usage policies. Throttling can be adjusted dynamically based on user behaviour, time of day, or detected threat levels. This helps prevent abuse while maintaining service quality for legitimate users.

- **API Gateways:** Utilizing API gateways provides a centralized point to enforce rate limiting, authentication, and other security policies. API gateways can handle traffic management and load balancing, and provide additional security features such as request validation, anomaly detection, and caching to enhance performance and security.
- **Quota Management:** Assigning usage quotas to different API consumers ensures that resources are used appropriately. Quotas can be based on subscription levels, user roles, or specific use cases. This prevents any single user or application from monopolizing resources and encourages fair usage.
- **Self-Service Portals:** Providing developers with self-service portals to monitor their API usage and manage their access keys promotes transparency and encourages responsible usage. It simplifies key rotation, access revocation processes, and allows developers to receive real-time feedback on their API consumption.

2.7 Code Injection

Embracing a Future-proof Approach to Code Injection Defence

Code injection attacks involve inserting and executing malicious code within an application's runtime environment, potentially leading to unauthorized access, data manipulation, or system compromise. In the Android ecosystem, code injection threats have evolved with the increasing complexity of applications, the use of third-party libraries, and the adoption of dynamic features such as reflection and code generation.

As attackers continuously refine their techniques, developers must adopt a proactive stance toward secure coding practices and vulnerability management. Integrating automated code analysis tools, embracing DevSecOps principles, utilizing AI-driven security solutions, and fostering a culture of security-first development contribute to building resilient applications that adapt to emerging threats and stand the test of time.

Engaging Curiosity: A Thought Experiment

- **Have you ever wondered how a seemingly harmless input could allow attackers to execute malicious code within your app?**

  Imagine a user enters a seemingly innocent comment on your app, but it contains hidden code that, when processed, allows the attacker to take control of your server. How would you detect such an attack? What coding practices could you adopt to prevent malicious inputs from being executed?

- **What if a popular third-party library you are using contains hidden vulnerabilities that could compromise your entire application?**

  You rely on a third-party library for a critical feature, but it turns out to have a vulnerability that allows attackers to inject malicious code. How would you discover such a vulnerability? What steps could you take to ensure that third-party libraries are secure before integrating them into your app?

- **Can you imagine the potential damage if a reflection-based attack manipulated your app's behaviour without you even realizing it?**

Reflection allows your app to execute code dynamically, but it can also be exploited by attackers to manipulate your app's behaviour. How would you detect such an attack? What precautions could you take to limit the use of reflection and prevent it from being abused?

2.7.1 Injection Techniques

Thwarting Invaders

Various injection techniques can be used to exploit code injection vulnerabilities in Android applications, requiring vigilant countermeasures:

- **Deserialization Attacks:** These occur when untrusted data is deserialized into objects without proper validation. In Android, insecure deserialization can lead to arbitrary code execution, privilege escalation, or denial-of-service attacks. Attackers craft malicious serialized objects that, when deserialized, execute unintended code paths. Using safe serialization practices and avoiding the deserialization of untrusted inputs are crucial defences.
- **Reflection and Dynamic Code Execution:** Apps that utilize reflection or dynamically execute code, such as loading code from external sources or using scripting engines, may expose themselves to code injection risks. Attackers can manipulate inputs to alter the behaviour of reflection APIs or inject malicious code into dynamically executed content. Limiting the use of reflection and dynamic execution and implementing strict input validation can mitigate these threats.
- **Dependency Injection Attacks:** In applications using dependency injection frameworks, attackers may exploit misconfigurations or vulnerabilities to alter the application flow, inject malicious components, or override existing dependencies with malicious ones. Ensuring proper configuration and validation within dependency injection frameworks is essential.
- **Software Bill of Materials (SBOM) Attacks:** Advanced supply chain attacks that target software dependencies through compromised components that evade traditional SBOM analysis. Attackers inject malicious code into legitimate libraries or create malicious packages with names similar to popular dependencies, exploiting automated dependency management systems and trust relationships in software supply chains.
- **Insecure Use of WebViews and Hybrid Applications:** Modern hybrid apps that use WebViews or frameworks like React Native can be susceptible to JavaScript injection or bridge attacks, where malicious scripts interact with the native code, leading to code execution in the application context. Implementing strict security measures in WebViews and hybrid frameworks is imperative.

2.7.2 Secure Coding Practices

Building Resilient Code

Implementing secure coding practices is crucial for preventing code injection vulnerabilities and maintaining the security of Android applications. These practices align with our proactive security ethos:

- **Input Validation:** This involves ensuring that user-supplied data meets specific criteria before processing it in the app. Input validation can prevent many types of injection attacks by rejecting illegitimate or malicious input. For example, ensuring that numeric fields contain only digits or that email fields contain valid email addresses can prevent attempts to inject harmful code.
- **Output Encoding:** This is the process of converting data into a format that is safe for output, particularly in contexts like HTML or JavaScript. In Android apps, output encoding is essential when displaying user-supplied data in a WebView to prevent XSS attacks. Proper encoding ensures that any potentially dangerous characters are rendered harmless.
- **Parameterized Queries:** This technique involves using placeholders for user input in SQL queries, separating data from code. In Android, parameterized queries can be implemented using SQLite's '?' placeholder for user-supplied input in SQL queries. This prevents SQL injection attacks by ensuring that user input is treated as data, not executable code.
- **Secure Deserialization:** Avoid deserializing data from untrusted sources. If deserialization is necessary, use libraries that enforce type constraints and implement strict input validation. Employing serialization formats that are less prone to injection attacks, such as Protocol Buffers or JSON with strict parsing, enhances security.
- **Limiting Reflection and Dynamic Execution:** Minimize the use of reflection and dynamic code execution. If required, enforce strict controls and validation to prevent misuse. Ensure that any dynamically loaded code comes from trusted sources and is verified for integrity.
- **Safe Dependency Management:** Use dependency management tools that verify the integrity of third-party libraries. Regularly audit dependencies for known vulnerabilities using tools like OWASP Dependency-Check, Snyk, or WhiteSource Bolt. Keeping dependencies updated reduces exposure to known vulnerabilities.
- **Secure Coding Frameworks:** Leveraging secure coding frameworks, libraries, or development tools that provide built-in protection against common injection vulnerabilities can significantly enhance application security. For example, using ORM libraries like Room for database access or security-focused libraries like OWASP's ESAPI can reduce the risk of introducing vulnerabilities.

2.7.3 Static and Dynamic Analysis

Unveiling Hidden Vulnerabilities

Conducting static and dynamic analysis of code is essential for identifying and mitigating code injection vulnerabilities in Android applications. These analyses ensure vigilant oversight:

- **Static Code Analysis:** This involves analysing the application's source code without executing it. Static analysis tools scan the source code for patterns that indicate potential vulnerabilities, including code injection vulnerabilities. These tools can identify insecure coding practices, such as improper input handling or the use of dangerous APIs, helping developers address issues early in the development process.
- **Dynamic Code Analysis:** This involves analysing the application while it is running to identify vulnerabilities that may not be apparent in the source code. In Android, dynamic analysis tools monitor running applications for behaviours indicative of vulnerabilities, such as unexpected system calls, file operations, or memory accesses.

Dynamic analysis can uncover issues like race conditions or insecure data handling that static analysis might miss.

- **Fuzz Testing:** Also known as fuzzing, this technique involves providing random, malformed, or unexpected input to an application to identify vulnerabilities. Fuzz testing is particularly effective for uncovering injection vulnerabilities, boundary conditions, or error-handling flaws. In Android, fuzz testing can be used to test input fields, APIs, or other points of user interaction.
- **AI-Powered Code Analysis:** Leverage artificial intelligence and machine learning in static code analysis tools to detect complex vulnerabilities. Tools like DeepCode AI by Synk can analyse code semantics and patterns to identify potential injection points that traditional tools might miss.
- **Interactive Application Security Testing (IAST):** IAST combines static and dynamic analysis during runtime testing, providing real-time insights into an application's security. IAST tools monitor applications as they run, identifying vulnerabilities in real-world conditions, and are particularly effective for detecting injection flaws.
- **Runtime Application Self-Protection (RASP):** Integrate RASP solutions that monitor application behaviour at runtime and can detect and block injection attacks as they occur. RASP adds a layer of defence within the application, identifying anomalous activities such as unexpected code execution paths or dangerous API calls.

2.7.4 Proactive Patch Management and DevSecOps

Staying Ahead of Threats

Applying timely patches and updates is crucial for addressing known vulnerabilities and reducing the risk of code injection attacks in Android applications. This proactive approach keeps us ahead of evolving threats:

- **Timely Patching:** This involves regularly updating your app's dependencies to their latest versions, often including security patches that fix known vulnerabilities. This means keeping the Android SDK, libraries, and other dependencies up-to-date in Android. Automated tools can help track dependency versions and notify developers when updates are available.
- **Vulnerability Management:** This is the process of identifying, classifying, prioritizing, remediating, and mitigating application vulnerabilities. In the context of Android, this could involve subscribing to security bulletins and advisories related to Android development, using tools to monitor your app for known vulnerabilities, and prioritizing fixes based on the severity and exploitability of the vulnerabilities. Proactive vulnerability management ensures that security issues are addressed promptly, reducing the risk of exploitation.
- **Automated Updates:** Whenever possible, enable automated updates for dependencies and libraries to ensure that applications receive security patches and updates as soon as they are released. This minimizes the window of exposure for newly discovered vulnerabilities and helps maintain a strong security posture.
- **Automated Vulnerability Scanning:** Incorporate continuous vulnerability scanning into the CI/CD pipeline using tools like SonarQube, Veracode, or Fortify. This ensures that vulnerabilities are identified and addressed before deployment.

- **Shift-Left Security (DevSecOps):** Embracing DevSecOps involves integrating security practices early in the development process. This includes secure coding training for developers, integrating security tools into development environments, and fostering collaboration between development, security, and operations teams.
- **Real-Time Threat Intelligence Integration:** Utilize real-time threat intelligence feeds to stay informed about emerging vulnerabilities and attack vectors. Subscribing to platforms like MITRE ATT&CK or Cyber Threat Alliance keeps developers aware of the latest threats impacting Android applications.

2.8 Data Leakage

Securing Data in a Connected World

Data leakage refers to the unauthorized transmission or exposure of sensitive information, such as personal data, financial records, or proprietary business information. In today's interconnected digital landscape, the protection of sensitive data is more critical than ever. With evolving regulations and advancing technologies, adopting robust encryption practices and proactive data leak prevention strategies is essential to safeguard user information and maintain trust.

Fostering a culture of data stewardship and prioritizing regulatory compliance helps ensure the privacy and security of user information in the digital age.

Engaging Curiosity: A Thought Experiment

- **Have you ever wondered what would happen if your personal data were stored in plaintext, vulnerable to any prying eyes?**

  Imagine your app stores user data like passwords or credit card information in plaintext on the device. If the device is lost or stolen, how easily could an attacker access this data? What encryption methods could you use to protect sensitive information, even if the device falls into the wrong hands?

- **What if your sensitive information was intercepted while being transmitted over an unsecured network?**

  You are sending sensitive data over a public Wi-Fi network, and an attacker intercepts it. How would you know if your data was compromised? What encryption protocols could you implement to ensure that data is secure, even if the network is not?

- **Can you imagine the legal and financial consequences if your app failed to comply with data protection regulations?**

  Your app collects user data but fails to comply with regulations like GDPR or CCPA. What penalties could you face? How would you handle a data breach notification to users and regulators? What steps could you take to ensure compliance with data protection laws?

2.8.1 Storage Vulnerabilities

Protecting Your Data

Storage vulnerabilities arise when sensitive information is not adequately protected on a device, making it susceptible to unauthorized access. Addressing these vulnerabilities is key to resilient data protection:

- **Insecure Data Storage:** Android provides several options for data storage, such as Shared Preferences, SQLite databases, and the file system. However, these storage mechanisms should not be used to store sensitive information like passwords, encryption keys, or personal data in plaintext. Failing to secure data at rest can lead to significant breaches if the device is compromised. Leveraging encrypted storage solutions and ensuring data is encrypted before being stored can mitigate these risks.
- **Weak Encryption:** When encrypting data, it is crucial to use strong encryption algorithms (e.g., AES-256) and follow best practices for key management. Use AndroidKeyStore to generate and protect cryptographic keys. Avoid key export and ensure keys are bound to device integrity (e.g., require user authentication). Adopting end-to-end encryption for data storage can significantly enhance security.
- **Improper File Permissions:** Android uses a permission-based security model to restrict access to files and directories. It is vital to set permissions to prevent unauthorized access carefully. For example, use private mode (MODE_PRIVATE) when creating files so they can only be accessed by your app, reducing the risk of other apps accessing sensitive data.
- **Side-Channel Data Leakage:** Information disclosure through indirect channels, including sensor data patterns, power consumption analysis, electromagnetic emissions, and timing attacks. These sophisticated techniques can extract sensitive information like cryptographic keys or personal data without direct access to storage systems, exploiting physical characteristics of device operation.

2.8.2 Transmission Security

Securing Data in Transit

Ensuring the security of data transmission between Android devices and remote servers is crucial to prevent interception or tampering by attackers. These measures uphold our commitment to secure connectivity:

- **Secure Communication Protocols:** When your app communicates with servers, always use secure protocols like HTTPS with TLS (Transport Layer Security). Avoid sending sensitive information over unencrypted connections, as this can be intercepted by attackers. Android's Network Security Configuration allows you to enforce secure communication for your app without needing to change its code, ensuring all data in transit is protected. Implementing forward secrecy within TLS can further enhance the security of data in transit.
- **Certificate Validation:** Implement certificate pinning in your app to ensure it communicates only with the intended servers. Certificate pinning involves storing a copy of the server's certificate or public key within the app, which is then used to verify the server's identity during communication. This technique helps prevent man-in-the-middle attacks where an attacker intercepts and potentially alters your app's network

traffic. Regularly updating pinned certificates and utilizing automated tools for managing certificate lifecycles can improve reliability and security.

2.8.3 Regulatory Compliance

Meeting Data Protection Standard

Compliance with regulatory standards and data protection laws is essential for ensuring the privacy and security of user data stored or processed by Android applications. Adhering to these standards reinforces our proactive responsibility:

- **Data Protection Regulations:** Adhering to data protection laws, such as the General Data Protection Regulation (GDPR) or the California Consumer Privacy Act (CCPA), is crucial for safeguarding user privacy rights and preventing unauthorized data processing or disclosure. These regulations often require businesses to implement specific security measures, obtain user consent for data collection, and provide users with control over their data. Staying informed about updates to these regulations and implementing compliance automation tools can streamline adherence to legal requirements.
- **Industry Standards:** Following industry-specific security standards and best practices is vital for ensuring compliance and protecting sensitive data. For example, the Payment Card Industry Data Security Standard (PCI DSS) provides guidelines for securing payment information. At the same time, the Health Insurance Portability and Accountability Act (HIPAA) outlines requirements for protecting healthcare data. Leveraging industry-specific security frameworks and conducting regular audits can ensure compliance and strengthen security.
- **Data Breach Notification:** Establishing procedures for promptly notifying users and regulatory authorities in case of a data breach or unauthorized data disclosure is essential for complying with legal requirements and mitigating potential harm to affected individuals. Timely notification can help users take necessary actions to protect themselves and reduce the impact of the breach. Utilizing automated breach detection and notification systems can improve response times and ensure compliance.

2.8.4 Data Leak Prevention

Minimizing Data Loss

Preventing data leakage requires a proactive approach to identify and mitigate potential risks throughout the application lifecycle. These strategies enhance our resilience against leaks:

- **Encryption at Rest:** Sensitive data stored on the device should be encrypted to prevent unauthorized access in case of device theft or loss. Using Android's Keystore system or encrypted shared preferences provided by the Jetpack Security library can help ensure that sensitive data remains protected, even if the device is compromised. Implementing robust key management practices and regular encryption key rotation can further enhance data security.
- **Data Minimization:** Following the principle of data minimization, collecting and storing only the minimum amount of data necessary for the application's functionality can significantly reduce the risk of data exposure in the event of a breach. Minimizing the amount of sensitive data stored also minimizes the potential impact of a data leak.

Conducting regular data audits and implementing data retention policies can help enforce data minimization practices.

- **Data Loss Prevention (DLP) Solutions:** Implementing DLP solutions can help monitor and control the movement of sensitive data within an organization's network and endpoints, preventing unauthorized access or leakage. DLP tools can identify, monitor, and protect sensitive information, ensuring that data is only accessible to authorized users and is not transferred outside the organization without proper authorization. Integrating DLP solutions with other security measures, such as encryption and access controls, can provide a comprehensive approach to data protection.

2.9 Device Exploitation

Securing Tomorrow's Devices Against Emerging Threats

Device exploitation refers to the act of leveraging vulnerabilities or weaknesses in Android devices to gain unauthorized access or control or compromise the integrity of the device. As the Android ecosystem continues to expand with new technologies such as the Internet of Things (IoT), 5G connectivity, and an increasing reliance on mobile devices, the risks associated with device exploitation have grown more complex and sophisticated.

Embracing next-generation endpoint security solutions, implementing robust device management practices, and fostering user education initiatives help ensure the security and integrity of tomorrow's Android devices while maintaining an edge in the evolving threat landscape.

Engaging Curiosity: A Thought Experiment

- **Have you ever wondered how a single vulnerability in your device's bootloader could lead to a complete takeover by malicious actors?**

  A vulnerability in the bootloader allows an attacker to install malicious firmware, giving them complete control over your device. How would you detect such an attack? What steps could you take to secure the bootloader and prevent unauthorized modifications?

- **What if zero-day exploits were silently compromising your device, with no patches available to protect you?**

  A zero-day exploit targets a vulnerability in your device's operating system; no patch is available yet. How would you detect if your device was compromised? What proactive measures could you take to minimize the risk of zero-day attacks?

- **Can you imagine the potential chaos if attackers exploited your mobile device's weaknesses, accessing sensitive data and controlling your apps?**

  Attackers exploit a weakness in your device, gaining access to your emails and messages and even control over your apps. How would you respond to such an attack? What tools or practices could you use to secure your device and prevent future exploitation?

2.9.1 Rooting Techniques

Understanding the Risks

Rooting involves gaining privileged access to the Android operating system, allowing users to bypass built-in security restrictions and install unauthorized applications or modify system files. While rooting can offer greater control over the device, it also introduces significant security risks:

- **Magisk and Systemless Rooting:** Newer rooting methods like Magisk enable "systemless" rooting, modifying the device without altering the system partition. This makes it harder for security mechanisms to detect rooted devices, increasing the risk of undetected exploitation by malicious actors.
- **Bootloader Exploitation:** Attackers may exploit vulnerabilities in the device's bootloader to gain persistent root access. Such exploitation can lead to the installation of malicious firmware or custom ROMs that are difficult to detect and remove.
- **Security Implications:** Advanced rooting techniques can disable Android's built-in security features, making devices more susceptible to malware, data breaches, and unauthorized access. Rooted devices may bypass security policies (SafetyNet/Play Integrity) enforced by applications or enterprise management systems, posing significant risks in organizational contexts.
- **Detection and Mitigation:** Developers and security solutions are incorporating advanced root detection methods, including behavioural analysis and monitoring for root access commands. Encouraging users to avoid rooting and educating them on the associated risks remains crucial.

2.9.2 Zero-day Vulnerabilities and Exploit Chains

The Unforeseen Threats

Zero-day vulnerabilities are security flaws or weaknesses in software or hardware that are unknown to the vendor and unpatched, making them attractive targets for attackers. These vulnerabilities are particularly dangerous because they can be exploited before the vendor has a chance to release a patch or mitigation.

- **Sophisticated Exploits:** Attackers develop advanced exploits targeting core components of the Android operating system, such as the kernel, media frameworks, or hardware drivers. These exploits can lead to remote code execution, privilege escalation, and complete device compromise. Recent trends show an increase in firmware-level attacks, including exploits targeting the bootloader and baseband processors, which can lead to persistent compromise even after OS updates.
- **Exploit Kits and Malware Frameworks:** The availability of exploit kits and modular malware frameworks in underground markets makes it easier for attackers to exploit zero-day vulnerabilities at scale. These tools often incorporate obfuscation and anti-analysis techniques to evade detection.
- **Over-the-Air (OTA) Update Hijacking:** Attackers may target the OTA update mechanism, delivering malicious updates that exploit zero-day vulnerabilities to compromise devices. Secure update practices, including update signing and integrity verification, are critical defences.

- **Vendor Response:** A timely response from vendors is crucial when zero-day vulnerabilities are discovered. This includes implementing vulnerability disclosure policies, coordinating with security researchers and industry partners, and promptly releasing security patches. Effective communication with users about potential risks and available mitigations is also essential.
- **Defence Strategies:** To protect against zero-day attacks, organizations and individuals should implement proactive security measures, such as intrusion detection systems (IDS), anomaly detection, and endpoint protection solutions. Regular monitoring and threat intelligence can help detect and mitigate zero-day exploits targeting Android devices, reducing the potential impact of these attacks.

2.9.3 Device Management Solutions

Maintaining Control in a Complex Landscape

Device management solutions provide organizations with centralized control and visibility over Android devices deployed in enterprise environments. These solutions enable the enforcement of security policies, monitoring of device compliance, and an effective response to security incidents:

- **Mobile Device Management (MDM):** MDM solutions allow organizations to enforce security policies, remotely manage and monitor devices, and protect against unauthorized access, data breaches, and other security threats. Features such as remote wiping, password enforcement, and app management help maintain control over devices and ensure compliance with organizational security standards.
- **Mobile Application Management (MAM):** MAM focuses on controlling access to corporate data and resources by managing application permissions, enforcing app whitelisting or blacklisting, and implementing containerization or sandboxing to isolate sensitive data. This approach provides granular control over app behaviour and data access, reducing the risk of data leakage or unauthorized access.
- **Endpoint Detection and Response (EDR):** EDR solutions are designed to detect, investigate, and respond to security incidents on Android devices. These solutions monitor device activities, detect anomalies, and provide real-time alerts for potential threats, such as malware infections, suspicious behaviours, and unauthorized access attempts. EDR enhances an organization's ability to respond swiftly to security incidents and mitigate risks.
- **Device Inventory:** Maintaining an accurate inventory of managed devices is essential for tracking device status, ownership, and usage patterns. Device inventory systems can generate reports or alerts to identify security risks or compliance violations, enabling proactive management of devices and ensuring they remain secure.
- **Remote Wipe and Lock:** It is crucial to provide administrators with the ability to remotely wipe or lock devices in case of loss, theft, or security incidents to prevent unauthorized access to sensitive data. Remote wipe and lock capabilities help protect corporate data and maintain security even when devices are compromised or go missing.
- **Remote Attestation:** Implementation of cryptographic verification systems that allow remote servers to verify device integrity, detect tampering, and validate the trustworthiness of device hardware and software components. This approach provides continuous assurance of the device's security state without requiring physical access to the device.

- **Hardware Security Module (HSM) Protection:** Securing cryptographic operations and key storage within dedicated hardware security modules that provide tamper-resistant environments. Modern Android devices increasingly rely on HSMs for secure key generation, storage, and cryptographic operations, making HSM security critical for overall device protection.

2.9.4 User Education and Security Culture

Empowering Users in a Changing Environment

Educating users about device security risks, best practices, and security hygiene is essential for preventing device exploitation and protecting sensitive data. These efforts build a vigilant security culture:

- **Device Security Best Practices:** Users should be educated about Android device security best practices, such as avoiding rooting, keeping devices updated with the latest security patches, and using built-in security features like encryption and screen locks. Encouraging users to enable features like biometric authentication and two-factor authentication (2FA) can further enhance device security.
- **Risk Awareness:** Users should be made aware of the risks associated with unauthorized modifications to Android devices, including exposure to malware, loss of data privacy, and compromise of sensitive information. Educating users about the potential consequences of these actions can discourage risky behaviours and promote safer device usage.
- **Safe Browsing Habits:** To prevent exploitation, users should be advised to exercise caution when downloading apps, clicking on links, or sharing sensitive information online. Users should also be taught to recognize and avoid potential security threats like phishing attacks, malicious websites, and untrusted app sources.

Looking Ahead

Traversing the dynamic landscape of Android threats reveals that securing Android apps is not merely a one-time effort but an ongoing commitment to vigilance and innovation. This chapter has highlighted the myriad threats that developers must contend with. Each of these threats underscores the importance of adopting a proactive and comprehensive approach to security, one that integrates rigorous testing, continuous monitoring, and a deep understanding of emerging vulnerabilities.

Secure coding, supply chain integrity, API security, and device integrity checks (e.g., Play Integrity) are essential strategies in defending against common attack vectors. Additionally, regular security audits and threat modelling can help identify and address vulnerabilities before they are exploited. In conclusion, navigating the Android threat landscape requires a multifaceted strategy that combines technical expertise, proactive defence mechanisms, and a commitment to continuous improvement.

Moving forward, it is crucial to integrate security into the entire app development lifecycle rather than treating it as an afterthought. Automation through DevSecOps pipelines and AI-powered security tools are becoming essential in identifying and mitigating threats early. The upcoming chapters will explore practical techniques and best practices for implementing security at every stage, ensuring that Android applications are functional, user-friendly, and fortified against emerging threats. Embracing a security-first mindset enables developers to contribute to a safer mobile ecosystem for all users.

Chapter 3

Android App Testing Essentials

The first step is to establish that something is possible; then probability will occur.

–Elon Musk

Elon Musk, the visionary entrepreneur, emphasizes the importance of taking the initial step to explore and validate the feasibility of an idea or concept. Once feasibility is established, the likelihood of success increases as efforts are directed towards realizing that possibility.

In the area of testing Android applications, this quote emphasizes the significance of conducting thorough assessments to determine the feasibility of ensuring the security, functionality, and performance of the applications. By initiating the testing process, developers or security experts can uncover potential vulnerabilities, identify areas for improvement, and enhance the overall quality of the application. Just as Musk suggests that taking the first step towards possibility leads to eventual probability, initiating testing processes is the first step towards ensuring the reliability and trustworthiness of Android applications, ultimately increasing the likelihood of delivering a secure and high-quality product to users.

DOI: 10.1201/9781003640332-4

A LAYMAN'S PERSPECTIVE

Become the Picasso of Android App Evaluation

Welcome to the area of Android application testing, where the journey to creating secure and reliable mobile experiences begins. This chapter explores the critical role that testing plays in crafting Android applications that not only stand out in performance but also excel in safeguarding user data.

Think of your favourite Android app as a finely tuned machine designed to serve a specific purpose with precision and reliability. Whether it is helping you stay connected with loved ones, manage your finances, or entertain you during moments of downtime, every app presents both an opportunity and a risk. A well-designed app enhances digital life, but a poorly secured one can expose users to cyber threats, data breaches, and privacy violations.

The path to creating seamless and secure experiences is riddled with challenges. Developers must ensure that apps function flawlessly across a multitude of devices, optimize performance for responsiveness, and, most importantly, protect sensitive data from security vulnerabilities. This is where rigorous Android app testing comes into play.

Imagine testing as the quality assurance process that distinguishes robust, secure apps from their vulnerable counterparts. Just as a skilled craftsman meticulously inspects every detail of a masterpiece, security-focused developers subject their applications to rigorous scrutiny, identifying vulnerabilities, fortifying defences, and ensuring compliance with security best practices.

Android app testing involves a structured approach to evaluating an app's resilience against threats such as data leaks, insecure authentication mechanisms, weak encryption, and potential backdoors. By proactively identifying and addressing these issues, developers can prevent security breaches before they occur.

This chapter will uncover the strategies and techniques used in testing Android applications. To achieve comprehensive testing, developers rely on a variety of toolsets tailored specifically for Android apps. These tools assist in automating repetitive tasks, simulating real-world attack scenarios, and providing actionable insights into potential weaknesses.

Let's explore this journey into the world of secure Android application development, where meticulous attention to detail, a commitment to quality, and a passion for innovation converge to create mobile experiences that are not only seamless but also safeguarded against ever-evolving threats.

3.1 Testing Android Apps

Unlocking Quality Through Testing

Testing your app is a bit like making sure your favourite recipe turns out just right every time. You know how you check each ingredient before you mix them together? That is like unit testing, making sure each part of your app works perfectly on its own, like checking each ingredient to make sure it is fresh.

Then, when you start mixing everything together, you want to make sure the flavours blend well. That is integration testing, which checks that all the different parts of your app work together smoothly, like making sure all the ingredients in your dish complement each other.

Now, imagine you have made your dish and want to make sure it tastes excellent from start to finish. That is system testing, checking the whole recipe from cooking to serving, just like checking your app from opening to using all its features.

However, a delicious dish is not just about taste but also about presentation. It is important to make sure your app looks good and feels easy to use, just like you would like your dish to look appetizing and be easy to eat. That is user interface (UI) and usability testing, making sure your app is not only functional but also user-friendly.

Just as you want your dish to be delicious every time, an app should perform well, even when many people use it. That is where performance testing comes in, making sure your app runs smoothly no matter how many users are on it, just like making sure your recipe works even when cooking for a big family gathering.

Of course, it is also required for your app to be safe and secure, just like you would want your food to be safe to eat. So, security testing is going to make sure your app protects users' information from any bad actors, just like making sure your recipe does not have any harmful ingredients.

Then there is compatibility testing, which is going to make sure that your app works on different devices and with different versions of Android, just like making sure your recipe works with different types of cookware and ovens. And finally, localization testing is going to make sure your app is welcoming to everyone, no matter where they are from or what language they speak, just like making sure your dish can be enjoyed by people from all over the world.

So, testing your app is a bit like making sure your favourite recipe is perfect every time you cook it, checking each ingredient, making sure everything blends together well, and making sure it looks good, tastes great, and is safe for everyone to enjoy.

3.1.1 Functional Testing

Validating Core App Functions

Functional testing is a critical phase in the application testing life cycle. It verifies that each app's function operates according to the required specifications.

The primary goal is to ensure that the application behaves as expected and that all components interact seamlessly to deliver the desired outcome.

Functional testing aims to identify functional gaps, inconsistencies, and defects by simulating real-world scenarios, ensuring the overall quality and reliability of the final product.

The following subsections detail various types of functional testing methods:

3.1.1.1 Unit Testing

Purpose: The primary aim of unit testing is to validate the functionality of individual units within the application. It ensures that each component operates correctly in isolation, which is crucial for the stability of complex applications.

Process: Developers write automated test cases covering various input scenarios for individual units, such as classes, functions, ViewModels, or Composables. These tests run frequently during development to catch regressions early.

Benefits: Unit testing enhances code reliability and maintainability. It allows developers to refactor code with confidence, knowing that tests will catch any unexpected errors. This practice also accelerates the development process by enabling faster identification and resolution of bugs.

3.1.1.2 Integration Testing

Purpose: Integration testing aims to expose issues in the interactions between integrated units. It is essential for ensuring that various components of the app work together as intended.

Process: This involves creating test suites that simulate interactions between components, including APIs, databases, and external services. Tests validate data flow, API contracts, and inter-component communication.

Benefits: It provides assurance that the app's architecture is robust and that components integrate well. This reduces the risk of integration issues in production and ensures a better user experience.

3.1.1.3 System Testing

Purpose: System testing assesses the application's compliance with the specified requirements. It provides a comprehensive evaluation of the app's end-to-end functionality and overall performance.

Process: Testers prepare test cases that cover all aspects of the application, including user interactions, transaction processes, and performance under various conditions. These tests are often conducted in an environment closely resembling the production setting.

Benefits: It validates the application's readiness for release. System testing helps uncover discrepancies between the actual product and its specifications, ensuring that the final product meets both user expectations and quality standards.

3.1.2 UI/UX Testing

User Experience Assurance

UI/UX testing is an essential aspect of the application testing process. It focuses on evaluating the application's user interface (UI) and user experience (UX).

The primary goal of UI/UX testing is to ensure that the application functions correctly and provides a smooth, intuitive, and engaging user experience. This involves assessing the app's design, layout, and interactive elements to ensure they meet both the intended standards and user expectations.

By identifying and rectifying issues related to usability, visual appeal, and accessibility, UI/UX testing plays a crucial role in enhancing the overall user satisfaction and the application's success.

The following subsections detail the different types of UI/UX testing methods:

3.1.2.1 UI Testing

Purpose: The purpose of UI testing is to ensure that the application's user interface aligns with the required standards of functionality, performance, and design. It aims to deliver a seamless and visually appealing experience to the user.

Process: UI testing involves creating and executing test cases that cover all aspects of the app's user interface, including:

- Verifying the correct display and functionality of UI elements.
- Ensuring responsiveness to different screen sizes and orientations.
- Checking compatibility with various devices and operating systems.
- Assessing performance under different network conditions.

Benefits: The benefits of thorough UI testing include:

- A polished and professional user interface.
- Improved user confidence and satisfaction.
- Reduced likelihood of usability issues post-release.
- A more inclusive experience for users with disabilities.
- Potentially higher ratings and better reviews on app stores.

3.1.2.2 Usability Testing

Purpose: Usability testing is conducted to evaluate the app's efficiency, effectiveness, and overall user satisfaction. It focuses on optimizing the user experience to foster app adoption and loyalty.

Process: The usability testing process typically involves:

- Recruiting participants representing the app's target demographic.
- Observing participants as they complete predefined tasks within the app.
- Collecting qualitative and quantitative data regarding user performance and satisfaction.
- Analysing the results to identify pain points and areas for enhancement.

Benefits: Key benefits of usability testing include:

- Actionable insights from actual users leading to user-centric design decisions.
- Identification of frustration points and obstacles within the app.
- Enhanced user engagement and lower abandonment rates.
- A more intuitive and seamless user journey.
- Direct contributions to the app's success through improved user retention.

3.1.3 Performance Testing

Stress-testing the Stability

Performance testing is a critical aspect of the application testing process that focuses on evaluating how an application performs under various conditions.

The primary objective is to ensure that the application handles expected user loads efficiently, responds promptly, and optimizes resource utilization. It helps identify potential bottlenecks, scalability issues, and performance degradations before the application is deployed to production.

Performance testing provides insights into an application's reliability, stability, and efficiency by simulating real-world usage scenarios and stress conditions.

The following subsections detail different types of performance testing methods:

3.1.3.1 Load Testing

Purpose: Load testing is conducted to evaluate an app's performance under various user load conditions, from regular usage to peak traffic scenarios.

Process: Test scenarios mimic real user behavior to measure response time, throughput, and resource consumption under normal and peak loads.

Benefits: The primary benefit of load testing is the identification and resolution of performance bottlenecks. This ensures that the app can handle high user demand without performance degradation, maintaining a consistent and reliable experience.

3.1.3.2 Stress Testing

Purpose: Stress testing aims to determine the app's resilience and stability under extreme conditions.

Process: Test scenarios push the app to its limits, such as high traffic surges or poor network conditions, to observe its behaviour under stress and identify failure points.

Benefits: The process helps uncover performance-related issues, stability concerns, and potential failure points in the app's architecture. It ensures the app remains functional and responsive, even in challenging situations.

3.1.3.3 Resource Usage Testing

Purpose: Resource usage testing is essential for monitoring and optimizing how an app utilizes critical system resources such as CPU, memory, and battery.

Process: Developers use profiling tools to track the app's resource consumption patterns. These tools provide insights into inefficient resource usage, allowing targeted optimizations.

Benefits: Efficient resource usage is crucial for minimizing battery drain and maintaining device performance. This testing ensures that the app runs smoothly across various devices and scenarios, improving the overall user experience.

3.1.4 Security Testing

Strengthening Defences

Security testing is a vital component of the application testing process. It ensures that an application is protected from vulnerabilities that could be exploited by malicious actors.

The primary objective is to identify and rectify security weaknesses, safeguard sensitive data, and maintain application integrity, confidentiality, and availability.

Developers can enhance application security by conducting thorough security assessments and ensuring compliance with industry standards and regulations.

Security testing involves various techniques to evaluate an application's defensive measures comprehensively.

The following subsections detail different types of security testing methods:

3.1.4.1 Penetration Testing

Purpose: Penetration testing aims to simulate real-world cyberattacks on an Android application to evaluate its security posture. It is designed to uncover vulnerabilities that could be exploited by malicious entities, thereby assessing the app's defence mechanisms.

Process: The penetration testing process includes:

- **Planning:** Defining the test scope and objectives.
- **Reconnaissance:** Gathering information to understand how the application functions and identifying potential weaknesses.
- **Exploitation:** Attempting to exploit known vulnerabilities using various tools and techniques.
- **Analysis and reporting:** Documenting findings and providing recommendations for mitigation.

Benefits: Penetration testing provides several benefits, including:

- Identifying security weaknesses before attackers can exploit them.
- Validating the effectiveness of existing security measures.
- Ensuring the protection of sensitive data by maintaining confidentiality, integrity, and availability.
- Complying with security standards and regulations can help avoid legal and financial repercussions.

3.1.4.2 Code Review

Purpose: Code review is a systematic evaluation of the application's source code. It is conducted to find and fix security vulnerabilities and coding errors, and ensure adherence to security best practices.

Process: The process includes:

- **Manual Review:** Security experts scrutinize the code for logic errors and security flaws.
- **Automated Scanning:** Tools analyse the code to detect common vulnerabilities and enforce secure coding standards.
- **Peer Reviews and Pair Programming:** Developers collaboratively review and refine the code to ensure security best practices are followed.

Benefits: The benefits of code review include:

- Early detection of security risks reduces the potential for future breaches.
- Assurance that security controls are correctly implemented.
- Improvement in code quality and maintainability.
- Promotion of a security-focused culture within the development team.

3.1.4.3 Static and Dynamic Analysis

Purpose: Static (SAST) and dynamic (DAST) analysis detect vulnerabilities pre- and post-deployment. Modern workflows integrate IAST (Interactive Application Security Testing) for real-time scanning during execution, combining code and runtime analysis for DevSecOps pipelines.

Process: The process includes:

- **Static Analysis:** Uses automated tools to scan the source code for patterns indicative of security risks.
- **Dynamic Analysis:** Monitors the app during execution, identifying vulnerabilities such as memory leaks or unhandled exceptions.
- **Integration with Continuous Integration (CI)/Continuous Delivery (CD) Pipelines:** Provides continuous security assessments.

Benefits: The combined use of static and dynamic analysis offers comprehensive benefits, including:

- Thorough coverage of security testing across the application's lifecycle.
- Identification and remediation of security risks in both pre-deployment and post-deployment stages.
- Enhanced application performance and reliability due to early detection of non-security-related bugs.

3.1.5 Compatibility Testing

Seamless Functionality across Ecosystems

Compatibility testing is crucial for ensuring that an Android application functions seamlessly across a diverse range of devices and environments.

The primary goal is to validate that the application delivers a consistent and optimal user experience, regardless of device specifications, operating system versions, or third-party integrations.

This testing includes device and API/library compatibility assessments to identify and address potential issues that could impact usability and performance.

Thorough compatibility testing enhances user satisfaction, expands market reach, and reduces post-release support costs.

The following subsections detail different types of compatibility testing methods:

3.1.5.1 Device Compatibility Testing

Purpose: The purpose of device compatibility testing is to ensure that an Android application operates as intended across a diverse range of devices, each with varying screen sizes, resolutions, hardware specifications, and operating system versions. This testing aims to guarantee a uniform and optimal user experience regardless of the device used.

Process: The process involves creating and executing test scenarios that simulate different device configurations. This includes assessing the app's performance on various physical devices, utilizing emulators to mimic specific devices, and employing cloud-based testing services that offer access to many device types and conditions. The testing encompasses checking the app's UI elements, functionality, performance, and behaviour under different device states. Testing must now account for foldable displays (multi-resume states), tablets, and ChromeOS devices using WindowSizeClass for adaptive layouts.

Benefits: The benefits of thorough device compatibility testing include:

- **Enhanced User Satisfaction:** By ensuring the app works well on all targeted devices, user satisfaction is maximized.
- **Broader Market Reach:** Compatibility with a wide range of devices increases the potential user base.
- **Reduced Support Costs:** Identifying and fixing issues early reduces the need for extensive post-release support.

3.1.5.2 API and Library Compatibility Testing

Purpose: API and library compatibility testing is conducted to verify that the application correctly utilizes Android APIs and third-party libraries across different versions of the Android platform. This ensures that the app does not encounter compatibility issues that could limit its functionality or availability to users.

Process: Developers must test the application against various versions of Android APIs and libraries, mainly focusing on deprecated features and ensuring backward compatibility. This involves using the AndroidX libraries and testing tools provided by the Android SDK to identify potential issues. Continuous integration and delivery (CI/CD) pipelines can be set up to automate the testing process across different API levels.

Benefits: The key advantages of API and library compatibility testing include:

- **Consistent App Behaviour:** Ensures that the app behaves consistently across different Android versions.
- **Future-proofing the App:** Keeps the app resilient against platform updates and changes.
- **Wider Compatibility:** Allows the app to serve a larger audience by supporting older devices and OS versions.

3.1.6 Regression Testing

Ensuring Consistency

Regression testing is a vital process in the application testing lifecycle aimed at ensuring that recent code changes have not adversely affected the existing functionalities of the application.

The primary objective is to verify that the previously developed and tested features continue to work correctly after modifications such as enhancements, patches, or configuration changes.

Regression testing helps maintain application stability and reliability by systematically re-running test cases while detecting unintended side effects.

It plays a critical role in detecting unintended side effects and ensuring that new updates do not introduce new bugs.

The following subsections detail different types of regression testing methods:

3.1.6.1 Continuous iIntegration (CI) Testing

Purpose: CI testing ensures application integrity by verifying that new code commits do not break or degrade existing functionality. It helps detect issues early, streamline development, and enhance code quality.

Process: CI testing involves setting up automated pipelines that trigger a series of regression tests upon every code commit. These pipelines are integrated with version control systems and employ automated build systems and test automation frameworks. Modern CI testing includes:

- **Automated Build Process:** Compiling code, running tests, and creating deployable application artefacts.
- **Automated Testing:** Utilizing frameworks for unit and integration testing to identify defects early.
- **Code Quality Checks:** Implementing static code analysis tools to enforce coding standards and detect potential vulnerabilities.
- **Integration with Version Control Systems:** Running regression tests automatically upon each code commit.

Benefits: The benefits of CI testing include:

- **Rapid Feedback:** Developers receive immediate information on the impact of their changes.
- **Reduced Integration Issues:** Frequent code integration reduces the complexity of merging changes.
- **Enhanced Application Quality:** Early detection of defects leads to higher quality and more secure Android applications.
- **Faster Time-to-Market:** Streamlined processes enable quicker release cycles.

3.1.6.2 Issue Retesting

Purpose: Issue retesting is focused on verifying that defects identified during previous testing cycles have been effectively resolved. It ensures that bug fixes do not introduce new issues and that the application remains secure after updates.

Process: The process of issue retesting includes:

- **Reiteration of Test Cases:** Executing the same test cases that initially identified the bugs.
- **Validation, not Exploration:** Focusing on validating bug fixes rather than comprehensive testing.
- **Regression Checkpoint:** Ensuring that the fixes do not cause regressions in other parts of the application.

Benefits: The key benefits of issue retesting are:

- **Assured Bug Resolution:** Confirms that the fixes are effective and lasting.
- **Enhanced User Satisfaction:** A stable and secure app leads to a better user experience.
- **Mitigation of Regression Risks:** Prevents new issues from arising due to changes in the codebase.
- **Optimized Deployment:** Contributes to a smoother release process with fewer post-deployment issues.

3.1.7 Accessibility Testing

Inclusive Design Validation

Accessibility testing is a crucial aspect of the application testing process that ensures applications are usable by individuals with various disabilities.

The primary goal is to verify compliance with accessibility standards, ensuring an inclusive user experience for people with visual, auditory, motor, or cognitive impairments.

This type of testing not only enhances the usability and user satisfaction for people with disabilities but also improves the overall quality and user experience for all users.

The following subsections detail different types of accessibility testing methods:

3.1.7.1 Accessibility Compliance Testing

Purpose: Accessibility Compliance Testing is essential to ensure that Android applications are not only usable but also enjoyable for individuals with disabilities. This testing verifies the application's conformance to established accessibility standards, such as Android's Accessibility Guidelines and the broader Web Content Accessibility Guidelines (WCAG) 2.1/2.2.

Process: The testing process includes a comprehensive review of the application's user interface and interaction elements. Testers simulate various disability scenarios to ensure that the app provides an equivalent experience for all users. This includes checking visual elements for colour contrast and size, auditory cues for clarity, and interactive elements for ease of use with assistive technologies. Manual testing is complemented by automated tools that can quickly identify potential issues.

Benefits: The benefits include:

- **Broader Market Reach:** Expands accessibility to users with disabilities.
- **Legal Compliance:** Reduces risks associated with accessibility regulations.
- **Enhanced Usability:** Improves design and user experience for all users.
- **Stronger Brand Image:** Demonstrates commitment to inclusivity.

3.1.7.2 Assistive Technology Compatibility Testing

Purpose: The goal of Assistive Technology Compatibility Testing is to ensure that the application seamlessly integrates with assistive technologies, which are vital for users with disabilities to access digital content. This form of testing is crucial for creating an inclusive user experience that accommodates the needs of all users, regardless of their physical abilities.

Process: This testing involves a thorough evaluation of the application's performance with various assistive technologies, such as screen readers, magnifiers, and voice recognition applications. Testers actively use these technologies to navigate the app, identifying any areas where the app fails to respond correctly or presents barriers to access. The process often includes feedback from actual users of assistive technologies to gain insights into the real-world challenges they face.

Benefits: The benefits include:

- **Increased User Satisfaction:** Enhances experience for users who rely on assistive devices.
- **Higher Retention Rates:** Ensures accessibility, leading to greater user engagement.
- **Competitive Advantage:** Establishes the app as a leader in inclusive design.

3.1.8 Compliance Testing

Adherence to Regulatory Protocols

Compliance testing is an essential aspect of application testing that ensures applications adhere to necessary legal, regulatory, and industry standards.

The primary objective is to verify that the application meets all relevant compliance requirements, which can include data protection regulations, security standards, and other operational policies. By conducting compliance testing, developers can ensure that their applications not only operate within the legal frameworks but also follow best practices for security and data handling.

This type of testing is crucial for mitigating legal risks, enhancing user trust, and ensuring the application's marketability.

The following subsections detail different types of compliance testing methods:

3.1.8.1 Regulatory Compliance Testing

Purpose: The purpose of regulatory compliance testing is to ensure the application complies with legal and regulatory requirements, such as GDPR (EU), CCPA (California), and other regional data protection laws.

Process: The process involves identifying the relevant regulations and standards, creating test cases that reflect the requirements of these regulations, and executing these tests to verify compliance. This often requires a thorough review of the app's data handling, storage, and processing practices.

Benefits: The benefits include:

- **Legal Compliance:** Avoids penalties and ensures adherence to regulations.
- **User Trust:** Builds credibility by safeguarding user privacy.
- **Improved Marketability:** Increases acceptance in regulated industries.

3.1.8.2 Security Standards Compliance Testing

Purpose: Security standards compliance testing aims to validate that the app meets established security benchmarks, such as the OWASP Mobile Top 10, which outlines critical risks in mobile applications. It also ensures adherence to industry-specific security frameworks and best practices.

Process: This involves mapping the app's security features against the chosen standards, conducting rigorous testing to identify any deviations, and implementing necessary measures to address gaps. The process includes reviewing code for vulnerabilities, testing encryption implementations, and assessing access controls, etc.

Benefits: The benefits include:

- **Stronger Security:** Protects against cyber threats and data breaches.
- **Enhanced Reliability:** Ensures safe user interactions and data handling.
- **Competitive Edge:** Positions the app as a secure and trustworthy solution.

3.1.9 Globalization Testing

Global Compatibility Adaptation

Globalization testing is a critical process in the application testing lifecycle that ensures an application is suitable for use in various regions worldwide.

The primary objective is to verify that the application can be easily adapted for different languages, cultures, and regional preferences, thereby providing a seamless and intuitive user experience to a global audience. This involves both localization and internationalization testing.

Localization focuses on adapting the app for specific locales. At the same time, internationalization ensures that the app's design and codebase are flexible enough to support multiple languages and cultural norms without significant re-engineering.

The following subsections detail different types of globalization testing methods:

3.1.9.1 Localization Testing

Purpose: Localization testing ensures that an Android application is fully adapted to the specific linguistic, cultural, and technical requirements of target users in different geographical regions. The purpose is to provide a seamless and intuitive user experience that feels native to each user, regardless of their location.

Process: The process involves:

- Identifying target locales for the application.
- Creating locale-specific resources such as strings, layouts, and region-specific assets.
- Implementing locale-sensitive handling of dates, numbers, and currency.
- Conducting thorough testing on devices set to the target locales.
- Iterating based on feedback to refine the localization.

Benefits: The benefits include:

- **Enhanced User Engagement:** Users are more likely to engage with an app that speaks their language and respects their cultural norms.
- **Increased Market Penetration:** Tailoring content to local markets can significantly boost the app's adoption in those regions.
- **Competitive Advantage:** A well-localized app can stand out in crowded marketplaces, attracting users who value localized experiences.

3.1.9.2 Internationalization Testing

Purpose: Internationalization testing verifies that the Android application's design and code-base are prepared for efficient localization. This ensures that the app can support multiple languages and cultural norms without requiring extensive re-engineering.

Process: The process includes:

- Designing a flexible architecture that separates content from functionality.
- Using Unicode for universal character encoding.
- Externalizing strings and other locale-sensitive elements from the code.
- Testing with pseudo-localization to expose hard-coded strings, layout truncation, and string concatenation issues.
- Validating with real-world scenarios to ensure the app behaves correctly across different locales.

Benefits: The benefits include:

- **Simplified Localization:** A well-internationalized app reduces the time and cost associated with localizing for new markets.
- **Future-proofing:** The app is ready to adapt to new languages and regions as opportunities arise.
- **Quality Assurance:** Ensures that the app's functionality remains consistent and reliable when localized.

3.2 Toolsets

Craft the Future with the Right Tools

Having the right tools can make all the difference! In this section, let's explore why using the right tools matters and how they can help you create incredible apps.

Imagine trying to build a sandcastle without a bucket or shovel. It would be pretty tough, right? Well, in Android development, having the right tools is like having that bucket and shovel; they make building your app much easier and more efficient.

Let's start with the Android Software Development Kit (SDK). Think of it as your toolbox filled with everything you need to build your app. From basic building blocks to advanced features, the SDK provides you with the tools to turn your ideas into reality.

Next up is Android Studio, your trusty workbench. With Android Studio, you can write code, design your app's layout, and test it out on virtual devices. It is like having a super-charged workshop right at your fingertips.

But why stop there? Tools like Firebase can take your app to the next level by providing features like user authentication, cloud storage, and analytics. It is like having a team of experts helping you build and grow your app.

And let's not forget about version control with Git. By keeping track of changes to your code and allowing you to collaborate with others, Git ensures that your app stays organized and up-to-date.

Finally, there are tools for automating tasks like testing and deployment. By streamlining these processes, you can save time and ensure that your app is ready for prime time.

So, why do these tools matter? Simply put, they make your life easier and help you build better apps faster. Whether you are a beginner or a seasoned developer, using the right tools can help you turn your ideas into reality and create apps that delight users around the world. So, let's roll up our sleeves and explore the world of tools!

3.2.1 Development Environments and IDEs

1. Android Studio

Description: Android Studio is the official IDE for Android app development, offering a comprehensive suite of tools for designing, building, and testing Android applications. It includes a visual layout editor for creating UIs, a code editor with advanced code completion and refactoring tools, a performance profiler for optimizing app performance, and built-in support for testing and debugging. Android Studio is built on the IntelliJ IDEA platform and is continuously updated with new features and improvements by Google.

Popularity: Android Studio is widely regarded as the most popular and recommended IDE for Android development due to its seamless integration with the Android SDK and continuous updates by Google.

2. Flutter

Description: Flutter is Google's UI toolkit for building natively compiled applications for mobile, web, and desktop from a single codebase using the Dart programming language. It provides a rich set of pre-built widgets for building beautiful and performant user interfaces, along with tools for layout and animation. Flutter apps are compiled into native machine code, resulting in high performance on both Android and iOS, and they offer a consistent experience across platforms.

Popularity: Flutter has been gaining rapid adoption among developers for its fast development cycle, expressive UI, and ability to create high-quality apps for Android and other platforms from a single codebase.

3. Gradle

Description: Gradle is a highly customizable build automation tool for building Android apps. It offers a Groovy-based DSL (Domain Specific Language) for scripting builds, making it flexible and powerful. Gradle's plugin ecosystem provides extensive support for tasks like dependency management, code compilation, and deployment, making it the default choice for Android projects.

Popularity: Extremely popular, the default build system for Android projects.

4. Kotlin Multiplatform Mobile (KMM)

Description: Kotlin Multiplatform Mobile allows developers to share business logic between Android and iOS applications while keeping native UI implementations. It enables code reuse for networking, data storage, and business logic layers, reducing development time and maintenance overhead for cross-platform projects.

Popularity: Growing rapidly as Google's recommended approach for cross-platform development.

5. JitPack

Description: JitPack is a package repository for JVM and Android libraries. It allows you to build GitHub projects on demand and publish them as Maven artefacts. It supports both public and private repositories from GitHub, GitLab, Bitbucket, and other Git hosting services.

Popularity: JitPack is gaining popularity due to its simplicity and integration with GitHub.

Other Tools

- **IntelliJ IDEA Community Edition:** It is the open-source version of the IntelliJ IDEA IDE, which serves as the foundation for Android Studio. While it lacks some of the Android-specific features of Android Studio out of the box, developers can extend its functionality with plugins to support Android app development. IntelliJ IDEA provides a robust code editor with features like code completion, refactoring, and version control integration, making it suitable for Java development.
- **Visual Studio with .NET MAUI:** The evolution of Xamarin, .NET Multi-platform App UI (MAUI) is Microsoft's modern framework for creating native mobile and desktop apps with C# and XAML from a single shared code-base. It allows developers to build for Android, iOS, Windows, and macOS with a unified development experience.
- **React Native:** It allows developers to build mobile apps using JavaScript and React. It is popular for cross-platform development but is not limited to Android. If you are interested in sharing code between Android and iOS, React Native is a good choice.
- **Bazel:** It is an open-source build system developed by Google. It is designed for building and testing applications at scale. It uses a Python-like syntax for defining build rules and offers features like hermetic builds and parallel execution. Bazel's focus on performance and reproducibility makes it suitable for large distributed teams and mono-repo development.

3.2.2 UI/UX Design and Prototyping Tools

1. Adobe XD (Experience Design)

Description: Adobe XD is a versatile design tool tailored for creating interactive prototypes, wireframes, and high-fidelity designs. Its features, such as component states and auto-animation, empower designers to create engaging user experiences for Android apps while seamless integration with other Adobe products enhances workflow efficiency.

Popularity: Widely adopted for its integration with other Adobe products and its comprehensive feature set tailored for UX/UI design.

2. Jetpack Compose

Description: Jetpack Compose is Android's modern toolkit for building native UI. It simplifies and accelerates UI development on Android with less code, powerful tools, and intuitive Kotlin APIs. Compose allows developers to build UI with declarative functions rather than XML layouts, making UI testing and prototyping more streamlined.

Popularity: Rapidly becoming the standard for Android UI development for all new Android projects.

3. Figma

Description: Figma is a browser-based design tool known for its collaborative features and versatility. Its real-time collaboration capabilities, coupled with robust design and prototyping features, make it an ideal choice for teams working on Android app designs. Figma's cross-platform compatibility and versioning system further enhance team collaboration and design iteration.

Popularity: Known for its collaborative features, cross-platform accessibility, and ease of use, making it a preferred choice for distributed design teams.

4. InVision

Description: InVision is a versatile prototyping tool that enables designers to create interactive prototypes with animations and gestures. It is widely used for its ease of use, extensive library of UI components, and robust collaboration features.

Popularity: Popularity stems from its user-friendly interface and comprehensive feature set, which caters to both individual designers and large design teams.

5. Axure RP

Description: Axure RP is a comprehensive prototyping tool known for its ability to create complex interactions and dynamic content. It is often used for high-fidelity prototypes and UX design, particularly for enterprise-level projects.

Popularity: Popularity lies in its advanced capabilities for creating interactive prototypes with rich interactions and conditional logic.

Other Tools

- **Framer:** It is a dynamic design and prototyping platform that blends visual design with advanced interactivity, supporting responsive layouts, innovative components, and rich animations. It enables designers to build highly interactive, production-like prototypes and even publish live web experiences.
- **Sketch:** It is primarily used for macOS and does not offer functionalities like prototyping or developer handoff as extensively as Figma or XD.
- **Balsamiq:** It focuses on simplicity and rapid wireframing, offering a sketch-style interface for quickly mocking up interfaces. It is a good tool for low-fidelity wireframing but may not be ideal for complex prototypes.

3.2.3 *Testing Frameworks and Libraries*

1. Espresso

Description: Espresso is a widely used testing framework for Android app UI testing. It provides APIs to simulate user interactions within the app, making it ideal for UI testing, such as button clicks, text inputs, and assertions on UI elements.

Popularity: Widely adopted for its simplicity and effectiveness in UI testing.

2. JUnit

Description: JUnit is a popular testing framework for Java and Android development. It provides annotations and assertions for writing and running unit tests, facilitating the testing of individual units or components of an Android application.

Popularity: Ubiquitous in the Android development community, considered a standard for unit testing.

3. Robolectric

Description: Robolectric is a unit testing framework that runs tests inside the JVM on the developer's workstation. It simulates the Android environment without needing a device or emulator. However, it has limitations with newer Android features and complex UI interactions, and many developers now prefer on-device testing for more reliable results.

Popularity: Still used but declining in favor of on-device testing approaches due to simulation limitations with modern Android features.

4. Appium

Description: Appium is an open-source tool for automating mobile applications, including Android apps. It supports multiple programming languages and test frameworks, allowing testers to write and execute automated tests for Android apps using familiar tools.

Popularity: Widely used for its cross-platform compatibility and support for multiple programming languages.

5. Firebase Test Lab

Description: Firebase Test Lab provides cloud-based infrastructure for testing Android apps across a wide range of devices and configurations, including physical and virtual devices. It now supports foldable devices, tablets, and Wear OS testing, with enhanced integration for Jetpack Compose UI testing.

Popularity: Increasing adoption among developers due to its integration with other Firebase services and ease of use for testing on real devices.

Other Tools

- **UI Automator:** It is an Android testing framework suitable for cross-app functional UI testing. It enables testing interactions across multiple apps and system apps, providing APIs to interact with UI elements across different apps. It is generally considered lower level compared to Espresso.
- **Calabash:** It is an open-source testing framework that enables writing and executing automated acceptance tests for Android and iOS apps. It allows testers to write tests in natural language and automate interactions with the app's UI.
- **Mockito:** It is a mocking framework for Java and Android testing. It allows the creation of mock objects to simulate the behaviour of real objects in tests, facilitating easier isolation of code under test. While not directly related to UI testing, it is a valuable tool for developers working with JUnit.

3.2.4 Performance Testing and Monitoring Tools

1. Android Profiler

Description: Android Profiler is a strong choice because it is built directly into Android Studio. Developers use it to profile CPU, memory, network, and battery usage. It helps identify bottlenecks and optimize app performance.

Popularity: Widely used among Android developers due to its integration with Android Studio.

2. Apache JMeter

Description: Originally designed to test web applications, JMeter can also be used for load testing and performance measurement of Android apps through HTTP requests. It remains relevant, especially for backend testing, but its Android-specific usage has alternatives.

Popularity: Popular among developers due to its versatility and extensive features.

3. Perfetto

Description: A powerful, open-source performance monitoring and tracing tool for Android and Linux systems. It captures detailed system-level data, including CPU scheduling, memory usage, disk I/O, and application lifecycle events. It helps developers diagnose performance issues like UI jank, slow app startup, and excessive background activity. It supports both on-device recording and real-time streaming to a host machine.

Popularity: Widely adopted by Android performance engineers and increasingly used in production app development.

4. Firebase Crashlytics

Description: Firebase Crashlytics is Google's crash reporting and analysis tool for mobile apps. It automatically captures and reports app crashes, exceptions, and errors, providing detailed crash reports and insights to help developers diagnose and fix issues quickly. It also offers features like real-time alerts and custom logging. Note that standalone Crashlytics was discontinued.

Popularity: Widely used and trusted by Android developers for its reliability, ease of integration, and comprehensive crash reporting capabilities as part of the Firebase suite.

Other Tools

- **Gatling:** It is an open-source load-testing tool primarily used for web applications but can also be used to test Android apps' backend services and APIs. It offers a user-friendly scripting language for creating realistic user scenarios and provides detailed reports on performance metrics.
- **Android Performance Tuner:** It is a tool provided by Google Play Console that helps developers optimize their apps' performance and improve user experience. While it is gaining traction, it might not be as widely adopted as the other tools.

3.2.5 Security and Static Analysis Tools

1. MobSF (Mobile Security Framework)

   Description: MobSF performs SAST/DAST for Android, iOS, and Flutter apps, including API security testing and malware detection.
   Popularity: Growing popularity within the mobile security community due to its comprehensive features and active development.

2. APKTool

   Description: APKTool is a tool for reverse engineering Android APK files. It allows security researchers to decompile, modify, and recompile applications for analysis. It helps users understand how an app is structured and identify potential security issues.
   Popularity: Essential in the Android security toolkit, widely used for analysing app binaries and identifying vulnerabilities.

3. Frida

   Description: Frida is a dynamic instrumentation toolkit that allows security researchers to inject JavaScript into running Android applications for runtime manipulation and analysis. Note that Frida requires root access for many operations on Android 10+ devices due to enhanced security restrictions.
   Popularity: Highly popular among mobile security researchers for its dynamic analysis capabilities and versatility in bypassing security measures, though its effectiveness is limited on modern Android versions without root access.

4. SpotBugs

   Description: SpotBugs is the spiritual successor of FindBugs, offering static analysis of Java bytecode to find bugs in Java programs. It excels at detecting a wide range of security vulnerabilities and code quality issues. It offers plugins for popular IDEs like Eclipse and IntelliJ IDEA, making it easy to integrate into the development workflow.
   Popularity: SpotBugs has gained popularity in the Java community, including Android development, as a more actively maintained alternative to FindBugs.

5. Lint (Android Lint)

   Description: Lint is a static code analysis tool that checks Android project source files for potential bugs and optimization improvements for correctness, security, performance, usability, accessibility, and internationalization. Developers can create custom rules to enforce specific coding standards and practices relevant to their projects.
   Popularity: Lint comes integrated with Android Studio and Gradle, making it a widely used tool in Android development.

6. SonarQube

Description: SonarQube is an open-source platform for continuous code quality inspection. It performs automatic reviews with static code analysis to detect bugs, code smells, and security vulnerabilities in 20+ programming languages. It easily integrates with various CI/CD tools like Jenkins, GitLab CI, and GitHub Actions. It has a large user community and regular updates, ensuring it stays relevant and up-to-date with the latest security standards.

Popularity: SonarQube is widely used in enterprise settings for code quality management, including Android projects.

Other Tools

- **Checkstyle:** It is a development tool to help programmers write Java code that adheres to a coding standard. It is primarily focused on coding style and conventions rather than finding bugs or vulnerabilities.
- **PMD:** Similar to Checkstyle, it focuses on identifying potential bugs and enforcing coding standards. It finds common programming flaws like unused variables, empty catch blocks, unnecessary object creation, and so forth.

3.2.6 Cloud-based and Remote Testing Servicing

1. Android Studio Emulator

Description: The Android Studio Emulator is an official emulator provided by Google as part of the Android Studio IDE. It allows developers to emulate various Android devices with different configurations, screen sizes, and Android versions for testing their applications. With features like hardware acceleration and support for Google Play Services, it offers a comprehensive environment for app development and testing.

Popularity: Very popular, especially among developers, due to its integration with Android Studio.

2. Genymotion

Description: Genymotion is a feature-rich Android emulator designed for both developers and testers. It provides a wide range of virtual devices with different Android versions and hardware configurations, enabling realistic testing scenarios. With its high performance, easy setup, and support for advanced features like GPS simulation and network quality emulation, Genymotion streamlines the app development and testing process.

Popularity: Popular among both developers and testers, particularly for its speed and flexibility.

3. Firebase Test Lab for Android

Description: Firebase Test Lab is a cloud-based app-testing infrastructure provided by Google. It allows you to test your Android apps across a wide range of devices and device configurations. It supports both manual and automated testing and integrates seamlessly with the Firebase platform.

Popularity: Widely used among Android developers for its ease of integration with the Firebase ecosystem.

4. Amazon Web Services (AWS) Device Farm

Description: AWS Device Farm is a cloud-based mobile app testing service provided by Amazon Web Services (AWS). It enables you to test your Android apps on real devices hosted in the AWS cloud. It supports automated testing across a large selection of Android devices.

Popularity: Trusted by enterprises and developers due to its comprehensive device coverage and integration with other AWS services.

Other Tools

- **Sauce Labs:** It provides a cloud-based testing platform for web and mobile applications. It offers automated testing for Android apps on a wide range of devices and OS versions. It supports parallel testing, real-time analytics, and integrations with popular CI/CD tools.
- **Bitbar Cloud:** Now part of SmartBear, it allows you to test your Android apps on real devices hosted in the cloud. It supports automated testing using popular testing frameworks like Appium and Espresso. Additionally, it offers detailed test reports and integrations with CI/CD pipelines.

3.2.7 Debugging and Profiling Tools

1. ADB (Android Debug Bridge)

Description: ADB is a versatile command-line tool that acts as a bridge between a developer's machine and an Android device or emulator. It facilitates various debugging tasks, such as installing and debugging apps, accessing the device shell for command-line interaction, and transferring files between the device and the development machine. ADB is an essential tool for Android developers for debugging and troubleshooting their applications.

Popularity: Widely used among Android developers for its utility in various debugging tasks.

2. Flipper

Description: A Flipper is a modern, extensible debugging platform developed by Meta for Android, iOS, and React Native apps. It provides a desktop interface that connects to apps running on devices or emulators, enabling real-time inspection of network requests, database content, shared preferences, and UI layout hierarchy. With a plugin-based architecture, Flipper supports both built-in and custom debugging tools, making it highly adaptable to different project needs.

Popularity: Increasingly adopted, especially in cross-platform and large-scale apps.

3. LeakCanary

Description: LeakCanary is an open-source library designed to detect memory leaks in Android applications. It automatically monitors the app's memory usage and generates notifications when potential memory leaks are detected. LeakCanary provides detailed information about the leak, including the leak trace and heap analysis, to help developers promptly identify and fix memory leaks during development.

Popularity: Widely used for its effectiveness in detecting memory leaks and its seamless integration into the Android development workflow.

Other Tools

- **MAT (Memory Analyzer Tool):** It is a powerful tool for analysing Java heap dumps. It helps developers identify memory leaks and optimize memory usage by providing various reports and visualizations, including histogram analysis, leak suspects report, and dominator tree analysis. It may require more manual setup compared to LeakCanary.
- **Firebase Performance Monitoring:** It is a cloud-based tool that helps developers monitor and analyse the performance of their Android applications in real-time. It offers insights into app startup time, network performance, and UI responsiveness, allowing developers to identify and resolve performance issues efficiently.
- **Sentry:** It is a commercial real-time error-tracking tool designed to help developers monitor and fix crashes and errors in their Android applications. It captures and aggregates crash reports in real-time, providing detailed crash reports with stack traces, breadcrumbs, and contextual information to diagnose and prioritize issues for resolution.

3.2.8 *Version Control and DevOps Integration*

1. Git

Description: Git is a distributed version control system known for its speed and efficiency. It is widely used in Android development due to its branching and merging capabilities, which are essential for managing complex projects. Developers can work offline, commit changes locally, and synchronize with remote repositories, making collaboration seamless.

Popularity: Extremely high. Git is the de facto standard for version control in the application development industry.

2. GitHub

Description: GitHub provides a web-based interface for Git repositories. It offers features like issue tracking, pull requests, and project management tools, making it a favourite for open-source Android projects and collaborative development. GitHub's social features also encourage community engagement and contribution.

Popularity: Very high. GitHub is one of the most popular platforms for hosting Git repositories and collaborating on projects.

3. Jenkins

Description: Jenkins is an open-source automation server widely used for continuous integration and continuous delivery (CI/CD) of application projects, including Android applications. It provides a highly customizable environment through its vast collection of plugins, allowing developers to automate building, testing, and deployment processes efficiently. Jenkins can be easily integrated into existing development workflows and supports distributed builds across multiple platforms.

Popularity: Highly popular in the Android development community due to its flexibility and extensive plugin ecosystem.

4. GitHub Action

Description: GitHub Actions is a native CI/CD platform that enables automation of Android build, test, and deployment workflows directly within GitHub repositories. Workflows are defined using YAML files, making pipelines version-controlled and easy to manage. It supports custom triggers based on Git events like pushes or pull requests. Integrated runners provide Android SDK, Gradle caching, and dependency management for fast builds. Seamlessly deploys to Firebase, Google Play, or third-party services with minimal configuration.

Popularity: Extremely high among modern Android projects hosted on GitHub. Fast becoming the go-to CI/CD choice due to deep integration and ease of use.

5. CircleCI

Description: CircleCI is a cloud-based CI/CD platform designed to automate the application development lifecycle. It supports building, testing, and deploying Android applications with customizable workflows and parallelism. CircleCI's intuitive interface and extensive integrations with popular development tools make it a preferred choice for Android developers seeking scalable and efficient CI/CD solutions.

Popularity: Popular among Android developers, especially in teams preferring cloud-based CI/CD solutions.

Other Tools

- **Bitbucket:** Similar to GitHub, Bitbucket is another Git hosting platform but provides tighter integration with other Atlassian tools. It offers free private repositories for small teams.
- **Bitrise:** It is a cloud-based CI/CD platform tailored specifically for mobile app development, including Android applications. It provides a comprehensive set of pre-configured workflows and integrations with popular development tools, enabling developers to automate building, testing, and deploying Android apps with ease. Bitrise's focus on mobile app CI/CD pipelines simplifies the complexities of mobile development and accelerates time-to-market for Android applications.
- **Azure Pipelines:** Part of the Microsoft Azure cloud platform, it is a robust CI/CD tool. However, its adoption might be more prevalent for projects heavily invested in the Azure ecosystem and not necessarily the top choice for general Android development.

3.2.9 Database and Storage Management Tools

1. SQLiteStudio

   Description: SQLiteStudio is a powerful and user-friendly SQLite database manager. It provides a graphical interface for managing, browsing, and editing SQLite databases, making it easy for developers to visualize database structures, execute SQL queries, and manipulate data efficiently. SQLiteStudio is widely respected in the Android development community for its simplicity and effectiveness.
   Popularity: Widely used and respected in the Android development community.

2. DataStore

   Description: DataStore is Android's modern data storage solution that replaces SharedPreferences. It provides two implementations: Preferences DataStore for key-value pairs and Proto DataStore for typed objects. DataStore uses Kotlin coroutines and Flow, is thread-safe, and provides data consistency guarantees.
   Popularity: Rapidly becoming the standard for local data storage, officially recommended by Google to replace SharedPreferences.

3. Room Persistence Library

   Description: Room Persistence Library is an official part of Android Jetpack, providing a simple and efficient way to work with SQLite databases in Android apps. Room reduces boilerplate code by generating SQL queries at compile time and mapping query results to Kotlin/Java objects. It now offers full integration with Kotlin coroutines, Flow, and Jetpack Compose, making it the preferred choice for Android developers.
   Popularity: Extremely popular among Android developers due to its official support from Google and integration with other Jetpack libraries.

4. Firebase

   Description: Firebase Realtime Database is a cloud-hosted NoSQL database offered by Google as part of the Firebase platform. It enables real-time data synchronization across devices and platforms, making it ideal for building collaborative and reactive applications. With its SDKs for various platforms, including Android, Firebase Realtime Database simplifies backend development and allows developers to focus on creating engaging user experiences.
   Popularity: Very popular among Android developers for real-time data syncing and its integration with other Firebase services.

Other Tools

- **GreenDAO (Object Relational Mapper):** GreenDAO is a lightweight and efficient ORM library for Android that simplifies database operations by mapping SQLite tables to Java objects. It generates DAO (Data Access Object) classes for database CRUD (Create, Read, Update, Delete) operations, offering developers a fast and reliable way to interact with databases. It may not be as widely used as the Room Persistence Library.

- **SQLCipher for Android (Encrypted SQLite):** This is an open-source extension to Android's SQLite database that provides transparent 256-bit AES encryption of database files. It enhances data security for Android applications by encrypting sensitive data at rest, but it is not a core database management tool itself.

3.2.10 API Testing Tools

1. Postman

   Description: Postman is widely used for API testing due to its user-friendly interface, extensive features, and support for both REST and SOAP APIs. It allows you to create and execute requests, manage collections, and automate tests. It is excellent for both beginners and experienced testers.
   Popularity: Widely used for its intuitive interface and comprehensive feature set.

2. Insomnia

   Description: Insomnia is a powerful, open-source API client with a clean UI, excellent for designing, testing, and documenting APIs. It supports REST, GraphQL, and gRPC. It integrates well with version control via Git and offers robust environment management and automation capabilities. Popular among developers and testers alike.
   Popularity: Widely used, especially in developer communities; often considered a Postman alternative with a focus on simplicity and extensibility.

3. Rest-Assured

   Description: Rest-Assured is an open-source Java-based library for testing RESTful APIs. It integrates seamlessly with Java-based test frameworks and provides a fluent API for writing expressive test cases.
   Popularity: Moderately adopted among Java developers for API testing.

4. SoapUI

   Description: SoapUI is a comprehensive API testing tool supporting SOAP and REST APIs, with features for functional testing, load testing, and security testing. It shines in scenarios where SOAP web services are involved, but for purely RESTful APIs, the other two might be more popular choices.
   Popularity: Moderately adopted for its extensive capabilities in API testing.

Other Tools

- **Paw (RapidAPI):** It is a good alternative to Postman, especially for Mac users. It offers similar functionalities but might have a smaller user base. It has features for creating complex API requests, organizing collections, and automating tests.
- **Karate DSL:** It is an open-source testing framework for API testing, web service testing, and web UI automation. It allows tests to be written in a readable syntax based on Gherkin. However, its adoption might be limited due to its specific syntax and relative newness in the API testing landscape.

3.2.11 Analytics and User Behaviour Tools

1. Firebase Analytics

Description: Developed by Google, Firebase Analytics is a popular choice for mobile app tracking. It provides real-time insights into user behaviour, conversion rates, and engagement metrics. Key features include event tracking, user segmentation, and integration with other Firebase services.

Popularity: Highly popular due to its integration with other Firebase services and ease of use.

2. Google Analytics 4 (GA4)

Description: Google Analytics 4 provides enhanced mobile app tracking with event-based data collection, improved privacy controls, and machine learning insights. It offers cross-platform monitoring and integration with other Google services.

Popularity: Mandatory for all new Google Analytics implementations since Universal Analytics was discontinued.

3. Mixpanel

Description: Mixpanel is a commercial analytics platform that focuses on user engagement and retention. It allows for the tracking of specific user actions (events) and the analysis of user flows. It also provides cohort analysis, A/B testing, and funnel visualization.

Popularity: Well-known in the industry for its advanced analytics capabilities but less popular among developers due to its pricing model.

Other Tools

- **Amplitude:** It is a commercial analytics platform that emphasizes behavioural analytics. It helps to understand how users interact with the app and identify bottlenecks. Features include event tracking, retention analysis, and user segmentation.
- **Matomo (formerly Piwik):** It is an open-source web analytics platform that can also be used for mobile app analytics. It provides features such as user tracking, event tracking, and customizable dashboards. While it is not as widely used as Firebase or Google Analytics, it is popular among privacy-conscious organizations due to its self-hosted nature and data ownership.
- **Countly:** It is an open-source mobile analytics platform that offers real-time insights into user behaviour, push notifications, crash analytics, and more. It is especially favoured by developers who want to host their analytics infrastructure in-house.
- **AppsFlyer:** It is a commercial mobile attribution and marketing analytics platform that helps app developers track app installs, user engagement, and marketing ROI. It is commonly used by mobile marketers and app publishers to optimize their marketing spend.

3.2.12 Localization and Internationalization Tools

1. Localazy

   Description: Localazy is a cloud-based localization platform that offers automated translation management, over-the-air updates, and support for multiple platforms, including Android. It provides translator tools, integration with version control systems, and seamless integration with Android apps.
   Popularity: Gaining popularity among Android developers for its comprehensive features and ease of use.

2. CrowdIn

   Description: CrowdIn is a cloud-based localization platform that supports Android, iOS, web, and application localization. It provides features such as translation memory, machine translation, screenshot localization, and integration with version control systems.
   Popularity: Popular among Android developers and localization teams for its versatility and extensive feature set.

3. Transifex

   Description: Transifex is a localization management platform that supports Android, iOS, web, and application localization. It offers features such as translation memory, glossary management, file versioning, and integration with popular version control systems and CI/CD pipelines.
   Popularity: Widely used by enterprises and large-scale Android development teams for its advanced features and enterprise-grade support.

Other Tools

- **POEditor:** It is a localizsation management platform that supports Android, iOS, web, and other platforms. It offers features such as translation memory, terminology management, version control integration, and collaboration tools for translators.

3.2.13 Collaboration and Project Management Tools

1. Slack

   Description: Slack is a messaging app for teams, enabling communication through channels organized by project, topic, or team. It offers integrations with various tools and services, file sharing, and search functionality.
   Popularity: Widely used in professional environments for team communication and collaboration.

2. Microsoft Teams

   Description: Microsoft Teams is a collaboration platform that integrates with Microsoft Office 365. It offers chat, video meetings, file storage, and application integration, and facilitates teamwork and communication within organizations.

Popularity: Highly popular among businesses and enterprises for its integration with Office 365.

3. Google Workspace (formerly G Suite)

Description: Google Workspace includes Gmail, Google Drive, Google Docs, Google Sheets, Google Slides, and more. It offers cloud-based collaboration and productivity tools and enables real-time collaboration on documents, spreadsheets, and presentations.

Popularity: Dominant in both personal and professional environments for its seamless integration with Google services.

4. JIRA

Description: JIRA is a powerful Agile project management tool developed by Atlassian. It is based on Agile principles and supports Scrum, Kanban, or hybrid methodologies like Scrumban. Key features include tracking projects, customizable workflows, time tracking, and extensive reporting capabilities. JIRA integrates well with other products like GitHub, Slack, Trello, Salesforce, and Confluence.

Popularity: Very popular in enterprise environments and among application development teams.

5. Confluence

Description: While not strictly a project management tool, Confluence is a team collaboration application that allows teams to create, share, and collaborate on documents, plans, and project documentation. It features rich text editing, file sharing, and integration with other Atlassian products like JIRA.

Popularity: Widely used in organizations, particularly in combination with JIRA for project documentation and knowledge management.

Other Tools

- **Trello:** It is a visual project management tool that uses boards, lists, and cards to organize tasks and workflows. It provides a flexible and intuitive way to manage projects, track progress, and collaborate with team members. However, it may be more focused on task management than broader collaboration features.
- **Asana:** It is a project management tool designed to help teams organize, track, and manage their work. It offers features like task assignments, due dates, and project timelines. This is a user-friendly and versatile tool that caters to both Agile and traditional project management styles.
- **ClickUp:** It is a freemium (with paid options) project management platform that offers customizable features like task management, document collaboration, and goal tracking. It aims to replace multiple tools by integrating them into one platform.

3.2.14 Documentation and Code Maintenance Tools

1. Dokka & Dokka Gradle Plugin

   Description: Dokka is a documentation engine designed to work with Kotlin and Java
   projects. It can generate documentation in HTML, GitHub Flavored Markdown
   (GFM), or Javadoc format. It integrates well with Gradle builds and Kotlin projects.
   Popularity: It is widely adopted, especially within the Kotlin community.

2. Swagger

   Description: Swagger is an open-source framework for designing, building, and documenting APIs. While it is not specific to Android, it can be used to generate API
   documentation for Android projects. It allows developers to define API functionalities in a machine-readable format, which can then be used to create interactive
   documentation or client code. This is particularly useful for Android apps that
   interact with external APIs.
   Popularity: High, particularly in web API development, but also growing in popularity for Android APIs.

3. Hilt

   Description: Hilt is Google's recommended dependency injection (DI) framework for
   Android, built on top of Dagger. It reduces boilerplate by automating Dagger setup
   with annotations like @HiltAndroidApp. Provides built-in Android component
   bindings for activities, fragments, and services. Enables compile-time dependency
   resolution with minimal manual configuration. Simplifies testing and promotes
   consistent DI practices across Android apps.
   Popularity: Widely adopted in new Android projects as the standard DI solution.

4. Koin

   Description: Koin is a pragmatic, lightweight, and beginner-friendly dependency
   injection framework for Kotlin developers. It uses a simple DSL (Domain-Specific
   Language) model for defining modules and dependencies, with no reflection or
   proxy involved.
   Popularity: Growing in popularity due to its simplicity and Kotlin support.

Other Tools

- **Javadoc:** It is a traditional tool provided by Oracle for generating API documentation
  in HTML format from Java source code. While Javadoc remains relevant, newer tools
  like Dokka are gaining popularity.
- **Markdown:** It is a lightweight markup language with plain-text formatting syntax,
  often used to format documentation files. There are various tools and plugins available
  for converting Markdown documents to HTML or other formats.

Looking Ahead

As this chapter has illustrated, a thorough and methodical approach to testing and auditing not only uncovers vulnerabilities but also fortifies the app's resilience against emerging threats. By leveraging a combination of manual and automated testing techniques, developers can ensure their apps meet the highest security standards. The comprehensive toolsets available today provide an array of functionalities that empower developers to identify and mitigate potential risks efficiently. The journey from identifying security gaps to implementing robust solutions is an ongoing process, reflecting the dynamic nature of cyber threats.

Looking ahead, the future of Android app security will increasingly rely on advancements in AI and machine learning. These technologies hold the promise of revolutionizing the detection and response to security threats, offering predictive capabilities and real-time analytics that can significantly enhance defensive strategies. The integration of AI-driven tools into the testing and auditing workflows will enable developers to proactively address vulnerabilities before they can be exploited, thus fostering a more secure mobile ecosystem. Moreover, as the industry moves towards a more interconnected world, the principles and practices discussed in this chapter will serve as a foundational framework for securing the next generation of mobile applications.

By integrating comprehensive testing, rigorous auditing, and advanced toolsets into the development workflow, developers can build Android applications that are not only functional but also secure by design.

Part 2

The Secure Development Journey

Insecure code is often the result of deeper systemic issues rather than mere oversight. "Chapter 4: Decoding the factors influencing insecure code" examines the key contributors to vulnerabilities in Android apps, including:

- **Human and Organizational Challenges** – Knowledge gaps, tight deadlines, and misaligned incentives that prioritize speed over security.
- **Technical Debt and Legacy Systems** – Outdated frameworks and complex codebases that perpetuate insecure practices.
- **Team Dynamics and Cognitive Biases** – Communication breakdowns, overreliance on automation, and psychological factors that lead to overlooked risks.
- **External Risks** – Vulnerable third-party libraries and evolving threat landscapes that complicate security.

Security should never be an afterthought; it must be woven into every phase of development. "Chapter 5: Integrating security in app development process" outlines a holistic approach:

- **Planning and Requirements** – Defining security objectives early to set a strong foundation.
- **Design and Architecture** – Building threat-resistant frameworks from the ground up.
- **Implementation** – Applying secure coding practices to prevent common vulnerabilities.
- **Testing** – Identifying and mitigating risks before deployment.
- **Deployment and Maintenance** – Ensuring continuous security through updates and monitoring.

A structured Secure SDLC ensures that security is systematically enforced at every stage. "Chapter 6: Implementing secure SDLC for Android apps" provides a step-by-step guide:

- **Threat Modelling** – Proactively identifying and mitigating risks before development begins.
- **Secure Design and Coding** – Architectural best practices and defensive programming techniques.
- **Security Testing and Code Reviews** – Rigorous validation to catch vulnerabilities early.
- **Training and Awareness** – Keeping teams updated on evolving threats and best practices.
- **Secure Deployment and Incident Response** – Safely releasing apps and handling breaches effectively.

DOI: 10.1201/9781003640332-5

Decoding the Factors Influencing Insecure Code

The only way to do great work is to love what you do.

– Steve Jobs

Steve Jobs, an American businessman, inventor, and investor, emphasizes the importance of passion and dedication in achieving excellence. He suggests that genuine love and enthusiasm for one's work are essential ingredients for producing outstanding results.

In the world of Android application security, understanding the motivations and influencers behind insecure code is crucial. Developers who are genuinely passionate about creating secure apps are more likely to prioritize security measures and adhere to best practices. Conversely, those who lack passion or commitment may overlook security concerns, leading to the proliferation of insecure code.

Therefore, this quote underscores the significance of cultivating a genuine interest in security practices among Android developers to mitigate vulnerabilities and enhance app security. While developers might not always be passionate about security specifically, understanding the impact of insecure coding practices can lead to a dedication to writing more secure code.

DOI: 10.1201/9781003640332-6

A LAYMAN'S PERSPECTIVE

Unravel the Mystery behind Insecure Code

Welcome to the captivating world of application development, where every digital creation is a masterpiece waiting to be unveiled. Applications function like intricate puzzles, where every component must fit seamlessly. However, just like any puzzle, challenges arise, particularly in ensuring security and robustness against potential threats.

This chapter embarks on a journey into the nuanced arena of application security. Imagine applications as vast cities, with each building representing a different aspect of development. Within these digital metropolises, hidden vulnerabilities exist, akin to unlocked doors or unprotected windows in a skyscraper. Addressing these vulnerabilities is crucial to safeguarding the integrity of an application.

Let's explore more into the core of why some applications falter in their security measures. Sometimes, it is due to a lack of crucial information among those crafting the applications, or perhaps they are unaware of the latest tactics employed by cyber adversaries. Other times, constraints imposed by technology or the burden of dealing with outdated systems hinder the implementation of robust security measures.

Securing applications is an ongoing process that requires awareness, collaboration, and a shift in mindset. Just as a city's infrastructure demands coordinated efforts from planners, builders, and policymakers, securing applications necessitates a shared responsibility among developers, security teams, and business leaders.

Yet, the human element cannot be overlooked. Emotions, biases, and cognitive factors influence how individuals develop applications, underscoring the significance of understanding human psychology in ensuring application security. Moreover, fostering a culture of feedback and continuous improvement is paramount in strengthening the resilience of applications against emerging threats.

By recognizing the factors influencing insecure code and addressing them proactively, resilient applications can be created that stand firm against evolving threats. Let's embrace security as an integral part of development and work toward a safer digital future for all.

4.1 Knowledge Gaps and Misconceptions

From Blind Spots to Bright Insights

In the fast-evolving world of application development, knowledge gaps and misconceptions about security practices remain significant barriers to creating secure systems. These issues range from inexperienced developers being unaware of common threats to misunderstandings about critical security requirements, all of which can lead to vulnerabilities in code and potential breaches in system integrity.

This section explores the root causes of these gaps and offers actionable strategies to address them effectively. By bridging these knowledge divides, development teams can strengthen their defences and build applications that are not only functional but also secure.

4.1.1 Lack of Awareness of Secure Coding Practices

Awareness Gap

Developers who lack awareness of secure coding best practices are more likely to introduce vulnerabilities into their applications. This lack of understanding can manifest in several ways, each posing unique challenges to application security.

Challenges

- **Insufficient Knowledge:** Developers may not be well-versed in common security threats, attack vectors, or mitigation techniques, which can result in oversight of essential security measures.
- **Neglecting Security Considerations:** In many cases, developers might prioritize functionality over security, mistakenly assuming that as long as the application works, it is secure.
- **Inadequate Training:** A lack of education or training in secure coding principles often leads to gaps in knowledge and blind spots that can result in vulnerabilities.

Real-world Case Illustration

Consider an Android application that processes user-uploaded files or dynamic intents. If developers are unaware of improper intent handling or insecure deep link parsing, they may allow arbitrary app launching or data exfiltration via crafted URLs. This oversight enables attackers to manipulate app flow or access sensitive components, compromising both data integrity and user privacy.

Action Items

- **Education and Training:**
  - Conduct regular training sessions and workshops focusing on secure coding practices.
  - Provide resources such as coding guidelines, security documentation, and best practice checklists.
  - Cover critical topics like input validation, parameterized queries, secure authentication, and others.
- **Code Reviews and Peer Feedback:**
  - Encourage regular peer code reviews to identify and rectify security oversights early in the development process.
  - Foster a culture of constructive feedback and continuous learning within the team.
- **Security Champions:**
  - Designate security champions within development teams who are responsible for promoting security awareness and mentoring others.
  - These champions can act as focal points for security-related discussions and knowledge dissemination.
- **Integration with the Development Process:**
  - Integrate security checks into the development pipeline using tools like static analysis and dynamic testing.
  - Ensure that security considerations are embedded into every phase of the development life cycle, from design to deployment.

By proactively updating developers' knowledge, using state-of-the-art security tools, and fostering a security-aware development culture, organizations can significantly reduce vulnerabilities stemming from insecure coding practices. These modern practices not only improve the resilience of individual applications but also enhance overall user trust in the Android ecosystem.

4.1.2 Misunderstanding of Security Requirements

Security Lost in Translation

Developers might misinterpret or overlook security requirements, which can lead to inadequate security measures or introduce new vulnerabilities. These misunderstandings often stem from various systemic issues.

Challenges

- **Unclear or Ambiguous Specifications:** Vague or poorly defined security requirements can easily be misinterpreted by developers, resulting in improper implementation.
- **Communication Gaps:** Inadequate communication between stakeholders, such as project managers, security experts, and developers, often leads to misunderstandings or overlooked requirements.
- **Insufficient Expertise:** A lack of deep expertise in security principles among developers can lead to misjudgements about what security measures are necessary and how to implement them.

Real-world Case Illustration

Imagine an Android application that offers a file-sharing feature. The security requirements specify that data must be protected during transmission. However, due to a misinterpretation of these requirements and inadequate communication among stakeholders, the development team mistakenly omitted encryption for sensitive data. As a result, user files are transmitted without proper safeguards, exposing them to interception and potential misuse.

Action Items

- **Clearly Define Security Requirements:**
  - At the project's outset, establish precise and unambiguous security requirements.
  - Utilize use cases, threat modelling, and security architecture diagrams to provide clear context and understanding.
  - Explicitly state expectations for encryption, access controls, authentication, and other security measures to avoid misinterpretation.

- **Ongoing Communication:**
  - Maintain regular and open communication channels between security experts, project managers, and developers to ensure everyone is on the same page.
  - Address any ambiguities promptly and ensure all team members have a clear understanding of the security requirements.

- Feedback and Clarification:
  - Provide opportunities for continuous feedback throughout the development process.
  - Encourage developers to seek clarification whenever security requirements are unclear or seem ambiguous.

By clearly defining requirements, maintaining open lines of communication, and promoting continuous feedback, teams can proactively resolve misunderstandings. This collaborative approach ensures that security requirements are fully understood and effectively implemented, strengthening the overall security posture of Android applications.

4.2 Development Constraints

Challenges Shape Progress

In the fast-paced landscape of application development, various constraints can significantly influence the progress of projects and the decisions made throughout the development process. From tight deadlines that demand rapid completion to resource limitations that affect the allocation of efforts, these constraints present considerable challenges that developers must navigate effectively.

This section explores the typical constraints encountered during development and proposes strategies to overcome them while maintaining a focus on security. By understanding and addressing these constraints, development teams can enhance their ability to deliver secure and reliable application solutions, even in challenging circumstances.

4.2.1 Tight Deadlines

Racing Against the Clock

Tight deadlines are time constraints that necessitate the completion of tasks or projects within a limited timeframe. These deadlines can arise in various contexts, from high-pressure work projects to urgent personal commitments, often forcing developers to prioritize speed over thoroughness.

Challenges

- **Speed Over Security:** Developers may prioritize speed over security to meet deadlines, leading to rushed coding practices that overlook essential security measures.
- **Shortcuts and Omissions:** In their haste to meet deadlines, developers might sacrifice thoroughness, resulting in shortcuts, inadequate testing, and incomplete security reviews.
- **Increased Vulnerabilities:** The trade-off between speed and security increases the likelihood of introducing vulnerabilities and weaknesses into the application.

Real-world Case Illustration

Consider a development team working on a feature enhancement for an Android app. The company has set an aggressive deadline to roll out the update before a significant event. Due to the time crunch, developers skip essential security testing phases, fail to update third-party dependencies, and neglect to enforce the latest Android security guidelines. As a result, the update introduces security flaws, exposing user data and increasing the risk of attacks.

Action Items

- **Secure Coding Practices:** Implement coding practices that emphasize both efficiency and security. This includes prioritizing secure design principles, such as input validation and proper authentication mechanisms, even when under time pressure.
- **Task Breakdown:** Divide development tasks into smaller, manageable chunks. Set realistic deadlines for each task, balancing the need for speed with the requirement for quality and thoroughness.
- **Automated Security Testing:** Leverage automation tools for security testing to accelerate the detection of vulnerabilities without compromising on quality. Automated tools can help maintain a high standard of security checks even when time is limited.
- **Security-first Development Culture:** Foster a culture that values both quality and speed. Encourage collaboration between development and security teams to ensure that security is integrated into the development process from the outset.

By striking a balance between speed and security, teams can deliver high-quality, secure Android applications even under aggressive timelines. Leveraging modern security automation tools, adopting best practices from Google's Android security guidelines, and fostering a security-aware culture will significantly reduce risks while ensuring efficient and timely development.

4.2.2 Resource Constraints

The Budget Dilemma

Resource constraints, such as limited budget, time, or personnel, pose significant challenges to implementing robust security measures. When security initiatives lack adequate resources, development teams may struggle to address vulnerabilities effectively.

Challenges

- **Budget Limitations:** Organizations may allocate minimal funds for security efforts, limiting access to essential tools, training, and expertise.
- **Time Pressure:** Tight schedules often leave little room for thorough security assessments, making it challenging to identify and mitigate potential vulnerabilities.
- **Personnel Shortages:** Insufficient staffing can prevent a dedicated focus on security tasks, leading to gaps in security coverage.

Real-world Case Illustration

Consider an Android app development team working under severe resource constraints. With a limited budget, the team opts not to invest in expensive security tools or hire dedicated security professionals. Instead, they rely on ad-hoc manual testing and outdated security practices. Consequently, essential security assessments are incomplete, and vulnerabilities go undetected. This scenario leaves the application at risk of exploitation, potentially compromising user data and device integrity.

Action Items

- **Allocate Specific Resources for Security:**
  - **Budget:** Advocate for a dedicated security budget to ensure that adequate funds are available for essential security tools, training, and personnel.
  - **Time:** Allocate specific time for security tasks within project schedules, ensuring that security is considered an integral part of the development process.
  - **Personnel:** Ensure adequate staffing for security roles, whether through hiring dedicated security professionals or designating existing team members to focus on security.

- **Prioritize Security in Budgeting:**
  - Highlight the risks of underinvestment in security to stakeholders. Clearly convey the potential consequences of security breaches, including financial losses, reputational damage, and regulatory penalties, to secure necessary resources.

- **Leverage Existing Resources:**
  - Utilize open-source security tools and frameworks to perform essential security tasks without incurring additional costs. Collaborate with external security experts or consultants as needed to fill any gaps in expertise.

- **Cultural Shift: Foster a Security-first Mindset:**
  - **Education:** Educate all stakeholders about the importance of security and its impact on the organization's success.
  - **Advocacy:** Advocate for security within the organization, emphasizing that security is everyone's responsibility and should be prioritizsed alongside other development goals.

By strategically leveraging open-source tools, cloud-based automation, and a security-first culture that emphasizses security throughout the development lifecycle, teams can navigate resource constraints without compromising on security. These modern approaches help ensure that even in resource-limited environments, Android apps are developed with a robust security posture, reducing risks and enhancing overall application resilience.

4.3 Experience Management

The Science of Happy

Experience plays a crucial role in shaping the competency and approach of developers in application security. The spectrum of experience within development teams, ranging from novice programmers grappling with foundational concepts to seasoned veterans navigating complex security challenges, significantly influences the security posture of application products.

This section explores the management of experience-related challenges and how organizations can cultivate expertise, address overconfidence, and foster a culture of continuous learning to bolster their security practices. By effectively managing experience, development teams can mitigate vulnerabilities and strengthen their defences against evolving threats, ultimately contributing to the creation of more resilient and secure applications.

4.3.1 Lack of Experience

Navigating Uncharted Waters

Inexperienced developers often face challenges related to security knowledge, skills, and practical experience. Without a solid foundation in security principles, they may inadvertently introduce vulnerabilities into the codebase.

Challenges

- **Security Blind Spots:** A lack of familiarity with common security risks and mitigation techniques can result in developers missing critical security vulnerabilities.
- **Omissions:** Inexperience may lead to overlooking essential security practices, such as input validation, secure data storage, and proper encryption methods during development.
- **Risk Exposure:** The inexperience of developers increases the likelihood of introducing vulnerabilities, making applications more susceptible to attacks.

Real-world Case Illustration

Imagine a team of junior developers building a new feature for an Android application. Due to their limited experience, they might neglect best practices for input validation or fail to properly implement encryption for sensitive user data. As a result, the app may become vulnerable to common attacks such as SQL injection or data breaches, even though Android now provides advanced tools and libraries to assist with these tasks.

Action Items

- **Mentorship Programs:**
  - Pair less experienced developers with seasoned colleagues to provide guidance, support, and oversight.
  - Encourage knowledge sharing and learning through regular mentoring sessions.
  - Facilitate hands-on experience by involving junior developers in security-focused projects under the supervision of experienced mentors.

- **Training and Workshops:**
  - Offer opportunities for hands-on security exercises that simulate real-world scenarios.
  - Conduct workshops on secure coding practices, covering essential topics like threat modelling, secure design principles, and risk assessment techniques.
  - Provide access to online courses, certifications, and other learning resources focused on application security.

- **Continuous Learning:**
  - Promote professional development in security by encouraging developers to stay informed about emerging threats and security trends.
  - Support attendance at conferences, webinars, and security forums to facilitate ongoing education and exposure to new ideas and best practices.
  - Create a culture of learning where developers are motivated to improve their security knowledge continuously.

Remember, investing in skill development and creating a supportive, learning-focused environment is key to bridging the experience gap. Enhancing the security knowledge of every developer not only reduces the risk of vulnerabilities but also strengthens the overall security posture of the organizsation.

4.3.2 Overconfidence

The Dangerous Edge

Overconfidence can occur when developers underestimate security risks or believe they can handle vulnerabilities without proper validation. This overconfidence can lead to significant security oversights.

Challenges

- **False Sense of Security**: Overconfident developers may assume their code is flawless and free from vulnerabilities, leading to complacency.
- **Complacency**: Developers who are overly confident in their abilities may become resistant to feedback or unwilling to seek advice, reducing opportunities for improvement.
- **Risk Ignorance**: Overconfidence can cause developers to overlook potential vulnerabilities, assuming that their expertise alone will prevent security issues.

Real-world Case Illustration

Imagine a group of experienced Android developers working on a new app feature. Confident in their abilities and past successes, they choose to forego external validation and automated security scanning, relying on manual reviews alone. As a result, critical vulnerabilities remain undetected. These oversights could eventually lead to severe security breaches, undermining both user trust and the app's integrity.

Action Items

- **Cultivate Humility:**
  - Encourage developers to approach security with a critical mindset, understanding that even the most experienced developers can make mistakes.
  - Foster a culture where acknowledging and learning from mistakes is valued, reducing the stigma around seeking help or admitting uncertainties.

- **Seek Peer Reviews and Feedback:**
  - Regularly conduct code reviews to identify potential security issues and encourage developers to learn from each other's insights and experiences.
  - Create an environment where colleagues are encouraged to challenge assumptions and provide constructive feedback, promoting a culture of continuous improvement.

- **External Audits:**
  - Engage external security experts for independent assessments to validate assumptions and uncover blind spots that internal teams may overlook.
  - Regularly schedule external audits to ensure that security practices are kept up-to-date and aligned with industry standards.

- **Continuous Learning:**
  - Provide ongoing training and education focused on the latest security trends, techniques, and vulnerabilities.
  - Encourage developers to stay informed about emerging threats and continuously refine their skills and knowledge.

Remember, even the most experienced developers benefit from external validation and continuous learning. By cultivating a culture of humility, encouraging robust peer review processes, engaging external experts, and investing in ongoing education, organizsations can ensure that overconfidence does not undermine the security posture of Android applications.

4.4 Legacy Systems and Complexity

Modernize for Efficiency

Legacy systems and the inherent complexity of interconnected application architectures present formidable challenges in modern application development. As technology evolves, organizations often struggle to maintain and secure outdated codebases while navigating the complexities of systems composed of multiple components and dependencies.

This section explores the issues associated with legacy systems and interconnected architectures, highlighting the risks posed by outdated practices and complicated interdependencies. Strategies to modernize legacy codebases, enhance security measures, and mitigate vulnerabilities within complex systems are also provided. By addressing these challenges directly, organizations can streamline operations, strengthen defences, and lay the groundwork for a more resilient and secure application ecosystem.

4.4.1 Legacy Code and Practices

The Shadows of the Past

Legacy code and practices refer to existing codebases or development methodologies that were considered acceptable at the time of creation but have since become outdated or risky due to technological advancements.

Challenges

- **Outdated Components:** Legacy systems may rely on deprecated libraries, insecure APIs, or obsolete encryption algorithms that no longer meet current security standards.
- **Lack of Modern Security Features:** These codebases often lack the security features and protections available in newer software versions or frameworks, leaving them vulnerable to contemporary threats.
- **Risk Accumulation:** Over time, legacy code accumulates technical debt, making it harder to maintain, update, and secure. This increases the potential for security vulnerabilities and operational inefficiencies.

Real-world Case Illustration

Imagine an Android app developed several years ago using outdated libraries and legacy practices. The app might lack proper input validation, secure authentication, and modern encryption mechanisms. Consequently, it remains vulnerable to attacks even though current

Android frameworks offer safe alternatives. The absence of updated components and security features in the legacy codebase exposes the app to exploitation that modern code would typically resist.

Action Items

- **Gradual Refactoring:**
  - Refactor legacy code incrementally to introduce modern security practices without overwhelming the development process.
  - Prioritize refactoring efforts based on the risk level of components and the criticality of the features they support.

- **Leverage Platform Features:**
  - Explore and utilize security enhancements available in the platform (e.g., Android security libraries).
  - Update components to leverage built-in security mechanisms, such as advanced encryption and secure data handling APIs.

- **Code Reviews and Assessments:**
  - Conduct thorough code reviews to identify and remediate vulnerabilities, deprecated components, or insecure configurations.
  - Perform regular security assessments to ensure that legacy code meets current security standards and best practices.

- **Automated Tools:**
  - Use automated tools to identify security issues within legacy codebases, such as static code analysis tools and dependency checkers.
  - Prioritize the remediation of critical vulnerabilities and high-risk areas to minimize the risk of exploitation.

Remember, modernizing legacy code is a strategic investment in your applications' long-term security and maintainability. By gradually refactoring outdated components, leveraging the latest platform security enhancements, and embedding automated security assessments into your development process, you can significantly reduce technical debt and bolster your app's defences against contemporary threats.

4.4.2 Complexity and Interconnected Systems

The Web We Weave

Complex, interconnected systems present unique challenges for security. These systems involve multiple components, dependencies, and interactions, creating numerous attack surfaces and potential vulnerabilities.

Challenges

- **Interdependencies:** Components within the system often rely on each other, making security interdependent. A vulnerability in one component can have cascading effects on the entire system.

- **Overlooked Vulnerabilities:** The complexity of interconnected systems increases the likelihood of overlooked vulnerabilities or misconfigurations as it becomes more challenging to maintain a comprehensive view of the entire system.
- **Insufficient Access Controls:** Inadequate access controls and poor privilege management can lead to unauthorized access and data breaches, especially when multiple components and services interact.

Real-world Case Illustration

Imagine an Android app that leverages several third-party APIs for functionalities like payment processing, social integration, and cloud data storage. If these APIs are integrated without adhering to the latest security standards (for instance, neglecting proper validation of API tokens or failing to enforce encryption for data in transit), a vulnerability in one API could compromise sensitive user data. Furthermore, if the app's internal modules are not isolated using modern architectural techniques (such as microservices or containerization), a breach in one component may expose the entire system to attack.

Action Items

- **Security Architecture and Design:**
  - Implement security principles that account for the complexity of the system, such as zero trust, defence in depth, least privilege, and secure by design.
  - Use architectural techniques like microservices, containerization, and service-oriented architecture (SOA) to isolate components and minimize the impact of a security breach.

- **Threat Modelling and Risk Assessment:**
  - Conduct regular threat modelling and risk assessments to identify potential vulnerabilities and attack vectors within the system.
  - Consider system boundaries, interactions, and dependencies to ensure a comprehensive understanding of the security landscape.

- **Security Controls:**
  - Implement robust security controls, such as network segmentation, to isolate critical components and reduce the attack surface.
  - Use strong encryption for data in transit and at rest to protect sensitive information from unauthorized access.
- Monitor system behaviour for anomalies and potential security incidents, leveraging logging and monitoring tools to detect and respond to threats promptly.

By embracing modern architectural strategies, continuously assessing risks, and integrating the latest security tools and Android features, organizations can manage the inherent complexity of interconnected systems. This holistic approach not only reduces the attack surface but also ensures that each component of the system is secured, thereby bolstering the overall security posture of Android applications.

4.5 Quality Control Shortcomings

Seal the Leaks

Effective quality control measures are essential for ensuring the reliability, functionality, and security of applications. However, inadequacies in testing practices and oversight can compromise the integrity of codebases and expose applications to vulnerabilities.

This section examines the challenges arising from quality control shortcomings, such as insufficient testing procedures and lack of code reviews and oversight. Strategies to enhance quality control measures are proposed, emphasizing comprehensive testing, automated tools, and collaborative review processes. By addressing these shortcomings, organizations can strengthen their defences against potential threats, uphold quality standards, and instil confidence in their application products.

4.5.1 Inadequate Testing

Testing in the Dark

Inadequate testing poses significant risks to both application quality and security. When testing is insufficient, vulnerabilities and weaknesses may remain undetected, leading to potential exploitation and operational failures.

Challenges

- **Undetected Vulnerabilities:** Inadequate testing allows security flaws to slip through the cracks, leaving the application exposed to potential attacks.
- **Release Risks:** Unidentified issues can delay application delivery, affecting brand reputation, customer trust, and potentially leading to costly post-release patches and updates.
- **Fragmented Testing Practices:** Many development teams still rely on siloed testing approaches. Without integrating static application security testing (SAST)), dynamic application security testing (DAST), and interactive application security testing (IAST) into the CI/CD pipeline, the testing process becomes fragmented. This results in inconsistent security assessments that fail to cover all aspects of the application, from the front-end code to the backend APIs and third-party components.

Real-world Case Illustration

Consider an Android app feature with unvalidated input fields that was developed under tight deadlines. If testing only covers basic functionality and overlooks security-specific test cases such as parameterized queries, secure authentication checks, or robust data sanitization, these fields may be left vulnerable to injection attacks (like SQL injection or cross-site scripting). Modern testing techniques can automate these checks, but critical vulnerabilities may go unnoticed without their integration.

Action Items

- **Comprehensive Testing Strategy:**
  - Implement a robust testing framework that includes unit testing, integration testing, and security testing. This ensures that both functionality and security are thoroughly assessed.
  - Prioritize security assessments alongside functional and performance testing to identify vulnerabilities early in the development process.

- **Automated Tools:**
  - Utilize automated testing tools such as static code analysis (SAST), dynamic analysis (DAST), interactive analysis (IAST), and penetration testing to detect security flaws, code errors, and misconfigurations more efficiently.

- Automated tools can help identify potential issues before they make it into production, reducing the risk of vulnerabilities being exploited.

- **Continuous Integration (CI)/Continuous Deployment (CD) Integration:**
  - Integrate security testing into the continuous integration/continuous deployment (CI/CD) pipeline to automate vulnerability scanning and code analysis.
  - Embedding security checks in the CI/CD process ensures that security is continuously assessed throughout the development lifecycle, reducing the risk of introducing vulnerabilities.

- **Clear Criteria and Requirements:**
  - Define clear testing criteria, security requirements, and acceptance criteria to guide the testing process.
  - Prioritize security validation alongside other testing activities to ensure that security is a primary focus throughout the development process.

Robust testing is crucial for ensuring that Android applications are resilient against modern threats. By integrating comprehensive automated testing, embedding security checks into the CI/CD pipeline, and defining clear security acceptance criteria, organizations can detect and mitigate vulnerabilities early in the development process. These modern practices not only protect sensitive user data but also support faster, more reliable software delivery, ultimately building trust and maintaining the security posture of your mobile applications.

4.5.2 Lack of Code Reviews and Oversight

Security Gaps in the Details

A lack of code reviews and oversight can lead to vulnerabilities and weaknesses in the codebase. When developers skip or inadequately conduct reviews, critical security issues may go unnoticed, compromising the application's security and integrity.

Challenges

- **Missed Vulnerabilities:** Security checks omitted during development can leave potential vulnerabilities unaddressed.
- **Coding Errors:** Unidentified flaws or misconfigurations can persist in the code, potentially leading to security breaches or functional errors.
- **Noncompliance Risks:** Failure to adhere to coding standards, best practices, or regulatory requirements can expose the organization to legal and reputational risks.

Real-world Case Illustration

Imagine an Android app developed without mandatory code reviews. In this scenario, issues, like hardcoded API keys, insecure integration with third-party services, or the use of deprecated libraries, may persist throughout the codebase. These issues can lead to unauthorized access or data manipulation, compromising user privacy and the overall security integrity of the application.

Action Items
- **Mandatory Code Reviews:**
  - Implement a process for thorough code reviews that is mandatory for all code changes, focusing on security best practices, coding standards, and compliance requirements.
  - Regular code reviews help catch security vulnerabilities, coding errors, and potential compliance issues early in the development process.

- **Guidelines and Checklists:**
  - Establish clear review criteria and checklists that address common security vulnerabilities, performance issues, and architectural concerns.
  - Use these guidelines to ensure that code reviews are consistent and comprehensive, covering all critical aspects of the codebase.

- **Automated Code Analysis:**
  - Employ static code analysers and quality metrics to identify potential security issues, code smells, and areas for improvement automatically.
  - Automated code analysis tools can supplement manual reviews, providing an additional layer of security and quality control.

- **Collaborative Culture:**
  - Foster a culture of collaboration and feedback within the development team, encouraging developers to learn from each other's insights and experiences.
  - Promote knowledge sharing and continuous learning to help developers improve their skills and understand the importance of security in coding practices.

Robust code reviews and oversight are crucial for maintaining high-quality, secure Android applications. By mandating security-focused code reviews, standardizing guidelines and checklists, integrating automated code analysis into the CI/CD pipeline, and fostering a culture of collaboration and continuous learning, organizations can significantly reduce the risk of security breaches and ensure that vulnerabilities are caught early. This holistic approach helps protect sensitive user data, improves overall code quality, and ensures that applications remain resilient in today's fast-evolving threat landscape.

4.6 Cultural and Incentive Misalignment

The Misalignment Trap

An organization's cultural and incentive landscape plays a pivotal role in shaping its approach to security. When incentives and priorities are misaligned, security measures may be marginalized, exposing the organization to heightened risks. Furthermore, cultural perceptions surrounding security can significantly impact the effectiveness of security practices and the willingness of stakeholders to prioritize security considerations.

This section explores the challenges stemming from cultural and incentive misalignment, examining the implications of underinvestment in security initiatives and the cultural perceptions that undermine robust security practices. Strategies to realign incentives, cultivate a security-conscious culture, and foster organizational commitment to security objectives are proposed. By addressing these underlying issues, organizations can mitigate risks, fortify their defences, and cultivate a culture of security resilience.

4.6.1 Incentives and Priorities

Prioritizing Progress Over Protection

Misaligned incentives and priorities can severely jeopardize an organization's security posture. When security takes a backseat to other business objectives, the consequences can be dire.

Challenges

- **Underinvestment in Security**: Organizations may prioritize speed, innovation, or cost savings over security initiatives, leading to inadequate investment in essential security measures.
- **Risk Exposure**: Neglecting security considerations in favour of other goals exposes applications to unnecessary vulnerabilities, increasing the risk of breaches and data loss.
- **Balancing Goals**: Striking the right balance between security and other business objectives is crucial for sustainable growth and resilience.

Real-world Case Illustration

Imagine an Android app development team under pressure to launch a new feature to capture market share. In their drive to meet aggressive deadlines, they bypass comprehensive security testing and overlook necessary security reviews. As a result, vulnerabilities remain in the codebase. Later, these weaknesses are exploited, leading to a data breach that not only affects user trust but also incurs significant remediation costs and reputational damage.

Action Items

- **Incorporate Security Metrics:**
  - Use Key Performance Indicators (KPIs) and Service Level Agreements (SLAs) to measure security effectiveness. This ensures that security is a visible and quantifiable aspect of performance.
  - Tie performance evaluations, bonuses, and rewards to security outcomes, incentivizing teams to prioritize security alongside other goals.

- **Establish Accountability:**
  - Clearly define roles and responsibilities for security within the organization, ensuring that every team member understands their part in maintaining security.
  - Emphasize security as a core business value, integrating it into the company's mission, vision, and everyday practices.

- **Educate Decision-Makers:**
  - Highlight the risks associated with underinvestment in security, including the potential for data breaches, financial losses, and reputational damage.
  - Stress the impact of security failures on brand reputation, customer trust, and regulatory compliance, encouraging decision-makers to prioritize security investments.

- **Integrate Security into Processes:**
  - Include security considerations in project planning, resource allocation, and risk management processes to ensure that security is not an afterthought.
  - Prioritize security requirements throughout the development lifecycle, from design to deployment and beyond.

Aligning security incentives and priorities with overall business objectives is essential for building resilient and trustworthy Android applications. By integrating measurable security metrics, establishing clear accountability, educating decision-makers, and embedding security into every phase of development, organizations can protect themselves against evolving threats while supporting innovation and growth. This holistic approach ensures that security becomes a fundamental part of business strategy, ultimately reducing risk and enhancing the organization's competitive edge.

4.6.2 Cultural Perception of Security

The Cultural Blind Spot

The cultural perception of security significantly influences an organization's ability to establish robust security practices. Understanding these perceptions is crucial for addressing security challenges effectively.

Challenges

- **Business Priorities:** Organizations often prioritize speed, innovation, or cost savings over security. When security is perceived as a hindrance to productivity or profitability, it tends to be deprioritized.
- **Lack of Awareness:** Employees, managers, and executives may not fully understand the impact of security breaches or the importance of their role in maintaining a secure environment.
- **Risk Tolerance:** Some organizations have a higher tolerance for risk, believing that security incidents will not directly affect them or that the costs of prevention outweigh the benefits.
- **Historical Precedence:** If an organization has not experienced significant security incidents in the past, there may be a false sense of security or complacency regarding future risks.

Real-world Case Illustration

Imagine an Android app development team in a company that prides itself on rapid innovation. With management pushing for faster time-to-market, security reviews and threat modelling sessions are either rushed or skipped entirely. As a result, vulnerabilities are introduced and later exploited. Even if these flaws are minor individually, their combined effect can lead to a significant breach, undermining user trust and damaging the company's reputation.

Action Items

- **Education and Advocacy:**
  - Educate stakeholders about the risks of cyber threats and the importance of proactive security measures. Use real-world examples to illustrate the potential consequences of neglecting security.
  - Advocate for security as a core business value, emphasizing its importance to the organization's long-term success and stability.

- **Training and Support:**
  - Provide resources for security awareness and skills development, including training sessions, workshops, and e-learning courses tailored to different roles within the organization.

- Empower employees to recognize, report, and mitigate risks by equipping them with the knowledge and tools they need to act effectively.

- **Open Dialogue:**
  - Encourage transparency regarding security incidents and vulnerabilities, fostering a culture of openness and continuous improvement.
  - Promote collaboration and knowledge-sharing across teams to enhance collective understanding and response to security challenges.

Transforming the cultural perception of security requires a concerted effort across all organizational levels. By integrating targeted training, measurable security metrics, open cross-functional collaboration, and embedding security into core business processes, organizations can shift from a reactive, risk-tolerant stance to a proactive, security-first mindset. This holistic approach not only protects against evolving threats but also builds a resilient foundation that supports innovation and sustainable growth in Android app development.

4.7 External Challenges

Adapting Amidst Shifting Winds

Navigating the external landscape presents a myriad of challenges for organizations involved in application development. From dependencies on third-party components to stringent regulatory compliance requirements, external factors can significantly impact the security and integrity of application products.

This section explores the external challenges faced by organizations, including the risks associated with third-party dependencies and the complexities of regulatory compliance and legal requirements. Strategies to mitigate these challenges are provided, emphasizing the importance of proactive monitoring, collaboration with vendors, and adherence to regulatory frameworks. By effectively addressing external challenges, organizations can adapt to shifting winds, fortify their defences, and sustain resilience amidst dynamic environments.

4.7.1 Dependency on Third-party Components

The Third-party Puzzle

The use of third-party components is commonplace in application development due to their ability to accelerate growth, reduce costs, and add functionality. However, integrating external libraries, frameworks, or SDKs without proper vetting can introduce significant security risks.

Challenges

- **Supply Chain Vulnerabilities:** Third-party components may harbour vulnerabilities or malicious code, making applications that rely on them susceptible to exploitation.
- **Inadequate Oversight:** Without proper monitoring, organizations may unwittingly include risky components, which can lead to security breaches and data leaks.
- **Compliance Challenges:** Using third-party components without verifying their licensing terms or ensuring they meet regulatory requirements can lead to legal and compliance issues.

Real-world Case Illustration

Consider an Android app that relies heavily on third-party libraries for core functionalities such as user authentication and data processing. Suppose these dependencies are not routinely updated or vetted using modern Software Composition Analysis (SCA) tools (such as Snyk, GitHub Dependabot, or Gradle plugins with real-time CVE integration). In that case, the app may become susceptible to supply chain attacks like those exploiting Log4j vulnerabilities. Outdated libraries or unpatched vulnerabilities could allow attackers to bypass authentication mechanisms or leak sensitive user data, ultimately jeopardizing compliance and user trust.

Action Items

- **Regular Monitoring and Updates:**
  - Continuously monitor third-party dependencies for security vulnerabilities and ensure they are regularly updated to the latest versions.
  - Apply patches promptly to address known vulnerabilities and reduce the risk of exploitation.

- **Vetting Process:**
  - Implement a thorough vetting process to evaluate third-party components before integration. Consider factors such as the component's reputation, track record, community support, and frequency of updates.
  - Conduct security assessments to ensure that the component meets your organization's security standards.

- **Guidelines and Policies:**
  - Establish clear procedures for managing third-party dependencies, including guidelines for version control, vulnerability management, and license compliance checks.
  - Maintain an inventory of all third-party components used in your applications and regularly review them for potential security or compliance issues.

- **Collaboration with Vendors and Developers:**
  - Stay informed about security updates, patches, and changes from third-party vendors and developers. Maintain open lines of communication to address any emerging threats quickly.
  - Collaborate with third-party maintainers to ensure timely updates and adherence to security best practices.

Securing the application supply chain in modern Android development requires a proactive, multi-layered approach. By continuously monitoring dependencies with automated SCA tools, enforcing a robust vetting process, establishing clear management policies, and collaborating closely with vendors and the developer community, organizations can significantly reduce the risk of third-party vulnerabilities. These updated practices ensure that your applications remain secure, compliant, and resilient against emerging threats even as the mobile ecosystem evolves.

4.7.2 Regulatory Compliance and Legal Requirements

Navigating the Maze

Failure to comply with relevant regulations and legal requirements can have severe consequences for organizations. Understanding why these challenges occur and their impact on businesses is crucial for navigating the complex legal landscape.

Challenges

- **Legal and Financial Liabilities:** Non-compliance exposes companies to hefty fines, legal battles, and financial losses. Violating laws or contractual obligations can severely impact an organization's economic stability.
- **Reputational Damage:** Public perception is critical. Non-compliance can tarnish a company's reputation, eroding trust among customers, partners, and stakeholders and leading to long-term damage.
- **Business Disruption:** Legal actions can disrupt operations, divert resources, and hinder growth. Compliance failures can result in business closures, bankruptcy, or loss of market position.

Real-world Case Illustration

Consider an Android app that collects, processes, and stores sensitive user data without adequately integrating modern consent mechanisms, encryption, or data minimization practices. If the app fails to adhere to privacy regulations such as General Data Protection Regulation (GDPR), California Consumer Privacy Act (CCPA), or Health Insurance Portability and Accountability Act (HIPAA), the organization could face not only regulatory enforcement actions and lawsuits but also widespread reputational damage. The ensuing financial penalties and operational disruptions could severely hinder business growth and market position.

Action Items

- **Stay Informed:**
  - Continuously monitor regulations (GDPR, CCPA, HIPAA, and emerging EU DMA/DSA), industry standards, and legal requirements that apply to your organization and products.
  - Understand your obligations based on your industry, geographic region, and the types of data you handle, ensuring that your practices align with current laws.

- **Regular Audits and Assessments:**
  - Conduct regular compliance reviews and audits to ensure adherence to regulatory requirements. This should cover areas like data privacy, security, accessibility, and consumer protection.
  - Use the findings from these audits to address gaps in compliance and improve your organization's security posture.

- **Ethical Behaviour and Accountability:**
  - Handle consumer data responsibly, ensuring that data collection, storage, and processing practices comply with legal and ethical standards.
  - Differentiate your business by prioritizing compliance and building a culture of accountability and transparency, which can enhance customer trust and loyalty.

Compliance is not merely a regulatory burden; it is a strategic imperative that protects an organization from legal risks, financial losses, and reputational damage. By continuously monitoring legal developments, automating compliance audits, fostering an organizational culture of ethical data handling, and embedding security into every stage of development, organizations can build resilient, compliant Android applications that instil trust and drive long-term success.

4.8 Communication and Resistance to Change

Speak to Transform

Effective communication and a willingness to embrace change are integral components of a dynamic and resilient organization. However, challenges often arise when communication channels falter and resistance to change impedes progress, notably in the area of security initiatives.

This section explores the obstacles posed by communication breakdowns and inertia within organizations, examining their impact on security practices and the development process. Strategies to enhance communication and collaboration among stakeholders and address resistance to change are provided, emphasizing the importance of clear protocols, cultural shifts, and effective change management processes. By overcoming these challenges, organizations can foster a culture of transparency, adaptability, and continuous improvement, ultimately strengthening their security posture and resilience in the face of evolving threats.

4.8.1 Communication and Collaboration Challenges

The Tower of Babel

Effective communication and collaboration are the cornerstones of successful application development, particularly in ensuring robust security practices. However, challenges often arise when security teams, development teams, and other stakeholders fail to align their efforts.

Challenges

- **Misunderstandings:** A lack of clear communication can lead to misinterpretations of security requirements, risks, or vulnerabilities, resulting in security gaps or misaligned priorities.
- **Silos:** Teams operating in isolation may overlook critical security issues due to inadequate collaboration and lack of information sharing.
- **Incomplete Features:** Misalignment between security requirements and their implementation can result in incomplete or insecure features, undermining the overall security posture of the application.

Real-world Case Illustration

Consider a cross-functional Android app development team working under a fast-paced agile framework. If security experts, developers, designers, and testers do not communicate effectively, the security requirements can become lost in translation. For instance, if security-related feedback is not promptly shared via integrated collaboration platforms, critical issues (such as insecure API usage or improper handling of sensitive data) might be deprioritized. The result is an application with insecure features, exposing it to potential breaches and undermining overall integrity.

Action Items

- **Communication Tools:**
  - Utilize collaboration tools and platforms to facilitate seamless information sharing among team members. Tools like Slack, Microsoft Teams, or project management software can enhance real-time communication and document sharing.
  - Create dedicated channels for feedback, cross-team discussions, and issue resolution to ensure that security concerns are addressed promptly and effectively.

- **Clear Protocols:**
  - Establish clear guidelines for reporting security issues, including defined workflows for escalating concerns and requesting assistance from relevant stakeholders.
  - Implement standard operating procedures for handling security incidents, ensuring that all team members understand their roles and responsibilities in maintaining security.

- **Integration into Planning:**
  - Ensure that security considerations are integrated into project planning from the outset. This includes incorporating security checkpoints into development processes and release management.
  - Regularly review and update security practices to align with evolving threats and industry standards, fostering a proactive approach to security.

- **Cultural Shift:**
  - Foster a culture of transparency and accountability where security is viewed as a shared responsibility across all teams.
  - Encourage open dialogue and knowledge-sharing across teams, promoting a collaborative environment where security is prioritized and integrated into every aspect of development.

A unified, collaborative approach to security is vital for building secure Android applications. By leveraging modern communication tools, establishing clear protocols, integrating security early into planning, and fostering a culture of transparency and continuous learning, organizations can ensure that security is embedded throughout the development process. This holistic approach not only enhances the app's security but also aligns with business goals, resulting in a more resilient, trustworthy product.

4.8.2 Inertia and Resistance to Change

Anchored in the Past

Resistance to change is a common challenge within organizations, particularly when it comes to implementing new security initiatives. Overcoming inertia can be daunting, but it is essential for maintaining a robust security posture.

Challenges

- **Comfort with the Familiar:** Employees, managers, and executives may prefer existing practices due to familiarity or habit, resisting new approaches that require learning and adaptation.

- **Fear of Disruption:** Change can disrupt routines, workflows, and established norms, creating uncertainty and discomfort among employees.
- **Risk Aversion:** People may perceive change as risky, especially if they are uncertain about the benefits or fear adverse outcomes associated with new security measures.

Real-world Case Illustration

Consider a cross-functional Android app development team operating in a company with a long history of relying on established legacy security practices. When a proposal is made to integrate modern DevSecOps tools (such as automated security scans within the CI/CD pipeline or new code review platforms with built-in security checks), there is significant pushback. Executives and team leads worry that these changes might disrupt the existing workflow or delay product launches. As a result, critical updates that would protect the app against vulnerabilities introduced by recent threats remain unimplemented, exposing the app and user data to unnecessary risks.

Action Items

- **Change Management Processes:**
  - Implement structured approaches to manage change, such as change management frameworks (e.g., ADKAR, Kotter's 8-Step Change Model) that guide organizations through the transition process.
  - Clearly communicate the need for security improvements, outlining the benefits and potential risks of maintaining the status quo to garner support from all stakeholders.

- **Education and Rationale:**
  - Educate stakeholders about the rationale behind security changes, providing clear explanations of how new measures will improve security and protect the organization.
  - Highlight the benefits of enhanced security, such as reduced risk of breaches, improved customer trust, and compliance with regulatory requirements.

- **Feedback and Participation:**
  - Solicit input from affected parties to ensure that their concerns and suggestions are considered during the change process.
  - Address concerns and objections collaboratively, demonstrating a commitment to finding solutions that work for everyone involved.

- **Lead by Example:**
  - Demonstrate commitment to security at all levels of the organization, with leaders setting the tone for embracing change and prioritizing security.
  - Foster a culture of agility and resilience where adapting to new challenges and evolving threats is seen as an opportunity for growth and improvement.

Overcoming inertia and resistance to change is essential for maintaining a robust security posture in Android app development. By implementing structured change management processes, providing targeted education and training, fostering open dialogue, and demonstrating strong leadership commitment, organizations can shift cultural perceptions. This unified approach helps integrate modern security practices (such as automated testing, DevSecOps, and continuous improvement) into every aspect of development, ensuring that security remains a core, proactive element of the business strategy.

4.9 Psychological Factors

Embrace your Inner Dialogue

Across the application development arena, understanding the psychological factors that influence developer behaviour is paramount to fostering a culture of security and innovation. This section explores the interplay between cognitive biases, the pressure for feature expansion, and the underestimation of threats, examining how these psychological phenomena shape decision-making processes and impact application security.

Cognitive biases and ingrained mental shortcuts can lead developers astray, potentially compromising the integrity and security of applications. Moreover, the relentless pressure to expand features in competitive markets can result in rushed development cycles and neglect of security considerations, exposing applications to vulnerabilities. Additionally, the tendency to underestimate threats can leave applications vulnerable to exploitation, highlighting the importance of comprehensive threat assessments and proactive security measures.

By acknowledging and addressing these psychological factors, organizations can empower developers to make informed decisions, prioritize security, and fortify their applications against emerging threats.

4.9.1 Cognitive Biases

Blind Spots in Decision-Making

Cognitive biases are ingrained behaviours and thought patterns that can significantly influence developer actions, potentially leading them astray and necessitating corrective actions.

Challenges

- **Limited Cognitive Capacity:** Developers often face information overload, tight deadlines, and complex problem-solving tasks. To cope, they rely on mental shortcuts (heuristics) that can introduce biases. For example, the availability bias may prompt developers to choose solutions based on readily remembered examples, even if those examples are not the most suitable.
- **Prior Experience and Familiarity:** Biases can emerge from prior experiences with specific solutions. For instance, belief perseverance bias may cause developers to focus excessively on code they believe contains a bug, even when evidence suggests otherwise.
- **Individual Problem-Solving Styles:** Developers exhibit different problem-solving styles. Hyperbolic discounting bias, which favours immediate rewards, might influence their choice of solutions. While these biases can lead to quick outcomes, they can also result in negative consequences if not managed properly.

Real-world Case Illustration

Consider a scenario where developers, confident in their established methods, assume that a particular authentication module is secure. Relying on past experiences and ignoring new threat intelligence, they conduct minimal testing and dismiss external reviews. As a result, subtle vulnerabilities (such as improper error handling or edge-case flaws in biometric integration) remain undetected, compromising the application's security.

Action Items

- **Challenge Assumptions:**
  - Encourage teams to question assumptions and consider alternative perspectives when evaluating security risks, threat scenarios, or mitigation strategies. This practice can help reduce the impact of biases on decision-making.

- **Raise Awareness:**
  - Provide training, education, and awareness programs to highlight common cognitive biases and their impact on decision-making.
  - Emphasize the importance of objectivity, scepticism, and critical thinking in security analysis and risk management.

- **Implement Decision-making Frameworks:**
  - Utilize decision-making frameworks, checklists, or peer review processes to mitigate the influence of cognitive biases.
  - These tools can help ensure a more systematic and evidence-based approach to security assessment, incident response, and vulnerability management.

Cognitive biases can subtly erode an organization's security posture if left unaddressed. By challenging assumptions, raising awareness, implementing structured decision-making frameworks, and fostering a culture of collaboration, organizations can help developers make more objective, informed security decisions. This holistic approach not only mitigates the impact of cognitive biases but also ensures that the security measures within Android app development remain robust, current, and aligned with industry best practices.

4.9.2 Pressure for Feature Expansion

The Tug-of-War

In the fast-paced world of application development, the pressure to deliver new features and functionalities is ever-present. Organizations strive to stay competitive, innovate rapidly, and meet customer demands. However, this drive for feature expansion can have unintended consequences if not managed carefully.

Challenges

- **Rushed Development Cycles:** The urgency to release new features quickly can lead to rushed development cycles. Developers may cut corners, skip thorough testing, or bypass security considerations, resulting in vulnerabilities creeping into the codebase and compromising the application's security posture.
- **Feature Delivery vs. Security:** When faced with tight deadlines, organizations may prioritize feature delivery over security. New features are often seen as revenue generators or market differentiators. Unfortunately, this can lead to neglecting security best practices, leaving applications exposed to potential threats.
- **Testing and Validation Neglect:** In the race to launch features, testing and validation may take a back seat. Insufficient time or resources allocated for comprehensive testing can result in undetected vulnerabilities that are only discovered after exploitation.

Real-world Case Illustration

Imagine an Android app development team competing in a crowded market. In order to capture market share, they prioritize rapid feature rollout, such as adding new functionalities without integrating full-scale security reviews or automated testing into their CI/CD pipeline. As a result, while the app boasts innovative features, hidden vulnerabilities (such as insecure API calls or poor data validation practices) remain undetected. These vulnerabilities later become the target of malicious actors, leading to data breaches that damage customer trust and the company's reputation.

Action Items

- **Prioritization Process:**
  - Implement a prioritization process that considers security implications alongside business requirements and market demands.
  - Evaluate the impact of each proposed feature on security, stability, and reliability.

- **Risk Assessments and Analyses:**
  - Conduct risk assessments, impact analyses, or cost-benefit analyses for proposed features.
  - Understanding the security risks associated with each change enables informed decision-making.

- **Involve Security Experts:**
  - Engage security experts, architects, or risk managers early in the feature planning phase.
  - Seek their guidance, feedback, and validation regarding security considerations, trade-offs, and alternatives.

Rapid feature expansion can drive business growth but it must be carefully balanced with robust security measures. By integrating security into every phase of the development lifecycle through continuous threat modelling, automated testing, and cross-functional collaboration, organizations can innovate without compromising the integrity and trustworthiness of their Android applications. This holistic approach not only protects user data but also enhances long-term business resilience and compliance with evolving security standards.

4.9.3 Underestimation of Threats

Playing it Safe

The underestimation of threats is a significant issue in application development. It occurs when developers do not fully assess or anticipate the potential security risks associated with their applications.

Challenges

- **Lack of Comprehensive Threat Modelling:** Threat modelling is a structured approach that involves identifying potential threats and vulnerabilities and developing countermeasures to mitigate risk. If this process is not comprehensive, some threats may go unnoticed, leaving the application vulnerable.
- **Failure to Prioritize Security:** In the rush to meet project deadlines and deliver new features, security can sometimes be overlooked or deprioritized, leading to severe consequences later.

Real-world Case Illustration

Consider an Android app development team that, based on previous success with basic input validation, neglects to update its threat model to account for recent vulnerabilities in network communication protocols or advanced injection techniques. As a result, the app's security assessment fails to identify potential data breaches or injection attacks. This oversight could leave sensitive user data exposed and compromise the application's overall functionality.

Action Items

- **Prioritize Security:**
  - Ensure that security is a priority from the beginning of the development process, not an afterthought.
  - Integrate security practices throughout the application development lifecycle to build secure applications from the ground up.
- **Conduct Thorough Threat Assessments:**
  - Regularly conduct threat modeling using frameworks like STRIDE and tools like Microsoft Threat Modeling Tool to understand and anticipate potential security risks.
  - Stay informed about the latest security threats and vulnerabilities to protect applications proactively.
- **Implement Security Best Practices:**
  - Adopt security best practices, such as input validation and encryption. Input validation prevents improperly formatted data from entering an application system, while encryption secures data in transit and at rest.
- **Stay Informed:**
  - The world of cybersecurity is ever-evolving. Staying informed about emerging security threats and vulnerabilities can help developers stay one step ahead and protect their applications from potential risks.
- **Continuous Learning and Improvement:**
  - Encourage developers to be open to learning and adapting to new security practices and technologies. Continuous learning and improvement are essential for staying ahead of evolving threats and ensuring application security.

By addressing the psychological factors that impact security decision-making, organizations can foster a culture of security awareness and resilience, empowering developers to make informed decisions that prioritize security and protect applications from emerging threats.

4.10 Reliance on External Factors

At the mercy of what might be

In the dynamic landscape of application development, reliance on external factors such as AI, automation, code libraries, and frameworks is increasingly prevalent. While these external resources offer efficiency, innovation, and convenience, they also introduce unique challenges and potential vulnerabilities.

This section explores the implications of over-reliance on external factors and provides actionable strategies to mitigate associated risks. From AI-driven authentication systems to third-party code libraries, understanding the potential vulnerabilities and implementing proactive measures is crucial to safeguarding applications against exploitation and cyber threats.

4.10.1 Reliance on Artificial Intelligence (AI) and Automation

The AI Dependency Dilemma

The rapid evolution of AI and automation technologies has transformed security practices by enabling the automation of routine tasks and the rapid detection of patterns and anomalies. Modern Android development now leverages AI-driven security tools that integrate directly into CI/CD pipelines and development environments like Android Studio. However, over-reliance on these systems can still introduce vulnerabilities if they are not correctly implemented, regularly audited, or complemented by human judgement.

Challenges

- **Automated Detection Limitations:** While AI models can scan vast codebases and runtime data for vulnerabilities, they may produce false positives or miss context-specific issues. Sophisticated attackers are now using adversarial machine learning techniques to deceive these systems, potentially bypassing AI-driven defences.
- **Lack of Fallback Mechanisms:** AI-driven authentication systems or anomaly detection tools might rely on complex algorithms to verify user identities or monitor behaviour. If these systems lack robust fallback mechanisms, such as multi-factor authentication (MFA) or manual review protocols, an attacker could exploit weaknesses or trigger false negatives, leading to unauthorized access.
- **Insufficient Continuous Oversight:** Relying solely on automation without periodic human audits can allow biases or outdated threat models to persist. As AI models are only as good as the data and assumptions they are built upon, they require continuous monitoring, updates, and integration with human expertise to remain effective.

Real-world Case Illustration

Consider an Android app that depends heavily on AI-driven authentication for user login and anomaly detection to monitor for unusual behaviour. In this scenario, if the underlying AI model is not regularly audited or updated, it may fail to detect novel attack vectors or be tricked by adversarial inputs. For instance, an attacker could craft inputs designed to manipulate the AI model's behaviour, resulting in unauthorized access despite the automated controls. Without proper fallback mechanisms, such as additional layers of multi-factor authentication or manual code reviews, critical vulnerabilities may remain unaddressed, especially when using AI-generated code without security review.

Action Items

- **Regular Audits:**
  - AI models should be regularly audited for biases and vulnerabilities. This can help identify potential weaknesses and take corrective actions before attackers exploit these vulnerabilities.
  - Conduct routine assessments of AI algorithms to ensure they perform as expected under different scenarios, reducing the risk of false positives or negatives.

- **Integrate Multi-factor Authentication (MFA):**
  - Implementing multi-factor authentication (MFA) can serve as a backup to AI-driven authentication systems. Even if the AI system is compromised, the attacker would still need to bypass additional security layers provided by MFA.
  - Combining AI-based and traditional authentication methods adds an extra layer of security, making it more difficult for attackers to gain unauthorized access.

- **Enhance Human Oversight:**
  - Provide users with clear instructions on what to do in case of AI failure or false positives. This can help minimize the impact of such incidents and ensure a quick recovery.
  - Develop user-friendly guidelines and support systems to handle potential issues related to AI-based security measures.

While AI and automation have immense potential in enhancing security measures, they should be used judiciously and in conjunction with traditional security measures to ensure robust and foolproof security. It is also important to remember that technology is just one piece of the puzzle, a comprehensive security strategy should also include user education, robust policies and procedures, and a culture of security awareness.

4.10.2 Overreliance on Code Libraries and Frameworks

The Framework Trap

The widespread use of code libraries and frameworks accelerates Android app development by offering ready-made solutions and reducing development time. However, overreliance on these third-party components can introduce significant security risks, particularly if they are not rigorously vetted or maintained.

Challenges

- **Supply Chain Vulnerabilities:** Third-party libraries may harbour known vulnerabilities or even malicious code if they are not updated or monitored continuously. Advanced dependency scanning tools now reveal that even widely used frameworks can be exploited if they lag behind current security patches.
- **Inadequate Oversight:** Developers sometimes integrate external components without performing comprehensive security assessments. Without automated tools and formal processes in place, outdated or risky libraries can persist in the codebase, potentially exposing the application to exploits.
- **Compliance and Licensing Issues:** Failing to verify licensing terms or ensure that third-party components meet modern regulatory and security standards can lead to legal complications, in addition to technical vulnerabilities.

Real-world Case Illustration

Consider an Android app that uses outdated or transitive dependencies with hidden vulnerabilities, especially in widely used but minimally maintained open-source libraries (e.g., utility SDKs with excessive permissions or logging of sensitive data). These libraries could have known security vulnerabilities that have been patched in newer versions. However, if the developer is unaware of these updates or neglects to update the libraries, the app remains vulnerable to these known security risks. This oversight could lead to data breaches or other forms of cyberattacks.

Action Items

- **Evaluate and Manage:**
  - Implement strict controls and processes for evaluating and managing third-party dependencies. Regularly update dependencies to their latest secure versions and monitor security advisories for known vulnerabilities.
  - Conduct a thorough assessment of third-party libraries before integration, considering factors such as the library's security history, maintenance activity, and community support.

- **Code Reviews:**
  - Conduct thorough code reviews to identify and mitigate any potential security risks introduced by third-party components. This helps ensure that any vulnerabilities or security issues are detected and addressed before deployment.
  - Incorporate security-specific checks into the code review process to focus on identifying weaknesses related to third-party integrations.

- **Custom Solutions:**
  - For critical, security-sensitive functionalities, consider using lightweight alternatives or building custom solutions. This reduces dependency on external code and gives developers more control over the security aspects of their applications.
  - Evaluate whether third-party libraries are necessary for each functionality and opt for in-house development when security or performance is a priority.

- **DevSecOps Approach:**
  - Adopt a DevSecOps approach by integrating security practices into the DevOps process. Ensure that security considerations are accounted for from the initial stages of development. This includes practices such as automated security testing and continuous monitoring for vulnerabilities.
  - Use automated tools to scan dependencies for known vulnerabilities continuously, and integrate these scans into the CI/CD pipeline for real-time feedback.

- **Team Education:**
  - Educate the development team about the importance of security and keep them updated on the latest security threats and best practices. Regular training sessions and workshops can enhance awareness and preparedness among developers.
  - Encourage a culture of security mindfulness, where developers are proactive about identifying and addressing security risks.

By balancing the use of external resources with internal oversight and security best practices, organizations can leverage the benefits of AI, automation, and third-party libraries while minimizing their risks. A comprehensive approach that includes regular audits, robust policies, and a proactive security culture is essential to protect applications against emerging threats.

4.11 Feedback and Improvement Loops

From Insight to Innovation

In the context of application development, feedback is a vital catalyst for progress and innovation. Effective feedback mechanisms enable organizations to identify areas for improvement, address vulnerabilities, and enhance security posture.

This section explores the importance of robust feedback loops in bolstering security measures and outlines actionable strategies to cultivate a culture of continuous improvement. From stakeholder engagement to incident response readiness, organizations must integrate feedback loops seamlessly into their development processes to fortify security postures and adapt proactively to evolving threats and requirements. Through a commitment to continuous learning and improvement, organizations can harness the power of feedback to drive innovation and resilience in their application development endeavours.

4.11.1 Inadequate Feedback Loops

Closing the Loop

In the dynamic landscape of application development, the absence of effective feedback mechanisms can have far-reaching consequences for security. Organizations that lack robust feedback loops struggle to identify and address security issues promptly, becoming vulnerable to exploitation, data breaches, and compliance violations.

Challenges

- **Delayed Detection and Response**: Organizations may miss emerging threats or vulnerabilities without timely feedback. Delayed detection hampers their ability to respond effectively, leaving critical security gaps unaddressed.
- **Adaptation Challenges**: Security practices must evolve alongside risks, requirements, and vulnerabilities. Inadequate feedback impedes adaptation, increasing the likelihood of security incidents and making it difficult to keep up with the evolving threat landscape.

Real-world Case Illustration

Consider an Android app development process without established feedback loops. Security vulnerabilities discovered after app release may remain unaddressed for extended periods, creating opportunities for malicious actors to exploit these weaknesses. This can lead to reputational damage, financial losses, or regulatory penalties, ultimately compromising the organization's standing and trust with its users.

Action Items

- **Stakeholder Engagement:**
  - Establish mechanisms to gather feedback from users, security experts, auditors, and other stakeholders. This collaborative approach ensures that a wide range of perspectives is considered in identifying and prioritizing security issues.
  - Use feedback to proactively remediate weaknesses and continuously improve security measures, ensuring that security is integral to the development process.

- **Incident Response Readiness:**
  - Implement comprehensive incident response procedures, including well-defined reporting channels and communication protocols. This ensures that incidents are detected and reported promptly, enabling swift resolution.
  - Regularly test and update incident response plans to keep them current and effective in addressing emerging threats and vulnerabilities.

- **Learn and Improve:**
  - Conduct post-mortem reviews, lessons learned exercises, and root cause analyses after security incidents. This helps identify systemic issues, process enhancements, and corrective actions that can prevent similar incidents in the future.
  - Encourage a culture of transparency and accountability, where security incidents are viewed as learning opportunities rather than failures.

- **Integrate Feedback Loops:**
  - Embed feedback loops into the development lifecycle, CI/CD pipeline, or agile processes to ensure that security concerns are addressed continuously. This integration allows for real-time feedback and quick iteration, enhancing the overall security posture of the application.
  - Foster a collaborative environment where developers, security teams, and other stakeholders work together to address security concerns throughout the application development journey.

By integrating robust feedback loops into their development processes, organizations can enhance their ability to detect, respond to, and mitigate security threats. A proactive approach to feedback and continuous improvement not only strengthens security but also drives innovation and resilience, enabling organizations to adapt to evolving threats and maintain a competitive edge.

Looking Ahead

Understanding the factors that contribute to insecure code is essential for developing robust and secure Android applications. This chapter has explored a broad spectrum of influences. Each of these elements plays a role in shaping the security landscape, highlighting the need for a holistic approach to secure coding.

Security is not a static goal but an ongoing process that requires continuous learning, collaboration, and adaptation. Addressing insecure code demands a shift in mindset. By acknowledging and tackling these challenges head-on, development teams can create more resilient applications that stand up to evolving threats. The journey toward secure development is iterative, and by integrating security best practices at every stage, organizations can cultivate a culture of security that strengthens both their applications and their teams.

Looking ahead, developers and security professionals must remain vigilant, leveraging automation, security training, and policy refinements to bridge existing gaps. As the Android ecosystem continues to evolve, so must our security approach. The insights gained in this chapter lay the foundation for a more secure development paradigm, guiding the industry toward a future where security is an integral part of the development process rather than an afterthought.

Chapter 5

Integrating Security in App Development Process

It takes 20 years to build a reputation and five minutes to ruin it. If you think about that, you will do things differently.

– Warren Buffett

Warren Buffett, an American businessman, investor, and philanthropist, emphasizes the importance of reputation and the potential consequences of neglecting security. It highlights the fact that a single security breach or incident can have significant and lasting repercussions for an organization or individual.

In the context of securing the Android application development lifecycle, this quote serves as a reminder of the critical role that security plays in safeguarding the reputation and trustworthiness of an application and its developers. By prioritizing security throughout the development lifecycle, developers can mitigate the risk of security breaches and protect the integrity of their applications. It encourages developers to adopt a proactive approach to security, investing time and resources into implementing robust security measures to prevent potential reputational damage.

DOI: 10.1201/9781003640332-7

A LAYMAN'S PERSPECTIVE

Embedding Security in Every Step

Welcome to the dynamic world of Android application development, where every tap, swipe, and interaction has the power to shape digital experiences for millions. This journey is not just about coding functionalities but about embedding security at every stage to ensure user trust and data protection.

Imagine yourself as an architect tasked with designing a skyscraper, not just to stand tall but to ensure the highest levels of safety for its occupants. Before laying a single beam, meticulous planning and foresight are required to anticipate and mitigate potential threats. Similarly, Android developers must construct digital structures that are not only feature-rich but also resilient against cyber threats. Our journey begins with understanding user needs and expectations, forming the foundation for applications that not only perform seamlessly but also protect sensitive data from vulnerabilities.

In an era where data breaches and privacy violations frequently make headlines, securing Android applications is a fundamental responsibility. Much like a fortress shielding its inhabitants, our apps must be built to defend users' personal information against unauthorized access and malicious exploitation. By integrating robust security measures at the core of our applications, ethical duties are fulfilled while establishing trust and credibility, strengthening user loyalty in an increasingly competitive digital landscape.

However, security is not a one-time effort; it is an ongoing commitment requiring continuous vigilance and adaptation. The cyber threat landscape is ever-evolving, necessitating proactive security updates and defensive strategies. Developers must adopt a mindset of constant learning and improvement, regularly assessing vulnerabilities, patching potential threats, and fortifying applications against new attack vectors. Embedding a culture of security awareness into our development process ensures that our apps remain resilient amidst emerging digital threats.

Furthermore, fostering security-conscious development extends beyond our immediate teams. Through education, collaboration, and adherence to best practices, colleagues and partners can be empowered to prioritize security in their projects, contributing to a more secure digital ecosystem. Encouraging a collective approach to cybersecurity enhances not only our individual applications but also the broader Android development community, making security a shared responsibility.

By prioritizing security throughout the Android development lifecycle, more than just technical excellence is achieved; this contributes to a digital world where privacy is respected and data integrity is safeguarded. This journey is committed to building applications that exceed user expectations while upholding the highest standards of security and trust.

5.1 Planning and Requirements Gathering

Building the Right Foundation

This section emphasizes the importance of thorough requirements gathering, laying the foundation for creating outstanding Android applications.

Imagine building a house without a plan or setting sail without a map. Similarly, crafting an Android app without understanding user needs is like wandering blindfolded. Thus, our journey begins with highlighting the significance of meticulous requirements gathering.

The value of stakeholder interviews, surveys, and workshops is stressed for gaining insights into user expectations and functional needs. Understanding the diverse Android user base is paramount, spanning demographics and cultures.

Moreover, ensuring compliance with regulations like General Data Protection Regulation (GDPR) and Health Insurance Portability and Accountability Act (HIPAA) is crucial for protecting user privacy. Finally, prioritizing security requirements tailored for the Android platform, covering aspects like data sensitivity and access controls, is essential.

Let's see how these steps contribute to laying the groundwork for an Android app that exceeds user expectations while safeguarding their data and privacy with unwavering diligence.

5.1.1 Engaging Stakeholders and User Needs

Aligning Stakeholder Insights

The first step in building a secure Android application is engaging with stakeholders to gather insights and expectations. This involves:

- **Stakeholder Interviews:** Conduct interviews with individuals or groups who have a vested interest in the application, such as business leaders, developers, and end-users. These interviews help uncover expectations, pain points, and specific security requirements.
- **Surveys:** Utilize surveys to collect feedback from a broader audience. This helps in understanding user preferences, behaviours, and security concerns, which can guide the development process.
- **Workshops:** Organize workshops with stakeholders from different areas of expertise. These collaborative sessions facilitate brainstorming, define requirements, and align on security objectives, ensuring a comprehensive approach to application security.

5.1.2 Addressing Android User Diversity

Recognizing User Variation

A successful Android application must cater to a diverse user base, taking into account various factors such as:

- **Cultural and Demographic Diversity:** Android users come from different cultural backgrounds and possess varying levels of technological literacy. It is essential to consider cultural norms, language preferences, and accessibility needs when designing your app.
- **Geographic and Technical Considerations:** Factors like network connectivity, bandwidth limitations, and regional regulations can significantly impact the user experience and security requirements. Tailoring your application to address these considerations ensures it performs well across different regions.
- **Localization and User Experience:** Customizing the user interface, content, and design elements to resonate with users from different backgrounds enhances user engagement and satisfaction.

5.1.3 Understanding Compliance Requirements

Mapping Compliance

Compliance with relevant regulations is crucial for protecting user data and avoiding legal pitfalls. Key regulations to consider include:

- **GDPR (General Data Protection Regulation)**: Applicable to European users, GDPR mandates user consent for data processing, the right to access personal data, and stringent data protection measures.
- **CCPA (California Consumer Privacy Act)**: Applicable to California residents, CCPA grants consumers the right to know what personal information is collected and to request its deletion.
- **HIPAA (Health Insurance Portability and Accountability Act)**: For healthcare-related applications, HIPAA requires safeguarding patient information through rigorous security protocols.
- **COPPA (Children's Online Privacy Protection Act)**: For apps involving children under 13, COPPA requires obtaining parental consent and enforcing strict privacy protections.
- **Digital Services Act (DSA) and Digital Markets Act (DMA)**: For apps serving EU users, these regulations impose additional obligations on digital platforms, including content moderation and interoperability requirements.
- **PCI DSS (Payment Card Industry Data Security Standard)**: For apps handling payments, PCI DSS outlines standards for secure payment processing, including data encryption and regular security assessments.

5.1.4 Documenting and Prioritizing Security Needs

Prioritizing Protection

A critical aspect of planning is documenting and prioritizing security requirements. This involves:

- **Security Requirements Documentation**: Identify potential threats, vulnerabilities, and necessary security controls. This documentation serves as a blueprint for securing the application.
- **Prioritization and Risk Assessment**: Assess the potential impact of security breaches and the likelihood of their occurrence. Prioritize security measures based on these assessments to mitigate the most significant risks effectively.
- **Data Sensitivity Assessment**: Categorize the types of data collected, processed, and stored by the application based on their sensitivity. This helps in implementing appropriate security controls.
- **Implementing Robust Security Mechanisms**: Ensure robust authentication mechanisms such as biometric authentication, passkeys (FIDO2/WebAuthn), strong passwords, or token-based authentication. Prioritize passkeys as they eliminate phishing risks and provide better user experience. Encrypt data both in transit and at rest using industry-standard algorithms like HTTP Secure (HTTPS)/Transport Layer Security (TLS) and Advanced Encryption Standard (AES).
- **Access Controls**: Implement role-based access controls to limit user permissions and prevent unauthorized access to sensitive functionality or data.

5.1.5 Threat Modelling and Security Traceability

Building Security Foundations

Threat modelling is an essential practice in identifying and mitigating potential security threats. It involves:

- **Identifying Threats:** Utilize structured threat modeling methodologies to systematically uncover security and privacy risks. STRIDE (Spoofing, Tampering, Repudiation, Information Disclosure, Denial of Service, Elevation of Privilege) provides a foundational framework for identifying technical security threats. For a business-aligned, risk-centric approach, PASTA (Process for Attack Simulation and Threat Analysis) integrates threat modeling with business objectives, regulatory compliance, and adversarial simulation. When privacy is a key concern, particularly for GDPR or data protection compliance, LINDDUN offers a specialized methodology focused on privacy threats such as linkability, identifiability, and unawareness. Combining these approaches enables comprehensive threat identification that addresses both security vulnerabilities and privacy risks across the system lifecycle.
- **Risk Assessment:** Evaluate the likelihood and potential impact of identified threats to prioritize mitigation efforts.
- **Mitigation Strategies:** Develop strategies to address identified threats, which may include implementing technical controls, altering processes, or providing user training.
- **Security Requirements Traceability Matrix (SRTM):** Maintain a matrix that maps security requirements to specific features and tests. This ensures all security requirements are addressed throughout the development process and enhances accountability by assigning responsibility to specific team members.

Real-world Scenarios: Lessons from BeFitHealth

To illustrate the importance of thorough planning and requirements gathering, consider the case of BeFitHealth, a fitness tracking application that encountered security challenges due to inadequate planning. This scenario highlights how neglecting critical security considerations during the early stages of development can lead to significant risks.

Scenario 1: Inadequate Security Requirements

BeFitHealth was designed as a cutting-edge fitness tracking app, offering features like heart rate monitoring, step counting, and GPS-based activity tracking. The development team prioritized user experience and aesthetics, creating a sleek interface that quickly gained popularity. However, in their rush to launch, they overlooked a critical aspect: identifying and classifying sensitive user data.

During the planning phase, the team failed to ask essential questions, such as:

- What types of data will the app collect?
- How sensitive is this data?
- What are the potential risks if this data is exposed?

As a result, health metrics (e.g., heart rate, sleep patterns) and personal identifiers (e.g., names, email addresses) were stored and transmitted without adequate protection. This lack of planning led to significant exposure risks, including potential data breaches and misuse of sensitive information. For example, an attacker could exploit weak encryption to access users' health data, leading to privacy violations and reputational damage for BeFitHealth.

Key Aspects to Address (Scenario-based)

- **Identify Sensitive Data:** Classify all user data according to its sensitivity. For BeFitHealth, this includes health metrics, personal identifiers, and any other data that could potentially harm the user if exposed.
- **Threat Modelling:** Conduct comprehensive threat modelling sessions to identify and mitigate potential vulnerabilities. This includes understanding how data flows within the app and the potential attack vectors.
- **Regulatory Compliance:** Ensure the app complies with relevant data protection laws like GDPR or HIPAA, depending on the user base's location.
- **Security Policies and Standards:** Develop and implement robust security policies and standards to guide the development team from the planning phase onward.

Scenario 2: Overlooking Regulatory Compliance

When BeFitHealth was first launched, the team focused on global scalability but failed to account for the legal and regulatory requirements of different regions. The app was made available in Europe and the United States, two regions with stringent data protection laws: GDPR (General Data Protection Regulation) in Europe and HIPAA (Health Insurance Portability and Accountability Act) in the United States.

The team did not conduct a thorough review of these regulations during the planning phase. For instance:

- **GDPR:** Under this regulation, users must provide explicit consent for data collection, and they have the right to access, modify, or delete their data. BeFitHealth did not implement these features initially.
- **HIPAA:** Under this act, health data must be encrypted both at rest and in transit, and access must be strictly controlled. BeFitHealth's encryption practices were insufficient to meet these requirements.

This oversight led to compliance issues, with the app failing to meet the legal standards in both regions. As a result, BeFitHealth faced potential fines (up to 4% of global revenue under GDPR) and damage to its reputation. Users in Europe and the US began questioning the app's trustworthiness, leading to a drop in downloads and active users.

Key Aspects to Address (Scenario-based)

- **Regulatory Compliance:** Conduct a thorough review of all applicable regulations in the regions where the app will be launched. Ensure that data collection, processing, and storage practices are compliant.
- **Security Requirements Definition:** Clearly define security requirements based on regulatory needs. This includes data encryption, user consent mechanisms, and data access controls.
- **Regular Compliance Audits:** Implement regular audits to ensure ongoing compliance with all relevant laws and regulations. This proactive approach helps identify and rectify compliance issues before they lead to legal action.

5.2 Design and Architectutre

Build a Shield, Not Just an App

In today's digital age, where smartphones have become gateways to our personal and professional lives, the security of Android applications is more critical than ever. Think of your app as a fortress that protects valuable user data from potential threats. With the increasing prevalence of cyberattacks and data breaches, reinforcing your app's defences through secure design and architecture is essential.

A cornerstone of secure app development is threat modelling. Threat modelling is akin to crafting a detailed blueprint to foresee and counter potential risks to your app's security. By thoroughly examining your app's architecture, you can identify vulnerabilities and weaknesses, allowing you to proactively safeguard against potential breaches.

For Android applications, effective threat modelling is particularly crucial due to the platform's open nature and diverse ecosystem. With new threats constantly emerging, threat modelling helps maintain the security and integrity of the app, thereby preserving user trust.

However, threat modelling is not a task for one person. It requires collaboration among various experts, including security professionals, analysts, and developers. Together, they assess, analyse, and mitigate security risks, ensuring the app remains resilient against potential threats.

The following sections explore key secure design principles and architecture patterns that can fortify your Android application. By incorporating these practices, you can enhance your app's security and strengthen user trust. Let's explore the details and build a fortress for your Android application in this ever-evolving digital landscape.

5.2.1 Secure Design Principles

Designing with Safety in Mind

To build a secure application, it is essential to adhere to fundamental secure design principles. These principles act as guidelines to minimize vulnerabilities and enhance security:

- **Principle of Least Privilege**: Grant users and components the minimum level of access necessary to perform their functions. This reduces the attack surface and limits potential damage from compromised components.
- **Defence in Depth**: Implement multiple layers of security controls to provide redundancy. If one control fails, additional layers continue to protect the application.
- **Fail-Safe Defaults**: Design systems to default to a secure state in the event of a failure. This prevents unauthorized access when unexpected issues arise.
- **Economy of Mechanism**: Keep the design simple and straightforward. Simplicity reduces the chance of errors and makes the system easier to understand and secure.
- **Complete Mediation**: Ensure that every access request to a resource is thoroughly checked for proper authorization, preventing unauthorized access.

5.2.2 Secure Architecture Patterns

Building Resilient Apps

In addition, to secure design principles, employing secure architecture patterns helps mitigate security risks by structuring your application in a way that inherently reduces vulnerabilities:

- **Modular Architecture:** Use Android app modularization (dynamic feature modules) to isolate sensitive functionality (e.g., payment or health modules), reducing attack surface and enabling differential security controls.
- **Zero Trust Architecture:** Adopt zero trust principles such as enforcing continuous device integrity checks (via Play Integrity API), certificate pinning, and context-aware access controls beyond authentication.
- **Service-Oriented Architecture (SOA):** Apply SOA principles to modularize the application. Modularization allows for easier management and security of individual components, enhancing the overall security posture.
- **Supply Chain Security Architecture:** Implement software bill of materials (SBOM) tracking and dependency vulnerability scanning to address supply chain attacks.

5.2.3 Data Protection

Safeguarding Sensitive Information

Protecting user data is a critical component of application security. Implementing robust data protection measures ensures the confidentiality, integrity, and availability of sensitive information:

- **Encryption:** Encrypt data both in transit and at rest using industry-standard encryption algorithms. Encryption ensures that even if data is intercepted or accessed without authorization, it remains unreadable.
- **Secure Storage:** Utilize secure storage mechanisms provided by Android, such as the Keystore system, to store sensitive information securely.
- **Data Anonymization and Masking:** Where possible, anonymize and mask sensitive data to protect user privacy while preserving the utility of the data for analysis and other purposes.

5.2.4 Application Programming Interface (API) Security

Fortifying API Interactions

APIs are a critical interface for applications, making their security paramount. Securing APIs helps protect against unauthorized access and data breaches:

- **Authentication and Authorization:** Use secure protocols like OAuth 2.1 or OpenID Connect to authenticate users and authorize access to APIs. This ensures that only legitimate users can interact with your application.
- **Rate Limiting:** Implement rate limiting to control the number of requests a client can make to your APIs. This helps prevent abuse and mitigates the risk of denial-of-service attacks.
- **Input Validation and Sanitization:** Rigorously validate and sanitize all inputs to APIs to prevent injection attacks and ensure the integrity of the data processed by your application.
- **API Gateway Security:** Implement API gateways with threat protection, including bot detection and anomaly-based rate limiting.
- **Zero Trust API Design:** Verify every API request regardless of source, implementing mutual TLS (mTLS) for service-to-service communication.

Real-world Scenarios: Lessons from BeFitHealth

To illustrate the importance of secure design and architecture, let's consider some real-world scenarios faced by BeFitHealth, a fitness-tracking application that encountered significant security challenges due to inadequate design. These scenarios highlight how poor design decisions can lead to vulnerabilities that compromise user data and trust.

Scenario 1: Poor Authentication Mechanisms

BeFitHealth initially implemented weak authentication mechanisms, relying solely on simple passwords without any additional verification. Users were allowed to create passwords as short as four characters, with no requirements for complexity (e.g., no mandatory use of uppercase letters, numbers, or special characters).

This approach made the app highly susceptible to unauthorized access. Attackers could easily compromise user accounts through brute-force attacks (systematically trying all possible password combinations) or password guessing (using common passwords like "1234" or "password").

For example, an attacker could use automated tools to guess weak passwords and gain access to user accounts. Once inside, they could view sensitive health data, modify user profiles, or even impersonate users to perform malicious actions. This not only exposed users to privacy violations but also damaged BeFitHealth's reputation as a secure platform.

Key Aspects to Address (Scenario-based)

- **Strong Authentication:** Implement multifactor authentication (MFA) to provide an additional layer of security. This could include SMS-based OTPs, authenticator apps, or biometric verification. For example, even if an attacker guesses a user's password, they would still need the second factor (e.g., a one-time code sent to the user's phone) to gain access.
- **Authorization Controls:** Ensure robust authorization controls are in place, restricting user access based on roles and permissions. This minimizes the potential damage from compromised accounts. For instance, a regular user should not have access to administrative functions, and sensitive data should only be accessible to authorized personnel.
- **Regular Security Assessments:** Conduct regular security assessments and penetration tests focused on authentication mechanisms to identify and address weaknesses before they can be exploited. For example, simulate brute-force attacks to test the strength of password policies and identify vulnerabilities in the authentication process.

Scenario 2: Inadequate Data Flow Security

During the design phase, BeFitHealth failed to secure data flows within the application. Sensitive data, including user health metrics (e.g., heart rate, sleep patterns) and personal identifiers (e.g., names, email addresses), was transmitted in plaintext between the app and backend servers.

This lack of encryption made the data highly susceptible to interception by attackers. For instance, if a user is connected to an unsecured public Wi-Fi network, an attacker on the same network could use packet sniffing tools to capture unencrypted data.

In one of the incidents, attackers intercepted health data transmitted by BeFitHealth users, including sensitive information like weight, blood pressure, and exercise routines. This data was later sold on the dark web, leading to privacy violations and legal repercussions for

BeFitHealth. The incident highlighted the critical importance of securing data flows during the design phase.

Key Aspects to Address (Scenario-based)

- **Secure Data Transmission:** Use end-to-end encryption (such as TLS) to secure data in transit. This ensures that even if data is intercepted, it cannot be read without the encryption keys. For example, implement TLS 1.3, the latest version of the protocol, to ensure strong encryption and protection against known vulnerabilities.
- **Data Flow Analysis:** Conduct a thorough analysis of how data flows through the application to identify all points where data could be exposed. Implement encryption and other security measures at these points. For instance, create a data flow diagram to visualize how data moves between the app, servers, and third-party services and identify potential weak points.
- **Regular Data Security Audits:** Perform regular security audits to ensure that all data flows remain secure. This includes verifying that encryption protocols are up to date and properly implemented. For example, conduct quarterly audits to check for vulnerabilities like outdated encryption algorithms or misconfigured TLS certificates.

5.3 Implementation

Shift Left, Secure Right

The implementation phase is where your security efforts truly come to life. "Shifting left" means integrating security practices early in the development process, allowing you to "secure right", that is, deliver a secure application at deployment. This section explores essential practices and tools that developers should adopt to write secure code for Android applications.

5.3.1 Secure Coding Guidelines

Crafting Resilient Code

Adhering to secure coding guidelines is foundational to preventing vulnerabilities and ensuring your application is robust against attacks. Here are some key principles:

- **Input Validation and Sanitization:** Always validate and sanitize all inputs to prevent injection attacks, such as SQL injection or command injection. Use allow-lists (whitelists) to define acceptable input values, ensuring that only expected data is processed by the application.
- **Output Encoding:** Encode outputs to prevent cross-site scripting (XSS) attacks. Proper encoding ensures that any data sent to the user is safe and cannot be used to inject malicious scripts.
- **Error Handling and Logging:** Implement comprehensive error handling to manage exceptions securely. Avoid exposing sensitive information through error messages and logs. Ensure that logs are stored securely and do not contain sensitive data that could be exploited if accessed by unauthorized users.
- **Secure Storage of Sensitive Data:** Follow best practices for securely storing sensitive data, such as using the Android Keystore system. This prevents unauthorized access to sensitive information, such as user credentials or payment information.

- **Avoid Hardcoding Secrets:** Never hardcode secrets, such as API keys or credentials, within the source code. Instead, use secure storage solutions or environment variables to manage these secrets.
- **Secure Dependencies:** Use trusted libraries and frameworks, regularly updating them to mitigate known vulnerabilities. Avoid using deprecated or untrusted third-party components that could introduce security risks.
- **Supply Chain Security:** Verify integrity of all dependencies using checksums or digital signatures. Implement dependency pinning and automated vulnerability scanning for third-party libraries.

5.3.2 Code Reviews and Static Analysis

The Art of Code Scrutiny

Regular code reviews and static analysis are critical components of a secure development process:

- **Peer Code Reviews:** Conduct regular peer code reviews to identify potential security issues early in the development process. Reviews provide a fresh perspective, helping to catch errors or insecure practices that the original developer might have missed.
- **Automated Static Analysis:** Utilize static analysis tools to automatically scan the codebase for vulnerabilities and coding flaws. These tools can identify common security issues, such as buffer overflows, injection vulnerabilities, and insecure use of APIs.
- **Software Composition Analysis (SCA):** Implement tools that specifically track open-source components and their known vulnerabilities (CVEs).

5.3.3 Security Tools and Frameworks

Leveraging Security Solutions

Leveraging security tools and frameworks can significantly enhance your application's security posture:

- **Secure Development Frameworks:** Use secure development frameworks that offer built-in security features, such as input validation, output encoding, and secure session management. Frameworks with security best practices embedded reduce the likelihood of introducing vulnerabilities.
- **Automated Security Testing Tools:** Utilize automated security testing tools to continuously scan for vulnerabilities during development. These tools help identify issues like SQL injection, XSS, and insecure data storage, allowing for timely remediation.
- **Dependency Management Tools:** Use tools to manage and update dependencies, ensuring they are free from known vulnerabilities. Tools like dependency checkers can alert you to outdated libraries or frameworks that need security patches.

5.3.4 Secure Configuration

Tailoring Security Settings

Proper configuration is crucial for maintaining application security across different environments:

- **Secure Defaults:** Configure the application with secure defaults to minimize the risk of misconfiguration. For instance, ensure that default passwords are changed and default access permissions are restrictive.
- **Configuration Management:** Implement configuration management practices to ensure consistent and secure configurations across all environments, development, testing, and production. This practice reduces the risk of inconsistencies that could lead to security vulnerabilities.
- **Environment-specific Configurations:** Use environment-specific configurations to manage settings securely. This includes using different keys, secrets, and endpoints for development, testing, and production environments to prevent leakage of sensitive information.

Real-world Scenarios: Lessons from BeFitHealth

To illustrate the importance of secure implementation practices, consider these real-world scenarios faced by BeFitHealth, a fitness tracking application that encountered security issues due to inadequate implementation practices. These scenarios highlight how poor implementation decisions can lead to vulnerabilities that compromise user data and app functionality.

Scenario 1: Inadequate Input Validation

In its initial implementation, BeFitHealth neglected to enforce strict input validation. User input fields, such as login forms, search bars, and profile editors, were not properly validated or sanitized. This oversight created vulnerabilities where attackers could inject malicious code through these fields.

For example:

- **SQL Injection:** Attackers could input malicious SQL queries into the login form, allowing them to bypass authentication or extract sensitive data from the database.
- **Cross-site Scripting (XSS):** Attackers could inject malicious scripts into user input fields, which would then execute in the browsers of other users, potentially stealing session cookies or redirecting users to phishing sites.

One of the incidents involved an attacker exploiting an XSS vulnerability in BeFitHealth's profile editor. The attacker injected a script that stole session cookies, allowing them to hijack user accounts and access sensitive health data. This incident not only compromised user privacy but also disrupted the app's functionality, leading to user complaints and negative reviews.

Key Aspects to Address (Scenario-based)

- **Input Validation:** Implement comprehensive input validation to ensure that only expected and safe data is processed by the application. Using allow-lists (whitelists) for input validation can effectively mitigate injection attacks. For example, validate that email fields contain only valid email addresses and that numeric fields contain only numbers. Reject any input that does not conform to expected formats.
- **Regular Code Reviews:** Conduct regular code reviews specifically focused on input validation practices. Ensure all developers adhere to secure coding guidelines, particularly

around input handling. For instance, during code reviews, check for the use of parameterized queries to prevent SQL injection and output encoding to prevent XSS.

- **Security Testing:** Integrate security testing tools that automatically scan for injection vulnerabilities during the development process. Automated testing can quickly identify and highlight insecure code, allowing developers to remediate issues promptly. For instance, use tools like OWASP ZAP or Burp Suite to test for SQL injection and XSS vulnerabilities. Incorporate these tools into the continuous integration (CI)/continuous deployment (CD) pipeline for continuous security testing.

Scenario 2: Hardcoded Secrets

BeFitHealth initially hardcoded API keys and credentials within the source code. For example, the app's backend API keys, third-party service credentials, and encryption keys were embedded directly in the codebase.

This practice exposed sensitive information to anyone with access to the codebase, including:

- **Developers:** While developers may have legitimate access, accidental leaks (e.g., sharing code on public repositories) could expose these secrets.
- **Attackers:** By decompiling the app, attackers could easily extract hardcoded secrets and use them to gain unauthorized access to backend systems or third-party services.

In one incident, an attacker decompiled the BeFitHealth app and extracted the Google Maps API key. They used this key to exceed usage limits, resulting in significant financial costs for BeFitHealth. Additionally, the attacker accessed user location data stored in the backend, further compromising user privacy.

Key Aspects to Address (Scenario-based)

- **Secure Storage of Secrets:** Use secure storage mechanisms, such as the Android Keystore system, to store sensitive information securely. This prevents unauthorized access even if the app's code is decompiled. For example, store API keys and credentials in the Android Keystore, which provides hardware-backed security and ensures that secrets are inaccessible to attackers.
- **Avoid Hardcoding:** Never hardcode secrets in the source code. Instead, use environment variables or secure vaults to manage secrets dynamically based on the environment. This practice minimizes the risk of exposing sensitive information. For instance, use Android App Attestation and cloud-backed token services. For third-party keys, enforce strict restrictions (package name, SHA-256 cert fingerprint, IP allowlists).
- **Dynamic Secrets Management:** Implement dynamic secrets management to rotate secrets automatically and reduce the risk of exposure. For instance, use tools like HashiCorp Vault to generate and rotate API keys dynamically.
- **Regular Security Audits:** Conduct periodic security audits to ensure that no secrets are hardcoded in the application code. These audits should be comprehensive, covering all aspects of the codebase to identify any inadvertent hardcoding of sensitive data. For example, use tools like GitGuardian or TruffleHog to scan the codebase for hardcoded secrets and ensure compliance with security policies.

5.4 Testing

Write Secure, Build Secure

Testing is a critical phase in the development of secure Android applications. It is not enough to write secure code; you must also rigorously test your application to ensure that security measures are effective and that vulnerabilities are identified and mitigated before the app is deployed. This section explores the different types of security testing and the tools and strategies that can help ensure your app is robust against potential threats.

5.4.1 Types of Security Testing

The Security Testing Spectrum

A comprehensive security testing strategy includes various testing methodologies, each providing unique insights into the security posture of your application:

- **Static Analysis:** This involves analysing the app's source code for potential vulnerabilities without executing the program. Static analysis tools can identify issues such as insecure coding practices, hardcoded secrets, and improper error handling.
- **Dynamic Analysis:** Unlike static analysis, dynamic analysis tests the application in a runtime environment. This helps identify vulnerabilities that occur only during execution, such as memory leaks, improper session handling, and insecure runtime configurations.
- **Penetration Testing:** Penetration testing simulates real-world attacks to identify and exploit vulnerabilities. This type of testing provides a deeper understanding of how an attacker could potentially breach the application's defences and helps prioritize vulnerabilities based on risk.
- **Fuzz Testing:** Fuzz testing involves providing the application with random or unexpected inputs to identify potential crashes or vulnerabilities. This method is particularly useful for uncovering buffer overflows and other memory-related vulnerabilities.
- **Manual Code Review:** Conducting manual code reviews allows security experts to examine the codebase for potential security issues that automated tools might miss. This process is invaluable for identifying complex vulnerabilities that require human intuition and experience.
- **Interactive Application Security Testing (IAST):** IAST tools test the app in a running state, combining elements of both static and dynamic analysis. These tools provide more context-aware insights into the application's behaviour, identifying vulnerabilities in real-time as the application runs.
- **Runtime Application Self-protection (RASP):** RASP tools monitor and protect the app in real-time. They detect and respond to attacks as they happen, adding an additional layer of security by preventing exploitation of vulnerabilities during runtime.
- **Container Security Testing:** For apps using containerized backends, implement container image scanning and runtime protection.
- **API Security Testing:** Dedicated testing for API endpoints including GraphQL injection, REST parameter pollution, and OAuth flow vulnerabilities.

5.4.2 Automated Testing Tools

Streamlining Security Checks

Automated tools play a crucial role in a security testing strategy by providing continuous, repeatable, and scalable testing processes:

- **Static Application Security Testing (SAST):** SAST tools analyse source code or compiled code to identify vulnerabilities without executing the program. These tools help detect security flaws early in the development process.
- **Dynamic Application Security Testing (DAST):** DAST tools analyse the running application for vulnerabilities by interacting with it in real-time. These tools simulate external attacks on the application and are effective in identifying runtime vulnerabilities.
- **Mobile App Security Testing Tools:** These tools are specifically designed to identify vulnerabilities unique to mobile applications, such as insecure data storage, improper use of mobile APIs, and weaknesses in network communication.

5.4.3 Manual Security Testing

Hands-on Security Testing

While automated tools are powerful, they cannot replace the intuition and experience of skilled security professionals:

- **Code Reviews:** Manual code reviews by experienced developers and security experts can uncover subtle security issues that automated tools might miss. Regular code reviews are an essential part of a robust security testing strategy.
- **Security Audits:** Comprehensive security audits assess the overall security posture of the application. These audits involve a detailed review of the application architecture, code, configurations, and deployment environment.

5.4.4 Continuous Integration and Continuous Deployment (CI/CD)

Seamless Security Integration

Integrating security testing into the CI/CD pipeline ensures that security is a continuous concern throughout the development lifecycle:

- **Security Integration:** Integrate security testing tools into the CI/CD pipeline to ensure continuous security testing. This approach helps catch vulnerabilities early and prevents insecure code from reaching production.
- **Automated Testing:** Automate security tests to run with every build, providing immediate feedback on security issues. Automated tests ensure that new vulnerabilities are identified as soon as they are introduced into the codebase.
- **Security Gates:** Implement security gates in the CI/CD pipeline to prevent the deployment of builds that do not meet security standards. Security gates enforce security policies and ensure only compliant code is released.
- **DevSecOps Integration:** Implement security as code with policy-as-code frameworks like Open Policy Agent (OPA) for automated security policy enforcement.
- **Container Pipeline Security:** Secure container registries with image signing and vulnerability scanning at build time.

Real-world Scenarios: Lessons from BeFitHealth

To illustrate the importance of comprehensive security testing, consider these real-world scenarios faced by BeFitHealth, a fitness tracking application that experienced security challenges due to insufficient testing practices. These scenarios highlight how inadequate testing can leave critical vulnerabilities undetected, leading to significant risks once the app is deployed.

Scenario 1: Insufficient Security Testing

BeFitHealth initially conducted minimal security testing, focusing primarily on functional testing to ensure the app worked as intended. While functional testing confirmed that features like step counting, heart rate monitoring, and GPS tracking functioned correctly, it did not address security vulnerabilities.

As a result, several critical security issues were not detected before release. For example:

- **Authentication Bypass:** A vulnerability in the login mechanism allowed attackers to bypass authentication and access user accounts without valid credentials.
- **Data Leakage:** Sensitive user data, such as health metrics and personal identifiers, was inadvertently exposed through insecure API endpoints.

Once the app was deployed and used by a large number of users, these vulnerabilities were exploited by attackers. In one incident, attackers gained unauthorized access to thousands of user accounts, leading to privacy violations, reputational damage, and financial losses for BeFitHealth. The company had to temporarily pull the app from stores to address the issues, resulting in lost revenue and user trust.

Key Aspects to Address (Scenario-based)

- **Comprehensive Security Testing**: Implement a robust and thorough testing strategy that covers all types of security testing, including static and dynamic analysis, penetration testing, and fuzz testing. This ensures a comprehensive assessment of the application's security. For example, use static analysis tools like SonarQube to identify insecure code and dynamic analysis tools like OWASP ZAP to detect runtime vulnerabilities.
- **Automated and Manual Testing**: Utilize both automated tools and manual reviews to ensure comprehensive coverage of potential security issues. Combining automated tools with manual testing provides a balanced approach to identifying vulnerabilities. For instance, use automated tools to scan for common vulnerabilities (e.g., SQL injection, XSS) and conduct manual code reviews to identify complex issues that tools might miss.
- **Regular Testing Cycles**: Conduct regular security tests throughout the development lifecycle to continuously identify and address vulnerabilities. Regular testing ensures that new vulnerabilities are caught early and that the application remains secure as it evolves. For example, integrate security testing into the CI/CD pipeline to automatically test every code change and provide immediate feedback to developers.

Scenario 2: Overlooked Dynamic Analysis

BeFitHealth's testing strategy focused primarily on static analysis, which involves reviewing the app's code for vulnerabilities without executing it. While static analysis identified some issues, such as hardcoded secrets and insecure coding practices, it failed to detect runtime vulnerabilities.

For example:

- **Memory Management Issues:** The app experienced memory leaks during runtime, causing it to crash or become unresponsive. These issues were not identified during static analysis.
- **Runtime Permissions:** The app requested excessive permissions at runtime, such as access to the camera and microphone, even when these features were not needed. This raised privacy concerns among users.

In one case, an attacker exploited a runtime vulnerability to escalate privileges and gain access to sensitive system resources. This allowed them to extract user data and modify app behaviour, further compromising user privacy and app functionality.

Key Aspects to Address (Scenario-based)

- **Dynamic Analysis Implementation:** Incorporate dynamic analysis into the security testing strategy to identify vulnerabilities that manifest during the execution of the app. Dynamic analysis helps catch runtime issues that static analysis might miss. For example, use tools like Burp Suite or AppScan to simulate app behaviour and identify vulnerabilities such as memory leaks and insecure runtime permissions.
- **Real-World Attack Simulation:** Use penetration testing to simulate real-world attacks and identify vulnerabilities that static analysis might miss. Penetration testing provides a realistic assessment of the application's defences against potential attackers. For instance, hire ethical hackers to simulate attacks like privilege escalation and data exfiltration to identify and address vulnerabilities before they can be exploited.
- **Continuous Monitoring:** Implement continuous monitoring tools to detect and respond to security issues in real-time, ensuring that the app remains secure post-deployment. Continuous monitoring helps identify and mitigate security incidents as they occur. For example, use tools like Splunk or ELK Stack to monitor app logs and detect suspicious activity, such as unauthorized access attempts or data breaches.

5.5 Deployment and Maintenance

Securing the Real World

Ensuring the security of Android applications does not stop once the code is written and tested. Deployment and maintenance are critical phases where security must be diligently managed to protect the application in the real world. This section explores the best practices for deploying and maintaining secure Android applications, emphasizing the importance of proactive security measures to prevent breaches before they occur.

5.5.1 Secure Deployment Practices

Deploying with Confidence

Deploying an application securely involves setting up a robust environment that minimizes the attack surface and protects the application from potential threats:

- **Environment Hardening:** Harden the deployment environment by disabling unnecessary services, applying the latest security patches, and configuring secure settings. This minimizes the attack surface and reduces the risk of exploitation.
- **Secure Deployment Pipeline:** Ensure the deployment pipeline is secure by implementing strong access controls, regular audits, and logging of all deployment activities. A secure pipeline prevents unauthorized changes and ensures that only trusted code reaches the production environment.
- **Environment Isolation:** Isolate production, staging, and development environments to prevent unauthorized access and reduce the risk of cross-environment contamination. This ensures that vulnerabilities or issues in non-production environments do not impact the production environment. Ensure debug builds are not deployable to production and disable logging in release builds.
- **Infrastructure as Code (IaC) Security:** Use tools like Terraform or CloudFormation with security scanning to ensure consistent, secure infrastructure deployment.

5.5.2 Post-Deployment Security

Staying Vigilant

Once the application is deployed, continuous monitoring and timely responses to security incidents are crucial for maintaining security:

- **Security Information and Event Management (SIEM):** Implement AI-powered SIEM solutions that can detect advanced persistent threats and zero-day attacks through behavioral analysis.
- **Runtime Application Self-Protection (RASP):** Deploy runtime protection that can automatically respond to attacks without human intervention.
- **Incident Response:** Develop and maintain a robust incident response plan that outlines clear procedures for detecting, reporting, and mitigating security incidents. A well-prepared team can respond swiftly to incidents, minimizing the impact and preventing further damage.
- **Patch Management:** Regularly update the application and its dependencies to address security vulnerabilities. Keeping the software up-to-date with the latest patches ensures that known vulnerabilities are promptly fixed, reducing the risk of exploitation.

5.5.3 Continuous Improvement

Learning and Adapting

Security is not a one-time effort but an ongoing process that requires continuous improvement and adaptation to emerging threats:

- **Regular Security Assessments:** Conduct regular security assessments to identify and address new vulnerabilities. This proactive approach helps maintain a strong security posture by continuously evaluating and improving security measures.
- **User Feedback and Bug Bounty Programs:** Leverage user feedback and bug bounty programs to identify and address security issues. Engaging the community helps uncover vulnerabilities that might have been missed during internal testing.
- **Security Training and Awareness:** Provide ongoing security training and awareness programs for the development and operations teams. Keeping teams informed about the latest security practices and emerging threats is essential for maintaining a high level of security.
- **Automate Security in CI/CD:** Integrate security testing and monitoring into the CI/CD pipeline for continuous security, including automated vulnerability scanning and compliance checks.

Real-world Scenarios: Lessons from BeFitHealth

To illustrate the importance of secure deployment and maintenance practices, consider these real-world scenarios faced by BeFitHealth, a fitness tracking application that encountered security challenges due to inadequate deployment and maintenance strategies. These scenarios highlight how poor practices in deployment and maintenance can lead to vulnerabilities that compromise the app's security and user trust.

Scenario 1: Insecure Deployment Pipeline

BeFitHealth initially had an insecure deployment pipeline, with insufficient access controls and auditing. The pipeline allowed unauthorized personnel to make changes to the codebase and deployment process without proper oversight.

For example:

- **Lack of Access Controls:** Developers and contractors had unrestricted access to the deployment pipeline, increasing the risk of malicious or accidental changes.
- **No Auditing:** Changes to the pipeline were not logged or reviewed, making it difficult to detect unauthorized modifications.

This insecure pipeline made the app susceptible to attacks. In one incident, an attacker exploited weak access controls to inject malicious code into the production environment. The malicious code stole user data and sent it to an external server, leading to a major data breach. The incident exposed thousands of users' health data, resulting in legal penalties, financial losses, and reputational damage for BeFitHealth.

Key Aspects to Address (Scenario-based)

- **Secure Deployment Pipeline:** Implement strong access controls to ensure that only authorized personnel can make changes to the deployment pipeline. Regularly audit the pipeline to detect any unauthorized modifications and ensure that all changes are logged and reviewed. For example, use role-based access control (RBAC) to restrict access to the pipeline based on job roles. Only senior developers or DevOps engineers should have permission to deploy code to production.

- **Environment Hardening:** Harden the deployment environment by disabling unnecessary services, applying security patches, and configuring secure settings. This reduces the risk of exploitation and helps maintain a secure production environment. For instance, disable unused ports, enforce TLS encryption for all communications, and apply the principle of least privilege to all services.
- **Regular Audits:** Conduct regular audits of the deployment pipeline and environment to ensure security measures are in place and effective. Audits help identify potential weaknesses and ensure compliance with security policies. For example, perform monthly audits to review access logs, verify patch levels, and check for misconfigurations in the deployment environment.

Scenario 2: Poor Incident Response

BeFitHealth lacked a robust incident response plan. When a security incident occurred, the team was unprepared and disorganized, leading to delays in addressing the issue.
For example:

- **Delayed Detection:** The team took several days to detect a data breach, during which attackers continued to access and exfiltrate user data.
- **Ineffective Mitigation:** Without a clear plan, the team struggled to contain the breach, leading to further exposure of sensitive data.
- **Poor Communication:** Users were not informed about the breach until weeks later, causing frustration and eroding trust in the app.

In one case, an attacker exploited a vulnerability in the app's backend to gain access to user accounts. The lack of a proper incident response plan meant that the breach was not contained quickly, and attackers were able to compromise thousands of accounts. The incident highlighted the critical importance of having a well-defined and practiced incident response plan.

Key Aspects to Address (Scenario-based)

- **Incident Response Plan:** Develop a comprehensive incident response plan that outlines clear steps for detecting, reporting, and mitigating security incidents. Ensure all team members are familiar with the plan and understand their roles and responsibilities in responding to incidents. For example, the plan should include steps like isolating affected systems, notifying stakeholders, and conducting a post-incident review.
- **Regular Drills:** Conduct regular incident response drills to ensure the team is prepared to handle security incidents efficiently and effectively. Drills help build confidence and ensure that the response plan is well-practiced and understood. For instance, simulate a data breach scenario and evaluate how quickly the team can detect, contain, and mitigate the incident.
- **Continuous Improvement:** Continuously review and improve the incident response plan based on lessons learned from past incidents and emerging threats. Regular updates to the plan ensure it remains effective and relevant in the face of evolving security challenges. For example, after each incident, conduct a post-mortem analysis to identify gaps in the response process and update the plan accordingly.

Looking Ahead

Integrating security into the application development lifecycle is not a one-time effort but an ongoing process that ensures Android apps remain resilient against evolving threats. By embedding security considerations, developers can proactively mitigate vulnerabilities before they become exploitable. A security-first mindset helps teams align their strategies with best practices, regulatory requirements, and user expectations, ultimately reducing risks while maintaining performance and usability. This holistic approach ensures that security is not an afterthought but a core component of the development process.

As mobile threats continue to evolve, it is imperative for us to stay ahead of these changes by adopting forward-thinking security practices, leveraging advanced tools, and fostering a security-first mindset within the teams. Moving into an era where mobile applications are increasingly central to our daily lives, the responsibility to safeguard user data and maintain trust becomes even more critical. In conclusion, the successful integration of security into the application development lifecycle is a dynamic and ongoing process.

Chapter 6

Implementing Secure SDLC for Android Apps

> Coming together is a beginning; keeping together is progress; working together is success.
>
> – Henry Ford

Henry Ford, an American industrialist and business magnate, founder of the Ford Motor Company, highlights the evolutionary journey of a team, from its formation to achieving success. While assembling a team marks the initial step, sustaining unity and collaboration is indicative of progress. However, true success is attained when the team harmoniously works together towards a common goal.

Within the realm of application development, the synergy and unity of a team play a crucial role across all stages of the secure software development life cycle (SDLC). Starting from the inception phase to the deployment of the product, seamless teamwork guarantees streamlined processes and the attainment of desired results. SDLC methodologies underscore the significance of collaborative efforts among developers, testers, and stakeholders in accomplishing project goals with efficacy. Cultivating an environment of teamwork within application development teams amplifies productivity, fosters innovation, and ultimately leads to the triumph of their endeavours.

DOI: 10.1201/9781003640332-8

A LAYMAN'S PERSPECTIVE

Implementing Security from Conception to Completion

Imagine you are a banker entrusted with delivering a digital banking experience that seamlessly integrates convenience with ironclad security. In today's ever-evolving digital landscape, where cyber threats are relentless, the security of your mobile banking application is not just an optional feature; it is a fundamental necessity. This is where the secure software development life cycle (SDLC) becomes your strategic ally, guiding you through the intricate process of secure application development.

This chapter explores the SDLC, using the development of a secure Android banking application as a practical example. Each phase of the SDLC is examined to demonstrate how security can be systematically embedded from the initial planning stage to post-deployment maintenance. Each phase of the SDLC functions as a crucial layer of defence, reinforcing the app's resilience against potential vulnerabilities and security threats.

Let's traverse through:

- The intricate web of Requirements Gathering, where the bank sets the foundation for its digital revolution.
- Follow the exploration of the realm of Threat Modelling, where proactive measures are taken to identify and mitigate potential security risks.
- Witness the artistry of Secure Design as the bank architects a mobile banking application that seamlessly blends security, privacy, and usability.
- Experience the craftsmanship of Secure Coding, where developers wield their tools with precision to craft resilient and maintainable code.
- Step into the arena of Security Testing, where the application undergoes rigorous scrutiny to uncover vulnerabilities and weaknesses.
- Engage in the collaborative spirit of Code Review, where developers come together to ensure code quality and security resilience.
- Embrace the ethos of Security Training, as the bank invests in cultivating a security-conscious culture among its development teams and stakeholders.
- Witness the meticulous orchestration of secure deployment, where the application is launched into the digital realm with integrity, authenticity, and compliance at its core.
- Explore the realm of monitoring and maintenance, where proactive measures are taken to detect, mitigate, and remediate security threats.
- And finally, stand resilient in the face of adversity by confronting the inevitability of Incident Response, where swift and coordinated actions are taken to minimize the impact of security incidents and fortify defences against future attacks.

By embedding security at each stage of the SDLC, developers can significantly reduce the risk of security breaches and ensure compliance with industry regulations such as GDPR, PCI DSS, and OWASP Mobile Top 10. Through this structured approach, security ceases to be an afterthought and instead becomes an integral part of the application's DNA.

This chapter serves as a blueprint for integrating security into Android app development. By adopting a secure SDLC approach, developers, security teams, and stakeholders can collaborate to build applications that are both functional and resilient against evolving cyber threats. Let's embark on this journey to understand how a security-first mindset can transform the development of Android applications, ensuring they stand strong against modern security challenges.

6.1 Requirements Gathering

From Ambiguity to Clarity

The requirements-gathering phase is a pivotal step in developing a secure Android banking application. It ensures that the application not only meets business objectives but also adheres to rigorous security standards. This section outlines the key activities involved in gathering comprehensive and actionable requirements to establish a solid foundation for secure development.

6.1.1 Stakeholder Engagement and Market Research

Bridging Perspectives and Unveiling Insights

Effective requirements gathering begins with engaging stakeholders and conducting extensive market research. Stakeholders in a banking application typically include:

Key Stakeholders

- **Banking Executives:** Define the overarching business objectives, such as increasing customer engagement, enhancing operational efficiency, and driving revenue growth. They provide strategic direction and ensure that the application aligns with the bank's business goals while prioritizing long-term profitability and customer trust.
- **IT and Security Teams:** Responsible for the technical and security aspects of the application, these teams ensure that the app complies with both internal security policies and external regulations. They also assess the feasibility of various features from a technical standpoint and identify potential security risks to pre-empt vulnerabilities early in the development lifecycle.
- **End-users:** The customers who will use the application. Gathering their feedback through structured surveys, focus groups, and usability testing helps to understand their needs, preferences, and pain points. This ensures that the app delivers a user-friendly experience that meets customer expectations and fosters adoption and satisfaction.
- **Regulatory Bodies:** Compliance with regulations such as GDPR, PCI DSS, and other applicable regional financial regulations is mandatory in the banking sector. Engaging with regulatory experts helps ensure that the app meets all legal requirements and avoids costly penalties or reputational damage.

Methods of Engagement

- **One-on-One Interviews:**
  - **In-depth Stakeholder Interviews:** Conduct in-depth interviews with key stakeholders across various departments within the bank, including customer service, marketing, and IT. Gather insights into their specific needs, expectations, and pain points related to the mobile banking app. This process ensures alignment with organizational goals and facilitates buy-in from different stakeholders.
  - **Remote Interviews:** Utilize video conferencing tools(such as Zoom or Microsoft Teams) with end-to-end encryption for remote interviews. Record interviews for later reference while ensuring compliance with data protection regulations and obtaining proper consent.

- Survey Administration:
  - **Customer Surveys:** Administer targeted surveys to existing customers to capture quantifiable data on their usage behaviours, satisfaction levels, and feature preferences in mobile banking applications. Analyse the survey results to identify common trends and prioritize features accordingly.
  - **Survey Platforms:** Implement secure survey collection methods(platforms like SurveyMonkey or Google Forms) with proper data anonymization and retention policies aligned with privacy regulations. Use advanced survey logic to dynamically adjust question flow based on respondents' answers, enhancing the quality of collected data.
- Market Research:
  - **Industry Analysis:** Perform thorough market research to stay up to date with industry trends, competitors' offerings, and emerging technologies in the fintech space. This includes analysing customer demands, technological advancements, and regulatory changes to ensure the bank's mobile app remains competitive and meets evolving market needs.
  - **Data Analytics Techniques:** Employ data analytics tools such as Tableau, Power BI, or Google Analytics to analyse market trends, competitor offerings, and customer behaviour. Use ethical data collection methods and APIs from trusted sources instead of web scraping to gather structured data, aligning with privacy standards and avoiding legal risks.

6.1.2 Documentation of Functional Requirements

From Ideas to Precise Blueprints

Functional requirements define the specific behaviours and functions that the application must perform.

- Functional Requirements
  For a banking app, these might include:
  - **Account Management:** Users should have the ability to view account balances and transaction histories and manage multiple accounts. This includes features like account summaries, detailed transaction views, and the ability to export transaction data.
  - **Funds Transfer:** Enable users to transfer funds between their accounts, pay bills, and send money to other users within the same bank or to external accounts. Support multiple transfer types, including immediate, scheduled, and recurring payments.
  - **Notifications:** Provide real-time alerts for transactions, security updates, promotional offers, and other important activities. Users should have the option to customize their notification preferences for different types of alerts (e.g., SMS, email, push notifications).
  - **User Authentication:** Implement robust authentication mechanisms to ensure secure access. This includes support for passwords, biometrics (fingerprint, facial recognition), and multi-factor authentication (MFA) methods.
  - **Customer Support:** Offer various in-app support options such as live chat, callback requests, email support, and a well-organized FAQ section. This ensures that users can quickly get help when they encounter issues.

- **Detailed Identification of Functional Requirements**
  Develop detailed documentation outlining the functional requirements of the mobile banking application. This documentation should cover a wide range of features, including:
  - **Account Management:** Account creation, login/logout procedures, profile management, and account linking functionalities.
  - **Transaction History:** Displaying transaction details, filtering options, and export capabilities.
  - **Fund Transfers:** Domestic and international transfer functionalities, beneficiary management, and transaction limits.
  - **Bill Payments:** Support for various bill types (utilities, loans, credit cards), scheduling options, and payment reminders.
  - **Card Management:** Activation, blocking, and management of debit/credit cards associated with user accounts.
  - **Account Alerts:** Customizable alerts for transaction notifications and account activity.
  - **Customer Support:** In-app messaging, FAQ section, support ticket submission, and escalation procedures.
- **Collaborative Platforms:** Use collaborative documentation platforms like Confluence or Microsoft SharePoint to create detailed functional requirement documents. Incorporate version control features to track changes and facilitate collaboration among team members. Utilize formatting options such as tables and bullet points to organize information effectively.
- **Visual Aids and Use Case Diagrams**
  - **Use Case Diagrams:** Utilize visual aids such as use case diagrams, user stories, and wireframes to provide a clear understanding of each feature's implementation and user interaction.
  - **Prototyping Tools:** Utilize prototyping tools like Sketch or Figma to create interactive wireframes and mockups. Share prototypes via cloud-based platforms for real-time collaboration and feedback collection. Integrate with design systems to maintain consistency across different screens and components.
  - **UML Tools:** Employ UML tools such as Lucidchart or Visual Paradigm to create use case diagrams illustrating various user interactions. Link use cases to corresponding functional requirements within the documentation for traceability. Utilize collaborative features to gather feedback and iterate on diagram designs.

6.1.3 Identification of Non-functional Requirements

Setting the Stage Beyond Functionality

Non-functional requirements (NFRs) are essential for ensuring the app's performance, usability, security, and compliance. They define the quality attributes and constraints that the application must adhere to. Key non-functional requirements for a banking app include:

- **Performance**
  - **Response Times:** Specify acceptable response times for various operations (e.g., login, transaction processing). The app should provide a seamless and fast user experience even during peak usage times.

- Scalability: Ensure the application can handle increasing user loads effectively without performance degradation.
- Performance Testing: Utilize cloud-based load testing services like BlazeMeter or LoadNinja to simulate realistic user traffic and measure application performance. Integrate with monitoring tools like New Relic or Datadog to collect real-time performance metrics and identify performance bottlenecks. Implement caching mechanisms and content delivery networks (CDNs) to optimize response times.
- Usability
  - Intuitive UI Design: Prioritize intuitive user interface design that simplifies navigation and interaction. Ensure the app is easy to use for users of all ages and technical proficiencies.
  - Accessibility Features: Implement accessibility features to accommodate users with disabilities or special needs, such as screen readers, voice commands, and adjustable text sizes.
  - Usability Testing: Conduct remote usability testing sessions using platforms like UserTesting or Maze. Utilize screen sharing and video recording features to observe users' interactions with the application. Leverage heatmaps and session replay tools to identify areas of the application that may require improvement in terms of usability and user experience.
- Security
  - Authentication and Authorization: Implement robust authentication mechanisms such as biometrics, multi-factor authentication (MFA), and OAuth. Ensure proper authorization controls to prevent unauthorized access to sensitive functionalities.
  - Data Protection: Encrypt sensitive data both in transit and at rest using strong encryption standards (e.g., AES-256, TLS 1.3). Regularly update and patch software to protect against vulnerabilities.
  - Security Measures: Implement secure coding practices and security frameworks such as OWASP Top 10 to mitigate common security vulnerabilities. Conduct regular security audits and penetration tests using tools like OWASP ZAP or Burp Suite. Utilize encryption protocols like SSL/TLS to secure data transmission and implement multi-factor authentication (MFA) to enhance user authentication security.
- Compliance
  - Data Protection Regulations: Implement robust data protection measures to comply with regulations such as GDPR, CCPA (California Consumer Privacy Act), and other regional data privacy laws.
  - Financial Transaction Standards: Adhere to financial transaction standards such as PSD2 (Payment Services Directive 2) and PCI DSS (Payment Card Industry Data Security Standard). Implement secure payment gateways that comply with PCI DSS requirements for handling cardholder data securely. Utilize APIs and protocols specified by PSD2 to enable secure access to account information and payment initiation services.
  - Compliance Measures: Utilize encryption techniques (e.g., AES encryption) to secure sensitive data both in transit and at rest. Implement access controls and audit trails to track data access and ensure compliance with regulatory requirements.
- Interoperability
  - Compatibility with Banking Systems: Ensure compatibility with existing banking systems and core banking platforms through standardized APIs and data formats.
  - Industry-standard Protocols: Utilize industry-standard protocols such as ISO 20022 for financial messaging to facilitate seamless communication between the

mobile banking application and backend banking systems. Implement middleware solutions or integration platforms to abstract complexities and enable interoperability with legacy systems.

- **Third-party Integrations:** Leverage APIs and web services provided by third-party service providers (e.g., payment processors, credit bureaus) to integrate additional functionalities into the mobile banking application. Implement secure authentication mechanisms (e.g., OAuth 2.0) to establish trust and securely exchange data with third-party services. Conduct thorough testing and validation to ensure compatibility and reliability of integrations, considering factors such as latency, error handling, and data consistency.

6.1.4 Documentation and Prioritization of Security Requirements

Securing the Foundations

Security requirements are critical in ensuring the safety and integrity of the banking application. These requirements must be thoroughly documented and prioritized to address the most significant threats first.

- **Collaboration**
  - **Cross-Functional Teams:** Foster collaborative relationships among cross-functional teams, including business stakeholders, product managers, UX/UI designers, and application developers.
  - **Regular Meetings:** Conduct regular meetings, workshops, and brainstorming sessions to refine requirements, discuss technical feasibility, and resolve any conflicting priorities or challenges.
  - **Open Communication:** Maintain open communication channels to ensure transparency, address concerns promptly, and foster a shared understanding of the project's goals and objectives among all team members.
- **Agile Methodologies**
  - **Iterative Development:** Adopt agile methodologies to iteratively develop and enhance the mobile app, incorporating feedback from stakeholders and end-users throughout the development lifecycle.
  - **Agile Tools:** Use agile project management tools like Jira or Azure DevOps to plan and track project progress. Utilize Scrum or Kanban boards to visualize work items and prioritize tasks. Conduct sprint planning meetings to define sprint goals and allocate tasks to team members. Hold retrospective meetings to reflect on past sprints and identify areas for improvement.
- **Version Control:** Utilize Git as a version control system and host repositories on platforms like GitHub or Bitbucket. Create separate branches for feature development and utilize pull requests for code review and collaboration. Integrate with continuous integration (CI)/continuous deployment (CD) pipelines to automate the build and deployment process, ensuring that changes are thoroughly tested before being merged into the main codebase.
- **Continuous Integration/Continuous Deployment (CI/CD):** Implement CI/CD pipelines using tools like Jenkins or GitLab CI to automate the build, test, and deployment processes. Integrate automated testing frameworks like Selenium or Cypress to validate application functionality and performance. Utilize deployment strategies such

as blue-green deployments or canary releases to minimize downtime and risk during deployment.

- **Risk Prioritization:** Conduct a thorough risk assessment to evaluate the potential impact and likelihood of various security threats. High-priority requirements should be addressed early in the development process to minimize risks. This prioritization can be guided by conducting a threat modelling exercise to identify and assess the risks to the application.

6.2 Threat Modelling

Uncovering Risks to Designing Solutions

Threat modelling is a structured approach to identifying and addressing potential threats and vulnerabilities that could compromise an application's security. For an Android banking application, this process involves defining the app's attack surface, identifying critical assets, and anticipating potential threats. By understanding how attackers might exploit vulnerabilities, developers can proactively implement security measures to mitigate these risks.

6.2.1 Assemble a Cross-functional Team

Collaboration for Comprehensive Defence

A successful threat modelling process relies on a diverse team with varied expertise to identify threats from multiple perspectives:

- Security Experts
  - **Role:** Use advanced threat intelligence platforms and machine learning models to monitor emerging threats, including supply chain attacks and zero-day exploits targeting mobile banking infrastructure. Analyse threat reports and incident databases to proactively identify and mitigate risks.
  - **Contribution:** Investigate past security breaches in mobile banking to understand common attack patterns. Conduct penetration testing and vulnerability assessments to simulate real-world attacks and uncover weaknesses.
  - **Collaboration:** Work with developers and architects to integrate robust security measures into the app. Provide ongoing training and best practices to ensure a security-first approach in development and design processes.
- Developers
  - **Role:** Implement automated security scanning tools in the software development lifecycle (SDLC) to detect and fix security flaws in the Android banking app's codebase. Ensure that security is integrated at every stage of development.
  - **Contribution:** Adopt secure coding practices and frameworks like OWASP's Mobile Top Ten and SANS' Secure Coding Guidelines to prevent common vulnerabilities such as injection attacks, insecure data storage, and improper session handling. Conduct regular code reviews and use static and dynamic analysis tools.
  - **Collaboration:** Work with security experts to apply secure coding practices tailored to mobile environments and mitigate known security risks. Collaborate with business analysts to ensure security measures do not hinder user experience or business functionality.

- **Architects**
  - **Role:** Design the system architecture of the Android banking app with security at its core, incorporating defence-in-depth strategies to minimize the impact of potential breaches. Plan the architecture to ensure robust security controls.
  - **Contribution:** Define trust boundaries between the app, backend servers, and third-party services. Enforce strict access controls to prevent lateral movement by attackers. Implement security controls at the architectural level, such as network segmentation, encryption of data in transit and at rest, and secure cloud service configurations.
  - **Collaboration:** Use threat modelling tools like Microsoft Threat Modeling Tool or OWASP Threat Dragon to visualize and analyse potential security risks within the app's architecture. Work closely with developers to ensure security is integrated from the ground up.
- **Business Analysts**
  - **Role:** Identify critical business processes and assets within the Android banking app that could be targeted by threat actors, such as customer accounts, transaction data, and financial assets. Translate business requirements into technical specifications that prioritize security.
  - **Contribution:** Assess the potential impact of security incidents on business operations, customer trust, and regulatory compliance. Use tools like Business Impact Analysis (BIA) and Value Stream Mapping (VSM) to prioritize security requirements.
  - **Collaboration:** Work with stakeholders to ensure that security measures align with business goals and do not adversely affect user experience. Liaise with legal and compliance teams to ensure all regulatory requirements are met.

6.2.2 Create a Threat Model Diagram

Visualizing Vulnerabilities and Strengths

A threat model diagram visually represents the components, data flows, and potential vulnerabilities of the Android banking app.

- **Expand on Components and Data Flows**
  - **Identify and Map:** Identify all components of the Android banking app, including the mobile client, backend servers, APIs, and third-party integrations. Understand how these components interact and the flow of data between them.
  - **Document Data Flows:** Track the flow of sensitive data, including user authentication credentials, account information, transaction data, and audit logs. Document these flows using modelling languages like Unified Modelling Language (UML) or Data Flow Diagrams (DFD).
  - **Tools:** Use modern diagramming tools like Lucidchart or Draw.io integrated with secure collaboration platforms to document data flows, ensuring diagrams are encrypted and access-controlled. Ensure diagrams are up-to-date with system changes.
- **Elaborate on Trust Boundaries**
  - **Define and Analyse:** Define trust boundaries using techniques like trust boundary analysis and attack surface reduction. Ensure sensitive operations within the app are isolated from untrusted components.

- **Methodologies:** Apply threat modelling methodologies such as STRIDE (Spoofing, Tampering, Repudiation, Information Disclosure, Denial of Service, Elevation of Privilege) to identify potential security threats across trust boundaries, especially between the mobile app and backend services.
- **Detail Potential Attack Vectors**
  - **Brainstorm and Identify:** Conduct threat modelling workshops with the cross-functional team to brainstorm potential attack vectors and vulnerabilities specific to mobile banking, such as SQL injection, cross-site scripting (XSS), cross-site request forgery (CSRF), and man-in-the-middle (MITM) attacks. Use attack trees and other techniques to explore different paths an attacker might take.
  - **Leverage Intelligence:** Use threat intelligence feeds and security advisories to identify known attack vectors targeting similar mobile banking systems and incorporate this information into the threat model. Stay updated on the latest attack trends and tactics used by cybercriminals.

6.2.3 Identify Potential Threat Actors

Understanding the Adversaries

Understanding potential threat actors helps in assessing who might target the app and why.

- **External Threats**
  - **Analyse Motivations:** Understand the motivations driving different categories of threat actors targeting mobile banking apps, such as financial gain, ideological beliefs, or espionage. This includes cybercriminals seeking profit, hacktivists pushing agendas, state-sponsored actors pursuing strategic goals, and insider threats with ulterior motives.
  - **Study Tactics:** Familiarize with the tactics and techniques used by threat actors to achieve their objectives, including reconnaissance, exploitation, privilege escalation, and data exfiltration. This can involve social engineering, exploiting vulnerabilities, or deploying malware to compromise the app.
  - **Tools and Scenarios:** Use frameworks like MITRE ATT&CK Mobile or NIST SP 800-53 to analyze threat actor tactics and techniques specific to mobile banking apps. Conduct scenario-based exercises to prepare for potential attacks, ensuring readiness against real-world threats.
- **Insider Threats**
  - **Recognize Risks:** Consider the risks posed by insider threats, such as disgruntled employees or contractors with privileged access to the mobile banking app's backend systems. Insiders can misuse their access intentionally or be exploited by external actors through coercion or deception.
  - **Preventive Measures:** Implement user behaviour analytics (UBA) and privileged access management (PAM) solutions to detect and prevent insider threats. These tools monitor for unusual behaviour patterns and enforce least privilege access controls, reducing the attack surface. Regularly review access logs and conduct audits to maintain oversight.
  - **Training:** Conduct regular security awareness training to educate employees about the risks of insider threats and how to report suspicious activities. Foster a culture of security where employees understand their role in protecting sensitive information and feel empowered to act.

6.2.4 Enumerate Potential Threats and Attack Scenarios

Anticipating the Unthinkable

Identifying specific threats and attack scenarios is crucial for understanding how attackers might target the application.

- Provide Detailed Scenarios
  - **Describe Scenarios:** Develop specific threat scenarios tailored to the mobile banking context, such as a phishing attack targeting customers to steal login credentials or malware infections spreading through compromised mobile banking applications. Consider scenarios involving fake apps or app tampering that could deceive users or bypass security controls.
  - **Impact Assessment:** Consider the potential impact of each threat scenario on customer trust, financial stability, regulatory compliance, and brand reputation. Evaluate how different attack vectors could affect various parts of the system and the overall user experience, from data breaches to service disruptions.
  - **Documentation:** Use standardized formats like the Common Attack Pattern Enumeration and Classification (CAPEC) framework to document the steps an attacker could take to exploit vulnerabilities in the mobile banking app. Create detailed attack narratives to help visualize the threat landscape and inform mitigation strategies.

6.2.5 Assess the Likelihood and Impact of Each Threat

Weighing Risks with Precision

Assessing the likelihood and impact of identified threats helps prioritize mitigation efforts.

- Quantify Risk Factors
  - **Assign Values:** Assign quantitative values to risk factors such as likelihood of occurrence, impact severity, and time to detection and response. This helps in prioritizing which threats need immediate attention based on their potential to cause harm.
  - **Methodologies:** Use risk assessment methodologies such as the Common Vulnerability Scoring System (CVSS) or the Risk Management Framework (RMF) to prioritize threats based on their risk profile. Apply quantitative risk assessment methodologies like FAIR (Factor Analysis of Information Risk) or DREAD (Damage, Reproducibility, Exploitability, Affected Users, Discoverability) to calculate the likelihood and impact of each identified threat with precision.
- Consider Regulatory Compliance
  - **Ensure Compliance:** Adhere to industry regulations and standards such as the Payment Card Industry Data Security Standard (PCI DSS), General Data Protection Regulation (GDPR), and Basel Committee on Banking Supervision (BCBS) guidelines. Ensure that the app complies with relevant financial regulations to avoid legal and operational risks.
  - **Legal and Financial Consequences:** Assess the potential legal and financial consequences of non-compliance with regulatory requirements related to data protection, privacy, and financial security. Use compliance management platforms

to map regulatory requirements to specific threats and vulnerabilities identified in the threat model, implementing controls and security measures to meet these obligations.

6.2.6 Prioritize Mitigation Strategies

Strategic Shielding for Maximum Impact

After identifying and assessing threats, prioritize mitigation strategies to address the most critical vulnerabilities.

- Tailor Strategies to Threat Landscape
  - **Address Specific Threats:** Select mitigation strategies that address the specific threats and vulnerabilities identified during the threat modelling process. This includes both technical controls, such as encryption, and process improvements, like enhanced monitoring.
  - **Effective and Feasible:** Prioritize strategies based on their effectiveness in reducing the likelihood and impact of high-risk threats, as well as their feasibility of implementation within the organization's resource constraints. Implement security controls using a defence-in-depth approach, combining preventive, detective, and corrective measures to mitigate the full spectrum of potential threats and vulnerabilities.
- Iterative Improvement Process
  - **Continuous Monitoring:** Continuously monitor and update the threat model as new threats emerge or changes are made to the mobile banking app. Incorporate feedback from security assessments, incident response activities, and threat intelligence feeds to keep the model current.
  - **Regular Reviews:** Conduct periodic reviews and reassessments of the threat model to ensure its relevance and effectiveness in mitigating evolving security risks and compliance requirements. Regularly update the threat model to reflect changes in the app's architecture or new threat intelligence, maintaining a proactive stance.
- Risk Reduction
  - **High-risk Threats:** Start by identifying and addressing critical vulnerabilities. These are the ones that pose the highest risk to your application and its users, such as authentication bypass, data leakage, and remote code execution, prioritizing fixes to prevent severe security incidents.
  - **Feasibility:** Consider the feasibility of implementing mitigation strategies. Evaluate the effort required for each approach, prioritizsing strategies that strike a balance between security and functionality and carefully weighing trade-offs like impacts on user experience or performance.

6.3 Secure Design

Blueprints for Resilience

Secure design principles aim to build security into the application architecture from the outset. This involves applying design patterns that promote security, such as least privilege, defence-in-depth, and fail-safe defaults. For an Android banking application, secure design ensures that sensitive data is protected and critical functions are safeguarded against unauthorized access and tampering.

6.3.1 Principles of Secure Design

Foundations for Fortified Systems

The foundation of a secure application lies in adopting well-established security principles that ensure data confidentiality, integrity, and availability. These principles help prevent unauthorized access, data leakage, and fraud in financial applications.

Principle of Least Privilege (PoLP)

Every user, service, and process within an application should be given only the minimum permissions necessary to perform their functions. Excessive privileges increase the risk of data leakage and privilege escalation attacks.

In the context of a mobile banking application,

- A regular banking customer should only have access to their own account details and transactions. They should not be able to modify administrative settings.
- A customer support agent should only have read-only access to user data and should require explicit approval before performing sensitive actions like password resets.
- The app itself should not request unnecessary Android permissions, such as access to contacts or SMS, unless absolutely needed.

Fail-Safe Defaults

A system should default to a secure state in case of failure, ensuring that security is not weakened due to errors or malfunctions.

In the context of a mobile banking application,

- If a login attempt fails multiple times, the app should lock the account and require additional authentication (such as an OTP or biometric verification) instead of allowing unlimited attempts.
- If a payment API call fails, the system should prompt the user to retry rather than assuming the payment was successful.

Separation of Duties

A single user or process should not have unchecked control over critical operations. This prevents fraud and insider attacks.

In the context of a mobile banking application,

- A transaction above ₹1 lakh should require approval from two different levels of authentication, such as user confirmation via biometrics and an OTP.
- Backend administrators should not have direct access to modify customer financial records without a secondary verification process.

Minimize Attack Surface

The application should expose only necessary functionality, reducing potential attack vectors that attackers can exploit.

In the context of a mobile banking application,

- Disable debugging and logging in the production environment to prevent sensitive data leakage.
- Restrict API access to authenticated users only and enforce role-based access control (RBAC).

Defence-in-Depth

Instead of relying on a single security measure, applications should use multiple layers of security controls to protect critical assets.

In the context of a mobile banking application,

- Use multi-factor authentication (MFA) to enhance login security.
- Implement TLS encryption for securing communication channels.
- Encrypt sensitive data at rest using AES-256 encryption.

Security by Design

Security must be an integral part of the development lifecycle rather than being added as an afterthought.

In the context of a mobile banking application,

- Use threat modelling techniques to identify attack vectors before coding begins.
- Enforce secure coding guidelines to prevent injection attacks and other vulnerabilities.

Supply Chain Security

- All third-party dependencies, libraries, and components must be continuously monitored for vulnerabilities and supply chain compromises.
- In the context of a mobile banking application,
  - Implement Software Bill of Materials (SBOM) tracking for all dependencies.
  - Use dependency scanning tools integrated into CI/CD pipelines.
  - Establish vendor security assessment protocols for all third-party integrations.

6.3.2 Secure Architecture Patterns

Crafting Robust Frameworks

A secure architecture is essential for reducing risks and protecting user data, particularly in Android banking applications, where sensitive financial transactions and personal information are involved. Designing a secure architecture involves adopting robust security patterns that enforce strict access control, data protection, and continuous threat mitigation.

This section explores key security architecture patterns that help mitigate risks and ensure confidentiality, integrity, and availability (CIA) in banking applications.

Zero Trust Architecture (ZTA)

Zero Trust Architecture (ZTA), guided by principles from NIST 800-207 and models like BeyondCorp, ensures every access request undergoes continuous verification on the principle that no entity, whether inside or outside the network, is inherently trusted. Every access request must undergo strict verification, authentication, and authorization before being granted.

This approach is particularly critical in banking applications, where attackers constantly attempt to bypass authentication mechanisms, hijack sessions, or exploit weak API security.

Key Components of ZTA in Banking Apps

- **Continuous Authentication and Verification:** Every request from a user, device, or system must be authenticated before access is granted. Even after successful login, the app should periodically re-validate session tokens to prevent session hijacking. Implement adaptive authentication with machine learning-based behavioral biometrics, device attestation via Android SafetyNet or Play Integrity API, and contextual risk assessment.
- **Least Privilege Access Control:** Users should only have the minimum permissions required to perform their tasks. Transactions above a certain limit (e.g., ₹1 lakh) should require additional verification such as biometric authentication.
- **Micro-Segmentation:** Divide the banking system into smaller isolated zones to prevent unauthorized access. A compromised feature (e.g., transaction history) should not allow access to fund transfer functions.
- **Explicit Trust Boundaries:** Any request from an unrecognized device or IP should trigger additional verification (OTP, biometric, or security questions).

In the context of a mobile banking application,

- A user logging in from a new mobile device is denied access until they confirm their identity via OTP verification and biometric authentication.
- Before allowing a high-risk transaction (such as adding a new payee), the system enforces multi-factor authentication (MFA) to verify the user's identity.
- The app detects an unusual login attempt from a different country and automatically blocks the request until the user verifies via email.

Microservices Security

Modern banking applications often use a microservices-based architecture, where different functionalities (e.g., login, payments, transactions, notifications) are implemented as independent services communicating via APIs. While this improves scalability and modularity, it also introduces security risks if the services are not properly secured.

Security Challenges in Microservices Architecture

- Inter-service communication is vulnerable to interception (man-in-the-middle attacks).
- API exposure increases the attack surface, leading to potential API abuse.
- Unauthorized services might attempt to access sensitive financial data.

Key Security Practices for Microservices in Banking Apps

- **Mutual TLS (mTLS) for Secure Communication:** All inter-service communication must be encrypted using mutual TLS (mTLS) with automated certificate management to prevent eavesdropping and tampering.
- **OAuth 2.0 and JWT for API Authentication:** Every API request should be authenticated using OAuth 2.0 tokens and verified using JSON Web Tokens (JWT). Access tokens should have short expiration times to minimize risks.
- **Role-based Access Control (RBAC) and Attribute-based Access Control (ABAC):** Define strict roles and permissions to prevent unauthorized access. Implement dynamic authorization policies based on factors like user device, location, and transaction amount.
- **Service-level Encryption:** Each microservice should encrypt sensitive data before storing or transmitting it.

In the context of a mobile banking application,

- The authentication service verifies the user's identity and generates an OAuth 2.0 token, which is required to access the transaction service.
- A fraud detection microservice monitors transaction patterns and flags suspicious activities for review.
- The payment microservice encrypts all transaction details before sending them to the bank's core processing system.

MVC Security (Model-View-Controller)

The Model-View-Controller (MVC) architectural pattern separates an application into three distinct layers:
- Model – Handles data processing and database interactions.
- View – Manages UI components and user interactions.
- Controller – Handles logic and bridges the Model and View layers.

Security Best Practices for MVC in Banking Apps

- **Strict Input Validation and Parameterized Queries:** Prevent SQL injection by never concatenating user input into SQL queries. Use ORM frameworks like Room, Hibernate, or JPA to handle database interactions securely.
- **Sanitize User Input to Prevent XSS:** Always encode user-generated content before rendering it on the UI to prevent malicious script execution.
- **Implement Strong CSRF Protections:** Use CSRF tokens to verify that requests originate from a legitimate user session.
- **Enforce Secure Session Management:** Implement session timeouts and use secure session tokens to prevent session hijacking.

In the context of a mobile banking application,

- The View layer restricts users from entering JavaScript in input fields to prevent XSS attacks.
- The Model layer uses parameterized SQL queries to prevent SQL injection.
- The Controller layer validates all incoming API requests before processing transactions.

Security by Isolation

Security by Isolation ensures that critical components of a banking app operate in separate, protected environments, reducing the impact of a security breach.

Key Isolation Techniques for Banking Apps

- **Application Sandboxing:** The banking app should run in an isolated environment to prevent unauthorized access to system resources.
- **Containerization for Backend Services:** Use Docker containers and Kubernetes to isolate different backend services, ensuring that compromised services cannot affect others.
- **Secure Data Storage Isolation:** Store cryptographic keys in the Android Keystore rather than in local storage.
- **Process Isolation:** Sensitive processes (such as handling payments) should run in separate, sandboxed processes with minimum privileges.

In the context of a mobile banking application,

- The biometric authentication module runs in a separate process, preventing malware from accessing fingerprint data.
- Payment transactions are processed in an isolated container, preventing unauthorized apps from interfering with payment execution.

6.3.3 Data Flow and Trust Boundaries

Channelling Trust with Precision

Understanding data flow and trust boundaries is critical for securing an Android banking application. Data flow refers to how user data moves within an application – from input to processing, storage, and transmission between components. Trust boundaries are security checkpoints where data transitions between different systems, users, or security contexts, and they require additional security enforcement to prevent unauthorized access, data leakage, or privilege escalation.

A well-defined data flow and trust boundary model ensures that financial transactions, user authentication, and sensitive banking information remain protected from attacks such as data breaches, unauthorized access, and privilege escalation.

Data Flow Mapping

Data flow mapping is a crucial process that enables organizations to pinpoint where sensitive data is stored, processed, and transmitted, while also revealing vulnerabilities that could be exploited by attackers. By visualizing the flow of information, it becomes easier to identify and reinforce critical points with measures like encryption, authentication, and logging, ensuring robust protection for valuable data.

Key Components in Data Flow for a Banking App

- **User Input and Device Interaction:** Users enter credentials, PINs, biometrics, or transaction details via the app UI. Data is captured via text fields, biometric sensors, NFC, or camera (QR payments).
- **Application Processing and API Calls:** The app processes user input, encrypts sensitive data, and sends API requests. API requests must be validated, authenticated, and authorized before further processing.
- **Backend Processing & Data Storage:** The banking server processes the request (e.g., fund transfer, account balance check). Sensitive data is stored in encrypted databases using AES-256 or similar secure algorithms.
- **Data Transmission:** The response (transaction success, balance update) is transmitted back to the app. Data in transit must be protected using TLS 1.3 encryption with certificate pinning.
- **Logging and Auditing:** Every transaction is logged in secure logging systems for fraud detection and forensic analysis.

In the context of a mobile banking application,

- User initiates a fund transfer, then the app encrypts transaction details and sends them to the bank's API.
- API authenticates the request using OAuth 2.0 and JWT.
- Transaction is processed at the backend and recorded in the bank's database.
- Response is sent back to the app confirming the transaction success.

Defining Trust Boundaries

Trust boundaries are the points where data moves from one security domain to another, requiring additional security controls. Each boundary represents a potential risk area where data might be exposed to unauthorized users or attackers.

Key Trust Boundaries in an Android Banking App

- **User Device to Banking App:** Data from user input (passwords, biometrics) must be secured before transmission. Enforce secure authentication mechanisms like biometric authentication, PIN, and OTP verification.
- **Banking App to Backend Server:** All communication between the app and server should use TLS 1.3 encryption with certificate pinning. Implement API rate-limiting and anomaly detection to prevent brute-force attacks.
- **Internal Services within the Banking Backend:** Microservices must use mutual TLS (mTLS) authentication to prevent unauthorized internal access. Implement role-based access control (RBAC) to ensure that only authorized services can access critical financial data.
- **Backend Server to Third-party Services:** Data sent to payment gateways (UPI, Visa, Mastercard, etc.) should be encrypted and digitally signed to prevent tampering. Implement secure APIs with OAuth 2.0 authorization for third-party integrations.

In the context of a mobile banking application,

- A user attempts to log in from a new device, then the system detects the trust boundary shift and enforces multi-factor authentication (MFA) before allowing access.
- The banking app requests account balance details, then the backend validates the request and ensures only authorized users can access the data.

Enforcing Security Controls at Trust Boundaries

It involves implementing measures like authentication, authorization, and input validation to safeguard sensitive data and functionality at points where the app interacts with external systems, users, or other apps, ensuring a secure and trusted environment.

Key Security Controls in an Android Banking App

- **Authentication and Authorization at Each Trust Boundary:** Implement multi-factor authentication (MFA) for high-risk transactions. Use OAuth 2.0, OpenID Connect, and JSON Web Tokens (JWT) for secure API authentication. Enforce session timeouts and automatic logouts to prevent unauthorized access.
- **Encrypting Data at Rest and in Transit:** Encrypt stored user data using AES-256 with secure key management in Android Keystore. Use TLS 1.3 encryption with HSTS and disable weak ciphers. Apply end-to-end encryption (E2EE) for sensitive communications.
- **API Security Measures:** Implement strict input validation to prevent injection attacks (SQL injection, XML injection, API abuse). Use rate-limiting and anomaly detection to detect DDoS and brute-force attacks. Secure API endpoints with JWT authentication and role-based access control (RBAC).
- **Secure Logging and Monitoring:** Log all security-related events (failed logins, high-risk transactions). Implement SIEM (Security Information & Event Management) tools for real-time monitoring. Detect anomalous behaviour using AI-driven fraud detection systems.

In the context of a mobile banking application,

- A user logs in from a new location, then the app blocks access until the user completes OTP verification.
- An API request with an invalid JWT token is immediately rejected to prevent unauthorized access.
- Transaction details are encrypted before being stored in the bank's database, ensuring data confidentiality.

6.3.4 Authentication and Authorization Framework

Building Gateways of Confidence

A robust authentication and authorization framework is essential for securing an Android banking application. This framework verifies user identities and manages their access to different parts of the application based on roles and risk levels.

- **Authentication:** The process of verifying the identity of a user or device.
- **Authorization:** Determines what an authenticated user is allowed to do within the application.

Components of a Robust Authentication System

Implementing a robust authentication system involves creating a mechanism that securely verifies the identity of users before granting them access to the mobile banking application. This can be achieved through:

- **Traditional Methods:** Use strong password policies, including complexity requirements, expiration periods, and prevention of reuse.
- **Advanced Techniques:** Incorporate biometric authentication, such as fingerprint and facial recognition, to provide a seamless and secure user experience.
- **Passwordless and Phishing-Resistant Authentication:** Implement FIDO2/WebAuthn standards for passwordless authentication using device biometrics, hardware security keys, or platform authenticators. This approach eliminates password-related vulnerabilities and provides stronger protection against phishing attacks and credential stuffing.

Adaptive Risk-based Authentication

Adaptive risk-based authentication is a dynamic approach that assesses the risk associated with each login attempt and adjusts the authentication requirements accordingly. This approach enhances security by tailoring the authentication process to the perceived risk level of each attempt:

- **Low-risk Scenarios:** For login attempts deemed low-risk based on factors such as the user's usual location, recognized device, and normal behaviour patterns, the application may require only basic authentication methods like a password.
- **High-risk Scenarios:** For attempts considered high-risk, such as those from unfamiliar locations, devices, or abnormal behaviour patterns, the application may prompt the user to provide additional verification, such as a biometric scan or OTP, ensuring heightened protection.

Fine-grained Access Controls

Fine-grained access controls allow administrators to define detailed permissions and privileges for different users or user groups within the application. This ensures that users have access only to the features and data necessary for their roles:

- **User Role Definition:** Clearly define user roles and associated permissions. For example, a bank employee might have access to customer financial data, while a regular customer can only view their own account information and transaction history.
- **Granular Permissions:** Implement permissions at a granular level to control access to specific features and functionalities. This ensures that users have access only to the features and data necessary for their roles, minimizing exposure.
- **Dynamic Adjustments:** Enable the system to dynamically adjust access permissions based on changing roles, responsibilities, or detected security risks.

6.3.5 Defence-in-Depth principles

Layering Security for Resilience

Defence-in-depth is a security strategy that involves deploying multiple layers of security controls to protect against a wide range of threats and vulnerabilities. For an Android banking application, this means implementing security measures at various layers of the application stack, including the application layer, network layer, and data layer. Each layer of security controls serves as a barrier to prevent unauthorized access and mitigate potential attacks.

Multi-layered Security Controls

Application Layer: At the application layer, security controls focus on ensuring that the code and application logic are secure:
- **Secure Coding Practices:** Implement secure coding practices, such as input validation, output encoding, and secure session management, to prevent common vulnerabilities like SQL injection and cross-site scripting (XSS).
- **Authentication and Session Management:** Use robust authentication mechanisms and secure session management techniques to protect against unauthorized access and session hijacking.
- **Static and Dynamic Analysis:** Regularly perform static and dynamic code analysis to identify and fix vulnerabilities early in the development lifecycle.

Network Layer: At the network layer, security controls are designed to monitor and protect data as it travels across the network:
- **Firewalls and IDS/IPS:** Deploy firewalls, intrusion detection systems (IDS), and intrusion prevention systems (IPS) to monitor and filter network traffic, detecting and blocking malicious activities.
- **Network Segmentation:** Use network segmentation and access control lists (ACLs) to restrict access to sensitive resources and prevent lateral movement within the network.
- **Secure Communication Protocols:** Ensure that all communication between the client (Android app) and server uses secure protocols such as HTTPS and TLS/SSL.
- **Certificate Pinning:** It enhances the security provided by TLS/SSL by binding the application to a specific set of server certificates. This prevents attackers from using fraudulent certificates to impersonate the server.

Data Layer: At the data layer, security controls protect the integrity and confidentiality of data:
- **Encryption:** Implement data-at-rest and data-in-transit encryption to safeguard sensitive information stored on devices and transmitted over networks. Use strong encryption algorithms like AES-256 for robust protection.
- **Access Controls:** Utilize role-based access control (RBAC) and attribute-based access control (ABAC) to limit access to data based on user roles, permissions, and attributes.
- **Database Security:** Apply encryption to databases and ensure proper database configuration to prevent unauthorized access and data leakage.

6.3.6 Encryption and Key Management

Safeguarding Secrets

Encryption and key management are fundamental components of securing sensitive data in an Android banking application. Proper encryption practices ensure that data is unreadable to unauthorizsed parties, while secure key management ensures the protection and integrity of the cryptographic keys used in the encryption process.

Utilization of Industry-Standard Encryption Algorithms

Encryption algorithms transform plaintext data into ciphertext, which can only be decrypted using the appropriate cryptographic keys. For a mobile banking application, it is crucial to utilize robust, industry-standard encryption algorithms to protect sensitive data.

- **Advanced Encryption Standard (AES):** AES is widely used for encrypting sensitive data due to its strength and efficiency. AES-256, in particular, provides a high level of security and is suitable for encrypting customer credentials, transaction details, and personal information.
- **Rivest-Shamir-Adleman (RSA):** RSA is often used for encrypting small amounts of data and for secure key exchange. It provides strong security for transmitting encryption keys over insecure channels.

In the context of the mobile banking application, sensitive data should be encrypted using these industry-standard algorithms before being stored on servers or transmitted over the network. This ensures that even if an attacker gains access to the underlying storage or communication channels, the data remains protected.

Secure Key Management Practices

Key management involves generating, storing, distributing, and revoking cryptographic keys used for encryption and decryption. Secure key management practices are essential for maintaining the integrity and confidentiality of cryptographic operations.

- **Key Generation and Storage:** Cryptographic keys should be generated using secure methods and stored in a protected environment. Hardware Security Modules (HSMs), cloud-based Key Management Services (KMS), or the Android Keystore system can be used to securely store encryption keys, ensuring they are protected from unauthorized access and physical tampering.
- **Key Rotation:** Regular key rotation limits the exposure of cryptographic keys over time. By periodically changing keys, the risk of key compromise is reduced. Automated key rotation policies should be implemented to ensure timely updates.
- **Key Escrow and Recovery:** Key escrow mechanisms ensure that encrypted data can be recovered in the event of key loss or compromise. This involves securely storing backup copies of encryption keys and having a recovery process in place.
- **Access Controls and Auditing:** Implement strict access controls to restrict who can access and use cryptographic keys. Auditing mechanisms should be in place to monitor key usage and detect any unauthorized or suspicious activity. This helps prevent malicious insiders or unauthorized individuals from tampering with cryptographic operations or accessing sensitive data.

Additional Security Measures

- **Encryption of Data at Rest and in Transit:** Ensure that all sensitive data is encrypted both when stored (data at rest) and during transmission (data in transit). This provides comprehensive protection across all stages of data handling.
- **End-to-End Encryption (E2EE):** Consider implementing end-to-end encryption for sensitive communication within the application. E2EE ensures that data is encrypted on the sender's device and can only be decrypted by the intended recipient, providing the highest level of data protection.

6.3.7 Resilient Architectures and Failover Mechanisms

Designing for Durability

Resilient architectures and failover mechanisms are crucial for ensuring the continuous availability and reliability of an Android banking application. These strategies involve designing the system to withstand and recover from various failures, thereby minimizing service disruptions and ensuring high availability.

Design for High Availability

High availability (HA) ensures that a system or service remains operational and accessible to users with minimal downtime. Achieving HA involves implementing redundant components, load balancing, and clustering to distribute workloads and minimize the impact of hardware or software failures.

- **Redundant Components:** Deploy multiple instances of critical components such as application servers, database servers, and network infrastructure. These components should be distributed across geographically dispersed data centres to avoid single points of failure.
- **Load Balancing:** Use load balancers to evenly distribute incoming traffic among multiple servers. This not only improves performance during peak usage periods but also ensures that the application remains responsive if one or more servers fail.
- **Clustering:** Implement clustering for critical services, allowing multiple servers to work together to provide high availability and scalability. If one server in the cluster fails, others can take over its workload.

In the context of a mobile banking application, deploying multiple instances of application and database servers across different locations ensures that the application remains operational even if some servers fail.

Fault Tolerance

Fault tolerance is the ability of a system to continue operating correctly despite the occurrence of faults or errors. This involves detecting, isolating, and recovering from failures without causing service disruptions or data loss.

- **Graceful Degradation:** Design the application to continue functioning with reduced capabilities if certain components fail. For example, if a non-critical service becomes unavailable, the application can still operate without it.

- **Error Handling:** Implement robust error handling to manage and recover from unexpected errors gracefully. This prevents crashes and maintains data integrity.
- **Redundancy:** Incorporate redundant components and services that can take over in case of failure, ensuring continuous operation.

For a mobile banking application, fault tolerance might include the ability to handle server outages or network issues without affecting the user's ability to perform essential banking functions.

Disaster Recovery Capabilities

Disaster recovery (DR) refers to the process of restoring operations and data in the event of a catastrophic failure, such as a natural disaster, cyberattack, or major hardware failure.

- **Regular Backups:** Regularly backup critical data and configurations to geographically dispersed backup servers or cloud storage providers. Ensure backups are secure and up-to-date.
- **Failover Mechanisms:** Implement automated failover mechanisms to switch operations to backup servers or data centres if the primary ones fail.
- **Data Replication and Synchronization:** Use data replication to keep copies of critical data synchronized across multiple locations. This ensures that data can be quickly restored from backups in the event of a disaster.
- **DR Plans:** Develop and regularly update comprehensive disaster recovery plans that outline procedures for restoring operations and data, including communication strategies and responsibilities.

In a mobile banking context, this means ensuring that critical data is backed up and that there are clear, tested procedures for quickly restoring services after a disaster.

Minimization of Service Disruptions and Points of Failure

Minimizing service disruptions and points of failure involves proactive measures to identify and mitigate risks that could impact service availability and performance.

- **Continuous Monitoring:** Implement continuous monitoring of infrastructure and applications to detect and address issues before they lead to failures. Use automated tools to monitor system health and performance.
- **Proactive Maintenance:** Regularly perform maintenance on hardware and software to prevent failures. This includes applying updates and patches and performing routine checks.
- **Automated Failover:** Implement automated failover mechanisms that quickly detect and respond to failures, switching to backup systems with minimal disruption.
- **Security Audits and Penetration Testing:** Conduct regular security audits and penetration testing to identify and address vulnerabilities. This helps prevent security breaches that could lead to service disruptions.
- **Redundant Systems and Data Replication:** Ensure that critical systems have redundant components and that data is replicated across multiple servers or data centres to prevent loss from a single point of failure.

For an Android banking application, minimizing service disruptions could involve automated monitoring tools that alert administrators to issues, regular security testing, and ensuring that all critical components have backups and redundancies.

6.4 Secure Coding

From Vulnerabilities to Vigilance

Secure coding practices are essential for writing resilient code that protects against attacks and vulnerabilities. Developers must adhere to secure coding standards and avoid common pitfalls such as buffer overflows, improper input validation, and insecure data handling. This is particularly crucial in Android banking applications, where the security of sensitive user data is paramount. This section explores various practices and guidelines to ensure secure coding throughout the development process.

6.4.1 Adherence to Secure Coding Standards

Code Crafted with Care

Adhering to secure coding standards is fundamental in mitigating common vulnerabilities and ensuring the integrity and security of the application. Secure coding standards provide a comprehensive set of guidelines that developers should follow to prevent security flaws.

OWASP Mobile Top 10

- **Familiarization:** Understand and familiarize yourself with the OWASP Mobile Top 10, which outlines the most critical security risks to mobile applications.
- **Mitigation Controls:** Implement security controls such as input validation, output encoding, and proper authentication mechanisms to address the identified risks.
- **Vulnerability Mitigation:** Incorporate strategies to address vulnerabilities like insecure data storage, insecure communication, and poor authentication.
- **Example:** Utilize tools like OWASP ZAP (Zed Attack Proxy) for automated scanning of the application to detect vulnerabilities listed in the OWASP Mobile Top 10.

Android Secure Coding Guidelines

- **Adherence to Best Practices:** Comprehend and adhere to Google's recommended best practices for Android app security. These guidelines cover a wide range of security aspects, from data protection to secure communication.
- **Integration in Development:** Ensure that secure coding practices are integrated into the development process from the beginning.
- **Example:** Employ Android lint checks integrated with Android Studio to enforce adherence to secure coding guidelines throughout the development lifecycle. Regularly review and update code to comply with the latest Android secure coding recommendations and best practices.

Platform-specific Security Recommendations

- **Staying Updated:** Stay updated with platform-specific security recommendations provided by Android to mitigate emerging threats and vulnerabilities.
- **Monitoring Security Bulletins:** Regularly monitor Google's Android Security Bulletins and other relevant sources for announcements regarding security updates and patches.

- **Example:** Utilize Android's Security APIs such as SafetyNet Attestation and SafetyNet reCAPTCHA to detect device tampering and ensure the integrity of app communications.

Implementation Strategies

- **Training and Awareness:** Conduct regular training sessions and workshops for developers to stay updated on the latest secure coding standards and practices. Training should cover understanding security threats, secure coding techniques, and the importance of adhering to guidelines.
- **Code Review Checklists:** Incorporate secure coding standards into code review checklists to ensure compliance. Code reviews should focus on identifying and mitigating potential security vulnerabilities.
- **Automated Tools:** Use static code analysis tools like Android Lint, SonarQube, and other security-focused tools that enforce secure coding standards and detect violations early in the development process. Automated tools help in identifying issues that might be missed during manual reviews.

6.4.2 Leveraging Secure Coding Libraries and Frameworks

Toolkits for Trustworthy Development

Using established libraries and frameworks can significantly enhance security by providing well-tested and robust components. These libraries and frameworks encapsulate best practices and common security measures, reducing the likelihood of introducing vulnerabilities.

Android SDK Libraries

- **Built-in Security Features:** Utilize secure coding libraries like Android Jetpack and Google Play Services to leverage built-in security features and streamline development efforts.
- **Example:** Utilize Android Jetpack's Security library to implement secure data storage using EncryptedSharedPreferences and EncryptedFile classes, ensuring that sensitive data is encrypted both at rest and during use.
- **Example:** Leverage the Google Play Integrity API to assess device and application integrity, helping to detect tampering and ensure the trustworthiness of the operating environment.

Cryptographic Libraries

- Leverage cryptographic libraries provided by the Android SDK for secure data storage, encryption, and decryption.
- **Example:** Use the javax.crypto package for implementing encryption and decryption functionalities in the application, ensuring that sensitive information remains confidential and secure.

Third-party Libraries

- **Rigorous Vetting:** Vet third-party libraries rigorously for security vulnerabilities before integrating them into the application. This includes reviewing the library's source code, understanding its update frequency, and checking its security track record.

- **Example:** Integrate security-focused third-party libraries such as SQLCipher for encrypted database storage, ensuring that database content remains confidential, and OkHttp for secure communication over HTTPS, which provides mechanisms for SSL/TLS encryption.
- **Regular Updates:** Regularly update libraries to ensure patches for known security issues are applied promptly. Keeping libraries up-to-date mitigates risks associated with outdated components.
- **Example:** Regularly monitor the Common Vulnerabilities and Exposures (CVE) database and other sources for security advisories related to third-party libraries and dependencies. This proactive approach helps in identifying and addressing potential security vulnerabilities in the libraries used.

Implementation Strategies

- **Dependency Management:** Use tools like Gradle to manage dependencies and ensure the application uses the most secure and recent versions of libraries. Gradle can automate dependency updates and help track library versions.
- **Library Configuration:** Configure libraries securely to maximize their security benefits. For example, ensure OkHttp is set up to enforce SSL/TLS encryption and enable SSL pinning to prevent man-in-the-middle attacks.
- **Security Audits:** Conduct regular security audits of both first-party and third-party libraries to identify and mitigate any potential security risks. Automated tools like OWASP Dependency-Check can be used to scan for known vulnerabilities.

6.4.3 Implementation of Input Validation and Output Encoding

Guarding Data Integrity

Proper input validation and output encoding are critical to preventing injection attacks, such as SQL injection and cross-site scripting (XSS). Input validation involves verifying that incoming data is both expected and safe, while output encoding ensures that data is correctly processed before being rendered in the user interface.

Input Validation Techniques

- **Strict Input Validation:** Implement strict input validation to sanitize user inputs and prevent injection attacks such as SQL injection, Cross-Site Scripting (XSS), and OS command injection.
- **Example:** Implement input validation using Android's InputFilter interface to restrict input characters and formats. For instance, an InputFilter can be used to limit input to numeric characters only for a phone number field.
- **Example:** Utilize regular expressions (Regex) for complex input validation requirements, such as validating email addresses and passwords. Regex can ensure that inputs adhere to expected patterns, preventing malformed or malicious data.
- **Validation of Data Types, Lengths, and Formats:** Validate the data types, lengths, and formats of input data to mitigate the risk of malicious input manipulation.
- **Example:** Ensure that fields like usernames and passwords do not exceed specified lengths and contain only allowed characters. This helps prevent buffer overflow attacks and other injection vulnerabilities.

Output Encoding

- **Neutralizing Malicious Characters:** Apply output encoding techniques to neutralize malicious input characters and prevent unintended script execution.
- **Example:** Use HTML escaping libraries like Html.escapeHtml() to encode dynamic content displayed in WebView components. This prevents XSS attacks by ensuring that any HTML tags entered by users are displayed as text rather than being executed as code.
- **Platform-specific Encoding Functions:** Utilize platform-specific encoding functions to sanitize dynamic content before rendering it in the user interface.
- **Example:** Implement Content Security Policy (CSP) headers to restrict the sources of content and prevent the injection of malicious scripts into web views. CSP can significantly reduce the risk of XSS attacks by controlling which resources the web view is allowed to load.

Implementation Strategies

- **Centralized Validation and Encoding:** Create centralized functions for input validation and output encoding to ensure consistency and reusability across the application. This helps in maintaining a single source of truth for validation and encoding logic.
- **Security Libraries:** Utilize security-focused libraries that provide robust validation and encoding functions. Libraries like OWASP's Java Encoder can be used for output encoding to prevent XSS attacks.
- **Testing:** Regularly test inputs and outputs for common injection vulnerabilities using automated tools like OWASP ZAP. These tools can simulate attacks and help identify weaknesses in input validation and output encoding processes.

6.4.4 Adoption of Secure Authentication Mechanisms

Access Assured

Secure authentication mechanisms are essential for protecting user accounts and sensitive data. Robust authentication not only verifies user identities but also provides a foundation for other security measures, such as authorization and auditing.

OAuth 2.0

- **Secure and Standardized Authentication:** Implement the OAuth 2.0 protocol to enable secure and standardized authentication between the mobile application and the authentication server.
- **Example:** Implement the OAuth 2.0 authorization code flow with PKCE (Proof Key for Code Exchange) for secure authentication. The PKCE extension enhances security by preventing authorizsation code interception. For even higher assurance, explore emerging standards like FIDO for passwordless authentication.
- **Proper Token Management:** Ensure proper token management to mitigate risks associated with token leakage and misuse. This includes secure storage, transmission, and validation of tokens.
- **Example:** Utilize Google's Firebase Authentication SDK to simplify OAuth 2.0 integration and handle user authentication securely. For device integrity and secure

authentication, integrate Play Integrity API or App Attest alongside SafetyNet (which is being phased out). Firebase Authentication provides built-in methods for secure token management and validation.

OpenID Connect

- **Federated Authentication and SSO:** Leverage OpenID Connect for federated authentication and single sign-on (SSO) capabilities while maintaining security and privacy standards.
- **Example:** Integrate OpenID Connect identity providers such as Google Sign-In or Auth0 for seamless and secure user authentication. This allows users to authenticate using their existing accounts, reducing friction and enhancing security.
- **Secure Configuration:** Configure authentication flows to support various identity providers securely, ensuring that tokens are validated properly.
- **Example:** Configure OpenID Connect clients with appropriate redirect URIs and cryptographic keys to verify ID tokens securely. This ensures that only authorized clients can handle authentication tokens.

JSON Web Tokens (JWT)

- **Secure Data Transmission:** Utilize JWTs for secure transmission of authentication and authorization data between the client and server. JWTs are compact and can be easily transmitted via URLs, headers, or cookies.
- **Example:** Use libraries like Nimbus JOSE + JWT or Auth0's Java JWT library to validate and verify JWTs received from the authentication server. These libraries provide robust methods for parsing, validating, and verifying JWTs.
- **Cryptographic Signing and Integrity:** Employ cryptographic signing to ensure the integrity and authenticity of JWTs throughout their lifecycle. This prevents tampering and ensures that tokens can be trusted.
- **Example:** Implement JWT expiration and token revocation mechanisms to manage the token lifecycle securely. This includes setting short expiration times and providing mechanisms to revoke tokens in case of compromise.

Implementation Strategies

- **Secure Storage:** Store authentication tokens securely using Android's secure storage mechanisms, such as SharedPreferences with encryption or the Android Keystore system.
- **Regular Audits:** Conduct regular security audits of the authentication mechanisms to ensure they remain robust against emerging threats. Automated tools and manual reviews should be used to identify and mitigate potential vulnerabilities.
- **User Education:** Educate users on the importance of security practices such as using strong, unique passwords and enabling multi-factor authentication (MFA) where available.

6.4.5 Application of Secure Coding Practices

Fusing Fidelity with Protection

Beyond standards and libraries, adopting a mindset of security throughout the coding process is crucial. This involves integrating security into every stage of development, from design to deployment, ensuring a holistic approach to protecting the application.

Error Handling

- **Robust Mechanisms:** Implement robust error-handling mechanisms to gracefully handle unexpected situations and prevent information leakage.
- **Example:** Use try-catch blocks and exception-handling mechanisms to handle runtime exceptions and errors without exposing sensitive information. Ensure that error messages do not reveal implementation details that could aid attackers.
- **Secure Logging:** Log errors securely, avoiding the exposure of sensitive information in log files or error messages.
- **Example:** Use Android's logging APIs with appropriate log levels (e.g., Log.d(), Log.e()) to log errors and debug information securely. Ensure sensitive information, such as user data or authentication tokens, is never logged.

Least Privilege Principle

- **Minimal Permissions:** Adhere to the principle of least privilege by granting only necessary permissions and access rights to app components.
- **Example:** Utilize Android's permission system to request and enforce runtime permissions for sensitive operations such as accessing the camera or location. Request permissions only when needed and explain to users why the permissions are necessary.
- **Access Control:** Limit access to sensitive resources based on user roles and privileges to minimize the impact of potential security breaches.
- **Example:** Implement runtime permission checks using ContextCompat.checkSelfPermission() to ensure that the app only accesses permissions granted by the user. Design the application to segregate user roles and enforce access control rules.

Secure Session Management

- **Confidentiality and Integrity:** Implement secure session management techniques to maintain the confidentiality and integrity of user sessions.
- **Example:** Use Android's SharedPreferences API with MODE_PRIVATE to store session tokens securely in encrypted form. Ensure session tokens are handled with care and stored in a manner that prevents unauthorized access.
- **Session Timeout and Revocation:** Enforce session timeouts and implement mechanisms to securely manage session tokens.
- **Example:** Implement secure session cookies with HttpOnly and Secure flags to prevent client-side tampering and protect against session fixation attacks. Enforce session timeouts and provide mechanisms for users to log out and invalidate sessions.

Secure File Handling

- **Protect Sensitive Data:** Apply secure file handling practices to protect sensitive data stored on the device's file system.
- **Example:** Store sensitive files using Android's File Encryption API or encrypt files using AES encryption with randomly generated keys. Ensure that encryption keys are stored securely, preferably using Android's Keystore system.
- **Secure Deletion:** Ensure secure deletion of files to prevent data leakage through file remnants.
- **Example:** Implement secure file deletion using File.delete() with overwrite patterns or secure deletion libraries to ensure that deleted files cannot be recovered.

Implementation Strategies

- **Centralized Security Functions:** Develop centralized functions and utilities for common security tasks such as error handling, logging, permission checks, and encryption. This ensures consistency and reduces the likelihood of security oversights.
- **Regular Security Audits:** Conduct regular security audits and code reviews to identify and mitigate potential vulnerabilities. Automated tools and manual reviews should be used to ensure that secure coding practices are followed consistently.
- **Developer Training:** Provide ongoing training for developers to stay updated on the latest secure coding practices and emerging threats. Training should cover the importance of secure coding and practical techniques for implementing security measures.

6.5 Security Testing

Validating the Fortress

Security testing is a critical phase in the development of any application, particularly for banking apps where sensitive financial data is involved. This phase involves rigorously testing the application to identify and fix security issues using techniques such as static analysis, dynamic analysis, penetration testing, and vulnerability scanning.

Security testing ensures that all components are secure against potential threats and that any vulnerabilities are addressed before deployment. By integrating these security testing techniques into the development workflow, developers can ensure their Android applications are robust and resilient against evolving cyber threats.

6.5.1 Static Code Analysis

Peering into the Source

Static Code Analysis involves scrutinizing the application's source code and its dependencies without executing the program. This process helps identify security vulnerabilities and coding errors early in the development lifecycle, which is both cost-effective and efficient.

- **Tools**
  - **SonarQube:** A widely-used open-source platform for continuous inspection of code quality and security.
  - **Fortify:** Provides comprehensive static analysis to uncover security vulnerabilities.
  - **Checkmarx:** A static analysis tool that scans source code to detect security flaws.
  - **CodeQL:** It is the code analysis engine developed by GitHub to automate security checks. The results are shown as code scanning alerts in GitHub.

- **Best Practices**
  - **Integration with IDE:** Integrate static code analysis tools within the Integrated Development Environment (IDE) to provide real-time feedback to developers, allowing them to address issues as they code.
  - **Automated Scans:** Conduct automated scans regularly to detect potential vulnerabilities such as SQL injection, cross-site scripting (XSS), buffer overflows, and insecure cryptographic algorithms.

- **Thorough Examination:** Examine the application's source code and dependencies to identify security weaknesses and coding errors comprehensively.
- **Detailed Reporting:** Generate detailed reports with recommendations for fixing identified vulnerabilities, prioritizing them based on severity and potential impact. These reports should guide developers on how to address the issues effectively.
- **Education and Training:** Educate developers on common security pitfalls and the importance of addressing identified issues promptly. Continuous learning about the latest security threats and mitigation strategies is crucial.

- **Potential Scenario: Banking App Money Transfer Feature**

In a banking app's money transfer feature, static code analysis helps identify vulnerabilities such as SQL injection. This vulnerability could potentially allow attackers to manipulate transactions or steal sensitive user information. By detecting such issues early, developers can implement necessary security measures, ensuring the robustness of the application's security posture.

6.5.2 Dynamic Application Security Testing (DAST)

Real-time Probes for Robust Defences

Dynamic application security testing (DAST) involves evaluating the security of an application in its running state. This method simulates real-world attack scenarios to identify vulnerabilities that occur during runtime.

- Tools
  - **OWASP ZAP (Zed Attack Proxy):** A popular open-source tool for finding security vulnerabilities in web applications.
  - **Nikto:** An open-source web server scanner that performs comprehensive tests against web servers to identify potential issues and vulnerabilities.
  - **Burp Suite:** A powerful platform for performing security testing of web applications.

- Best Practices
  - **Real-world Attack Scenarios:** Mimic real-world attack scenarios to uncover runtime vulnerabilities by interacting with application interfaces and APIs. This approach helps **identify issues that only manifest when the application is running.**
  - **Security Control Assessment:** Assess the effectiveness of security controls such as input validation, output encoding, authentication, authorization, and session management. Ensure these controls are robust and properly implemented.
  - **Regular Testing:** Conduct DAST regularly to identify newly introduced vulnerabilities during application updates or changes to the underlying infrastructure. This ongoing testing ensures that new code changes do not compromise the application's security.
  - **Detailed Reporting:** Generate comprehensive reports detailing the vulnerabilities discovered, along with recommendations for remediation. Prioritize these vulnerabilities based on their severity and potential impact on the application.

- **Potential Scenario: Banking App Login Process**

During the login process of a banking app, DAST can help identify vulnerabilities such as insecure session management. Such vulnerabilities could potentially allow attackers to hijack user sessions, leading to unauthorized access to user accounts. By regularly conducting

DAST, these issues can be identified and mitigated to ensure secure user authentication and session management.

6.5.3 Mobile Application Security Testing (MAST)

Shielding Mobile Frontiers

Mobile application security testing (MAST) is tailored to address the unique security challenges of mobile applications. For an Android banking application, MAST is essential to ensure the app's robustness against mobile-specific threats.

- Tools
  - **Mobile Security Framework (MobSF):** An open-source framework that performs static and dynamic **analysis of mobile apps, including Android.**
  - **Drozer:** A comprehensive security and attack framework for Android that helps identify and exploit vulnerabilities in mobile applications.

- Best Practices
  - **Client-side Vulnerabilities:** Focus on identifying client-side vulnerabilities such as insecure data storage, improper handling of sensitive information, and weak authentication mechanisms. Ensure that sensitive data is not stored in plaintext and that appropriate encryption methods are used.
  - **Communication Security:** Evaluate the security of communication channels, including SSL/TLS implementation and certificate pinning, to prevent man-in-the-middle (MITM) attacks. Verify that all data transmitted between the mobile app and backend servers is encrypted and properly authenticated.
  - **Device-specific Testing:** Perform device-specific testing to ensure compatibility across different Android versions and device configurations. This includes testing on various devices and emulators to identify platform-specific vulnerabilities.
  - **Third-party Libraries:** Assess the security of third-party libraries and SDKs integrated into the application, as they can introduce vulnerabilities. Ensure these libraries are up-to-date and comply with security best practices.

- Potential Scenario: Biometric Authentication Feature

In the banking app's biometric authentication feature, MAST can help identify vulnerabilities such as insecure data storage of biometric templates. These vulnerabilities could compromise user privacy and authentication security if biometric data is not properly secured. By conducting thorough MAST, these risks can be mitigated, ensuring the secure implementation of biometric authentication.

6.5.4 Penetration Testing (PenTesting)

Simulating Breaches to Strengthening Defences

Penetration Testing involves simulating real-world attacks on an application to uncover vulnerabilities that could be exploited by malicious actors. This method provides a comprehensive assessment of the application's security posture from an attacker's perspective.

- Tools
  - **Metasploit:** An open-source framework for developing, testing, and using exploit code to conduct penetration tests.

- **OpenVAS:** An open-source vulnerability scanner used for network and application penetration testing.
- **Nmap:** A network scanning tool that discovers hosts and services on a network, useful for network reconnaissance and penetration testing.

- Best Practices
  - **Engage Skilled Professionals:** Employ skilled security professionals or ethical hackers to conduct penetration testing. Their expertise ensures a thorough and realistic assessment of the application's security.
  - **Thorough Reconnaissance:** Conduct thorough reconnaissance to identify potential attack vectors, including application endpoints, backend systems, and third-party integrations. This step is crucial for mapping out the attack surface.
  - **Simulate Real-world Attacks:** Simulate a variety of real-world attack scenarios, including network-based attacks, social engineering, and physical security breaches. This comprehensive approach helps identify vulnerabilities that could be exploited in different contexts.
  - **Regular Testing:** Conduct penetration tests regularly, especially after major updates or changes to the application. This ensures that new vulnerabilities are promptly identified and mitigated.
  - **Detailed Reporting:** Generate detailed reports that outline the vulnerabilities discovered, the methods used to exploit them, and the potential impact. Provide prioritized recommendations for remediation based on the severity and exploitability of the vulnerabilities.

- **Potential Scenario: API for Retrieving Account Balances**

In the banking app's API for retrieving account balances, penetration testing can help identify vulnerabilities such as API injection. This type of vulnerability could allow attackers to manipulate the API requests and gain unauthorized access to sensitive account information. By simulating such attacks, penetration testing helps uncover critical weaknesses that need to be addressed to protect user data.

6.5.5 Integration into CI/CD Pipeline

Embedding Security into Every Sprint

Integrating security testing into the Continuous Integration/Continuous Deployment (CI/CD) pipeline, a practice often called 'shifting left,' ensures that security is embedded throughout the development process. This proactive approach facilitates continuous monitoring and swift remediation of security issues.

- Tools
  - **Jenkins:** An open-source automation server that can integrate with various security testing tools for continuous security checks.
  - **GitLab CI/CD:** A comprehensive platform for continuous integration and delivery that supports integration with security testing tools.
  - **CircleCI:** Another CI/CD tool that can automate security testing as part of the development workflow.

- Best Practices
  - **Automated Security Checks:** Integrate security testing tools into the CI/CD pipeline to perform automated security checks at every stage of the development process. This ensures that security vulnerabilities are detected and addressed early.

- **Seamless Integration and Automation:** Utilize open-source CI/CD platforms like Jenkins and GitLab CI for seamless integration and automation. These platforms support various plugins and integrations that facilitate continuous security testing.
- **Trigger Security Tests on Code Commits:** Configure CI/CD pipelines to trigger security tests upon code commits and before deploying changes to production environments. This ensures that every code change is automatically checked for security vulnerabilities.
- **Deployment Gates:** Establish threshold criteria for security test results to prevent the release of vulnerable code. Implement gates that block deployment if critical vulnerabilities are detected, ensuring that only secure code is released to production.
- **Regular Updates and Maintenance:** Regularly update and maintain the security testing suite to address new and emerging threats. Ensure that the CI/CD pipeline is continually improved to enhance security coverage.
- **Container and Infrastructure Security:** Implement container image scanning and runtime protection. Integrate Infrastructure as Code (IaC) security scanning. Apply security policies as code with automated compliance verification.

- Potential Scenario: Banking App Payment Feature

Before deploying updates to the banking app's payment feature, integrating security tests into the CI/CD pipeline ensures that automated security checks are triggered. This process prevents the release of code with critical vulnerabilities that could compromise payment transactions, protecting both the users and the financial institution.

6.6 Code Review

Scrutiny for Strength

Code review is a systematic examination of the source code by peers to identify security flaws and ensure adherence to security standards. It helps to detect issues that automated tools might miss. In the context of Android banking applications, ensuring the security of the codebase is paramount. This section looks into the best practices and processes for effective code reviews in a secure and efficient manner.

6.6.1 Establishing Code Review Processes

Laying the Groundwork for Excellence

Establishing a structured and efficient code review process is essential for maintaining high standards of code quality and security in Android banking applications. The following steps outline how to set up an effective code review process:

- Define Objectives
  - Clearly outline the goals of the code review process, prioritizing security, code quality, and adherence to best practices.
  - Ensure the primary focus is on identifying potential security vulnerabilities and ensuring code efficiency, readability, and maintainability.

- Define Guidelines and Standards
  - Develop clear and concise guidelines and standards for conducting code reviews. These should encompass security best practices, coding conventions, and platform-specific considerations.

- Specify detailed criteria such as the maximum length of code blocks, preferred naming conventions for variables and functions, and common security checks (e.g., input validation, error handling).

- Documentation
  - Document the code review processes comprehensively, outlining the steps involved, roles and responsibilities, and criteria for acceptance.
  - Store this documentation in a centralized location such as a wiki or shared drive for easy access by all team members, ensuring everyone is aligned and informed.

- Assign Roles
  - Designate specific roles within the team, such as the author (developer who wrote the code), reviewer (person responsible for examining the code), and approver (person who finalizes the review process).
  - Establish clear responsibilities for each role to streamline the process and ensure accountability.

- Set Review Criteria
  - Establish clear criteria for when code should be reviewed. For example, all new features, bug fixes, and code changes above a certain threshold (e.g., lines of code changed) should undergo review.
  - Define specific scenarios where reviews are mandatory, such as changes to authentication logic, payment processing functions, or data encryption methods.

- Training
  - Offer training sessions or workshops to educate developers on the code review process, effective feedback techniques, and security principles.
  - Include specialized workshops on secure coding practices, such as mitigating OWASP Top 10 vulnerabilities and how to apply these principles in the context of Android banking applications.

- Implement Tools
  - Use tools like pull requests and automated code review systems to facilitate the review process. These tools help manage the workflow and ensure that all code changes are properly scrutinized.
  - Integrate code review tools with the version control system to streamline the review process and ensure traceability of changes.

- Continuous Improvement
  - Regularly update the code review process based on feedback from team members and evolving security standards.
  - Conduct periodic assessments of the code review process to identify areas for improvement and implement necessary changes.

6.6.2 Conducting Code Review Sessions

Analysing with Rigor

Conducting effective code review sessions is crucial for identifying potential issues, enhancing code quality, and fostering a collaborative environment. Here are the best practices for conducting these sessions:

- **Regular Sessions**
  - **Schedule Regular Code Review Sessions:** Integrate code review sessions into the development workflow, holding them at specific intervals, such as after the completion of a feature or before merging code into the main branch. This ensures that reviews are a consistent part of the development process.
  - **Coordination Tools:** Use tools like Zoom, Slack, or Microsoft Teams to coordinate these sessions and share code snippets for review. These platforms facilitate real-time communication and collaboration among team members.

- **Preparation**
  - **Understand the Context:** Reviewers should prepare by understanding the context of the code changes. This includes reviewing associated documentation, understanding the feature or bug fixes, and familiarizing themselves with relevant parts of the codebase.
  - **Local Testing:** Encourage reviewers to test the code locally, if possible, to gain a better understanding of its functionality and potential issues.

- **Focus on Security**
  - **Identify Security Vulnerabilities:** Emphasize the identification of security vulnerabilities during code reviews. Reviewers should pay special attention to areas prone to security issues, such as input validation, authentication, and data encryption.
  - **Security Checklists:** Implement specific security checklists tailored to banking applications, covering topics like secure data storage, secure communication channels, and protection against common vulnerabilities.

- **Constructive Feedback**
  - **Provide Specific and Actionable Feedback:** Encourage reviewers to provide constructive feedback that is specific, actionable, and respectful. This feedback should focus on improving code quality, addressing security concerns, and promoting best practices.
  - **Use Review Platforms:** Platforms like GitHub Pull Requests or GitLab Merge Requests provide features for commenting directly on lines of code, making it easier to provide targeted feedback and suggestions.

- **Collaborative Approach**
  - **Foster a Collaborative Environment:** Encourage a collaborative and respectful environment where team members feel comfortable discussing potential issues and suggesting improvements. Open communication and constructive feedback are key to effective reviews.
  - **Document Review Decisions:** Ensure that review decisions and discussions are documented, helping maintain a clear record of changes and the rationale behind them.

- **Knowledge Exchange**
  - **Mentorship Opportunities:** Use code review sessions as opportunities for knowledge exchange and mentorship. Experienced developers can share their insights and best practices with less experienced team members, fostering a culture of learning and growth within the team.
  - **Dedicated Channels for Discussion:** Use platforms like Slack or Discord to create dedicated channels for discussing code review findings and sharing insights. This helps in building a repository of knowledge and facilitating ongoing learning.

- Follow-up
  - **Ensure Feedback is Addressed**: Ensure that feedback is addressed and verify that changes are re-reviewed if necessary. This follow-up is essential to ensure that all identified issues are resolved.
  - **Track and Resolve Comments**: Establish a process for tracking and resolving review comments to ensure that nothing is overlooked and all issues are adequately addressed.

6.6.3 Leveraging Tools for Code Review

Technology as a Trustworthy Ally

Utilizing specialized tools can significantly enhance the code review process by automating checks, improving collaboration, and increasing efficiency. Here are key tools and best practices for leveraging them:

- Code Review Tools
  - **Integrated Platforms**: Utilize code review tools integrated into popular version control platforms such as GitHub, GitLab, or Bitbucket. These platforms offer robust features to facilitate thorough reviews.
  - **Pull Requests/Merge Requests**: Developers can create pull requests or merge requests, which peers can then review before merging into the main codebase. AI-powered code review tools like GitHub Copilot and Amazon CodeWhisperer can now assist in identifying potential security issues during the review process.
  - **Inline Comments and Code Diff Views**: These tools provide features like inline comments, where reviewers can comment directly on specific lines of code, and code diff views, which highlight changes between different versions of the code. This makes it easier to understand changes and provide targeted feedback.
  - **Automatic Code Formatting**: Utilize automatic code formatting features to enforce consistent coding standards and reduce the time spent on stylistic issues during reviews.

- Automated Testing
  - **Security and Unit Tests**: Integrate automated testing tools to run security tests, unit tests, and integration tests as part of the review process. Tools like Jenkins, CircleCI, or Travis CI can help automate these tests, ensuring that code changes are thoroughly tested before being merged.
  - **OWASP ZAP and Burp Suite**: Use security-focused testing tools to identify vulnerabilities in the application during the review process. Modern DAST tools now incorporate AI-based vulnerability detection and can integrate directly with CI/CD pipelines for continuous security testing.

- Issue Tracking
  - **Integration with Issue Trackers**: Link code review tools with issue tracking systems like JIRA to ensure that identified issues are tracked and resolved. This integration helps maintain a clear record of all identified issues and their resolution status.
  - **Prioritization and Management**: Use issue tracking to prioritize and manage the remediation of security vulnerabilities identified during code reviews. This ensures that critical issues are addressed promptly and efficiently.

- Feedback and Updates
  - **Feedback and Adaptation:** Regularly review the effectiveness of the tools and processes in place. Gather feedback from developers on the utility of the tools and make adjustments as necessary to improve the code review process.
  - **Tool Updates:** Stay updated with the latest features and improvements in the tools being used, ensuring that the development team benefits from the most advanced and efficient tools available.

6.6.4 Emphasizing Secure Coding Patterns

Crafting Code with Integrity

Promoting secure coding patterns during code reviews is essential to prevent vulnerabilities and ensure the robustness of an Android banking application. Here are key secure coding practices to emphasize:

- Input Validation
  - **Sanitization and Validation:** Implement robust input validation mechanisms to ensure that all user input is properly sanitized and validated before being processed by the application. This helps prevent common vulnerabilities such as injection attacks (e.g., SQL injection, cross-site scripting (XSS)).
  - **Whitelist Approach:** Use a whitelist approach for input validation, where only explicitly allowed characters and formats are accepted. This minimizes the risk of malicious input.
  - **Validation Libraries:** Utilize validation libraries and frameworks that provide built-in functions for common validation tasks, ensuring consistency and reducing the likelihood of errors.

- Output Encoding
  - **Sanitize User-generated Content:** Apply output encoding techniques to sanitize user-generated content, preventing XSS attacks. This involves encoding data before rendering it in HTML or other output formats to ensure it is safely displayed.
  - **Encoding Libraries:** Use libraries like OWASP Encoder to handle encoding tasks efficiently. These libraries provide functions to encode user input for various contexts, such as HTML, JavaScript, and URLs.

- Parameterized Queries
  - **Database Interactions:** Use parameterized queries or prepared statements when interacting with databases to prevent SQL injection attacks. This ensures that user input is treated as data rather than executable code.
  - **ORM Support:** Most modern ORM (Object-relational Mapping) libraries provide built-in support for parameterized queries, making it easy to implement and enforce this best practice across the application.

- Secure Configuration Management
  - **Sensitive Information Storage:** Store sensitive configuration settings (e.g., API keys, database credentials) securely and avoid hardcoding them in the source code. This helps protect sensitive information from unauthorized access.
  - **Environment Variables:** Use environment variables to manage sensitive information, ensuring that credentials are not exposed in the codebase. Configure these variables securely on the deployment environment.

- **Configuration Files:** Use configuration files with restricted access permissions to store sensitive settings. Ensure that these files are protected from unauthorized access and are not included in version control systems.
- **Secrets Management Tools:** Utilize secrets management tools like HashiCorp Vault to securely store and manage sensitive information. These tools provide robust access control and encryption mechanisms to protect secrets.

- **Error Handling**
  - **Safe Error Messages:** Implement error handling practices that do not expose sensitive information. Error messages should be user-friendly but should not reveal internal logic, stack traces, or sensitive data.
  - **Logging Practices:** Ensure logging practices capture relevant information for debugging and security monitoring without logging sensitive information. Use secure logging frameworks to handle logs appropriately.

- **Dependency Management**
  - **Regular Updates:** Regularly update third-party libraries and frameworks to mitigate risks from known vulnerabilities. Use tools like Dependabot or Snyk for dependency management to automate the detection of outdated or vulnerable dependencies.
  - **Security Advisories:** Monitor security advisories related to your dependencies and act promptly to apply necessary updates and patches.

6.6.5 *Fostering a Culture of Continuous Improvement*

Evolving Together for Lasting Quality

Creating a culture of continuous improvement within the development team is vital for maintaining high standards of code quality and security in an Android banking application. Here are strategies to foster this culture effectively:

- Collective Ownership
  - **Shared Responsibility:** Cultivate a sense of collective ownership within the development team, where everyone takes responsibility for the quality and security of the codebase. Emphasize that security is a shared responsibility, not just the concern of a few specialists.
  - **Regular Team Meetings:** Conduct regular team meetings and retrospectives to discuss the state of the codebase, review recent code changes, and identify any emerging issues or trends.
  - **Shared Accountability:** Reinforce shared accountability for code reviews by involving all team members in the process, ensuring that everyone contributes to maintaining high standards.

- Active Participation
  - **Set Clear Expectations:** Encourage active participation in code reviews by setting clear expectations for all team members to review and provide feedback on code changes. Make it part of the team's regular workflow.
  - **Review Dashboards:** Utilize code review dashboards and metrics to track participation, identify bottlenecks, and ensure that reviews are completed in a timely manner. Tools like GitHub Insights or GitLab Analytics can provide valuable data on review activity.

- **Incentives and Recognition:** Recognize and reward active participation and valuable contributions to code reviews to motivate team members and highlight the importance of the process.

- Learning from Reviews
  - **Identify Patterns and Issues:** Treat code reviews as learning opportunities to identify common patterns, recurring issues, and areas for improvement. Document these findings and share them with the team to promote collective learning.
  - **Knowledge Sharing Sessions:** Organize regular knowledge-sharing sessions or lunch-and-learn events where developers can present insights and lessons learned from recent code reviews.
  - **Documentation of Best Practices:** Maintain and regularly update documentation of best practices, common pitfalls, and effective solutions identified during code reviews. This helps in building a repository of knowledge that new and existing team members can refer to.

- Continuous Feedback Loop
  - **Integrated Feedback Mechanism:** Establish a continuous feedback loop between code reviews, development, and testing phases. Use feedback from code reviews to inform future development efforts, identify areas for additional testing, and refine coding standards and guidelines over time.
  - **Iterative Improvement:** Encourage iterative improvement by regularly revisiting and refining coding standards based on the feedback received. This ensures that standards evolve in line with emerging best practices and project needs.
  - **Cross-functional Collaboration:** Promote collaboration between development, testing, and security teams to ensure that feedback from each phase is integrated into the overall development process, leading to a more cohesive and secure codebase.

- Emphasize Security Awareness
  - **Security Training:** Provide ongoing training and resources to keep developers up-to-date with the latest security practices, trends, and threats. This helps in fostering a proactive security mindset.

- Security Champions:
  - Identify and empower security champions within the team who can advocate for security best practices and provide guidance during code reviews.
  - Security champions can act as liaisons between the development team and the security team, ensuring that security considerations are integrated into all stages of development.
  - Encourage security champions to stay current with the latest security trends and share their knowledge with the team through regular updates and workshops.

- Retrospectives and Continuous Improvement
  - **Regular Retrospectives:** Conduct regular retrospectives focused on the code review process itself. Discuss what is working well, what challenges are being faced, and how the process can be improved.
  - **Actionable Insights:** Derive actionable insights from retrospectives and implement changes to the code review process to address any identified issues or inefficiencies.

6.7 Security Training

Empowering Minds for Defence

Security training involves educating developers and stakeholders about the latest security threats, secure coding practices, and the importance of maintaining security throughout the SDLC. For a banking application, continuous security training ensures that the development team is equipped to handle evolving security challenges and implement robust security measures. This section outlines the key aspects of establishing and maintaining a robust security training program.

To ensure the effectiveness of security training programs, organizations should regularly assess participants' knowledge through quizzes, practical exercises, and simulated phishing attacks. Feedback from participants can also help refine the training curriculum and address any gaps in understanding.

6.7.1 Structured Security Training Curriculum

Building Blocks for Expertise

A structured security training curriculum should be meticulously designed to cover all aspects of application security relevant to Android applications. It should be designed to equip development teams with the knowledge and skills necessary to address security concerns in mobile application development.

Here are the detailed components:

- **Android-specific Security:** Covers platform security features (sandboxing, permissions model), common vulnerabilities (insecure storage, cryptography, communication), and secure coding best practices.
- **Secure Coding Practices:** Teaches defensive coding against vulnerabilities like SQL injection and XSS, and adheres to standards like OWASP and CERT Secure Coding.
- **Threat Modelling:** Focuses on identifying threats and using frameworks like STRIDE and DREAD to mitigate them.
- **Cryptography Fundamentals:** Introduces encryption, hashing, digital signatures, and secure protocols (AES, RSA).
- **Authentication Mechanisms:** Includes multi-factor authentication and OAuth alongside traditional methods.
- **Secure Communication Protocols:** Highlights HTTPS/TLS importance and configuration for data protection.
- **Secure Development Methodologies:** Integrates security practices into SDLC and DevSecOps phases to proactively address vulnerabilities.

6.7.2 Delivery Methods

Bridging Knowledge with Engagement

A variety of delivery methods ensures the training program is accessible, engaging, and effective. Here are the expanded options:

- **Instructor-led Sessions**
  - **Interactive Presentations:** Conducting interactive presentations led by experienced security professionals to engage participants and encourage discussions.

- **Live Demonstrations:** Performing live demonstrations of security concepts and techniques to enhance understanding.

- **Hands-on Exercises**
  - **Simulation Exercises:** Creating simulated environments where developers can practice identifying and mitigating security vulnerabilities in realistic scenarios.
  - **Capture the Flag (CTF) Challenges:** Organizing CTF challenges to gamify learning and encourage competition among participants.

- **Internal Documentation and Tutorials**
  - **Comprehensive Guides:** Detailed documents covering security protocols, processes, and practices.
  - **Video Tutorials:** Step-by-step visual guides for implementing security measures.

- **Workshops and Bootcamps**
  - **Intensive Learning:** Short, focused sessions that dive deep into specific security topics.
  - **Real-world Scenarios:** Case studies and live exercises to simulate real-world attacks and defences.

6.7.3 Online Resources

Learning Beyond Boundaries

Online resources can complement formal training, providing continuous education opportunities:

- **Access to Platforms**
  - **OWASP Mobile Security Project:** Providing access to resources such as the OWASP Mobile Security Testing Guide and OWASP Mobile Top 10.
  - **Coursera and Udemy Courses:** Recommending courses covering topics like mobile application security, cryptography, and secure coding practices.

- **Self-paced Learning Modules**
  - **Interactive Labs:** Offering interactive labs where developers can experiment with security tools and techniques at their own pace.
  - **Quizzes and Assessments:** Incorporating quizzes and assessments to reinforce learning and measure progress.

- **Educational Materials**
  - **Whitepapers and Case Studies:** Sharing whitepapers and case studies highlighting real-world security incidents and their lessons learned.
  - **Webinars:** Educational sessions hosted by industry leaders and vendors.

- **Forums and Community Groups**
  - **Stack Overflow:** A platform for getting answers to specific security-related programming questions.
  - **Reddit's r/cybersecurity:** A community for technical professionals to discuss cybersecurity news, research, threats, etc.
  - **LinkedIn Groups:** Professional groups focusing on cybersecurity and mobile security.

6.7.4 Certification Pathways

Marking Milestones of Mastery

Certifications validate the skills and knowledge of your team, ensuring they are up-to-date with the latest security practices:

- **Encouraging Certification**
  - **Training Support**: Offering training materials and resources to help developers prepare for certification exams.
  - **Exam Reimbursement**: Providing financial incentives such as exam fee reimbursements for developers who successfully obtain security certifications.

- **Validation of Expertise**
  - **Badge Programs**: Recognizing certified individuals with badges or credentials within the organization to showcase their expertise and promote their contributions to security.

- **Certifications**
  - Certified Information Systems Security Professional (CISSP):
    - Comprehensive Coverage: Covers eight domains of cybersecurity, including security and risk management, application development security, and more.
    - Industry Recognition: Widely recognized and respected certification.
  - Certified Secure Software Lifecycle Professional (CSSLP):
    - Focus on SDLC: Emphasizes incorporating security into all phases of the software development lifecycle.
    - Skill Validation: Validates skills in secure coding, threat modelling, and risk management.
  - GIAC Mobile Device Security Analyst (GMOB):
    - Specialized Knowledge: Focuses on mobile device security, including Android and iOS.
    - Practical Skills: Teaches practical skills for securing mobile devices and applications.
  - Google's Associate Android Developer Certification:
    - Android Expertise: Ensures a solid understanding of Android development, which is crucial for implementing robust security measures.

6.7.5 Cultivating a Security-Conscious Culture

From Awareness to Action

Building a security-conscious culture is essential for long-term security success:

- **Collaboration and Knowledge Sharing**
  - **Security Forums and Discussion Boards**: Establishing forums and discussion boards where developers can ask questions, share experiences, and seek advice from peers and experts.
  - **Internal Security Workshops**: Hosting regular workshops where developers can showcase their security-related projects and exchange ideas with colleagues.

- **Mentorship Programs**
  - **Pairing Mentors and Mentees:** Pairing junior developers with experienced mentors who can provide guidance, support, and feedback on security-related projects.
  - **Structured Mentorship Plans:** Developing structured mentorship plans outlining goals, milestones, and learning objectives for mentees.

- **Supportive Environment**
  - **Open-door Policy:** Encouraging an open-door policy where developers feel comfortable reaching out to security experts and leaders for assistance and guidance.
  - **Feedback Mechanisms:** Implementing feedback mechanisms to gather input from developers on the effectiveness of training programs and identify areas for improvement.
  - **Security Newsletters:** Regular updates on the latest security trends and threats.

6.7.6 Free/Open-source Tools and Resources

Empowering with Accessible Solutions

Utilizing free and open-source tools and resources can provide significant advantages for hands-on learning and practical application of security concepts:

- **MobSF (Mobile Security Framework):** A powerful framework for automated security testing of Android and iOS applications. Combines static, dynamic, and malware analysis for comprehensive security assessments.
- **OWASP Mobile Security Project:** Provides a wealth of free resources including guides, tools, and best practices for securing mobile applications.
- **Open Web Application Security Project (OWASP):** Offers free online courses, webinars, and documentation covering various aspects of application security, including mobile security.
- **SANS Institute:** Provides free whitepapers, webcasts, and newsletters focusing on cybersecurity topics, including mobile application security.
- **Coursera and Udemy:** While some courses may require payment, both platforms offer free courses on cybersecurity fundamentals and secure coding practices.
- **Capture the Flag (CTF) Platforms:** Many CTF platforms, such as Hack The Box and OverTheWire, offer free challenges and exercises for practizing and improving cybersecurity skills, including mobile security.

6.8 Secure Deployment

Launching with Confidence

Secure deployment practices are essential to ensure that an Android banking application is securely released into the production environment. This involves configuring servers, securing APIs, setting up secure communication channels, and maintaining ongoing vigilance to protect user data and financial transactions. A secure deployment strategy ensures that the application is resilient to attacks from the moment it goes live. This section outlines best practices and strategies for securely deploying an Android banking application.

In addition to secure deployment practices, it is essential to have a rollback plan in case of a failed deployment. Automated rollback mechanisms can help quickly revert to a stable version of the app, minimizing downtime and reducing the risk of security incidents.

6.8.1 Establishing Robust Deployment Pipelines

Streamlining Secure Deliveries

A robust deployment pipeline ensures consistent and reliable application deployments, minimizing the risk of introducing vulnerabilities during the deployment process. By integrating modern DevSecOps practices and continuous integration/continuous deployment (CI/CD) pipelines, teams can automate and secure their deployment workflows effectively.

Utilizing Modern DevSecOps Practices

DevSecOps integrates security into every stage of the software development life cycle (SDLC), promoting collaboration between development, security, and operations teams to ensure a secure deployment process.

- Comprehensive DevSecOps Approach
  - **Integration into SDLC:** Embed security practices into each phase of the SDLC, including planning, coding, testing, and deployment. Security should be a continuous focus rather than an afterthought.
  - **Maturity Assessment:** Utilize frameworks like the OWASP DevSecOps Maturity Model to assess and improve the maturity of your DevSecOps practices. Regular assessments help identify gaps and areas for improvement.
  - **Supply Chain Security:** Implement Software Bill of Materials (SBOM) generation and verification using tools like Syft and Grype to track and secure third-party dependencies throughout the development pipeline.

- Security Testing in CI/CD
  - **Dynamic Application Security Testing (DAST):** Incorporate tools like OWASP ZAP to perform automated dynamic security testing as part of the CI/CD pipeline. This helps identify runtime vulnerabilities.
  - **Static Application Security Testing (SAST):** Use tools like SonarQube for continuous code quality inspection and to detect code quality issues and potential vulnerabilities early in the development process.
  - **Dependency Management:** Implement Software Component Analysis (SCA) tools to scan for known vulnerabilities in dependencies for comprehensive supply chain security, ensuring that external components do not introduce security risks.

- Potential Example
  - **Feature Security:** When introducing features like peer-to-peer (P2P) payments, apply DevSecOps practices to ensure the security of transaction data and user information. Perform thorough security testing to validate the confidentiality and integrity of these transactions.

Continuous Integration/Continuous Deployment (CI/CD) Pipelines

CI/CD pipelines automate the build, test, and deployment processes, ensuring that code changes are consistently and reliably integrated and delivered.

- **Automated Builds and Tests**
  - **Continuous Integration (CI):** Utilize CI tools such as Jenkins, GitLab CI, or CircleCI to automate the process of building and testing your application. Every

code change should trigger a build and run a suite of automated tests, including unit tests, integration tests, and security tests.
- **Continuous Delivery (CD):** Implement continuous delivery to automate the deployment process to staging and production environments, ensuring that code changes are consistently and reliably deployed.

- **Staging Environments**
  - **Mirror Production:** Set up a staging environment that closely resembles your production environment. This helps in identifying and resolving issues that might not be apparent in a development setting.
  - **End-to-end Testing:** Perform thorough end-to-end testing in the staging environment to validate the functionality and security of the application before it goes live.

- **Code Reviews and Static Analysis**
  - **Peer Reviews:** Enforce mandatory code reviews by peers to ensure that every code change is scrutinized for potential security issues and adherence to coding standards.
  - **Static Analysis Tools:** Use static analysis tools like SonarQube or Veracode to automatically analyse your code for vulnerabilities, coding errors, and compliance with security best practices.

- **Infrastructure-as-Code (IaC)**
  - **Automation Tools:** Utilize IaC tools such as Terraform or Ansible to automate the provisioning and configuration of development, testing, and production environments. This ensures consistency across environments and reduces the risk of configuration drift.

6.8.2 Secure Code Signing Practices

Authenticating Every Byte

Secure code signing is essential for ensuring the authenticity and integrity of your Android banking application, preventing tampering and unauthorized modifications. This section outlines best practices for managing cryptographic keys, using digital certificates, and handling key rotation and revocation.

Cryptographic Key Management

Proper management of cryptographic keys is crucial for maintaining the security of code signing processes.

- **Safeguarding Cryptographic Keys**
  - **Key Storage:** Utilize hardware security modules (HSMs) or secure key management services offered by cloud providers (e.g., AWS KMS, Google Cloud KMS, Azure Key Vault) to store and protect sensitive cryptographic keys. Consider implementing Confidential Computing solutions for additional protection of keys in use.
  - **Open-Source Solutions:** Leverage Android App Signing with Google Play's key management or HashiCorp Vault for secure key storage and management.

- Access Controls
  - **Restrict Access:** Limit access to signing keys to authorized personnel only, employing strict access controls to prevent unauthorized access.
  - **Multifactor Authentication (MFA):** Implement MFA to enhance the security of access to signing keys, ensuring that only authorized users can access them.

Key Rotation and Revocation

Regularly rotating and revoking keys is vital to maintaining the security of your application over time.

- Regular Rotation
  - **Periodic Rotation:** Implement policies for periodic rotation of signing keys to reduce the risk of key compromise. Regularly rotating keys help maintain the security of your application.
  - **Automated Processes:** Utilize automated processes and tools to facilitate the regular rotation of keys, ensuring that key rotation is performed consistently and without errors.

- Compromise Handling
  - **Compromise Response:** Establish procedures for responding to key compromise incidents. This includes revoking compromised keys and re-signing applications with new keys to maintain the integrity and trust of your application.
  - **Communication Plans:** Develop communication plans to inform stakeholders, including users and partners, in the event of a key compromise to maintain transparency and trust.

Digital Certificates from Trusted CAs

Obtaining digital certificates from reputable CAs ensures the authenticity and integrity of your application.

- Use Strong Certificates
  - **Cryptographic Keys:** Generate and use strong cryptographic keys (2048-bit RSA or higher) for signing your APK files. This ensures that the signed code cannot be easily forged.
  - **Trusted CAs:** Obtain digital certificates from reputable CAs such as Let's Encrypt, DigiCert, or GlobalSign to validate the identity of the code publisher.

- Enhanced Certificate Security
  - **Certificate Transparency Logs:** Implement certificate transparency logs to monitor and verify the issuance of digital certificates, ensuring that no unauthorized certificates are issued for your application.
  - **Certificate Pinning:** Leverage open-source certificate pinning libraries like TrustKit or OkHttp to defend against man-in-the-middle attacks by ensuring your application only trusts specific certificates.

6.8.3 App Permission Configuration

Balancing Access with Assurance

Properly configuring app permissions is critical to minimizing the attack surface and protecting user privacy. This involves adhering to the principle of least privilege, utilizing runtime permissions effectively, and regularly reviewing and auditing permissions.

Principle of Least Privilege

Applying the principle of least privilege ensures that your application only requests access to the minimum set of permissions required for its intended functionality.

- **Minimal Permissions**
  - **Necessary Permissions Only:** Request only the permissions that are absolutely necessary for the app's functionality. Avoid requesting permissions that could compromise user privacy or security.
  - **Permission Groups:** Use Android's permission groups to limit the scope of permissions requested. Grouping permissions helps manage and reduce unnecessary access.

- **Potential Example**
  - **Accessing Contacts:** When accessing contacts for features like peer-to-peer (P2P) payments, request contacts access only when initiating a transaction to minimize data exposure. This ensures that the permission is used contextually and only when necessary.

Runtime Permission Enforcement

Implementing runtime permission checks within the application enhances transparency and user control over data access.

- **User Consent**
  - **Runtime Permission Model:** Utilize Android's runtime permission model to request permissions at runtime, providing users with context and explanations for why the permissions are needed. This helps users make informed decisions about granting permissions.
  - **User-friendly Libraries:** Employ open-source libraries like Dexter or EasyPermissions for managing runtime permissions in a user-friendly manner. These libraries simplify the process of requesting and handling permissions dynamically.

- **Graceful Handling**
  - **Handle Denials:** Gracefully handle scenarios where users deny permissions, ensuring that the app continues to function with limited capabilities. Provide alternative functionality or inform users about the limitations caused by denied permissions.

Review and Audit Permissions Regularly

Regularly reviewing and auditing the permissions your app requests is essential to ensure they are still necessary as the app evolves.

- Periodic Audits
  - **Regular Reviews:** Conduct regular audits of the permissions your app requests to ensure they remain necessary. As your app's features evolve, some permissions might no longer be required and should be removed to reduce potential security risks.
  - **Automated Tools:** Use automated tools to analyse and audit permissions periodically, ensuring compliance with the principle of least privilege.

- User Feedback
  - **Collect Feedback:** Collect and analyse user feedback regarding permissions to identify potential concerns or unnecessary permissions. Users can provide valuable insights into which permissions they find intrusive or unnecessary.
  - **Respond to Concerns:** Address user feedback by adjusting the requested permissions and providing clear communication about why certain permissions are necessary.

6.8.4 Secure Update Mechanisms

Keeping Applications Future-Ready

Maintaining the security of an application post-deployment involves implementing secure update mechanisms to ensure the integrity and authenticity of updates, as well as managing their distribution effectively.

Signed Updates

Ensuring that updates are properly signed is crucial for preventing unauthorized modifications.

- Integrity Checks
  - **Cryptographic Signing:** Ensure that all updates are cryptographically signed with the same key used for the initial release. This helps prevent unauthorized modifications and ensures the authenticity of the updates.
  - **Version Control:** Implement strict version control and validation mechanisms to ensure that only authorized updates are applied. This includes maintaining a record of all released versions and their signatures.

Update Validation

Implementing robust validation mechanisms ensures that updates are authentic and have not been tampered with.

- Integrity Verification
  - **Checksum Verification:** Use checksum verification to confirm the integrity of the update files. This ensures that the files have not been altered during the update process.
  - **Signature Validation:** Validate the cryptographic signatures of updates before applying them to ensure their authenticity and integrity.

- Rollback Mechanisms
  - **Revert Updates:** Provide the ability to rollback updates in case of issues. This ensures the application can revert to a stable state if an update introduces problems.

Gradual Rollouts

Deploying updates incrementally helps in detecting and addressing issues early without affecting the entire user base.

- **Phased Deployment**
  - **Incremental Rollouts:** Use gradual rollouts to deploy updates to a subset of users initially. This approach helps identify potential issues early and limits the impact on the entire user base.
  - **User Feedback:** Collect and analyse user feedback during the rollout process to quickly identify and address any issues.

Over-the-Air (OTA) Updates

Using secure protocols and tools for delivering OTA updates ensures the confidentiality and integrity of the update process.

- **Secure Protocols**
  - **HTTPS Delivery:** Implement secure protocols such as HTTPS for delivering OTA updates. This ensures that the updated data is encrypted during transmission, protecting it from interception and tampering.
- **Open-Source Tools**
  - **Play Integrity API:** Use Google Play's In-App Update API with Play Integrity API for secure OTA updates, ensuring device and app integrity during the update process.

App Store Distribution Channels

Leveraging official app stores for distributing updates ensures the updates are delivered securely and reach a wide audience.

- **Official App Stores**
  - **Google Play Store:** Publish updates through official app stores to leverage their built-in security measures. These platforms provide a secure and reliable way to distribute updates to a wide audience.
- **Automation Tools**
  - **Fastlane:** Utilize open-source tools like Fastlane to automate the deployment and release process to multiple app stores simultaneously. This streamlines the update process and ensures consistency across different platforms.

6.8.5 Integration of Monitoring and Logging

Proactive Visibility in Action

Effective monitoring and logging are essential for detecting and responding to security incidents in real time. This involves logging sensitive actions, using a Security Information and Event Management (SIEM) system, setting up alerting mechanisms, ensuring real-time visibility, and maintaining incident response readiness.

Log Sensitive Actions

Logging security-relevant actions helps in tracking and investigating potential security incidents.

- **Action Logging**
  - **Security-relevant Actions:** Log actions such as authentication attempts, changes to user accounts, and significant financial transactions. These logs are crucial for auditing and forensic analysis.
  - **Anonymization:** Ensure that logs do not contain sensitive information like passwords or personally identifiable information (PII) in plaintext. Use anonymization techniques to protect user privacy.

Use a SIEM

A SIEM system centralizes log collection and analysis, providing a comprehensive view of security events.

- **Centralized Logging**
- **Integration with SIEM:** Integrate with an SIEM system to centralize log collection and analysis. This helps in correlating events from different sources and identifying potential security threats.
- **Real-time Analysis:** Utilize the SIEM for real-time analysis and correlation of log data to detect and respond to suspicious activities promptly.

Alerting

Setting up alerts based on predefined thresholds helps in the early detection of unusual or suspicious activities.

- **Thresholds and Triggers**
  - **Define Alerts:** Set up alerts for unusual or suspicious activities based on predefined thresholds and triggers. Alerts should be actionable and specific to potential security threats.
  - **Incident Response:** Establish and document incident response procedures to ensure prompt and effective action in case of a security breach. Regularly update and test these procedures to maintain readiness.

Real-time Visibility

Real-time visibility into application performance and security events is crucial for proactive security management.

- **Monitoring Tools**
  - **Prometheus and Grafana:** Integrate open-source monitoring tools like Prometheus and Grafana for real-time visibility into application performance metrics, resource utilization, and security-related events.
  - **Custom Metrics and Dashboards:** Implement custom metrics and dashboards to monitor critical security indicators and detect anomalies or suspicious activities.

- **Example Use Case**
  - **P2P Payment Monitoring:** Monitor peer-to-peer (P2P) payment transactions in real time to detect anomalies or suspicious activities that may indicate fraudulent behaviour.

Anomaly Detection

Using machine learning for anomaly detection helps in identifying deviations from normal behaviour that may indicate security threats.

- **Machine Learning Algorithms**
  - **Anomaly Detection Models:** Utilize machine learning algorithms and open-source libraries like TensorFlow or Apache Spark for anomaly detection. These models help identify deviations from normal behaviour that may indicate security threats or unauthorized access.
  - **Tailored Detection Models:** Implement anomaly detection models tailored to detect specific security threats relevant to banking applications, such as account takeover attempts or fraudulent transactions.

Incident Response Readiness

Maintaining incident response readiness ensures that your organization can promptly detect, analyse, and remediate security incidents.

- **Incident Response Procedures**
  - **Frameworks and Playbooks:** Establish incident response procedures and playbooks using open-source incident response frameworks like TheHive or MISP. These tools facilitate prompt detection, analysis, and remediation of security incidents.
  - **Centralized SIEM Solutions:** Leverage open-source SIEM solutions like OSSIM or Elastic Stack for centralized logging, correlation, and analysis of security-related events across the application infrastructure.

6.8.6 Compliance and Regulatory Considerations

Aligning with Standards of Trust

Ensuring compliance with relevant laws and regulations is crucial for the secure deployment of an Android banking application. This involves adhering to industry standards, staying informed about regulatory requirements, obtaining user consent, and conducting regular audits.

Adherence to Industry Standards

Complying with industry standards helps ensure the security and integrity of your application.

- **PCI DSS (Payment Card Industry Data Security Standard)**
  - **Payment Data Security:** If your app handles payment card information, comply with PCI DSS to protect cardholder data. This includes implementing strong encryption and secure transmission protocols to protect payment data during transactions.

- **Compliance Frameworks:** Use open-source compliance frameworks and check-lists provided by organizations like OWASP to guide your adherence to PCI DSS requirements.

- **GDPR (General Data Protection Regulation)**
  - **Data Handling:** Ensure your app complies with GDPR and other data protection regulations, which dictate how user data should be handled, stored, and transmitted.
  - **User Consent:** Obtain explicit user consent for data collection and processing activities, providing clear and transparent information about how user data will be used.

- **Regular Audits and Assessments**
  - **Security Assessments:** Conduct regular security audits and assessments to ensure ongoing compliance with relevant standards and regulations. Utilize open-source vulnerability scanners and compliance automation tools to identify and remediate security gaps.
  - **Third-party Audits:** Engage independent third-party auditors to validate your app's compliance and identify potential security gaps. Regular third-party audits provide an objective assessment of your security posture.

Regulatory Requirements

Staying informed about and complying with regulatory requirements specific to the banking industry and mobile applications is essential.

- **Regulatory Intelligence**
  - **Stay Informed:** Stay informed about regulatory requirements by leveraging open-source resources such as compliance libraries, templates, and regulatory intelligence feeds available on platforms like GitHub or OWASP.
  - **Banking Industry Regulations:** Monitor regulatory requirements specific to the banking industry to ensure that your app remains compliant with all applicable laws and standards.

- **Implementation and Documentation**
  - **Compliance Documentation:** Maintain comprehensive documentation of your compliance efforts, including policies, procedures, and evidence of adherence to regulatory requirements. This documentation is essential for demonstrating compliance during audits and assessments.
  - **Automated Compliance Tools:** Utilize automated compliance tools to streamline the process of adhering to regulatory requirements. These tools can help monitor compliance status and generate reports for audit purposes.

6.9 Monitoring and Maintenance

From Stability to Sustainability

Post-deployment, continuous monitoring and maintenance are essential to detect and respond to security incidents. This includes monitoring application logs, updating security patches, and regularly auditing the application's security posture. For banking applications, ongoing monitoring helps identify and mitigate security threats in real time, ensuring the continued safety of user data and transactions.

When vulnerabilities are discovered during monitoring, it is crucial to prioritize them based on their severity and potential impact. High-risk vulnerabilities, such as those that could lead to data breaches or financial losses, should be addressed immediately, while lower-risk issues can be scheduled for future updates.

This section explores how adopting these practices can significantly enhance the security, performance, and longevity the Android apps.

6.9.1 Advanced Monitoring Solutions

Staying Ahead with Intelligent Insights

Advanced monitoring solutions are critical for maintaining the security, performance, and reliability of an Android banking application. These solutions leverage cutting-edge technologies to provide comprehensive visibility into the application's operations and user interactions. Key features are as following:

Real-time Analytics

Tools like Splunk, Dynatrace, and modern observability platforms like Grafana and OpenTelemetry collect and analyse data as it is generated, monitoring user transactions, login attempts, and API calls with enhanced ML-based anomaly detection.

- **Potential Scenario:** The real-time analytics tool detects a sudden increase in failed login attempts, triggering an alert for immediate investigation. This could indicate a brute-force attack on user accounts, allowing security teams to respond swiftly and mitigate the threat.

Anomaly Detection

Machine learning algorithms recognize normal behaviour patterns and flag deviations as anomalies.

- **Potential Scenario:** Anomaly detection flags a series of transactions initiated from a new geographic location for a specific user account. This triggers an alert for further investigation to determine if the account has been compromised, potentially preventing fraudulent activity.

User Activity Monitoring

Detailed monitoring of user actions helps detect potentially malicious activities.

- **Potential Scenario:** User activity monitoring detects a sudden spike in transaction volume for a specific user account outside of normal behaviour patterns. This raises suspicion of fraudulent activity, prompting immediate action to secure the account and prevent further unauthorized transactions.

Performance Metrics

Performance metrics help identify performance bottlenecks and ensure the application remains responsive and reliable.

- **Potential Scenario:** Performance metrics reveal a significant increase in response times during peak usage hours, indicating a potential server overload. This prompts proactive measures to optimize server resources and maintain optimal application performance during high-traffic periods.

Log Management

Centralized log management solutions like the ELK Stack (Elasticsearch, Logstash, Kibana) collect logs from various sources, including the application, database, and network components. Analysing these logs helps identify security breaches, track system errors, and understand user behaviours.

- **Potential Scenario:** Log management detects unauthorized access attempts to the application server from a suspicious IP address. This triggers an alert for immediate investigation and remediation to prevent potential security breaches.

Intrusion Detection Systems (IDS)

IDS solutions, such as Snort and Suricata or Zeek, monitor network traffic to detect suspicious activities or unauthorized access attempts. They utilize signature-based detection for known threats and anomaly-based detection for deviations from normal behaviour.

- **Potential Scenario:** In the banking app, the IDS detects multiple failed login attempts within a short period, surpassing the predefined threshold. This indicates a potential brute-force attack or credential-stuffing campaign targeting user accounts. The IDS triggers an alert, prompting security teams to investigate and implement measures such as account lockouts or additional authentication steps to thwart the attack.

Security Information and Event Management (SIEM) Platforms

SIEM platforms, such as OSSIM, ELK Stack, etc., aggregate and analyse log data from various sources for proactive threat detection and incident response. They configure correlation rules to detect patterns indicative of security incidents and integrate threat intelligence feeds to enhance detection capabilities. For more advanced operations, Security Orchestration, Automation, and Response (SOAR) platforms can be integrated to automate incident response workflows.

- **Potential Scenario:** The SIEM platform correlates login attempts with geolocation data and user access patterns to identify suspicious activities. It detects a series of login attempts from a foreign country during non-business hours, followed by access to sensitive banking information. This triggers an alert, prompting immediate investigation and remediation to prevent unauthorized access and potential data breaches.

Continuous Monitoring

Establishing continuous monitoring practices ensures real-time visibility into the security posture of the banking app. Endpoint detection and response (EDR) solutions monitor activities on devices accessing the app, while file integrity monitoring detects unauthorized changes to critical system files or application binaries.

- **Potential Scenario:** Continuous monitoring detects unusual activities on a user's device, indicating a potential malware infection. The EDR solution identifies unauthorized access attempts to sensitive banking data and unusual network communication patterns. Simultaneously, file integrity monitoring detects unauthorized modifications to critical application files. These findings trigger automated responses to quarantine the device, revoke access, and initiate incident response procedures to contain the threat and prevent further damage.

6.9.2 Proactive Maintenance Routines

Ensuring Seamless Functionality

Proactive maintenance is essential to ensure that an Android banking application remains secure, reliable, and efficient. It involves a combination of regular updates, system optimizations, and pre-emptive checks to prevent potential issues. Key considerations are as following:

Patch Management Processes

Establish procedures to promptly apply security patches and updates to mitigate known vulnerabilities in the Android app and its underlying infrastructure. Automate patch deployment where feasible to expedite the process and minimize exposure to exploits. Conduct regression testing after patching to ensure no adverse effects on app functionality.

- **Potential Scenario:** Patch management ensures that any known vulnerabilities in the banking app's authentication mechanism are promptly addressed to prevent unauthorized access. Automated patch deployment tools can schedule updates during non-peak hours to minimize disruption to banking services.
- **Tools:** Ansible, Puppet, Chef

Regular Updates

Regularly updating the application and its dependencies is crucial for security and functionality. This includes applying patches for the operating system, third-party libraries, and any frameworks used in the application. Failing to update can leave the application vulnerable to known exploits.

- **Potential Scenario:** A critical security vulnerability is discovered in the third-party authentication library used by the banking app. By promptly updating the library to the latest patched version, the bank mitigates the risk of potential data breaches or unauthorized access to user accounts, ensuring the continued trust and confidence of its customers.

Database Maintenance

Regularly optimize the database to ensure efficient data retrieval and storage. This includes indexing frequently queried fields, archiving old data, and performing routine backups. Regular backups ensure data can be restored in case of corruption or loss, and indexing improves query performance.

- **Potential Scenario:** During a routine database maintenance operation, outdated indexes are identified on the 'Transactions' table, leading to sluggish query performance during peak usage hours. By optimizing the database indexes and archiving historical transaction data, the bank ensures that customers can access their transaction history swiftly and efficiently, enhancing their overall banking experience.

Vulnerability Management Programs

Employ vulnerability scanning tools to identify weaknesses in the Android app's code, libraries, and configurations. Prioritize vulnerabilities based on severity and exploitability. Implement remediation measures such as code fixes, configuration changes, or compensating controls.

- **Potential Scenario:** Vulnerability scans identify a weakness in the encryption protocol used by the banking app, prompting an update to strengthen encryption and protect user data. Vulnerability management programs can also track the lifecycle of vulnerabilities from discovery to resolution, ensuring timely remediation.
- **Tools: Trivy,** Nessus, OWASP ZAP

Threat Intelligence Integration

Integrate threat intelligence feeds, leveraging standards like STIX/TAXII, into maintenance routines to stay informed about emerging threats and vulnerabilities relevant to the banking app. Utilize threat feeds from reputable sources to enrich vulnerability assessments and prioritize remediation efforts. Implement automated workflows to incorporate threat intelligence into patch management and vulnerability scanning processes.

- **Potential Scenario:** Integration of threat intelligence feeds enables the bank to proactively identify and mitigate security risks posed by new vulnerabilities or exploitation techniques. For example, if a new exploit targeting a specific version of the app's underlying framework is discovered, threat intelligence feeds can trigger immediate action to apply patches or implement compensating controls.

System Health Checks

Conduct periodic health checks on all components of the application's infrastructure, including servers, network devices, and storage systems. Tools like Nagios or Datadog can automate these checks, alerting administrators to issues like high CPU usage, disk space shortages, or network latency.

- **Potential Scenario:** During a routine health check, the monitoring tools detect unusually high CPU usage on the server responsible for processing real-time transaction alerts. This early warning allows the IT team to investigate and resolve the issue before it affects the app's performance, ensuring that users continue to receive timely notifications of their banking activities without disruption.

6.9.3 Regular Security Assessments

Auditing for Ongoing Assurance

Regular security assessments are crucial for identifying and mitigating vulnerabilities within the Android banking application. These assessments ensure the application remains resilient against emerging threats and maintains a high level of security. Here are some key types of security assessments that should be conducted regularly:

Penetration Testing

Engage professional security testers to simulate attacks on the application. Penetration testing involves attempting to exploit vulnerabilities to understand how an attacker might gain unauthorized access or cause damage. This hands-on testing provides insights into real-world security weaknesses that automated tools might miss.

- **Tools and Techniques:** Professional penetration testers use a variety of tools and techniques to simulate attacks on the application, such as Metasploit, Burp Suite, and custom scripts designed to exploit specific vulnerabilities.
- **Potential Scenario:** During a penetration test, a tester successfully exploits a vulnerability in the authentication process, gaining unauthorized access to sensitive user data. This discovery prompts immediate remediation efforts and reinforces the importance of robust authentication mechanisms.

Vulnerability Scanning

Vulnerability scanning uses the automated tools to scan the application for known vulnerabilities. These tools compare the application's code and configurations against a database of known issues, providing a comprehensive report on potential security gaps.

- **Tools and Techniques:** Automated vulnerability scanners like Nessus, OWASP ZAP, and Nikto help identify known vulnerabilities in the application by comparing its code and configurations against a database of known issues.
- **Potential Scenario:** A routine vulnerability scan detects several medium-risk vulnerabilities in the app's third-party libraries. The development team promptly updates the affected libraries to the latest versions, mitigating the identified risks.

Code Audits

Conduct thorough reviews of the application's source code to identify security vulnerabilities, ensure compliance with coding standards, and improve code quality. Automated tools can assist in identifying issues such as SQL injection vulnerabilities, cross-site scripting (XSS), and insecure coding practices.

- **Tools and Techniques:** Automated code auditing tools like Checkmarx, Fortify, and SonarQube assist in identifying security vulnerabilities within the source code. They provide detailed reports on potential issues and help developers improve code quality and security.
- **Potential Scenario:** During a code review and static analysis, a logic flaw in the app's authentication process is discovered. This flaw could potentially allow an attacker to

bypass authentication controls. The development team implements additional security checks to mitigate this vulnerability.

Compliance Audits

Ensure the application complies with relevant regulations and industry standards, such as PCI-DSS (Payment Card Industry Data Security Standard) and GDPR (General Data Protection Regulation). Compliance audits involve reviewing policies, procedures, and technical controls to ensure they meet the necessary requirements.

- **Tools and Techniques:** Tools such as Lynis and OpenSCAP can be used to conduct compliance audits, ensuring that the application meets relevant regulatory and industry standards.
- **Potential Scenario:** A compliance audit confirms that the banking app enforces strong password policies and encrypts sensitive user data stored on the device. Audits also verify that access controls are properly configured to limit privileged access to authorized personnel only.

6.9.4 Incident Response Procedures

Preparedness in Action

Incident response procedures are crucial for effectively managing security incidents when they occur. A well-defined and tested incident response plan helps in mitigating damage and ensuring a quick recovery.

Establishing an Incident Response Framework

Define Clear Procedures and Protocols: Define clear procedures and protocols for responding to security incidents involving the Android app.

- **Assign Roles and Responsibilities:** Assign roles and responsibilities to incident response team members to ensure everyone knows their specific tasks during an incident.
- **Develop Incident Response Playbooks:** Create incident response playbooks outlining step-by-step procedures for different types of security incidents. These playbooks should guide the team through scenarios like data breaches, malware infections, and DDoS attacks.
- **Conduct Tabletop Exercises and Simulations:** Regularly conduct tabletop exercises and simulations to test the effectiveness of incident response plans and improve team readiness. These exercises help the incident response team practice coordination and communication during simulated breach scenarios.
- **Tools and Resources:** Utilize both commercial and open-source tools to support your incident response activities. Freeware and open-source tools such as TheHive and MISP can be instrumental in incident response operations, offering functionalities for case management, threat intelligence, and collaborative analysis.

6.9.5 Cultivating a Security Culture

Embedding Awareness Across the Organization

Cultivating a security culture within the organization is crucial for prioritizing security at all levels, particularly in the context of an Android banking application. A security-focused culture helps prevent incidents and promotes best practices throughout the organization. Here are strategies and benefits to achieve and maintain a strong security culture.

Employee Training

Regular training sessions are conducted to educate employees on security best practices, emerging threats, and their roles in maintaining security. This includes topics such as phishing awareness, secure coding practices, and data protection policies.

- **Tools and Techniques:**
  - Security awareness platforms like KnowBe4 or Proofpoint Security Awareness Training
  - Interactive e-learning modules using platforms like SANS Security Awareness
  - Simulated phishing exercises with tools like PhishMe or Wombat Security Education Platform
  - Secure coding training platforms such as Secure Code Warrior or Codecademy's cybersecurity courses

- **Potential Scenario:** Employees undergo periodic security training that includes simulated phishing attacks using tools like PhishMe. Upon completion, they receive personalized feedback on their performance through the platform, reinforcing good security practices. As a result, employees become more vigilant and adept at identifying and mitigating security threats.

Security Policies

Comprehensive security policies and procedures are developed and enforced to cover all aspects of security, including data handling, access control, incident reporting, and acceptable use.

- **Tools and Techniques:**
  - Policy management platforms like Microsoft Compliance Manager or IBM Security Policy Management
  - Document repositories such as SharePoint or Confluence for storing and accessing security policies
  - Automated compliance monitoring tools like Qualys Policy Compliance or Tripwire Enterprise
  - Security policy templates provided by organizations like NIST or ISO

- **Potential Scenario:** An incident response policy is established outlining clear procedures for reporting security incidents. Employees are trained on the policy, and a centralized incident reporting system is implemented using tools like ServiceNow or JIRA Service Management. When a security incident occurs, employees follow the prescribed procedures, enabling a swift and coordinated response to mitigate the impact.

Leadership Commitment

Leadership demonstrates a strong commitment to security by prioritizing it, allocating resources, and setting a positive example for the organization.

- **Tools and Techniques:**
  - Executive dashboards for security metrics using tools like Splunk or Elastic Security
  - Regular security briefings facilitated by platforms like Zoom or Microsoft Teams
  - Investment in security tools and training with vendors like CrowdStrike or Palo Alto Networks
  - Participation in security initiatives like CISO forums or industry conferences

- **Potential Scenario:** The CEO champions a security-first approach by allocating a budget for a company-wide security awareness program. Executives actively participate in security briefings conducted via Zoom, engaging with the security team to understand and address emerging threats. This commitment cascades throughout the organization, fostering a culture where security is everyone's responsibility.

Cross-functional Collaboration

Collaboration between development, operations, and security teams is encouraged to integrate security into every stage of the software development lifecycle.

- **Tools and Techniques:**
  - Cross-functional security committees facilitated by collaboration platforms like Slack or Microsoft Teams
  - Secure collaboration platforms such as GitHub Enterprise or GitLab for version control and code reviews
  - Threat modelling tools like Microsoft Threat Modelling Tool or OWASP Threat Dragon
  - Secure coding guidelines and libraries provided by organizations like OWASP or SANS Institute

- **Potential Scenario:** Development teams work closely with security analysts to conduct threat modelling sessions during the design phase of a new feature using tools like OWASP Threat Dragon. Security requirements are integrated into the development process, and regular security reviews are conducted using platforms like GitHub Enterprise to identify and address potential vulnerabilities. This collaborative approach ensures that security is built in from the outset.

Open Communication

Open communication about security concerns and incidents is encouraged, fostering transparency and collaboration throughout the organization.

- **Tools and Techniques:**
  - Incident reporting channels integrated into collaboration platforms like Slack or Microsoft Teams
  - Anonymous reporting mechanisms provided by third-party services like EthicsPoint or Whispli
  - Security awareness campaigns facilitated by email or intranet announcements
  - Employee feedback surveys using platforms like SurveyMonkey or Google Forms

- **Potential Scenario:** An employee identifies a potential security vulnerability in the banking application and reports it through the designated incident reporting channel integrated into Slack. The security team investigates the issue, confirms the vulnerability, and promptly implements a fix. The employee's proactive reporting is acknowledged through an email announcement, reinforcing the importance of open communication and active participation in security efforts.

6.10 Incident Response

Turning Chaos into Control

Incident response is the process of identifying, managing, and mitigating security incidents. A well-defined incident response plan ensures that the development team can quickly and effectively address security breaches, minimizing their impact. For an Android banking app, a robust incident response strategy is crucial for maintaining user trust and protecting sensitive financial information.

After resolving a security incident, it is important to conduct a post-incident review to identify lessons learned and improve future response efforts. This review should include an analysis of what went well, what could have been done better, and any changes needed to prevent similar incidents in the future.

6.10.1 Activation of Incident Response Team

Assembling the First Responders

A coordinated team is the foundation of a successful response. When a security breach occurs, the incident response team springs into action to mitigate risks, protect data, and restore system integrity. Each member plays a critical role in resolving the situation with expertise and precision.

Potential scenario: A banking app experiences a breach in its authentication system, leading to unauthorized access to customer accounts.

Team Formation

Assemble a multidisciplinary response team that brings unique skills and perspectives to address different aspects of the incident.

- **Security Analysts:** Responsible for continuous monitoring and initial detection of security incidents. They analyse security alerts to determine if an incident has occurred and assess the severity and impact of the breach.
- **Forensic Experts:** Tasked with gathering and preserving digital evidence related to the incident. They perform detailed analyses to understand the breach's nature, including how it occurred and its potential impact.
- **IT and DevOps Personnel:** Execute the technical steps needed for containment, eradication, and recovery. This includes system administrators, network engineers, and application developers who work to secure the affected systems and restore normal operations.
- **Legal and Compliance Officers:** Ensure that the response actions comply with legal requirements and regulatory standards. They also manage any legal implications arising from the incident and coordinate with external regulatory bodies if needed.
- **Public Relations and Communications Specialists:** Handle all external communications, including media relations. They craft messages to manage the organization's public image, maintain customer trust, and provide timely updates.

- **Customer Support Representatives:** Address customer concerns and inquiries related to the incident. They provide necessary support and information to affected customers, ensuring transparency and maintaining trust.

Initial Assessment

Utilize open-source security monitoring tools such as Security Onion or OSSEC to conduct an initial assessment. Analyse network traffic, server logs, and system alerts to understand the extent of unauthorized access and potential vulnerabilities exploited.

Role Assignment

Allocate technical roles within the team. Ensure that team members are equipped with the necessary tools and access permissions to carry out their tasks effectively.

6.10.2 Established Incident Response Procedures

Executing a Strategic Playbook

When chaos arises, a structured approach is the key to resolution. Predefined incident response procedures act as a playbook, ensuring that every action is deliberate, efficient, and targeted at neutralizing threats.

Potential Scenario: Malicious code is detected in the banking app's payment processing module, potentially compromising transaction data.

- **Procedure Activation:** Trigger predefined incident response procedures tailored to address security incidents in Android app environments. These procedures may include steps for isolating affected systems, analysing malware samples, and restoring compromised data from backups.
- **Communication Channels:** Establish secure communication channels for incident response coordination, such as encrypted email, secure messaging platforms like Signal or Riot, and virtual collaboration tools like Jitsi or Nextcloud Talk. Ensure that communication protocols comply with privacy regulations and organizational security policies.
- **Documentation:** Maintain detailed records of incident response activities using open-source incident management platforms like TheHive or MISP. These platforms allow the centralization of documentation and facilitate collaboration among team members.

6.10.3 Thorough Investigation and Root Cause Analysis

Tracing Issues to Their Core

Understanding the cause is essential to preventing future breaches. Investigating incidents thoroughly uncovers vulnerabilities and equips the organization to fortify its defenes.

Potential Scenario: The banking app's customer database is breached, resulting in the exposure of sensitive personal information.

- **Forensic Examination:** Conduct a thorough forensic examination of affected systems and mobile devices using open-source tools like Autopsy or Volatility. These tools help identify malware artefacts, unauthorized access logs, and other indicators of compromise. Utilize mobile forensics tools like Autopsy, Andriller, or Santoku to extract and analyse application data, device logs, and system files.

- **Root Cause Analysis:** Investigate the root cause of the breach by examining the source code, configuration settings, and infrastructure architecture of the banking app. Perform static and dynamic code analysis using open-source tools like MobSF (Mobile Security Framework) to identify vulnerabilities such as insecure data storage, inadequate encryption, and improper input validation.
- **Lessons Learned:** Document findings from the investigation using open-source documentation platforms like BookStack or DokuWiki. Identify lessons learned to improve incident response procedures and enhance security controls. Share insights with development teams to prioritize security enhancements and address systemic weaknesses in the banking app's design and implementation.
- **Attack Path Mapping:** Create a detailed map of the attack path, documenting each step the attacker took, from initial compromise to data exfiltration or other malicious activities. Attack path mapping helps in visualizing the attack and identifying gaps in security controls.

6.10.4 Implementation of Containment Measures

Containing Breaches with Care

Swift containment prevents further damage. When an incident occurs, immediate action is necessary to stop the spread of harm and restore security.

Potential Scenario: An attacker exploits a vulnerability in the banking app's account transfer feature, leading to fraudulent transactions.

- **Immediate Response:** Implement containment measures using open-source security tools such as Suricata or Snort to mitigate the immediate impact of the security incident and prevent further unauthorized access. This may involve isolating compromised servers, disabling compromised user accounts, and blocking malicious IP addresses at the network perimeter.
- **Remediation Actions:** Apply security patches, updates, and configuration changes using open-source automation tools like Ansible or Puppet to address identified vulnerabilities in the banking app. Conduct code reviews and security testing using open-source tools like FindBugs or QARK (Quick Android Review Kit) to verify the effectiveness of remediation measures and ensure that no residual risks remain.
- **Continuous Monitoring:** Deploy open-source intrusion detection and prevention systems like Suricata or Snort to continuously monitor network traffic, application behaviour, and user activity for signs of malicious activity. Set up alerts and automated responses using open-source SIEM (Security Information and Event Management) solutions like OSSIM or ELK Stack to detect and block suspicious behaviour in real-time, minimizing the window of opportunity for attackers to exploit vulnerabilities.
- **Temporary Service Restrictions:** Implement temporary restrictions on certain services, such as disabling specific functionalities that were targeted, to reduce risk while the incident is being managed. This might include disabling certain APIs or restricting access to critical systems.

6.10.5 Transparent Communication with Stakeholders

Fostering Trust Through Clarity

Clear communication inspires confidence during crises. Sharing timely, accurate information with stakeholders mitigates uncertainty and reinforces trust in the organization's capabilities.

Potential Scenario: News of a security incident involving the banking app spreads on social media, causing concern among customers and investors.

- **Timely Communication:** Communicate transparently with affected stakeholders through multiple channels, including email notifications, press releases, and social media updates. Provide clear and concise information about the incident, its impact, and the steps taken to mitigate risks and restore normal operations.
- **Customer Notification:** Offer guidance and support to affected customers using open-source customer relationship management (CRM) platforms like SuiteCRM or SugarCRM. Provide instructions for resetting passwords, monitoring account activity, and reporting suspicious transactions. Provide access to customer support channels staffed by trained personnel who can address security-related inquiries and concerns.
- **Regulatory Reporting:** Comply with data protection regulations and industry standards governing incident reporting and disclosure. Notify regulatory authorities and relevant stakeholders in accordance with legal requirements and industry best practices, demonstrating transparency and accountability in managing security incidents.
- **Media and Public Relations:** Manage the reputational impact of the security incident by proactively addressing concerns and restoring trust in the banking app's security posture. Engage with customers, partners, and investors to communicate the organization's commitment to security and resilience, emphasizing ongoing efforts to strengthen defences and protect customer data against future threats.

Looking Ahead

In closing, the journey of integrating a Secure Software Development Life Cycle (SDLC) for Android applications represents a comprehensive and ongoing commitment to security at every stage. Implementing a Secure SDLC is not just a best practice but a necessity in today's evolving threat landscape. By integrating security at every phase, developers can significantly reduce vulnerabilities and build resilient applications. A proactive approach to security ensures that risks are identified early, reducing the cost and complexity of addressing them later in the development cycle.

As new technologies and attack vectors evolve, the principles outlined in this chapter serve as a guiding framework for fostering a culture of security, embedding it deeply within the fabric of Android application development. Developers and organizations must remain vigilant by continuously refining their security practices. Regular security training, robust code reviews, and ongoing monitoring are essential to maintaining a strong security posture. By embracing a security-first mindset and fostering a culture of secure development, teams can build Android applications that not only meet functional requirements but also withstand emerging threats, ultimately safeguarding user data and trust.

Part 3

Security Standards and Emerging Trends

Android's security is built on a multi-layered approach, combining platform safeguards, Google's security services, and developer best practices. "Chapter 7: Exploring Android Security & OWASP MASVS" covers:

- **Android's Security Model** – Platform hardening, sandboxing, and permission systems.
- **Application Security Fundamentals** – Secure app components, IPC mechanisms, and data protection.
- **OWASP MASVS Introduction** – How this industry-standard framework defines security requirements for mobile apps.
- **Real-World Applicability** – Aligning development practices with MASVS to mitigate risks.

A deep dive into the OWASP MASVS framework, "Chapter 8: OWASP MASVS Insights" translates its guidelines into actionable practices:

- **Secure Data Storage (MASVS-STORAGE)** – Preventing local data leaks.
- **Cryptography (MASVS-CRYPTO)** – Proper encryption implementation.
- **Authentication and Authorization (MASVS-AUTH)** – Robust access controls.
- **Network Security (MASVS-NETWORK)** – Safeguarding data in transit.
- **Platform Interaction (MASVS-PLATFORM)** – Secure OS integration.
- **Code Integrity (MASVS-CODE)** – Anti-tampering and obfuscation.
- **Privacy (MASVS-PRIVACY)** – Compliance with regulations like GDPR.

The future of Android security demands proactive adaptation. "Chapter 9: Anticipating Future Trends & Challenges" includes key trends such as:

- **DevSecOps Integration** – Embedding security into CI/CD pipelines.
- **Emerging Technologies** – Addressing risks in AI, quantum computing, and XR (Extended Reality).
- **Zero Trust and RASP** – Shifting from perimeter-based to continuous verification models.
- **Supply Chain Security** – Mitigating risks in third-party dependencies.
- **Biometric and Edge Security** – Protecting decentralized data and advanced authentication.

DOI: 10.1201/9781003640332-9

Exploring Android Security and OWASP MASVS

The future is not something we enter. The future is something we create.

– Leonard Sweet

Leonard Sweet, an American theologian, semiotician, church historian, pastor, and author, underscores the active role individuals and organizations have in shaping their future. His quote reminds us that the future is not a fixed destination or something that happens to us; it is a product of our deliberate actions, choices, and innovations. By taking initiative and embracing change, we can craft a future that aligns with our aspirations and values.

In the realm of Android application security, this quote highlights the importance of proactive measures in shaping a secure digital future. Rather than merely reacting to threats as they arise, developers and organizations have the opportunity to actively contribute to a safer environment by investing in innovative security solutions, fostering a culture of awareness, and collaborating to address emerging challenges. Understanding the intricacies of software and systems is essential; neglecting this can lead to vulnerabilities and risks. Therefore, stakeholders must prioritize ongoing education about best practices, potential vulnerabilities, and evolving threats to maintain application integrity and ensure user safety.

A LAYMAN'S PERSPECTIVE

Venturing into the Realm of Application Security

In the vast landscape of mobile technology, Android stands as a beacon of innovation, openness, and user empowerment. From its inception, Android was designed to foster creativity while prioritizing user privacy and security. This chapter explores the foundational principles that shape the design of Android, examining its open nature, robust developer support, and steadfast commitment to user control and security.

At its core, Android is more than just a mobile operating system (OS); it is a dynamic, community-driven ecosystem built on the robust Linux kernel. This open-source nature offers unparalleled flexibility, enabling developers to create diverse and innovative applications that enhance the mobile experience.

Whether through the structured environment of Java/Kotlin or the efficiency of native code in C/C++, Android provides a powerful canvas for development. However, with this power comes responsibility, ensuring that applications remain secure against ever-evolving threats. Security in application development is not just about reacting to threats; it is about proactive defence and best practices.

Central to the Android experience is the Android Runtime (ART), the virtual machine where applications are executed. Android applications are packaged in .apk files, which represent the vast possibilities that the platform brings to users worldwide. While this openness facilitates innovation, it also introduces security risks that developers must address proactively. Android's security model incorporates multiple layers of protection.

As security threats evolve, adhering to best practices becomes essential. This is where the Mobile Application Security Verification Standard (MASVS) comes into play. Developed by the Open Worldwide Application Security Project (OWASP), MASVS provides a structured framework for securing mobile applications, offering clear and practical guidelines for developers, security professionals, and application owners.

MASVS sets a benchmark for mobile app security, ensuring that security is an integral part of the development lifecycle rather than an afterthought. By integrating MASVS principles, developers can enhance the security posture of their applications, fostering user trust and compliance with industry standards.

7.1 Android Security Overview

Android – A Secure Ecosystem Built on Collaboration

In an era where digital security is paramount, Android stands as a beacon of innovation and trustworthiness within the mobile ecosystem. As the world's leading mobile operating system, Android has not only revolutionized the way users interact with technology but has also set a gold standard for openness, innovation, and, above all, security. This section explores the Android's multi-layered security architecture, unveiling the core principles that underpin its design and the robust measures it employs to safeguard user data, privacy, and device integrity.

Android's commitment to openness and collaboration is ingrained in its DNA. Built upon an open-source framework, Android fosters an environment where developers can unleash their creativity, pushing the boundaries of mobile technology while ensuring that security remains a top priority. Through rigorous security mechanisms such as sandboxing, permission-based access control, encryption, and hardware-backed keystores, Android strikes a delicate balance between openness and security, empowering users with granular control over their digital privacy.

Furthermore, Android's support for developers is unparalleled. With comprehensive tools, libraries, and security guidance, developers are equipped to create high-quality, secure applications that enrich the Android ecosystem. Google's proactive initiatives, including the expanded Android Security Rewards Program, AI-driven vulnerability detection, and enhanced SafetyNet API with new device integrity checks, underscore its commitment to fortifying the Android platform against emerging cyber threats.

7.1.1 Confidence on the Go: Android Security

A Comprehensive Approach to Mobile Security

Android, the leading mobile operating system globally, is renowned for its commitment to openness, innovation, and user empowerment. By embracing an open-source model, Android fosters a thriving ecosystem where developers can create diverse applications while prioritizing user privacy and security. This section explores the foundational principles of Android's design, highlighting its open nature, support for developers, and emphasis on user control and security.

Android's Open Architecture

- **Open-source Framework:** Android is built on an open-source foundation, fostering collaboration and innovation within the developer community. This open approach allows developers to contribute to and improve the platform, enhancing its capabilities and security.
- **Encouraging Innovation:** The open nature of Android enables developers to explore new ideas and push the boundaries of mobile technology, leading to a diverse range of applications and services.
- **Customization and Extensibility:** Developers can tailor the Android platform to meet specific needs, promoting a culture of creativity and collaboration. Despite this flexibility, Android employs robust security mechanisms such as sandboxing, SELinux policies, and encryption to protect user data and device integrity.
- **Security Measures:** Android uses process-level isolation with unique user IDs (UIDs), SELinux for enforcing mandatory access controls (MACs), and Binder IPC restrictions to ensure that applications operate securely in isolated environments.

Empowering Developers

- **Comprehensive Toolset:** Android provides developers with a comprehensive suite of tools, libraries, and documentation to streamline the app development process.
- **Android SDK and Android Studio:** Developers have access to the Android SDK and Android Studio IDE, enabling them to create high-quality, secure applications for the platform.
- **Security Guidance:** Android offers developers guidance and best practices to mitigate common security risks, fostering a culture of security awareness within the developer community.

- **Collaborative Security Initiatives:** Through initiatives like the Android Security Rewards Program and monthly security updates, Google works closely with developers to identify and address potential vulnerabilities, ensuring a secure platform for users.

User-centric Design

- **Granular Permissions Control:** Android empowers users with granular control over app permissions, allowing them to review and manage the data accessed by installed applications.
- **User-centric Features:** Features like runtime permissions and app sandboxing enable users to make informed decisions about their digital privacy and security.
- **Protection Against Threats:** Android employs various security measures to protect users from malware, phishing attacks, and other malicious activities that pose risks to user data and device integrity. For example, Android employs the Play Integrity API (which supersedes SafetyNet) for device integrity verification, anti-phishing protection, and encryption of user data.
- **Proactive Security Measures:** By proactively monitoring and addressing security threats, Android ensures that users can trust their devices to safeguard their personal information and digital assets. For example, the Android Privacy Sandbox initiative aims to limit cross-app data sharing for advertising, and Google Play Protect leverages machine learning for real-time malware detection.

7.1.2 Android Platform Building Blocks

Foundations of a Secure Ecosystem

The Android platform, developed by Google, has evolved into a comprehensive ecosystem encompassing a wide array of hardware configurations and software components. This section looks into the intricate building blocks that form the foundation of the Android experience, including kernel-level hardening techniques like Kernel Address Space Layout Randomization (KASLR) and control flow integrity (CFI).

Android Devices

- **Versatility:** Android's compatibility spans smartphones, tablets, wearables, automotive infotainment systems, smart TVs, gaming consoles, and set-top boxes.
- **Processor Agnosticism:** Android adapts to diverse processor architectures while leveraging specific hardware features such as ARM eXecute-Never (XN), Pointer Authentication Codes (PAC), Memory Tagging Extensions (MTE), and TrustZone with Confidential Compute Architecture (CCA) for enhanced security. Recent Android versions leverage ARM's Realm Management Extension (RME) for enhanced isolation between secure and non-secure worlds.
- **Innovation Landscape:** Hardware diversity fosters innovation and optimization opportunities for developers. Secure elements (SEs) (e.g., Titan M on Pixel devices) ensure sensitive data protection.

Android Operating System

- **Linux Kernel Foundation:** The Linux kernel provides essential system services and manages hardware resources.
- **Resource Access:** The Android OS offers a framework for accessing device functionalities such as camera modules, GPS sensors, and Bluetooth connectivity.
- **Security Mechanisms:** Implements Verified Boot, rollback protection, and A/B partition updates to enhance security and reliability.

Android Application Runtime

- **Java and Native Support:** Android apps are primarily developed in Java but can also utilize native code via the Native Development Kit (NDK).
- **Kotlin Adoption:** Embracing Kotlin as a first-class language enhances code safety and readability, reducing common programming errors that could lead to vulnerabilities. For example, Kotlin enhances type safety, null safety, and reduces common vulnerabilities like null pointer dereferences.
- **ART Optimization:** Ahead-of-time (AOT) compilation techniques optimize application performance and memory efficiency.
- **Sandboxing Model:** Applications operate within isolated environments, mitigating security risks and ensuring data integrity. For example, stricter SECCOMP-BPF filters and shadow call stacks are used to restrict syscalls and protect control flow integrity, significantly reducing attack surfaces.

World of Android Applications

- **Preinstalled Apps:** Essential functionalities provided by Google or device manufacturers, showcasing platform capabilities.
- **User-Installed Apps:** A vast selection of third-party application offerings available through the Google Play Store and other channels.
- **Personalization and Enrichment:** Users personalize their devices with apps ranging from productivity tools to multimedia experiences.

7.1.3 Google Security Services

Fortifying the Android Ecosystem

In the dynamic realm of digital security, Google stands as a beacon of innovation, continually advancing its suite of protective measures to safeguard users and their devices within the Android ecosystem. This section provides an in-depth exploration of the primary Google security services, elucidating their multifaceted functionalities and paramount importance in fortifying the integrity and resilience of the Android platform against emerging cyber threats.

Google Play

- **Gateway to Android:** Google Play serves as the quintessential gateway for Android users, offering a comprehensive ecosystem for app discovery, installation, and transactions.

- **Security Measures:** Integrates robust security measures such as community-driven reviews and app scanning protocols to ensure the integrity and safety of its vast application repository.
- **User and Developer Confidence:** Sets a high standard for app security, fostering confidence among users and developers in the safety and reliability of the Android platform.

Android Updates

- **Cornerstone of Security:** The Android update service is pivotal in addressing security vulnerabilities and software exploits, delivering timely updates and patches to Android devices.
- **Proactive Defence:** Proactively addresses known vulnerabilities and emerging threats, enhancing the overall security posture of the Android ecosystem.

App Services

- **Cloud Empowerment:** Empowers Android applications with cloud capabilities, facilitating seamless data backup, settings synchronization, and cloud-to-device messaging.
- **Security Enhancements:** Implements robust encryption protocols and secure communication channels to mitigate the risk of data breaches and unauthorized access, fostering user trust.

Play Integrity API

- Device Integrity and App Attestation: Enables developers to assess whether a request originates from a genuine Android device and a legitimate version of their app, helping detect rooted devices, emulators, and modified app binaries.
- Protect Against Fraud and Cheating: Provides integrity verdicts to help prevent abuse such as spoofing, cheating in games, and fraudulent transactions by verifying the authenticity of the app environment.
- Secure Backend Integration: Delivers cryptographically signed attestation results to your server, allowing you to make informed trust decisions while keeping sensitive logic off the client side.
- Ecosystem Trust and Compliance: Supports a safer Android ecosystem by helping developers maintain control over their app's integrity and comply with security and licensing requirements.

Android Device Manager

- **Lost Device Management:** Empowers users to locate and secure their devices through advanced location tracking and remote device management capabilities.
- **Data Security:** Mitigates potential data breaches and privacy infringements, enhancing overall device security within the Android ecosystem.

7.1.4 Android Security Program Overview

Ensuring Robust Security

In the ever-evolving landscape of mobile technology, security stands as a paramount concern. Android, being one of the most widely used mobile operating systems, places significant emphasis on fortifying its security architecture. The Android Security Program comprises several pivotal components that collectively aim to safeguard user data, privacy, and the integrity of the platform.

Design Review

- **Early Intervention:** Security measures commence early in the development lifecycle with thorough design reviews. For example, integration of secure boot chains, sandboxing policies, and threat modelling.
- **Expert Scrutiny:** Engineering and security resources scrutinize major platform features to integrate robust security controls into the system architecture.
- **Preventive Approach:** Vulnerabilities are pre-emptively identified and addressed to enhance platform resilience.

Penetration Testing and Code Review

- **Continuous Evaluation:** Android-originated and open-source components undergo rigorous security evaluations throughout the development lifecycle.
- **Multifaceted Review:** Assessments are conducted by the Android Security Team, Google's Information Security Engineering team, and independent security consultants.
- **Proactive Vulnerability Detection:** The goal is to proactively detect weaknesses and potential vulnerabilities, mirroring post-release scrutiny by external security analysts.

Open Source and Community Review

- **Transparency and Collaboration:** Android fosters transparency and collaboration through the Android Open Source Project (AOSP).
- **Community Participation:** The AOSP invites widespread community participation in security reviews, enhancing platform resilience.
- **Leveraging External Expertise:** Leveraging established open-source technologies like the Linux kernel, which undergoes extensive external security scrutiny, further strengthens the platform's security posture.

Incident Response

- **Comprehensive Framework:** Android maintains a comprehensive incident response framework to swiftly address emerging threats post-deployment.
- **Continuous Monitoring:** Dedicated security personnel continuously monitor discussions within both the Android-specific and general security communities. For example, security threat monitoring using telemetry data, automated exploit detection, and AI-based threat models.
- **Prompt Mitigation:** Legitimate vulnerabilities are promptly identified and mitigated through cloud-supported responses, ensuring effective risk mitigation.

Monthly Security Updates

- **Proactive Patching:** Google issues regular security updates (CVE-based patches) primarily for Pixel devices, with collaboration across OEMs to improve patch dissemination, though timeliness varies across manufacturers.

- **Project Mainline:** It allows critical security components (e.g., Media Codecs, DNS) to be updated via Google Play, reducing patch latency.
- **Collaborative Approach:** Now includes AI-driven vulnerability detection and expanded collaboration with external researchers via the Android Open Source Project (AOSP) to ensure timely patches and minimize vulnerabilities.

7.2 Android Security Features

Balancing Security and Experience

In the interconnected world of mobile technology, Android's approach to device security is a masterclass in balancing robust protection with an intuitive user experience. Android employs a layered security architecture where diverse mechanisms work in concert to defend against malicious actors while ensuring that users enjoy a seamless and engaging interaction with their devices.

This section examines the comprehensive suite of security features that constitute Android's formidable defence strategy. From foundational principles like App Sandboxing, App Signing, and mandatory access control (MAC) to advanced layers like biometric authentication, full-disk encryption, and trusted execution environment (TEE), each component plays a pivotal role in safeguarding user data and maintaining device integrity. Understanding these elements provides valuable insight into how Android mitigates risks, empowers users, and upholds trust in the platform for billions worldwide.

7.2.1 App Sandbox

Building Walls Around your Apps

The App Sandbox is a fundamental security feature in Android that isolates each app from others, preventing unauthorized access to sensitive data and system resources.

Core Security Aspects

- **Isolated App Environment:** Imagine each app on your Android device living in its own little walled garden. This is essentially what the App Sandbox does. It uses the concept of Linux users to isolate app resources, assigning each app a unique user ID (UID) and running it within its own process. This UID-based isolation enforces discretionary access control (DAC) at the Linux kernel level, ensuring that apps cannot directly access other apps' resources. Additionally, SELinux introduces mandatory access controls (MACs), further strengthening sandbox security by enforcing fine-grained policies.
- **Protection Against Malicious Apps:** By confining apps to their respective sandboxes, Android prevents malicious apps from accessing files or functionalities of other apps, thereby safeguarding user data and device integrity. This isolation ensures that even if one app is compromised, the attack is contained, protecting the rest of the system. Each app can only access its own data and resources unless explicit permissions are granted, creating a robust barrier against data breaches. Additionally, Kernel Address Space Layout Randomization (KASLR), seccomp filters, and Memory Tagging Extensions (MTE) in newer hardware further mitigate potential sandbox escape vulnerabilities. Android 13 introduces per-app language preferences sandboxing and enhanced

user-space memory protection through Control Flow Integrity (CFI) enforcement in user applications.

- **Inter-process Communication (IPC) and Attack Vectors:** While sandboxing isolates apps, they often need to communicate with each other using Binder IPC, intents, or content providers. However, these mechanisms introduce potential attack surfaces such as intent spoofing, insecure content providers, and man-in-the-middle (MITM) attacks. Developers should enforce secure IPC communication using explicit intents, signature-based permissions, and properly configured content provider access modes to prevent unauthorized data leaks.
- **Permission-based Access Control:** The sandboxing mechanism is complemented by permissions. Apps must declare the permissions they need in their manifest files, and users are prompted to grant or deny these permissions, ensuring least-privilege access and mitigating over-permissions risks. This model not only isolates apps but also empowers users to control their data exposure. With Scoped Storage (introduced in Android 10), Android has restricted access to external storage, requiring apps to use the Storage Access Framework (SAF) or MediaStore APIs to manage shared files securely.

7.2.2 App Signing

Verifying App Identity for Trust

App Signing is a crucial security measure in Android that ensures the integrity and authenticity of an application. Every Android app must be digitally signed with a cryptographic key before it can be installed on a device or published on the Google Play Store. This process helps verify that the app comes from a trusted source and has not been altered by a third party.

Essential Mechanisms

- **Digital Signature for App Authenticity:** The app signing process involves developers signing their apps with a private key, creating a digital signature that verifies the app's authenticity and integrity. The digital signature is then verified by the Android system when the app is installed or updated. When an app is signed, a hash of the app's contents is encrypted with the developer's private key. This hash is compared with a freshly generated hash on the device during installation. Any discrepancy indicates that the app has been tampered with.
- **Enhanced Security and User Trust:** Simplifying updates, app signing allows developers to use the same signing key for subsequent updates, enhancing user trust and security. By thwarting impersonation attempts, app signing bolsters the security of the app ecosystem and protects users from potentially harmful applications. The Android system ensures backward compatibility by maintaining trust for previously signed updates. If the app is re-signed with a different key, it will be treated as a different app, necessitating user action to uninstall the old version and install the new one. Developers are encouraged to safeguard their signing keys meticulously, as losing control of these keys can compromise their entire app portfolio. Using hardware security modules (HSMs) or secure key storage solutions can significantly mitigate the risk of key compromise.
- **Google Play's Additional Security Layer:** Google Play provides additional mechanisms such as Play App Signing, which offloads the signing key management to Google, providing an extra layer of security and reducing the risk of key compromise. Play App

Signing service manages the app signing key in a secure environment and uses separate keys for signing and distributing the app to users. It now supports APK Signature Scheme v4, offering stronger integrity checks and faster verification to protect against rollback attacks and unauthorized modifications.

7.2.3 Authentication

You Are Who You Say You Are

Authentication is the process of verifying a user's identity before granting access to an Android app. It ensures that only legitimate users can interact with the app's features and data. Poor authentication mechanisms can lead to security vulnerabilities, such as unauthorized access or data breaches.

Secure Access Control Pillars

- **Multi-layered Authentication Approach:** Android employs multiple authentication methods, including PINs, passwords, and biometrics (fingerprints, facial recognition). The Gatekeeper subsystem ensures secure PIN/password verification within a trusted execution environment (TEE), keeping authentication safe even if the main operating system is compromised. The Gatekeeper works in tandem with the Keymint HAL (the successor to Keymaster), ensuring that keys are protected even in the event of a kernel compromise.
- **Protected Confirmation for Critical Actions:** Enhanced security measures such as Protected Confirmation (introduced in Android 9) provide additional layers of protection, particularly for critical actions like financial transactions. It ensures that sensitive transactions can be confirmed by the user in a manner that cannot be tampered with by malware. Protected Confirmation uses a secure UI to display a confirmation prompt, leveraging the TEE to isolate and secure the confirmation process. This ensures that even if an attacker controls the main OS, they cannot tamper with the confirmation dialogue.
- **BiometricPrompt API for Biometric Authentication:** The BiometricPrompt API in Android 15 supports face and iris recognition alongside fingerprints, enhancing secure and user-friendly authentication. This API standardizes biometric authentication, making it easier for developers to implement secure and user-friendly authentication methods. The BiometricPrompt API abstracts the complexity of integrating multiple biometric authentication methods by providing a consistent and secure interface. It also supports device credential fallback, allowing users to authenticate with their PIN or password if biometric methods fail.
- **Two-factor Authentication (2FA) and Hardware-Backed Credentials:** Additionally, Android provides robust support for passkeys, a phishing-resistant replacement for passwords, which are often backed by hardware credentials, enhancing the security of user accounts and sensitive operations. These measures collectively ensure that authentication on Android is both secure and user-friendly, reducing the risk of unauthorized access. Hardware-backed credentials are stored in the TEE or a secure element (SE) and are used in conjunction with the StrongBox Keymaster, which adds an extra layer of security by using tamper-resistant hardware to generate, store, and use cryptographic keys.

- **Passkey Authentication**: Android 14+ supports FIDO2 passkeys natively through Credential Manager, enabling passwordless authentication with cryptographic key pairs stored in secure hardware or synchronized across devices.

7.2.4 Device Identifier Composition Engine (DICE)

Crafting Unique Identities

The device identifier composition engine (DICE) is a security architecture that establishes a robust, cryptographic identity for a device by combining a hardware-embedded secret with measurements of the boot software. At its core, DICE leverages a Unique Device Secret (UDS), a secret programmed into the hardware during manufacturing, and a cryptographic hash of the early boot code (or other immutable measurements) to compute a Compound Device Identifier (CDI). This CDI serves as a basis for generating cryptographic keys that are intrinsically bound to both the device's hardware and the specific software that is loaded during boot.

How Dice Works

1. **Hardware Root-of-Trust:** The process begins with the UDS, a secret value that is only accessible during the earliest stages of the boot process. By limiting its exposure, the UDS minimizes the risk of compromise even if later software layers become vulnerable.
2. **Software Measurement:** As the device boots, a cryptographic hash (or similar measurement) is computed over the first piece of mutable code (e.g., the bootloader or firmware). This measurement reflects the integrity of the software that is about to run.
3. **CDI Derivation:** The UDS and the measured hash are combined, typically using a keyed hash or a key derivation function, to produce the CDI. Because the CDI is directly tied to both the hardware secret and the exact software that has been booted, any alteration (such as a malicious firmware update or tampering with the boot sequence) will produce a different CDI.
4. **Key Derivation and Attestation:** Once the CDI is generated, it can be used to derive device-specific cryptographic keys. These keys may be used for signing attestation certificates or for encryption, thereby ensuring that critical operations (like secure communication or remote key provisioning) are only possible when the device is in a trusted state.

Real-world Scenario

Consider a mobile banking application that demands high assurance of device integrity. In this scenario:

- **Secure Boot Verification:** When the smartphone boots up, the DICE engine computes the CDI using the UDS and the hash of the boot code. This CDI is then used to derive an attestation key, which signs a certificate describing the device's current secure state.
- **Remote Attestation:** When a user logs into the mobile banking app, the application sends the attestation certificate to the bank's server. The server verifies the certificate against a known-good state. If the CDI does not match the expected value (indicating that the boot process may have been tampered with or the firmware updated to an unapproved version), the server denies access.

- **Preventing Fraudulent Transactions:** In the event an attacker attempts to load compromised firmware on the device to intercept sensitive banking information, the CDI derived by DICE would change, causing the attestation to fail. As a result, the banking app would not complete the login process, thereby protecting the user's financial data.

This scenario demonstrates how DICE not only secures the boot process but also extends its benefits to application-level security by ensuring that only devices with verified and trusted software states can perform sensitive operations.

7.2.5 Encryption

Keeping your Data Safe and Secret

Encryption is the shield that protects your data on Android devices. When enabled, it scrambles user data before storing it, rendering it indecipherable to unauthorized access attempts. This crucial defence mechanism safeguards against physical theft or unauthorized access, ensuring the confidentiality and integrity of user information.

Fundamental Components

- **File-based Encryption:** Modern Android devices use FBE exclusively, allowing individual files to be encrypted with different keys, enabling features like direct boot and granular access control. FBE leverages hardware-accelerated inline encryption for performance and security.
- **Hardware Acceleration for Encryption:** Modern Android devices leverage hardware-accelerated encryption via the ARM TrustZone and AES instruction sets, significantly improving performance and security. FBE also utilizes Inline Encryption (UFS and eMMC inline encryption hardware) to speed up encryption and decryption processes.
- **Block-level Encryption and Access Control:** FDE ensures that all user data is encrypted at the block level, meaning that the data is inaccessible without the proper decryption key, which is typically derived from the user's PIN, password, or biometric authentication. In contrast, FBE encrypts individual files with different keys, allowing for finer control over access permissions and improved performance, particularly in multi-user scenarios.
- **Adoption of Advanced Cryptographic Algorithms:** Android broadly utilizes Adiantum, an efficient encryption mode designed for devices without hardware AES acceleration, alongside established algorithms like ChaCha20-Poly1305 and AES-GCM, to ensure performant and secure encryption across all device tiers. This algorithm also offers resistance against certain cryptographic attacks that AES-GCM might be vulnerable to, such as cache-timing and power analysis attacks.
- **Data Encryption in Transit:** Android also supports encrypting data in transit using protocols like TLS (Transport Layer Security), ensuring that data remains secure as it moves between the device and external servers. These encryption measures collectively protect user data against a wide range of threats, from physical theft to network-based attacks.
- **Memory Encryption:** To protect data in memory, newer Android devices employ memory encryption techniques, such as DRAM encryption, to safeguard sensitive data against physical attacks that attempt to access data stored in volatile memory. This adds an additional layer of security to protect user data even when the device is in use.

7.2.6 Keystore

The Vault for Your App's Secrets

The Android Keystore is a secure storage system that helps apps protect sensitive data, such as encryption keys, authentication credentials, and digital certificates. It ensures that cryptographic keys are stored securely and never exposed to the app's code, reducing the risk of data leaks and unauthorized access.

Foundational Elements

- **Secure Storage:** Keys stored in the Keystore are protected from extraction, meaning they cannot be easily accessed by unauthorized parties. Keystore provides an abstraction layer, ensuring that keys are stored in a secure hardware module (if available) or in a protected software environment.
- **Restricted Usage:** Developers can specify how and when the keys can be used, such as requiring user authentication (like a fingerprint or password) before the keys can be accessed. This usage restriction is enforced by the Keystore, ensuring that keys are only used in accordance with the specified policies.
- **Hardware Backed:** On devices with secure hardware, keys can be bound to the device's trusted execution environment (TEE) or secure element (SE), providing an extra layer of security. The TEE is an isolated execution environment that runs alongside the main operating system, safeguarding keys from vulnerabilities in the main OS.
- **Key Derivation and Secure Boot Integration:** The encryption key is derived using the user's passcode and a hardware-protected key stored in the TEE (trusted execution environment). Rollback protection ensures that an attacker cannot downgrade the firmware to a vulnerable version to bypass encryption protections. Secure boot ensures the integrity of the entire boot process, preventing unauthorized modifications to the OS.
- **Cryptographic Operations:** The Keystore supports various cryptographic operations like encryption, decryption, signing, and verification. By offloading these operations to the secure hardware, the Keystore minimizes the risk of sensitive key material being exposed to the app's runtime environment.
- **Key Attestation:** This feature allows the device's secure hardware to verify that a key is stored securely and has not been tampered with. Key attestation provides cryptographic proof of the key's origin and security properties, ensuring that the key is genuine and has not been compromised.

Guidelines for Robust Key Management

- **Use KeyGenParameterSpec:** This API allows developers to define security properties like requiring user authentication for key usage. It also enables the specification of key purposes (e.g., encryption, signing) and key validity periods, enhancing key management and security.
- Prefer StrongBox: For high-security applications (e.g., payments, authentication), verify the presence of StrongBox, a dedicated security chip that provides tamper-resistant key storage and cryptographic operations.
- **Encrypt Sensitive Data Before Storing:** Even when storing data in local databases or SharedPreferences, encrypt it using Keystore-protected keys. Consider using

AES-GCM (Advanced Encryption Standard with Galois/Counter Mode) for authenticated encryption to ensure both confidentiality and integrity of the data.

- **Rotate Keys Regularly:** Implement a key rotation mechanism to minimize risks in case of a compromise. Periodically rotating keys helps mitigate the impact of key exposure and ensures that old keys cannot be reused by attackers. Consider using a key rotation schedule that aligns with your organization's security policies.

7.2.7 Security-enhanced Linux (SELinux)

A Guardian for Your Device

SELinux is a crucial security feature in Android that enforces strict access control policies to protect the system and apps from unauthorized actions. It operates on the principle of mandatory access control (MAC), meaning even if an app or process has root access, it cannot perform actions beyond what is explicitly allowed by the policy. Unlike traditional discretionary access control (DAC), where users and applications define permissions, SELinux policies are predefined and immutable at runtime, ensuring a more robust security model.

Core Advantages

- **Prevents Unauthorized Access:** SELinux ensures that apps and processes can only access the system components and data they are permitted to, reducing the risk of malware exploitation. It does so by enforcing Type Enforcement (TE), which confines processes to specific security domains.
- **Enforces Least Privilege Principle:** Each app runs in an isolated domain with minimal required permissions, limiting potential damage from security breaches. Even privileged system services have tailored SELinux policies, restricting their access to only essential resources.
- **Blocks Privilege Escalation:** Even if an attacker gains control over an app, SELinux prevents them from gaining higher privileges to control the system. This is achieved through Multi-Level Security (MLS) policies, which prevent processes from accessing higher security levels.
- **Protects System Integrity:** System-critical files and processes are strictly regulated, preventing unauthorized modifications. This is particularly important in preventing kernel exploits, where an attacker attempts to tamper with system processes.
- **Logs Security Violations:** SELinux records any policy violations, making it easier to detect and analyse security threats. These logs can be audited using tools like audit2allow, allowing developers to refine security policies without compromising protection.

SELinux Modes

- **Enforcing Mode:** Actively blocks actions that violate security policies. This is the default mode in Android and ensures that all unauthorized actions are stopped immediately.
- **Permissive Mode:** Logs violations but does not block them, used mainly for debugging and policy development. It helps developers fine-tune policies before deployment.

SELinux Policy Components

- **Types:** Define labels for files, directories, and processes.
- **Attributes:** Group multiple types for easier policy management.
- **Rules:** Define allowed actions between types, such as reading, writing, or executing.

7.2.8 Trusty Trusted Execution Environment (TEE)

A Secure Island for Sensitive Tasks

Trusty is a secure operating system (OS) that provides a trusted execution environment (TEE) for Android devices. It runs alongside the Android OS on the same processor but is isolated from the rest of the system by both hardware and software. This isolation ensures that even if the Android OS is compromised, the TEE remains secure. Trusty is a lightweight, real-time OS designed to execute security-critical operations with minimal overhead. Further, Android is evolving toward open, auditable Trusted Execution Environment (TEE) frameworks with better integration into Generic Kernel Image (GKI) and enhanced hardware-backed security, reducing reliance on proprietary TEEs.

Defining Characteristics of Trusty TEE

- **Isolation:** Trusty is isolated from the Android OS, protecting it from malicious apps and vulnerabilities in the Android system. This isolation is enforced through CPU privilege levels, ensuring TEE operations are handled in a more secure execution mode.
- **Hardware Support:** Trusty works with ARM and Intel processors, using ARM's TrustZone technology for ARM systems and Intel's Virtualization Technology for Intel systems. TrustZone creates two execution worlds: the Normal World (Android OS) and the Secure World (trusty TEE), ensuring sensitive operations are shielded from untrusted software.
- **Open Source:** Trusty is provided as a free and open-source alternative to other TEE systems, offering transparency and ease of debugging. This enables security researchers to audit and improve the TEE, reducing the risks of hidden vulnerabilities.
- **Application Security:** Trusty now supports secure multi-party computation, enabling privacy-preserving features in isolated processes to reduce security vulnerabilities. Trusted apps in Trusty run with strict memory isolation, preventing any form of cross-app interference.

How Trusty TEE Works

- **Runs on a Secure Microkernel:** Unlike Android's Linux-based OS, Trusty operates in a small, hardened microkernel designed for security. It has a minimal attack surface and implements secure system calls for trusted applications.
- **Communicates Securely with Apps:** Android apps can use the Trusty API (via secure inter-process communication (IPC)) to perform security-critical tasks without exposing sensitive information. This API allows for secure data storage, biometric authentication, and cryptographic operations.
- **Enforces Strict Access Controls:** Only trusted applications, verified at the hardware level, can interact with Trusty, minimizing attack surfaces. Trusty uses the root of trust mechanisms, ensuring only authenticated firmware and applications can execute in the Secure World.

Advanced Applications of Trusty TEE

- **Secure Payments:** Many mobile payment systems, such as Google Pay, rely on TEE for secure transactions. Trusty securely stores cryptographic keys and processes payment requests without exposing sensitive data to Android OS.

- **Biometric Authentication:** Trusty handles fingerprint and facial recognition data securely, ensuring that biometric credentials are never accessible to untrusted applications.
- **Digital Rights Management (DRM):** Premium content protection systems use TEE to enforce DRM policies, preventing unauthorized access and piracy.
- **Secure Boot and Firmware Integrity:** Trusty verifies system boot integrity by ensuring only authenticated firmware and OS components are loaded. This prevents attackers from injecting malicious firmware during boot-up.

7.2.9 Verified Boot

Guarding Your Device from the Start

Verified Boot is a security feature in Android that ensures the integrity of the operating system from the moment the device is powered on. It helps prevent malicious software (malware) from altering the system files or boot process.

How It Works

- **Bootloader Verification:** When the device starts, the bootloader checks the integrity of the Android OS.
- **Chain of Trust:** Each stage of the boot process verifies the next stage before executing it, using cryptographic signatures. This ensures that only trusted code runs.
- **Rollback Protection:** Enforces anti-rollback counters stored in hardware fuses or secure storage, preventing downgrade attacks. Android 14+ strengthens this with Dynamic System Updates (DSU) support and stricter attestation.
- **User Warnings:** If the system is modified or corrupted, the device may display a warning, lock the boot process, or enter recovery mode, preventing unauthorized access.

Importance for Security

- **Prevents Malware Injection:** Blocks unauthorized changes to system files through tamper-resistant verification mechanisms.
- **Protects Sensitive Data:** Ensures apps run on a secure, unmodified system, reducing the risk of data exfiltration by malware.
- **Strengthens App Security:** A secure OS ensures a safer environment for apps to operate without interference from compromised system components.

For Developers and Users

- **Developers:** They should avoid requiring root access, as it disables Verified Boot and weakens security.
- **Users:** They should keep their devices updated and avoid unlocking the bootloader unless necessary, as it compromises Verified Boot protections.

7.2.10 Safety Center

Your One-Stop Shop for Staying Secure

Safety Center is a centralized security and privacy hub introduced in Android to help users manage their device's security and privacy settings in one place. It provides an easy-to-understand dashboard that highlights potential security risks and offers guidance on how to address them.

Essential Attributes

- **Security Alerts and Recommendations:** Displays warnings about compromised passwords, malware, or unsafe settings. Uses machine learning algorithms to analyse user behaviour and identify potential risks dynamically.
- **Privacy Controls:** Shows which apps have accessed sensitive data (location, camera, microphone, etc.). Employs granular permission tracking to log the exact duration and frequency of access.
- **Google Play Protect Integration:** Scans apps for malware and alerts users if an app is harmful. Implements real-time heuristics-based threat detection to identify evolving malware patterns.
- **Security Status Indicators:** Uses color-coded indicators (e.g., red for urgent issues, green for a secure state). Integrates with security patches and firmware updates to ensure compliance with the latest security standards.
- **Actionable Steps for Developers:** Developers must ensure their apps follow security best practices to avoid triggering warnings. Apps should use encrypted storage, API-level security controls, and biometric authentication where applicable.

7.2.11 Cellular Security

Navigating the Mobile Lifeline

While apps like WhatsApp or Signal implement end-to-end encryption to secure your messages, traditional voice calls and SMS texts depend on the cellular network's inherent security mechanisms. However, these protections are only as robust as the network infrastructure itself, leaving room for vulnerabilities that adversaries can exploit. Understanding the security architecture of cellular networks is crucial for mitigating risks.

Android 14+ includes native support for 5G security features including enhanced encryption (256-bit), improved authentication protocols, and network slicing security. The platform now supports disabling legacy protocols (2G/3G) at the modem level through carrier configuration.

The Hidden Risks of Cellular Networks

Cellular networks are designed to keep you connected wherever you go. Features like handover (switching between cell towers as you move) and roaming (connecting to networks when you are abroad) make this possible. However, these same features introduce security challenges:

- **Location Tracking:** Each time a phone pings a tower, it reveals its approximate location. Attackers leveraging SS7 (Signalling System No. 7) vulnerabilities or passive IMSI (International Mobile Subscriber Identity) catching techniques can track movements with alarming accuracy.

- **Interception Risks:** Legacy technologies like 2G employ weaker encryption protocols (e.g., A5/1 cypher), making them susceptible to eavesdropping attacks through real-time decryption methods like rainbow table-based attacks.

The Threat of 2G Networks

Despite their obsolescence, 2G networks continue to pose a security threat due to their persistence in fallback scenarios. Even as carriers phase them out, adversaries exploit their weaknesses through:

- **False Base Stations (FBS):** Also known as "stingrays" or "IMSI catchers", these rogue cell towers deceive devices into connecting, allowing attackers to eavesdrop or manipulate traffic.
- **Connection Downgrading:** Using jamming techniques, attackers can coerce modern devices to fall back to 2G, where encryption is either weak or nonexistent.
- **Data Interception:** Once a device connects to an FBS, attackers can intercept SMS messages and voice calls and even inject malicious payloads into unencrypted traffic.

Disabling 2G Connectivity

Recognizing these vulnerabilities, Android has introduced mechanisms to disable 2G connectivity at the hardware level:

- **Why?** Preventing devices from connecting to 2G eliminates the risk of forced downgrades and FBS-based attacks.
- **How?** Android 14 introduces granular control over 2G connectivity, allowing users or enterprise policies to disable 2G at the framework level to prevent downgrade attacks, subject to carrier and device support. This means the device will not even scan for 2G networks.

7.2.12 Private Space

Creating Safe Havens within Apps

Imagine your Android device as a shared workspace, and within it, you have a secret office that only you can access. This secret office is the Private Space. It is a secure, isolated environment where you can keep sensitive apps and data away from anyone else who might use or access your device.

When you install an app inside the Private Space, it is like placing a brand-new copy of that app in your secret office. There is no shared data or crossover with the same app in the main area of your device. This means all user-generated content, downloads, and account information within the Private Space are entirely separate from the rest of the device.

Core Benefits

- **Data Isolation:** Since apps in the Private Space are installed in a separate Android profile, they operate in their own sandboxed environment. This minimizes the risk of data leakage between apps in different spaces. This differs from the Android Work Profile, which is designed for enterprise data separation, whereas Private Space is focused on personal user privacy.

- **Enhanced Privacy:** Sensitive apps do not appear in notifications, recent apps, settings, or even in other apps when the Private Space is locked. This ensures that any confidential information remains hidden unless explicitly accessed by the authorized user.
- **Reduced Attack Surface:** By compartmentalizing apps, you are effectively reducing the avenues through which malicious actors can attempt to exploit vulnerabilities. Even if an app in the main space is compromised, it will not have access to the data or apps in the Private Space.

Technical Considerations

- **Multi-user Framework Implementation:** The Private Space utilizes Android's multi-user framework, specifically adding a new profile type: android.os.usertype.profile .PRIVATE. Be aware that when the Private Space is locked or unlocked, the user profile is stopped or started respectively. Your app should handle these state changes gracefully.
- **Permission and Role Management:** To interact with the Private Space, especially if you are developing a launcher or settings apps, you need specific permissions like android.permission.ACCESS_HIDDEN_PROFILES. Additionally, acquiring the role android.app.role.RoleManager.ROLE_HOME is necessary to access private profiles.
- **Intent and Broadcast Handling:** Regular intents (like those for telephony) are routed to the main user and display notifications there. However, other intents remain within the Private Space. Your app should listen for broadcasts that indicate when the Private Space is locked or unlocked. Utilize the EXTRA_USER constant to reference the private profile user.
- **User Experience Considerations:** When the Private Space is locked, apps within it should remain invisible. Ensure your app does not inadvertently expose any private data through widgets, notifications, or other channels. If your app deals with file sharing or accessing media, make use of the system Sharesheet and Photo Picker to allow access across spaces, but only when appropriate and securely.
- **Secure Data Handling:** Data does not automatically migrate into Private Space. Developers should implement encrypted synchronization mechanisms if essential data sharing is required. All sensitive operations should incorporate end-to-end encryption and user confirmation before execution.

Private Space creates a secure fortress within your device by utilizing Android's robust multi-user capabilities to add an extra layer of security. Developers ensure their code respects these boundaries and handles segregation properly, empowering users with greater control over their privacy; a vital feature in our increasingly connected world.

7.2.13 OMAPI (Open Mobile API)

Bridging Security and Functionality

The Open Mobile API (OMAPI) is a standardized framework that facilitates secure communication between Android applications and secure elements (SEs) embedded within mobile devices. These secure elements – such as SIM cards, embedded SEs, or external SEs connected via NFC – are tamper-resistant hardware components designed to store sensitive data like cryptographic keys, payment credentials, or identity information securely.

OMAPI plays a pivotal role in enabling secure transactions, including mobile payments, authentication, access control, and identity management. By providing a robust interface for interacting with secure elements, OMAPI ensures that sensitive operations are isolated from the main operating system, mitigating risks such as malware attacks, unauthorized access, or data breaches.

Introduced in Android 9 (API level 28), OMAPI has been extended to support earlier versions of Android (down to API level 21) through libraries like org.simalliance.openmobileapi. Furthermore, with the introduction of the OMAPI Vendor Stable Interface in Android 13, hardware abstraction layers (HALs) can now directly communicate with secure elements, enhancing integration with advanced features like Keymaster and Identity Credentials.

Essential Advantages

- **Secure Communication:** OMAPI provides application protocol data unit (APDU)-level access, ensuring a robust and secure channel for data exchange with secure elements. All interactions are encrypted and authenticated, guaranteeing the confidentiality and integrity of sensitive data.
- **Compatibility:** OMAPI supports a wide range of devices and secure element types, making it highly versatile. Developers can leverage libraries like org.simalliance.openmobileapi to extend compatibility to older Android versions (from API level 21).
- **Access Control:** OMAPI enforces strict access control mechanisms, allowing only authorized applications to interact with secure elements. Unauthorized access attempts result in SecurityException errors, ensuring that sensitive operations remain protected.
- **Vendor Integration:** Android 15's OMAPI Vendor Stable Interface extends secure element access to wearables, enhancing IoT and ecosystem integration.se
- **Support for Multiple Secure Elements:** Devices may contain multiple secure elements, including universal integrated circuit cards (UICCs), embedded SEs, or host card emulation (HCE) modules. OMAPI seamlessly supports interaction with any of these components, ensuring flexibility across use cases.
- **Interoperability:** OMAPI adheres to global standards like GlobalPlatform , ensuring compatibility across different devices, manufacturers, and regions.

Architecture of OMAPI

- **Application Layer:** This is where the Android app resides. Developers use the OMAPI library to send APDU commands to the secure element and process responses. The app must explicitly request permissions to access the secure element.
- **Middleware Layer:** The middleware acts as a bridge between the app and the secure element. It handles tasks such as command routing, protocol translation, and access control enforcement. On Android, this layer is implemented through the SmartcardService component.
- **Secure Element Layer:** This layer consists of the physical secure element(s) embedded in the device. Each SE has its own operating system and supports various applets (small applications) that perform specific functions, such as payment processing, authentication, or identity management.

Use Cases of OMAPI

- **Mobile Payments:** OMAPI facilitates secure NFC-based payment solutions by enabling communication between payment applications and secure elements. Popular apps like Google Pay and Samsung Pay rely on OMAPI for storing payment credentials and performing contactless transactions.

- **Authentication:** Applications can leverage OMAPI to access cryptographic keys stored in secure elements for secure user authentication. This is particularly useful for implementing strong authentication mechanisms like FIDO2-based login or digital ID cards.
- **eSIM Management:** OMAPI supports eSIM provisioning and management, allowing seamless profile switching and activation. This is critical for modern devices that rely on eSIMs for connectivity.
- **Digital Signatures:** Applications requiring legally binding signatures (e.g., document signing apps) can use OMAPI to generate and manage cryptographic keys securely.
- **IoT Device Management:** In IoT ecosystems, OMAPI can facilitate secure provisioning and management of connected devices by storing device certificates and keys on the secure element.
- **Enterprise Security:** Organizations can use OMAPI to enhance employee authentication and data protection, ensuring that corporate apps interact securely with hardware-backed credentials.

Challenges and Limitations of OMAPI

- **Device Compatibility:** Not all devices have secure elements, and configurations may vary across manufacturers. Developers must account for these differences to ensure broad compatibility.
- **Complexity of Implementation:** Working with OMAPI requires a solid understanding of secure element technologies and APDU commands, which can be challenging for developers new to the field.
- **Performance Overhead:** Interactions with secure elements introduce additional latency compared to purely software-based solutions. Developers should optimize their apps to minimize performance impact.
- **Vendor-Specific Extensions:** Some manufacturers may introduce proprietary extensions to OMAPI, complicating cross-device compatibility.

7.3 Application Security Perspectives

Code Under the Microscope

In the realm of application security, understanding the intricate workings of mobile platforms like Android is crucial. As the digital landscape evolves, so do the methods and technologies aimed at fortifying the resilience of applications against a myriad of threats.

This section explores the various facets of application security within the Android ecosystem, revealing a multifaceted approach that encompasses the fundamental building blocks of Android apps, permission models, third-party applications, and inter-process communication mechanisms.

Examining these elements collectively provides a deeper understanding of the challenges and opportunities inherent in securing Android applications in an ever-evolving digital landscape. This comprehensive analysis not only sheds light on the underlying architecture of Android applications but also gets into the strategies employed to safeguard user privacy, protect sensitive data, and fortify the integrity of the system.

7.3.1 Android Application Building Blocks

The Nuts and Bolts of Android

Android is an open-source mobile operating system built on the Linux kernel, which serves as the core of the OS, much like the engine of a car. This openness allows for widespread contributions from developers worldwide, continuously improving the platform's robustness and security. However, this openness also introduces challenges, such as increased attack surfaces and the need for rigorous security hardening techniques.

Developers use Kotlin, Java, or C++ with Android 15's Jetpack Compose for declarative UI development, reducing UI-related vulnerabilities. Google now mandates Rust for new OS components to mitigate memory-safety vulnerabilities in native code.

Applications are distributed as APKs or Android App Bundles (.aab), with .aab being the standard format for Google Play distribution, which contains all the necessary components for the app to function on an Android device. APKs are digitally signed using developer keys, and Android enforces signature verification to prevent tampering and unauthorized modifications.

Key Elements

- **AndroidManifest.xml:** Imagine this as the blueprint or instruction manual for the app. It is like a detailed map that tells the Android system everything about the app, what it is capable of, what resources it needs, and how it should behave. For instance, it lists permissions the app needs, like access to your location or camera, to ensure your privacy and security.
- **Activities:** Think of Activities as different rooms in a house, each serving a specific purpose. When you open an app, you are essentially stepping into one of these rooms. Some rooms might be where you read messages, others where you edit photos, and so on. Activities are the interactive parts of the app where you do things like tap buttons, type text, or swipe through screens.
- **Services:** Consider Services as the background workers or assistants of the app. They are like the backstage crew, making sure everything runs smoothly. For example, think of a music streaming app, even if you are not actively using it, a Service keeps the music playing in the background. Similarly, chat apps might have a Service that listens for new messages even when the app is not open.
- **Broadcast Receivers:** These are like attentive listeners, always on standby for important messages or signals. Imagine them as antennas tuned to specific frequencies. When something noteworthy happens, like your battery running low or a new notification arriving, they catch that signal and can trigger actions in the app. So, if your battery is low, a Broadcast Receiver might prompt the app to switch to a power-saving mode to conserve energy.

7.3.2 Android Permission Model

Protecting Your Privacy

The Android Permission Model acts as a protective shield around your device's sensitive features, such as the camera, GPS, or Bluetooth. To access these features, apps must request permissions, which serve as a form of user consent.

This model fosters transparency, accountability, and user empowerment, allowing individuals to navigate the digital landscape with confidence, knowing their devices are protected by robust security measures.

Key Blocks

- **Application Sandbox:** Imagine the sandbox as a fortress within your device. Each app resides in its own secure space, isolated from other apps and the core system. This separation ensures that even if one app is compromised, it cannot easily access or tamper with the data of other apps or the system itself. This sandboxing mechanism acts as a fundamental barrier, preventing malicious actions from spreading and protecting your device's integrity.
- **Limited Access:** By default, apps have restricted access to sensitive resources like your contacts, messages, or location. They cannot just reach out and grab this data without your explicit consent. Android's permission system requires apps to request access to specific resources, and you have the final say in granting or denying these requests. This granular control over permissions minimizes the risk of unauthorized access to your personal information, safeguarding your privacy.
- **Protected APIs:** Behind the scenes, Android exposes various application programming interfaces (APIs) that allow apps to interact with device features like the camera, GPS, or Bluetooth. However, not all APIs are open for unrestricted use. Some, known as protected APIs, are gated behind permissions. These permissions act as gatekeepers, ensuring that only authorized apps with legitimate purposes can access these sensitive features. This layered approach to API access enhances security by preventing unauthorized apps from exploiting device capabilities for malicious purposes.
- **Runtime Permissions:** Android introduced the runtime permissions model to empower users with greater control over their data. When an app requests permission to access a sensitive resource, such as your location or microphone, you receive a prompt asking for your consent. This real-time permission granting enables you to make informed decisions about which apps can access your personal data and under what circumstances. By placing permission control directly in your hands, Android enhances transparency and accountability in-app permissions, bolstering overall security.
- **Permission Management:** Once you grant permission to an app, it retains that permission until you uninstall the app. This means you will not be repeatedly bombarded with permission requests every time you use the app. However, Android provides robust tools for managing permissions, allowing you to review and adjust app permissions at any time. Whether you want to revoke permission from a specific app or check which apps have access to your location, Android puts you in control, empowering you to tailor your device's security settings to your preferences.
- **User Control:** Android prioritizes user autonomy when it comes to privacy and security. You have the freedom to customize your device's permission settings according to your preferences and needs. Within the device settings, you can easily navigate through the list of installed apps, view their permissions, and make adjustments as necessary. This level of user control empowers you to maintain a balance between functionality and security, ensuring that your device operates according to your personal standards.
- **Security Measures:** Android's permission system incorporates robust security measures to fortify your device against potential threats. If an app attempts to access a protected feature without the necessary permissions, it encounters a security barrier, preventing unauthorized access. This proactive enforcement of permissions at the

lowest system level serves as a critical line of defence, thwarting malicious attempts to exploit vulnerabilities and ensuring the integrity of your device's security posture.

7.3.3 Understand Third-party Applications

Be App Aware

In today's digital age, understanding the security implications of third-party applications is crucial. Android goes the extra mile to ensure users are informed about the permissions these apps require and the potential impact on their privacy and security.

Before downloading any app, Android provides detailed information about the permissions it requires, allowing users to make informed decisions. Once an app is installed, users are not bombarded with permission requests, ensuring a seamless experience while maintaining security.

Foundational Aspects

- **Empowering Users:** This proactive approach empowers users to take control of their security and privacy settings. By presenting permission requests before installation, Android ensures that users are aware of the data and resources an app intends to access. This transparency enables users to assess the app's trustworthiness and decide whether it aligns with their security preferences.
- **Enhanced Security:** Moreover, Android's upfront notification strategy contributes to enhanced security by preventing unauthorized access to sensitive data. Users are less likely to unwittingly grant permissions to malicious apps when they are provided with clear information about the app's intentions upfront. This proactive measure significantly reduces the risk of potential security breaches and protects users from malicious activities.
- **Seamless User Experience:** Android's commitment to providing a seamless user experience extends to its approach to permissions. Unlike platforms that bombard users with permission requests during app usage, Android minimizes disruptions by only requesting permissions at the time of installation. This ensures that users can enjoy their apps without constant interruptions, enhancing overall user satisfaction.
- **Transparency Matters:** Transparency is key to fostering accountability within the app ecosystem. Android's practice of displaying app permissions encourages developers to be transparent about their app's functionalities and data access requirements. This transparency not only builds trust between users and developers but also allows users to hold developers accountable for their app's behaviour.

7.3.4 Interprocess Communication

Behind the Scenes of Multitasking

Interprocess communication (IPC) is the mechanism that allows different apps or components within an app to communicate with each other on an Android device. It is like a secure channel that ensures efficient and safe data exchange between apps, maintaining the overall security of the device.

Android encourages developers to use recommended IPC frameworks to ensure that communication between apps is both efficient and secure, safeguarding user data and protecting against potential vulnerabilities.

How Android Securely Manages IPC

- **Binder:** Think of Binder as a super-efficient and secure hotline between apps. When one app needs to talk to another, it can pick up the Binder phone and make a call. This call is super-fast and secure, thanks to a special technology built into Android. It is like having a direct line to the information you need without any risk of someone eavesdropping on your conversation.
- **Services:** Consider Services as specialized assistants within apps. They offer specific functions or information that other apps might need. These services can be accessed securely using the Binder technology, which ensures controlled and safe communication. It functions like a personal assistant who shares only the necessary information, eliminating the risk of leaking private data to unauthorized parties.
- **Intents:** Intents are like requests or announcements sent out to the Android system. When an app wants to perform a certain action, like showing a webpage or notifying the user about something, it sends out an Intent. The Android system then finds the right app or component to handle that request, ensuring that tasks are completed efficiently and securely. It is akin to broadcasting your needs to the entire Android ecosystem but with safeguards in place to protect your privacy and security.
- **Content Providers:** Imagine Content Providers as secure vaults where apps store and share data. For example, your contacts list is stored in a Content Provider. Apps can access data from these vaults securely without risking any unauthorized access or tampering. Additionally, apps can create their own vaults to share their own data securely with other apps. It is like having a bank vault for your data, with strict security measures in place to ensure that only authorized users can access it.

7.4 OWASP MASVS Overview

Mobile App Security Blueprint

In the fast-paced realm of mobile application development, security is not just an option; it is a fundamental necessity. As the digital landscape continues to evolve, the need for robust security measures has become more critical than ever. The OWASP Mobile Application Security Verification Standard (MASVS) emerges as a key framework designed to address this imperative. MASVS provides a comprehensive guide to fortifying mobile applications against a wide range of potential threats lurking in the digital shadows.

This section provides an overarching view of the key facets encapsulated within OWASP MASVS, highlighting its significance, implementation strategies, and the continuous cycle of adaptation it embodies. From laying foundational principles to navigating the intricacies of secure coding and fortifying against attacks, MASVS serves as a steadfast companion in the journey toward creating mobile applications that not only function seamlessly but also safeguard the sanctity of user data and privacy.

7.4.1 MASVS Intro

The Key to Mobile App Trust

In the world of mobile app development, security is paramount. That is where the OWASP Mobile Application Security Verification Standard (MASVS) comes in. MASVS is your go-to guide for fortifying your app against threats.

MASVS functions as a rulebook, ensuring no security loopholes are left open during development. By integrating security measures seamlessly, it protects user data from hackers. Implementing MASVS instils a culture of security, enhancing user trust and protecting against cyber threats.

What sets MASVS apart is its adaptability; it is regularly updated to address emerging risks. Staying informed and using the latest version is crucial for developers, ensuring mobile apps remain secure in the ever-evolving digital landscape.

- **Overview:** The OWASP Mobile Application Security Verification Standard (MASVS) is a collaborative effort developed by cybersecurity experts within OWASP to provide a clear framework for mobile app security. It serves as a dynamic resource, regularly updated to address emerging threats and evolving industry trends, ensuring it remains relevant and effective. MASVS is designed to provide developers with clear instructions on integrating security measures into every phase of app development, from initial design to deployment and beyond.
- **Purpose and Importance:** MASVS functions as a comprehensive rulebook for developers, guiding them to fortify mobile apps against potential threats. It provides a checklist-like guide to ensure no security loopholes are left open during app development, addressing common security problems that could compromise user data. By embedding security measures from the outset, MASVS helps protect personal information and builds user trust, making mobile apps as secure as possible.
- **Implementation and Benefits:** MASVS guides developers in integrating security measures into every stage of app development and testing, acting as a shield against unauthorized access and data breaches. It equips developers with the necessary tools and insights to create secure mobile applications, enhancing user trust by prioritizing security and privacy. By adhering to MASVS guidelines, developers can protect both the app and its users from cyber threats, fostering a secure and reliable mobile environment.
- **Continuous Updates and Adaptation:** MASVS is regularly updated to remain relevant and effective in the rapidly evolving digital landscape, incorporating feedback from developers and keeping pace with industry trends. Staying informed and using the latest version of MASVS is essential for developers and security professionals to ensure mobile apps are equipped to address emerging threats and vulnerabilities effectively.

7.4.2 Mobile Application Security Model

The Mobile App Shield

Imagine your mobile device as a fortress, guarding your most valuable possessions: your personal data. Just as a fortress needs strong walls and vigilant guards to protect its treasures, your mobile apps require robust security measures to safeguard your information from digital threats.

The Mobile Application Security Model provides a comprehensive framework divided into various groups, each addressing critical aspects of mobile security. Let's look into these groups and explore how they ensure the safety and integrity of your mobile experience.

- **MASVS-STORAGE (Secure Data Storage):** Think of your mobile device as a vault, and inside that vault are your most valuable possessions, your personal data. This group focuses on implementing extra layers of security around that vault to ensure that even if someone gains access, they cannot retrieve your sensitive information. It is like having a hidden safe within your already secure vault, ensuring data remains protected against unauthorized access and potential breaches.

- **MASVS-CRYPTO (Encryption):** Encryption is akin to a secret language your device uses to scramble your data into unreadable text, which only those with the correct key can decipher. This group ensures that your secrets stay safe, even if intercepted by unauthorized parties. Encryption protects data in transit and at rest, securing communications and stored information from prying eyes.

- **MASVS-AUTH (Authentication and Authorization):** Picture your mobile app as a fortress with gatekeepers who control entry based on identity and authorization. This group ensures that only authorized individuals have access to specific areas or functions within an app. It enforces strong authentication mechanisms and limits access to resources, safeguarding against unauthorized use.

- **MASVS-NETWORK (Secure Network Communication):** Your mobile device acts as a messenger, delivering requests and receiving responses over the internet. This group ensures that all communications are securely encrypted and protected from interception or tampering. It is like sending your letters through a secure courier service, guaranteeing they arrive safely and unchanged.

- **MASVS-PLATFORM (Platform Security):** Imagine your mobile device as a bustling city, with different neighbourhoods representing different apps. This group ensures that each app interacts securely with the operating system and other apps, preventing conflicts and vulnerabilities. It focuses on maintaining a secure environment where apps can operate without compromising each other's security.

- **MASVS-CODE (Secure Coding):** An app's code is like the blueprint of a building. This group emphasizes the importance of writing secure code to prevent vulnerabilities that attackers could exploit. By adhering to secure coding practices, developers build apps that are resistant to common attacks such as injection, buffer overflow, and insecure deserialization.

- **MASVS-RESILIENCE (Resistance to Attacks):** This group equips your app with defensive measures to withstand attacks, ensuring it can continue functioning even under adverse conditions. It involves implementing protections against reverse engineering, tampering, and other forms of exploitation, making the app resilient against malicious activities.

- **MASVS-PRIVACY (Protecting User Privacy):** Users trust apps with their personal information, and this group focuses on respecting and safeguarding that trust. It ensures that user data is collected, stored, and processed in compliance with privacy standards and regulations. By following these guidelines, developers can build apps that protect user privacy and handle sensitive data responsibly.

7.4.3 Secure App Ecosystem

Security That Connects

In the world of mobile app development, security is paramount. Think of your app as a fortress, with each system it connects to as a potential entry point for attackers. From servers to Bluetooth devices, vulnerabilities can be found everywhere, and it is crucial to safeguard against these potential weaknesses.

Security is not an afterthought; it is a mindset ingrained from the very beginning of the app creation process. Developers must encrypt data, adhere to industry standards like OWASP, and regularly update their apps to fend off threats. However, security extends beyond code; it encompasses everyone involved in the development process, from developers to testers and managers.

- **Building a Secure Fortress Around Your App:** Imagine your app as a house, with various systems it interacts with, such as servers, APIs, Bluetooth devices, and even cars, acting as different entry points. Each entry point could have vulnerabilities that attackers might exploit. Building a secure app is akin to constructing a fortress, where every component is designed and tested to resist potential attacks.
- **Security – A Mindset from Day One:** Security should be a fundamental aspect of the app development process from the start. Developers need to follow strict guidelines to keep threats at bay, including encrypting sensitive data, adhering to industry standards like OWASP, and regularly updating the app to address new vulnerabilities. Security awareness should be instilled in everyone involved in app creation, ensuring a holistic approach to safeguarding the app.
- **Staying Ahead in the Ever-changing World of Apps:** The mobile app landscape is constantly evolving, with new technologies and threats emerging regularly. Developers and security experts must keep learning and adapting to stay ahead of potential attackers. Organizations like OWASP provide resources and training to help developers stay informed about the latest security practices, ensuring they can build secure apps that withstand evolving threats.

7.4.4 MASVS Applicability

Security for All Apps

When it comes to ensuring mobile apps are secure, the Mobile App Security Verification Standard (MASVS) acts as a comprehensive checklist, helping both businesses and developers ensure that their apps meet industry-standard security requirements, regardless of how they are built.

- **Native Apps:** Native apps are designed specifically for a particular platform, such as Java or Kotlin for Android. MASVS guidelines cover these apps, ensuring they are built securely to leverage the full potential of the platform while maintaining robust security measures.
- **Cross-platform and Hybrid Apps:** Cross-platform and hybrid apps are designed to work on multiple platforms, often using frameworks that may introduce security risks if not properly managed. MASVS helps developers address these potential issues, ensuring the apps are secure and consistent across different environments.
- **Preloaded Apps:** Preloaded apps come installed on devices from manufacturers and often have elevated privileges, making them potential targets for attackers. MASVS provides guidelines for assessing and securing these apps, ensuring they do not introduce vulnerabilities to the device.
- **SDKs (Software Development Kits):** SDKs are collections of tools and libraries that developers use to build apps more efficiently. However, they can also bring security risks if not properly vetted. MASVS helps developers ensure that the SDKs they use are secure and do not compromise the app's integrity.

Looking Ahead

This chapter serves as a pivotal junction in our exploration of Android security, emphasizing the significance of robust security measures in the evolving landscape of mobile technology. By dissecting the key components of Android security, ranging from device to application perspectives, this chapter laid the groundwork for understanding the multifaceted nature of protecting Android applications. This chapter not only illuminates the current security frameworks but also sets the stage for future advancements in this critical field.

The principles and insights gained from this chapter will be instrumental in navigating the complex world of mobile security. The rapid pace of technological innovation necessitates a proactive and forward-thinking mindset. Developers must remain vigilant and adaptive to emerging threats while embracing new tools and methodologies that enhance security. By continuously refining and evolving our security strategies, Android applications can remain resilient and secure against an ever-changing threat landscape.

Furthermore, the introduction to OWASP Mobile Application Security Verification Standard (MASVS) emphasized the value of a structured approach to security assessment. As a widely accepted framework, MASVS helps developers and security professionals establish robust security baselines for Android applications. Moving forward, adopting these security principles early in the development lifecycle will not only enhance app security but also build user trust and compliance with industry standards. The next chapters will explore practical implementation techniques to further strengthen Android app security in real-world scenarios.

Chapter 8

OWASP MASVS Insights

> Arise, awake, and stop not till the goal is reached.
>
> – Swami Vivekananda

Swami Vivekananda, an Indian Hindu monk, philosopher, author, and teacher, emphasis a call to action, urging individuals to awaken their inner potential and pursue their goals with unwavering determination. He emphasizes the importance of persistence and perseverance in the face of obstacles, inspiring people to relentlessly strive towards their aspirations.

In the context of mobile application security, Swami Vivekananda's quote encourages developers to remain steadfast in their efforts to secure Android applications. The journey of securing mobile apps can be challenging and demanding, requiring continuous vigilance and dedication. By adopting Vivekananda's mantra of "arise, awake, and stop not", developers can commit themselves to the ongoing process of improving the security posture of Android applications. This quote serves as a reminder that achieving security excellence requires persistent effort and a resolute mindset, aligning with the ethos of constant improvement advocated by the OWASP Mobile Application Security Verification Standard (MASVS).

DOI: 10.1201/9781003640332-11

A LAYMAN'S PERSPECTIVE

A Comprehensive Study of OWASP MASVS

In today's digital age, smartphones have evolved into indispensable companions, seamlessly handling everything from banking transactions to social interactions. However, as our reliance on mobile applications grows, so does the need for robust security. Just as doors are locked to safeguard physical belongings, securing mobile applications against cyber threats is crucial.

This is where the Mobile Application Security Verification Standard (MASVS) steps in. MASVS is not just a checklist; it is a comprehensive security framework designed to guide developers and organizations in fortifying mobile applications against potential vulnerabilities. Rather than merely serving as a certification standard, MASVS functions as a trusted security advisor, offering actionable recommendations to strengthen app security at every stage of development.

Understanding MASVS: A Security Consultant for Your Mobile Apps

Think of MASVS as a seasoned security consultant for your smartphone applications. Unlike conventional security models that rely solely on certification, MASVS adopts a transparent and systematic approach to security assessment. It provides a structured methodology that enables testers to scrutinizse an app's architecture, examine its source code, review project documentation, and analyse user interaction scenarios, all to uncover and mitigate potential security risks.

The Scope and Limitations of MASVS

While MASVS is an invaluable resource, it is essential to understand its scope. Consider it a specialized security expert focused on addressing specific threats rather than a one-size-fits-all shield against all cyber dangers. MASVS primarily addresses the most critical security aspects of mobile applications, ensuring they adhere to best practices in data protection, cryptography, authentication, network security, platform interaction, and resilience against reverse engineering.

The Testing Methodology: A Blend of Technology and Human Intuition

Ensuring compliance with MASVS requires a combination of advanced security technologies and human expertis. Security testers leverage automated tools and manual techniques, akin to combining a superhero's arsenal with the deductive prowess of a seasoned investigator. Through meticulous testing and analysis, they identify security flaws, reinforce defences, and protect user data from potential breaches.

MASVS as a Developer's Mentor

MASVS is not just a tool for security professionals; it also serves as a guiding framework for app developers. By following MASVS guidelines, developers can build inherently secure applications from the ground up. Furthermore, organizsations can tailor MASVS to meet their specific security needs, ensuring that their applications remain resilient against evolving threats in the ever-changing digital landscape.

Embracing MASVS for a Secure Digital Future

Ultimately, MASVS is a beacon of security wisdom, empowering developers and organizations to create more resilient mobile applications. By embracing its principles and integrating its recommendations into the development lifecycle, it becomes possible to cultivate a digital ecosystem where users can confidently engage with mobile applications without fear of cyber threats.

8.1 MASVS-STORAGE

Secure Data Handling: Protecting Sensitive Information

Imagine your smartphone as a treasure trove, brimming with valuable possessions: your identity, financial details, cherished memories, and more. Just like in real life, you entrust different apps with handling these digital treasures. Each app has its own little vault within your phone's treasure trove, where it stores sensitive data such as your login credentials, private messages, and preferences.

Now, the security of these digital vaults is paramount. Without adequate protection, it is akin to leaving your valuables strewn about in a crowded marketplace, vulnerable to prying eyes and nimble fingers.

Secure storage in Android applications acts as the guardian of these digital treasures, employing various safeguards to ensure that your sensitive information remains shielded from unauthorized access and potential breaches.

Consider your phone's storage as a vast landscape with different zones: private enclaves accessible only by the app itself, and public areas where any app or user could stumble upon your secrets. It is crucial for developers to implement robust security measures across all these zones, regardless of whether the data storage is intentional or inadvertent.

Think of secure storage as fortifying the walls of each app's vault within your phone's treasure trove. It is like installing multiple layers of security mechanisms such as encryption, access controls, and integrity checks to fortify these digital strongholds against intruders and data leaks.

Moreover, secure storage is not just about protecting intentional data storage. It also encompasses guarding against unintentional leaks that could occur due to missteps in utilizing the phone's capabilities, like backups or logging mechanisms.

In essence, secure storage is not merely a feature; it is a fundamental principle that underpins the trustworthiness of Android applications. It is about instilling confidence in users that their digital treasures are safeguarded with the utmost care, fostering a sense of security and peace of mind in an increasingly interconnected world.

So, the next time you entrust your personal information to an Android app, rest assured that secure storage is there, standing guard like a stalwart sentinel, ensuring that your digital treasures remain safe and sound within the confines of your smartphone's treasure trove.

8.1.1 MASVS-STORAGE-1: Secure Sensitive Data Storage

Fort Knox for Your Secrets

MASVS-STORAGE-1 defines a clear mandate: sensitive data must be stored securely. This requirement is crucial for maintaining the confidentiality, integrity, and trustworthiness of mobile applications, especially those handling user credentials, personal information, financial records, or session identifiers.

Failing to meet this requirement can lead to serious data breaches, particularly in rooted or compromised devices. Even in standard user environments, malicious apps or physical attackers may attempt to exploit poorly protected storage mechanisms. Developers must therefore implement a storage strategy that assumes hostile access while minimizing exposure.

Classifying and Identifying Sensitive Data

Before applying secure storage principles, developers must clearly identify what constitutes sensitive data in the context of their application. Common examples include:

- **Authentication Credentials:** such as usernames, passwords, OAuth access or refresh tokens.
- **Personally Identifiable Information (PII):** including name, address, phone number, email, and national ID numbers.
- **Financial and Transactional Data:** including account balances, transaction histories, or payment card information.
- **Health Data:** in medical or wellness apps, data such as heart rate, symptoms, or diagnostic results.
- **Cryptographic Secrets:** such as private keys, API keys, or symmetric encryption keys used for local encryption.

Once this data is identified, the next step is selecting appropriate storage mechanisms and applying strong protective controls.

Secure Storage Locations

Android offers multiple storage options, each with different risk profiles:

- **Internal App Storage** (/data/data/<package_name>/): Accessible only to the app, this location is sandboxed by the operating system. However, on rooted devices or those with privilege escalation, an attacker can still read this directory. Sensitive data here should be encrypted before being written.
- **External Storage** (e.g., /sdcard/, /storage/emulated/0/): This location is shared across apps and user-accessible. Data here is exposed to any app with storage permissions and even to USB-connected devices. Sensitive data must never be stored on external storage, even temporarily.
- **Shared Preferences:** Suitable for small key-value data. By default, these reside in internal storage (/data/data/<package_name>/shared_prefs/) but are not encrypted unless explicitly protected. Avoid storing secrets like passwords or tokens here in plaintext.
- **SQLite Databases:** Used for structured data. These are stored internally but require encryption for storing sensitive values. Developers can use libraries such as SQLCipher for transparent, file-level encryption of databases.
- **KeyStore System:** A hardware-backed storage (on supported devices) for cryptographic keys. It ensures that keys are stored outside the app's memory space and are never exposed in plaintext. The KeyStore is the preferred mechanism for managing encryption keys and signing credentials securely.

Best Practices for Safeguarding Sensitive Data

To effectively adhere to MASVS-STORAGE-1, developers should implement a layered security approach:

- **Encrypt Sensitive Data Before Storage:** Use AES-256 in GCM mode (AES-GCM) or similarly strong authenticated encryption algorithms. Keys should be generated and retrieved via the Android Keystore using KeyGenParameterSpec and encrypted data stored in internal files or EncryptedSharedPreferences.
- **Isolate Encryption Keys from Encrypted Data:** Never store both the encryption key and the encrypted data in the same location. For example, a user's password hash should be encrypted using a key from the Keystore, and the resulting cipher stored in a different internal file.
- **Leverage EncryptedFile and EncryptedSharedPreferences APIs:** These Jetpack Security components abstract key management and use AES-GCM for secure encryption. They use per-app Keystore keys and offer file-level and key-value encryption. Note that these APIs are now in maintenance mode; for new projects, consider direct Android Keystore integration with modern cryptographic libraries.
- **Use SQLCipher for Encrypted Databases:** SQLCipher is an open-source extension for SQLite that adds transparent 256-bit AES encryption. The encryption key should be generated dynamically and protected using the Android Keystore.
- **Avoid Storing Authentication Data Persistently:** For access tokens and session identifiers, store them in memory during the session lifecycle and persist them only when required for long-term authentication, ensuring they are encrypted.
- **Restrict Data Retention Periods:** Design your app so that sensitive data is removed once it's no longer needed. Examples include deleting cached responses on logout or clearing encrypted tokens after session expiration.
- **Disable Auto-backup for Sensitive Files:** Android's Auto Backup (API 23+) and cloud backup may include internal app data unless explicitly excluded. Use the android:allowBackup="false" flag in the manifest and place sensitive files in the no_ backup directory.
- **Apply Correct File Permissions:** Files stored in internal directories inherit restrictive permissions by default (MODE_PRIVATE), but avoid accidentally relaxing these permissions (e.g., MODE_WORLD_READABLE), which are deprecated for security reasons.
- **Protect In-memory Sensitive Data:** Clear memory buffers and strings containing sensitive data immediately after use. Avoid using immutable objects like Java strings for passwords or secrets, as they can persist in memory longer than necessary.

Common Pitfalls

Even well-meaning developers can fall into insecure storage patterns. Common mistakes that violate MASVS-STORAGE-1 include:

- Storing sensitive data like JWT tokens in unencrypted SharedPreferences.
- Writing logs that include full request or response bodies containing sensitive fields (e.g., passwords or API keys).
- Caching PDF reports or confidential images in external storage for viewing purposes.
- Backing up internal files containing PII without proper exclusions, leading to unintended cloud exposure.
- Using hardcoded symmetric keys within the application binary, which can be extracted via reverse engineering.

8.1.2 MASVS-STORAGE-2: Prevent Sensitive Data Leakage

Lock Down Your Leaks

MASVS-STORAGE-2 mandates that the mobile app must prevent leakage of sensitive data. This control focuses on ensuring that sensitive information is not accidentally exposed in unprotected areas of the device or app environment, such as logs, caches, backups, or inter-process communication channels.

The Importance of Preventing Data Leakage

Mobile applications often handle various forms of sensitive user data, including passwords, session tokens, personally identifiable information (PII), credit card numbers, and health-related records. Insecure storage or improper data handling can cause these details to leak into unintended locations on the device. Once leaked, even temporarily, such data becomes a potential target for exploitation by malicious applications, attackers with physical access, or forensic tools, particularly on compromised or rooted devices.

Common Data Leakage Vectors

Some typical ways through which sensitive data unintentionally leaks include:

- Logging confidential details such as API responses, user credentials, or tokens using Android logging utilities like Log.d() or Log.i().
- Storing sensitive data in temporary files or cache directories without proper restrictions.
- Allowing sensitive content to remain in the clipboard, which can be accessed by other apps.
- Saving user data in external storage or shared preferences without encryption or proper access controls.
- Failing to configure backup settings, thereby including sensitive data in automatic cloud backups.
- Including confidential information in crash reports or diagnostic data.
- Allowing WebView components to cache and store sensitive content.

Secure Development Practices to Prevent Data Leakage

To comply with MASVS-STORAGE-2, Android developers must rigorously apply secure design and coding principles throughout the app's lifecycle. Below are the key practices, each explained with practical technical details to help developers eliminate common data leakage risks.

- **Avoid Logging Sensitive Data at All Stages of the App Lifecycle:** Android provides logging utilities such as Log.d(), Log.i(), Log.w(), and Log.e() that are extremely useful during development. However, when used carelessly, these logs can expose highly sensitive information such as API tokens, user credentials, or personal identifiers. Developers should ensure that production builds do not log such data. This can be enforced by placing sensitive logging behind a BuildConfig.DEBUG condition and ensuring that ProGuard or R8 rules strip out these log statements during release compilation. Furthermore, sensitive objects (e.g., User, Token, CardDetails) should implement toString() cautiously to avoid accidental leakage when such objects are logged.

- **Use Internal Storage Exclusively for Sensitive Files and Data:** Android applications have access to both internal and external storage. Internal storage (accessed via methods like getFilesDir() or getCacheDir()) is private to the application and not accessible by other apps, making it suitable for storing sensitive information. On the contrary, external storage (e.g., using Environment.getExternalStorageDirectory()) is world-readable and can expose data even without root access. Sensitive data such as configuration files, session tokens, and cached API responses should be stored in internal directories only, with clearly defined lifecycles, such as secure deletion after use and during logout.

- **Disable or Restrict Data from Being Included in System Backups:** Android's backup mechanism can automatically save app data to a user's Google account. If this includes sensitive files, they may be unintentionally backed up to the cloud in plaintext. Developers should disable backups entirely if not needed by setting android:allowBackup="false" in the AndroidManifest.xml. For apps that do require backups, developers should use the <fullBackupContent> configuration to exclude specific files or directories containing sensitive data. This ensures that even if the backup is enabled, critical data like session information, authentication tokens, or biometric settings are not uploaded.

- **Minimize Use of Clipboard for Sensitive Content and Ensure Timely Clearing:** Android's clipboard system is accessible across applications and does not provide access control. If sensitive data, such as OTPs, passwords, or transaction details, is copied to the clipboard, any app running on the device can potentially read it. Developers should avoid placing sensitive data into the clipboard unless it is absolutely necessary for user convenience. In such cases, the app should clear the clipboard immediately after use using the ClipboardManager service, thus minimizing the exposure window.

- **Prevent WebView Components from Caching Sensitive Data:** WebViews are often used in mobile apps to render web-based content. However, by default, WebView components cache pages, store form data, and maintain history, all of which can lead to sensitive data leakage. When displaying content that includes personal or transactional data, developers should disable caching (WebSettings.setCacheMode(WebSettings.LOAD_NO_CACHE)) and disable saving form data. Additionally, developers should invoke methods like clearHistory() and clearCache(true) after the WebView has finished loading sensitive content, and avoid using WebView for highly sensitive operations unless the content is well-sanitized and hosted securely.

- **Ensure Crash Reporting Tools Are Configured to Exclude Sensitive Information:** Many developers integrate third-party crash reporting tools like Firebase Crashlytics, Sentry, or Bugsnag. These tools collect stack traces, log snippets, and device state at the time of failure. If these logs inadvertently contain sensitive user data, it becomes a serious privacy issue. Developers should take care to sanitize logs before submission, mask confidential fields, and use tagging mechanisms to prevent the collection of high-risk data. Some crash reporting tools allow configuration to filter out or redact certain fields at runtime before they are transmitted to the server.

- **Always Use Private Mode When Accessing Shared Preferences or Writing Files:** Shared preferences are often used to store simple key-value data such as user settings or flags. By default, developers should use MODE_PRIVATE when creating or accessing shared preferences or files. This mode ensures that the data is readable and writable only by the application itself. For example, storing a user token using getSharedPreferences("secure_prefs", MODE_PRIVATE) ensures proper isolation. Developers should also consider adding an encryption layer using the AndroidX Security library (EncryptedSharedPreferences) for an added layer of protection.

- **Review and Control Behaviour of Third-party Libraries and SDKs:** Many third-party libraries collect diagnostic information or maintain their own caches and logs. These behaviours can result in sensitive data being unintentionally stored or transmitted. Developers must audit all third-party dependencies, especially analytics, advertising, or payment SDKs, to ensure they do not violate MASVS-STORAGE-2 principles. This includes reviewing their documentation, runtime behaviour, and configurations to disable or limit data collection features.

8.2 MASVS-CRYPTO

Secure Cryptographic Operations: Enhancing Data Security

Let's explore a bit deeper into the analogy of cryptography being like a secret code and how it is used to protect sensitive information on your phone.

Imagine your phone is like a treasure chest full of valuable items - your passwords, financial details, and personal information are the treasures inside. Now, this treasure chest is small and portable, which is convenient for you, but it also means that if someone gets their hands on it, they could easily plunder your treasures.

Cryptography is like a magical lock that you put on your treasure chest to keep it safe. It scrambles all your valuable information into a jumbled mess that looks like gibberish to anyone who does not have the magic key to unscramble it. So, even if someone manages to lay their hands on your treasure chest (your phone), they will not be able to make sense of what is inside without the key.

Now, just like any lock, there are different types of cryptographic methods, some stronger than others. The controls in this category are like expert guidelines that developers follow to make sure they are using the best, strongest locks for your treasure chest. They ensure that developers use techniques that have been tried and tested, following industry standards, like using the sturdiest locks available.

But here is the thing: even if you have the strongest lock in the world, if you are careless with the key, your treasures are not completely safe. That is where key management comes in. These controls also focus on how developers handle and safeguard those magic keys. They ensure that keys are generated securely, stored in safe places, and protected from falling into the wrong hands.

So, think of cryptography and these controls as your ultimate guardians, making sure your treasures stay safe and sound inside your treasure chest, even if the chest itself gets into the wrong hands.

8.2.1 MASVS-CRYPTO-1: Strong Cryptography Usage

State-of-the-art Cryptography

Strong cryptography forms the backbone of secure Android app development. MASVS-CRYPTO-1 emphasizes that mobile applications must employ cryptographic algorithms that are both modern and aligned with current industry standards. This requirement is not merely about encryption for the sake of it, it is about applying cryptography correctly, using robust algorithms, and managing keys securely to protect sensitive data both at rest and in transit.

Importance of Using Strong Cryptography

Modern attackers have access to sophisticated tools and computing power, rendering outdated or misapplied cryptographic schemes ineffective. The use of deprecated algorithms such as MD5 or SHA-1, or incorrect implementations of otherwise strong ciphers (e.g., using ECB mode with AES), creates significant risk. MASVS-CRYPTO-1 requires developers to follow both cryptographic strength and secure implementation guidelines to ensure resilience against cryptanalysis, brute-force attacks, and other forms of exploitation.

Industry Best Practices in Cryptographic Usage

Android developers must adopt practices that go beyond simply invoking encryption APIs. Key considerations include:

- **Algorithm Selection**: Use strong and widely accepted cryptographic algorithms such as AES-256-GCM for symmetric encryption and RSA with at least 3072-bit keys for asymmetric encryption. For hashing, SHA-256, SHA-3, and BLAKE3 are preferred due to their collision resistance and robustness. Avoid outdated and insecure algorithms like MD5, SHA-1, DES, and RC4, as they are vulnerable to known attacks and offer insufficient protection against modern threats.
- **Cipher Modes**: The mode of operation determines how blocks of plaintext are encrypted and has direct implications on security. ECB (Electronic Codebook) mode must be avoided due to its vulnerability to pattern analysis. Instead, use CBC (Cipher Block Chaining) with random IVs or GCM (Galois/Counter Mode) which provides both encryption and authentication. For GCM, ensure that nonces are never reused, as this can completely undermine the encryption.
- **Key Management**: Encryption strength is only as good as the security of its keys. Android's Keystore system should be used for key storage, especially with hardware-backed protection (trusted execution environment or StrongBox). Keys should never be hardcoded or stored in plain text within the app. Implement periodic key rotation policies, enabling keys to be replaced or revoked if compromised, and always track key lifecycle metadata like creation and expiration dates.
- **Randomness**: Secure cryptography demands unpredictability. Use SecureRandom for generating cryptographic materials such as keys, IVs, salts, and nonces. Avoid using java.util.Random or timestamp-based generators, as they are not cryptographically secure and can lead to predictable output. For critical operations, consider seeding SecureRandom with entropy from a secure hardware source to further improve randomness.
- **Padding Schemes**: Padding ensures that plaintext messages align with the cipher's block size, but insecure padding can lead to padding oracle attacks. Use established padding mechanisms like PKCS#7 for block ciphers or OAEP (Optimal Asymmetric Encryption Padding) for RSA operations. Avoid creating custom padding logic, as even small mistakes can expose encrypted data to decryption without the key.
- **Hashing Practices**: Hash functions are used extensively, from storing passwords to ensuring data integrity. For secure password hashing, use memory-hard functions such as PBKDF2 (with high iterations), bcrypt, scrypt, or Argon2. Avoid fast hashes like SHA-256. These algorithms are designed to be computationally expensive, making brute-force and dictionary attacks more difficult. Always use a unique salt per user/password combination to mitigate rainbow table attacks.

- **Digital Signatures**: Digital signatures ensure the authenticity and integrity of data or code. Use strong algorithms such as ECDSA with P-256 or RSA-PSS instead of legacy formats like DSA. Ensure that the signature is validated using the correct public key and verify the integrity of the entire certificate chain when certificates are used. Avoid trusting unsigned or self-signed data without verification, especially in environments involving server communication or software updates.
- **MACs and Integrity Checks**: Message Authentication Codes (MACs) are essential to detect tampering and ensure the authenticity of messages. HMAC with SHA-256 is the recommended standard for secure MACs. Never use checksums, CRCs, or simple hashes as substitutes, as they are not designed for cryptographic integrity and can be easily spoofed. MAC keys should be kept separate from encryption keys and securely stored using the Keystore.
- **Signature Verification**: Implement rigorous checks when verifying digital signatures. This includes validating the certificate chain, checking the issuer, expiration date, and revocation status. Do not assume a signature is valid just because it exists, ensure that the signature matches the signed data and comes from a trusted authority. Failing to do so can result in accepting forged content as legitimate, undermining app security.

Common Pitfalls

Despite the availability of secure libraries and frameworks, developers frequently make mistakes that undermine security. These include:

- Using hardcoded keys or secrets in the source code, allowing easy extraction through reverse engineering.
- Reusing IVs or nonces across encryption operations, which can severely compromise data confidentiality.
- Implementing custom encryption logic or "home-grown" cryptographic algorithms, which often introduce subtle and critical flaws.
- Failing to update cryptographic libraries, thereby missing important security patches and vulnerability fixes.
- Relying on weak encryption schemes or outdated ciphers, assuming that any form of encryption is secure.
- Not implementing cryptographic key rotation, leading to prolonged use of compromised or ageing keys.
- Using cryptographically weak PRNGs which produce predictable output, jeopardizing the randomness required for secure key generation and nonce creation.
- Employing weak MACs or omitting them entirely, thus failing to protect against tampering and message forgery.
- Misapplying or skipping signature verification, leaving the app vulnerable to spoofed or tampered data that appears legitimate.

Integration with Android Security Infrastructure

Android provides built-in support for cryptographic operations through libraries such as javax.crypto, java.security, and the Android Keystore system. Leveraging these native capabilities helps ensure cryptographic materials are handled within secure boundaries, especially when hardware-backed modules are used.

Additionally, Android Jetpack Security (such as EncryptedSharedPreferences and EncryptedFile) offers high-level abstractions that automatically apply secure defaults and cryptographic hygiene, reducing the risk of misconfiguration.

Alignment with Compliance and Regulatory Expectations

Proper cryptographic implementation is often a regulatory necessity. Whether aligning with GDPR, HIPAA, PCI-DSS, or regional data protection laws, using strong cryptography is essential for demonstrating due diligence in safeguarding user data. MASVS-CRYPTO-1 helps developers maintain compliance through enforceable, auditable cryptographic standards.

8.2.2 MASVS-CRYPTO-2: Secure Crypto Key Management

Keys You Can Trust

In secure mobile application development, cryptographic key management plays a pivotal role. While encryption algorithms are generally robust and battle-tested, their security is significantly diminished if the associated keys are poorly handled. MASVS-CRYPTO-2 addresses this crucial aspect by emphasizing that key management should align with established industry best practices to prevent unauthorized access, misuse, or compromise.

Importance of Proper Key Management

Cryptographic keys are the most sensitive elements within a cryptosystem. Compromise of a key often leads to a complete breakdown of data confidentiality or integrity. For Android applications, especially those dealing with sensitive operations like financial transactions or health data processing, strong key management is not just a recommendation, it is a necessity.

A well-structured key management strategy ensures the following:

- Keys are generated securely using strong entropy sources.
- Keys are stored in a secure container, such as the Android Keystore system.
- Keys are never hardcoded in the application binary or stored in plaintext.
- Keys are associated with usage constraints and access control policies.
- Expired or unused keys are securely retired and replaced.

Key Management Considerations

Android provides several facilities to help developers implement proper key management. Central to this is the Android Keystore system, which allows cryptographic keys to be stored in a hardware-backed secure environment when supported by the device.

Key considerations when implementing key management in Android apps include:

- **Use Android Keystore for Key Storage:** Android Keystore securely stores cryptographic keys in a container isolated from the application using trusted execution environment (TEE) or StrongBox (on supported devices). This prevents keys from being extracted even if the app or OS is compromised. For high-risk apps, validate key attestation to confirm hardware backing.

- **Enforce Key Usage Restrictions:** When generating keys, define their purpose explicitly using parameters like PURPOSE_ENCRYPT, PURPOSE_DECRYPT, or PURPOSE_SIGN. This ensures keys are only used for specific cryptographic operations, reducing the chance of unintended misuse.
- **Apply User Authentication Binding:** Keys can be configured with the setUserAuthenticationRequired(true) flag and tied to biometric prompts or PIN-based authentication. This enforces that only an authenticated user can use the key, adding a strong second layer of protection.
- **Avoid Exportable Keys:** Always opt for non-exportable key material using setKeyExportable(false) where applicable. Exportable keys can be vulnerable to memory scraping or malicious exfiltration, especially on rooted or compromised devices.
- **Generate Keys on the Device:** Key generation should happen within the secure environment provided by Android Keystore using KeyGenerator or KeyPairGenerator. Avoid transmitting keys from a server to the device unless using secure key wrapping techniques.
- **Limit Key Lifetime and Rotate Keys Periodically:** Define an expiration date using setKeyValidityEnd() or rotate keys manually after a defined threshold (e.g., number of encryptions). This minimizes the risk of prolonged key exposure or cryptanalytic attacks.
- **Revoke and Replace on Device Compromise:** Implement a mechanism to detect signs of rooting or tampering using the Play Integrity API or reputable third-party attestation services. In such cases, revoke sensitive keys, invalidate existing sessions, and require re-authentication or re-keying.
- **Zeroize Memory After Use:** Sensitive data such as derived keys, passphrases, or intermediate results should be cleared from memory immediately using null assignments or secure memory clearing methods to prevent data leakage through heap dumps or forensic analysis.

Common Pitfalls

Beyond basic implementation, developers must be vigilant against subtle but serious issues that undermine cryptographic security. Below are common pitfalls and advanced threats to effective key management in Android applications:

- **Lack of Key Rotation Policies:** Failure to implement periodic key rotation allows long-term exposure of keys, increasing susceptibility to cryptographic attacks. Keys should be rotated after a set time period or number of uses, and rotation mechanisms should include secure archival and revocation of old keys.
- **Unrestricted Key Access Across App Components:** Keys must be tightly scoped to specific components or operations. Without enforced access control, other app modules, third-party SDKs, or even malware could misuse or leak keys. Use Keystore access constraints like user authentication and app-specific binding.
- **Reliance on Deprecated Keystore APIs:** Using outdated Keystore implementations or cryptographic providers can result in weaker protections and compatibility issues. Developers should adopt modern APIs like KeyGenParameterSpec and KeyInfo, and avoid fallback to insecure legacy algorithms.
- **Weak Key Derivation from User Input:** Deriving cryptographic keys from user-provided data like passwords without secure KDFs is dangerous. Techniques like PBKDF2 with high iteration counts or Argon2id should be used to add computational hardness and thwart brute-force attempts.

- **Insecure Export of Cryptographic Keys:** Exported keys must be encrypted using secure wrapping mechanisms such as AES-GCM or RSA-OAEP. Export should only occur over secure, mutually authenticated channels. Unwrapped or plaintext keys transmitted via insecure APIs or storage channels are highly vulnerable.
- **Misuse or Multipurpose Use of Keys:** Using the same key for both encryption and digital signatures violates the principle of cryptographic separation. Each key should be bound to a single, well-defined purpose to prevent collision and leakage scenarios.
- **Poor Key Generation Practices:** Cryptographic keys must be generated using true random sources, such as Android's SecureRandom with proper seeding. Avoid using static seeds, timestamps, or predictable patterns, which can make keys guessable or reproducible.
- **Unsafe Import and Memory Handling of Keys:** Imported keys should be wrapped immediately using Keystore mechanisms and never held in plaintext memory longer than necessary. Any temporary storage or object referencing sensitive keys must be cleared or zeroized promptly.
- **Insufficient Protection of Keys at Rest:** Keys stored outside Keystore (e.g., in app files, preferences, or SQLite databases) should always be encrypted with a securely derived master key. Ideally, such master keys should be hardware-bound via the Keystore and inaccessible outside the secure environment.

Industry Best Practices and Standards

Adhering to global cryptographic and key management standards further strengthens compliance and security posture. Notable standards and practices include:

- **NIST SP 800-57** for key management lifecycle guidelines.
- **OWASP Mobile Security Testing Guide (MSTG)** recommendations for secure cryptographic implementation.
- **FIPS 140-2** validation for cryptographic modules, especially in regulated industries.
- **Hardware Security Module (HSM)** integration in enterprise-grade applications to offload key storage and operations to highly secure external devices.

8.3 MASVS-AUTH

Adaptive Authentication: Tailoring Security Measures

Imagine your mobile app as a fortress protecting your treasure trove of personal information. Just like a fortress has its guards and gates, your app has authentication and authorization acting as its gatekeepers.

Authentication is like the fortress's gatekeeper checking IDs. It ensures that only the rightful owner, you, can enter. In the digital world, this could be using your fingerprint, a PIN, or a special code sent to your phone. It is like saying, "Hey, it is really me!"

Authorization, meanwhile, is what happens after you are inside the fortress. Different areas of the fortress might be off-limits to certain people. For example, you might not be allowed into the king's chambers unless you are a trusted advisor. Similarly, in your app, authorization determines what parts of the app you can access and what actions you can take.

Why all the fuss? Well, just as you would not want strangers wandering into your fortress and rifling through your belongings, you do not want unauthorized users snooping around your app and accessing your personal data. Strong authentication and authorization are the locks and keys keeping your information safe from prying eyes.

Implementing these measures in an app strengthens its defences, ensuring that only authorized individuals can access specific features. Security mechanisms like biometrics provide advanced ID verification, multi-factor authentication requires multiple forms of identification, such as a key and a secret code, and industry best practices establish a gold standard for securing digital environments.

Remember, it is not just about your app standing strong, it is about the entire ecosystem, including the servers it communicates with, being fortified against potential threats. Think of it as creating an impenetrable fortress to safeguard your digital treasures.

8.3.1 MASVS-AUTH-1: Secure Authentication Protocols Implementation

Who Gets In? Login Tight, Access Granted

Authentication and authorization form the cornerstone of any secure mobile application. In the context of Android app development, especially when handling sensitive transactions or accessing personal data, adhering to secure authentication and authorization protocols is not optional, it is essential.

MASVS-AUTH-1 emphasizes the need for mobile applications to use strong, standardized mechanisms for authentication and authorization. The goal is to protect against identity spoofing, credential theft, session hijacking, and privilege escalation, all of which can critically undermine the app's security posture.

Importance of Secure Authentication and Authorization

In Android applications, especially those dealing with financial services, healthcare, or enterprise data, user identity must be verified with high assurance, and access to features and data must be precisely controlled. The integrity and confidentiality of user sessions must be preserved across all usage scenarios, including login, token refresh, and session termination.

Authentication confirms the user is who they claim to be, while authorization ensures that the authenticated user is allowed to perform the requested operation. These two processes are interdependent and must be implemented with industry standards to minimize the risk of breaches.

Best Practices for Secure Authentication

Developers should consider the following best practices:

- **Use Standards-Based Authentication Protocols:** Adopt widely supported and secure protocols such as OAuth 2.0 with PKCE (Proof Key for Code Exchange) for authorization delegation and OpenID Connect (OIDC) for federated identity management. PKCE is mandatory for public clients like mobile apps, ensuring secure token handling. These standards provide robust mechanisms for token issuance, revocation, and scope control, and are compatible with most identity providers and mobile SDKs.
- **Avoid Authentication in WebViews:** Do not perform authentication within embedded WebViews, as they lack proper isolation from the app's JavaScript context and are vulnerable to credential theft via injection attacks. Instead, use external browsers or

Chrome Custom Tabs with the OAuth 2.0 Authorization Code Flow and PKCE to ensure secure, sandboxed authentication.

- **Leverage System-Level Biometric Authentication:** Use Android's BiometricPrompt API for biometric authentication, which leverages trusted execution environments (TEE) or StrongBox hardware to securely verify fingerprints or facial data. Avoid deprecated APIs like FingerprintManager or custom biometric dialogs, which are susceptible to spoofing and interception.
- **Utilize Android Account Manager Securely:** For enterprise or system-wide account integration, use Android's Account Manager and Confirm Credentials API. These platform-level tools enable centralized credential validation and token management while reducing the app's direct exposure to sensitive login information.
- **Avoid Custom Authentication Schemes:** Refrain from developing proprietary authentication logic, token formats, or homegrown login systems, as they often contain critical security flaws. Instead, rely on well-maintained SDKs from trusted identity providers that are regularly updated for compliance and security patches.
- **Store Credentials Using Android Keystore:** Authentication tokens and cryptographic keys should be stored securely using the Android Keystore System, preferably with hardware-backed storage (e.g., Titan M or StrongBox). Avoid storing sensitive data in SharedPreferences, internal files, or SQLite databases without encryption, as these can be accessed on rooted devices or through memory dumps.
- **Never Hardcode Secrets in App Binaries:** Avoid embedding API keys, passwords, or other secrets directly in the app code or resources. Even with obfuscation, tools like JADX or apktool can extract them. Instead, provision secrets dynamically after user authentication and bind them to device-specific attributes using secure channels.
- **Transmit Authentication Data Over Encrypted Connections:** Never send credentials, tokens, or session data over unencrypted connections. Always use TLS 1.3 (preferred) or at minimum TLS 1.2, with strict certificate validation enforced. For high-risk applications, implement certificate pinning to defend against man-in-the-middle (MITM) attacks.
- **Bind App to Web Domain Using Android App Links:** Use Android App Links (powered by Digital Asset Links) to cryptographically associate your app with your official web domain. This prevents phishing attacks and stops unauthorized apps from intercepting authentication callbacks during federated login flows.
- **Implement Robust Session Management:** Ensure secure session handling by supporting token expiration, refresh, and server-side revocation. Refresh tokens should only be issued through secure authentication flows. Upon logout, invalidate session tokens on the server to prevent reuse, even if the local token remains valid.
- **Enforce Account Lockout and Threat Detection:** Implement rate limiting or account lockout policies after repeated failed login attempts to deter brute-force attacks. Additionally, notify users of suspicious login activity and require additional verification (e.g., CAPTCHA or re-authentication) before allowing sensitive operations.
- **Follow Secure Password Handling Practices:** Enforce strong password policies, including length and complexity requirements. Store passwords using salted hashing algorithms such as bcrypt or Argon2, and never store passwords in plaintext—not even temporarily in memory during processing.
- **Validate Tokens on the Server Side:** Always validate authentication tokens server-side by checking critical claims such as issuer (iss), audience (aud), expiration (exp), and cryptographic signature. Never assume a request is legitimate based solely on the presence of a token; client-side checks can be bypassed.

- Adopt Passwordless Authentication Methods: Explore modern passwordless options such as device-bound push notifications, time-based one-time passwords (TOTP), or secure biometric login. These approaches reduce user friction and eliminate risks associated with password reuse, phishing, and weak credential management.

Best Practices for Secure Authorization

Authorization must enforce what a user can and cannot do within the application. Best practices include:

- **Implement Server-Side Access Control Models:** Enforce authorization using Role-Based Access Control (RBAC) or Attribute-Based Access Control (ABAC) on the server. RBAC assigns permissions based on user roles (e.g., admin, user), while ABAC allows dynamic policies based on attributes such as location, device type, or subscription level. This ensures access decisions cannot be manipulated on the client side.
- **Validate Authorization on Every Request:** Perform authorization checks on every backend request, regardless of client-side validations. Mobile apps can be reverse-engineered or automated using tools like Frida or Burp Suite, so never trust the client to enforce access rules.
- **Use Scoped Access Tokens:** Issue access tokens with narrowly defined scopes (e.g., read:profile, write:settings) to limit privileges. Scoped tokens reduce the impact of token leakage and support fine-grained control over what actions a user or app component can perform.
- **Prevent Bypassing Authorization Logic:** Ensure authorization logic cannot be circumvented even in compromised environments. Sensitive operations—such as fund transfers, data exports, or administrative actions—must include additional server-side context checks, including device fingerprinting, session history, and user behavior analysis.
- **Restrict Access to Sensitive APIs:** Internal endpoints used for debugging, administration, or diagnostics must be disabled in production or strictly protected. Expose them only to authenticated and authorized entities using verifiable identity assertions that are independently validated by the backend server.

Threat Scenarios and Mitigation

Weak authentication and authorization expose mobile apps to various risks:

- **Credential Stuffing:** Attackers use previously leaked usernames and passwords from data breaches to automate login attempts. Mitigation includes rate-limiting login attempts, enforcing strong password policies, using CAPTCHA, and promoting multi-factor authentication (MFA).
- **Token Theft:** Access or refresh tokens stored insecurely (e.g., unencrypted in local storage) or transmitted over HTTP can be intercepted and reused. Use encrypted storage (Keystore or EncryptedSharedPreferences), enforce HTTPS-only APIs, and implement short-lived tokens with secure refresh flows.
- **Privilege Escalation:** Poor server-side role validation can allow users to invoke high-privilege functions by altering request parameters (e.g., changing their role ID or account number). Authorization logic must be context-aware and must not rely on client-side roles.

- **Hardcoded API Secrets:** Secrets embedded in APKs can be extracted using reverse engineering tools, leading to unauthorized access to backend services or third-party APIs. This risk is mitigated by storing secrets server-side and requiring user or device authentication before provisioning tokens.
- **Authentication Material Exposed in WebViews:** If credentials are entered into an embedded WebView instead of a system browser, malicious JavaScript or app-injected scripts can steal input. Authentication should always be redirected to the system browser or trusted identity provider's secure screen.
- **Unlinked Mobile and Web Identities:** Without using Digital Asset Links or Shared Web Credentials, attackers can publish a fake app that mimics the login UI of a legitimate app. Binding app and web origins cryptographically ensures that only verified apps are trusted during federated login.
- **Missing Token Validation:** Apps that accept tokens without verifying their expiration or signature are vulnerable to replay and forgery attacks. Every token must be validated using cryptographic checks to ensure it was issued by a trusted authority.

8.3.2 MASVS-AUTH-2: Secure Local Authentication

Local Login, Seamless Access

Local authentication is a critical control point in mobile applications, especially when the application handles sensitive data, executes high-privilege operations, or operates in regulated domains such as finance, healthcare, or government services. MASVS-AUTH-2 emphasizes the need for secure implementation of local authentication, aligning closely with Android's platform guidelines to prevent impersonation, bypass, and abuse.

Understanding Local Authentication

Local authentication refers to verifying the user's identity on the device without necessarily involving a backend server. Common methods include PIN, password, pattern, biometric authentication (fingerprint, face recognition), or a combination thereof. These methods are typically used to unlock the app, access sensitive features, or approve sensitive transactions. In Android, local authentication mechanisms are often integrated through the BiometricPrompt API or the older FingerprintManager, though the latter is deprecated.

It is critical to distinguish between authentication (verifying identity) and authorization (granting access). Applications must not enforce authorization based solely on local authentication results. For high-impact operations, the backend should independently authorize the action based on a securely issued access token or server-side policy validation.

Platform Best Practices

Android developers should adhere to platform-recommended practices to ensure the reliability and security of authentication workflows. Below are key considerations:

- **Use the BiometricPrompt API:** Use the BiometricPrompt API (available from API level 28 and above, with BiometricManager for compatibility checks on lower API levels), which provides a system-managed and tamper-resistant UI for biometric authentication. This ensures consistency, usability, and security across different OEM implementations.

- **Fallback Authentication**: Implement secure fallback options such as device PIN, pattern, or password when biometric data is unavailable or fails. This should be done using the setAllowedAuthenticators() method with BIOMETRIC_STRONG | DEVICE_CREDENTIAL flags. However, avoid allowing fallback to non-biometric credentials for *sensitive transactions* (such as money transfers or device de-registration), unless those credentials are verified using trusted platform security (e.g., system credential confirmation using the Keyguard).
- **Do Not Store Biometric Data**: Avoid storing raw or processed biometric data locally in the app or transmitting it to servers. Android ensures this through hardware-backed trusted execution environment (TEE), and apps must never attempt to duplicate or bypass this.
- **Use Strong Biometric Classifications**: Ensure the app enforces strong biometric types (e.g., 3D face recognition, fingerprint scanners with anti-spoofing) by setting the biometric strength level to BIOMETRIC_STRONG. Weak biometric types, such as some facial recognition systems or voice authentication, should be explicitly excluded from authentication.
- **Display System UI for Authentication**: Do not create custom biometric prompts or overlays, as these can be spoofed or lead to phishing attacks. The system-provided prompt ensures integrity and a secure user experience. Additionally, biometric authentication should be explicitly bound to the event or transaction being confirmed (such as authorizing a payment). Avoid passive or session-based biometric use, as these can be replayed or misapplied.
- **Rate Limiting and Lockouts**: Utilize built-in rate limiting mechanisms provided by the Android framework. For instance, repeated biometric failures should automatically trigger fallback to device credentials and enforce a timeout period.
- **Secure Cryptographic Binding**: Where local authentication gates access to cryptographic operations (such as key unlocking), use the Android Keystore system to bind cryptographic keys to successful biometric or device credential authentication. For example, keys can be created using KeyGenParameterSpec with setUserAuthenticationRequired(true) to ensure they're unusable unless the user authenticates. If the app implements a custom PIN or passcode, it should not be treated as secure unless it is bound to a secure keystore entry. Storing app-defined PINs without using KeyStore protection is discouraged and undermines the trustworthiness of authentication.
- **Context-aware Authentication**: Adjust authentication requirements based on the sensitivity of actions. For instance, unlocking the app could require just biometric authentication, but approving a high-value transaction should demand additional authentication or step-up mechanisms.
- **Avoid Storing Session Flags Insecurely**: Do not persist authentication status using SharedPreferences or SQLite without encryption and strict access control. Any flag indicating that a user has authenticated should be stored in memory or a secure, ephemeral location.
- **Re-authentication for Sensitive Operations**: Enforce re-authentication for critical actions, such as changing a PIN, accessing stored credentials, or modifying security settings. This minimizes risk from unauthorized access in cases of unattended device access.
- **Key Invalidation on Biometric Enrolment Change**: Configure keys to become invalid when a new biometric (e.g., fingerprint or face) is enrolled. This is critical to defend against unauthorized biometric enrolment attacks. Use the setInvalidatedByBiometricEnrollment(true) flag in KeyGenParameterSpec to force reauthentication and key regeneration upon biometric changes.

- **Avoid Local-only Authorization Decisions**: Applications must not rely solely on local authentication to authorize sensitive operations like fund transfers, profile updates, or deregistration. Backend validation should be mandatory. For example, a server should verify tokens issued after biometric authentication before processing a withdrawal, preventing attackers from bypassing controls on a compromised device.

Common Pitfalls

Even when developers integrate local authentication into their apps, security can be compromised due to design or implementation oversights. Below are common mistakes that undermine the security posture of local authentication on Android:

- **Implementing Custom Biometric Prompts**: Some developers attempt to create custom UI for biometric input to achieve branding or UX uniformity. However, custom prompts lack the trusted path and security boundaries enforced by the platform. Attackers can spoof these UIs, leading to phishing attacks where users believe they are authenticating, but are actually interacting with a fake screen.
- **Relying Solely on Biometric Success Without Cryptographic Binding**: Simply checking for biometric success (e.g., a Boolean result) is insufficient. Without binding authentication to a secure keystore-backed cryptographic operation, attackers could spoof or manipulate the outcome. Biometric authentication should be tightly coupled with secure key usage, such as unlocking an encryption key stored in the Android Keystore.
- **Storing Biometric Results or Device Credentials Insecurely**: Apps should never attempt to access or store raw biometric data or passwords. Any attempt to log, cache, or store such data, even temporarily, in SharedPreferences, internal storage, or external logs opens avenues for compromise. Sensitive authentication artefacts must be kept strictly within platform-managed, hardware-protected zones.
- **Allowing Weak Biometric Methods Without Enforcing Strong Authentication**: Devices may support low-assurance biometric types such as 2D facial recognition or non-secure voice recognition. Apps must restrict usage to strong biometric authenticators only (classified as BIOMETRIC_STRONG). Failure to do so can expose the app to spoofing using photographs, voice recordings, or masks.
- **Not Handling Biometric Hardware Absence or Degradation Gracefully**: Some devices may lack biometric hardware, or it may become unusable due to sensor damage, OS restrictions, or user revocation. Apps must detect these conditions and offer secure fallback options (like system-managed device credentials), without disabling authentication entirely or bypassing it.
- **Failing to Invalidate Authentication Keys Upon New Biometric Enrolment**: When users add new biometric data (like a new fingerprint), attackers could have temporary access to the device and register their own biometrics. If the app doesn't invalidate authentication-bound cryptographic keys using setInvalidatedByBiometricEnrollment (true), the compromise remains undetected. The app should force reauthentication and key regeneration in such scenarios.
- **Enforcing Sensitive Actions Locally Without Server-side Authorization**: Sensitive actions, such as transferring funds, changing profile information, or disabling 2FA, must not rely solely on local biometric success. Server-side validation is critical. For example, an attacker with a rooted device could fake a local biometric result unless the server enforces a secondary token or policy check.

- **Using App-defined PINs That Are Not Keystore-protected:** Many apps implement their own 4- or 6-digit passcodes or PINs for added security. However, if these are stored or validated without Android Keystore integration, they can be extracted or bypassed via static analysis or device compromise. Such PINs should be securely bound to the device's trusted environment using keystore-stored HMACs or encrypted storage.
- **Reusing Biometric Success Across Unrelated Operations:** Biometric authentication must be bound to specific actions or events (e.g., confirming a payment or unlocking a secure note). Reusing a prior authentication success for a different context introduces replay risks. Each biometric prompt should be freshly triggered and tightly scoped to its associated operation.
- **Lack of Proper Session Timeout or Reauthentication Controls:** Once the user authenticates, apps often maintain the session indefinitely or rely on long-lived flags. This is dangerous if the user walks away from the device. Apps must implement idle timeouts and demand reauthentication after a period of inactivity or before sensitive operations.
- **No User Feedback or Logs on Authentication Events:** If the user is not informed when authentication events occur (especially failed attempts), security awareness drops. Apps should log authentication attempts and optionally notify users, especially for sensitive actions, so that abnormal patterns can be noticed and reported.

8.3.3 MASVS-AUTH-3: Additional Authentication Protection

Lockdown Mode, Extra Layer of Safety

In the context of mobile application security, merely authenticating users at login is insufficient for protecting high-risk functionalities. MASVS-AUTH-3 emphasizes the need for step-up authentication or reauthentication when a user attempts to perform particularly sensitive operations. This ensures that even if a session remains valid, high-value actions are protected by an additional layer of assurance.

Understanding Sensitive Operations

Sensitive operations refer to app functionalities that, if exploited, could result in data breaches, financial loss, unauthorized transactions, or privacy violations. These include, but are not limited to:

- Initiating high-value financial transactions (e.g., transferring funds, paying bills)
- Changing authentication credentials (e.g., updating passwords, security PINs)
- Modifying user profile data with security implications (e.g., changing email address, phone number)
- Accessing sensitive data (e.g., viewing tax returns, health records, account statements)
- Disabling security features (e.g., biometric authentication, device binding)

Protecting such operations with additional authentication mechanisms greatly reduces the risk posed by session hijacking, device theft, or unauthorized access through shared sessions.

Approaches to Implement Additional Authentication

Mobile applications should introduce contextual or risk-based authentication challenges during high-risk workflows. These may include:

- **Biometric Reauthentication:** Leverages device-level biometric sensors such as fingerprint readers or facial recognition. Using Android's BiometricPrompt API, the app can prompt the user to reauthenticate before performing critical actions like fund transfers. This approach ensures that the person interacting with the device is the legitimate owner, adding a seamless but strong security layer without requiring password reentry.
- **Device-based PIN or Pattern:** Uses the operating system's secure lock screen mechanism to verify user identity. By invoking Android's KeyguardManager, the app can request the user to confirm their device PIN, password, or pattern before executing sensitive changes, such as disabling multi-factor authentication within the app. This leverages system-level authentication mechanisms already trusted by the user and the OS.
- **Reentry of Account Password:** Often required for extremely sensitive operations that could compromise account integrity or data confidentiality, such as exporting private cryptographic keys or deactivating an account. Asking users to input their password again, even if already logged in, ensures that stolen devices or hijacked sessions cannot perform irreversible actions without explicit credential confirmation.
- **Time-bound Authentication:** Imposes a validity window on authenticated sessions. For instance, if a user's session is older than a predetermined time frame (e.g., 10 minutes), the app requires reauthentication before allowing sensitive operations. This limits risks related to session hijacking or unattended devices by ensuring recent user presence and consent.
- **Transaction-specific OTP (One-Time Password):** Provides an additional dynamic verification factor. When a user initiates high-risk actions, such as adding a new beneficiary, the app sends a unique OTP via SMS, email, or an in-app messaging service. The user must enter this code to confirm the operation. OTPs provide cryptographically strong, short-lived codes that mitigate risks associated with stolen credentials or session tokens. Transaction-specific OTPs should be delivered via secure channels such as in-app notifications or authenticator apps. Avoid SMS unless no alternative exists, due to SIM-swapping and interception risks.
- **In-app Approval via Push Notification:** especially useful for multi-device or multi-channel workflows. For example, when a transaction is initiated from a web interface or secondary device, the primary mobile app receives a push notification requesting user approval. This confirms device possession and intent directly from the user's trusted device, effectively mitigating unauthorized remote actions.
- **Multi-factor Authentication (MFA) Prompt as an Additional Layer:** Goes beyond initial login requirements. Even if MFA was used during authentication, critical post-login actions should trigger lightweight MFA challenges, such as entering an app-generated one-time code or biometric verification, to reaffirm identity before execution. Importantly, developers must avoid relying solely on session tokens or single-factor authentication for these operations, as that would leave them vulnerable to session theft or replay attacks.

Risk-Adaptive Authentication

Beyond static step-up mechanisms, modern applications increasingly employ risk-adaptive authentication. This approach evaluates contextual signals, such as device reputation, geolocation anomalies, behavioural biometrics, and IP address integrity, to determine if additional authentication is needed.

For example:

- A login attempt from an unrecognized country may prompt for biometric reauthentication even if the session is technically valid.
- A rapid sequence of actions within the app inconsistent with typical user behaviour may trigger a password challenge before permitting a fund withdrawal.

Developers should also ensure that reauthentication is triggered on contextual state changes, such as switching networks (e.g., from Wi-Fi to mobile data), a locked-to-unlocked device state, SIM card changes, or rapid screen rotations suggesting potential overlays. These conditions can indicate suspicious behaviour, and triggering step-up authentication in such scenarios adds a layer of defence without major UX disruption.

User Experience Consideration

While securing sensitive operations is critical, developers must balance security with usability. Overly aggressive authentication prompts can frustrate users and degrade the app experience. Strategies to improve UX without sacrificing security include:

- Using biometric reauthentication over password reentry, which offers a smoother user journey
- Allowing a grace period after successful reauthentication (e.g., 5 minutes) to prevent repetitive prompts
- Clearly communicating the reason for authentication prompts to users, reinforcing trust

8.4 MASVS-NETWORK

Secure Communication Channels: Detecting Suspicious Activities

Imagine your mobile app as a messenger sending packages back and forth across the internet. These packages contain important information, maybe your messages, pictures, or banking details. Naturally, you would want these packages to be delivered securely, just like you would want your mail to arrive safely at its destination.

To achieve this, developers employ sophisticated security measures akin to locking these packages in a secure vault before sending them out. They do this through a process called encryption, where the data is transformed into a secret code that only the intended recipient can decode. Additionally, they double-check the identity of the receiver, similar to verifying someone's ID before handing over confidential documents.

However, just as there are potential risks with sending physical mail, there are also vulnerabilities in transmitting data over the internet. Developers may accidentally weaken these security measures by incorrectly configuring their app's communication pathways or using less secure methods. It is like forgetting to lock the vault or using a flimsy lock that can be easily bypassed.

This is where the Mobile App Security Verification Standard for Network Communication steps in. It acts as a stringent set of guidelines to ensure that your app always maintains the highest level of security when communicating over the internet. It ensures that developers not only lock the vault securely but also use the most robust locks available, even in the face of potential pitfalls.

Specifically, this standard verifies that your app establishes a private, encrypted tunnel for data to travel through. It is akin to your packages being transported through a secret, underground tunnel, safe from prying eyes and potential tampering. Additionally, it checks whether developers choose to trust only well-known and reliable sources, further fortifying the security perimeter. It is like insisting that your packages are only handled by reputable courier services, minimizing the risk of interception or tampering.

8.4.1 MASVS-NETWORK-1: Secure Network Traffic

Data on the Move? Worry-free Transfers

Securing network communication is fundamental to protecting mobile applications from eavesdropping, tampering, and man-in-the-middle (MitM) attacks. MASVS-NETWORK-1 mandates that all network traffic must be protected in transit using industry-standard cryptographic protocols and hardened configurations. Android applications often communicate with remote APIs, cloud endpoints, and third-party services, making it imperative to enforce strict transport-level protections.

Importance of Secure Network Communication

Mobile devices operate over diverse network environments, including open or untrusted Wi-Fi networks. Without proper encryption and validation mechanisms, sensitive information, such as credentials, tokens, financial data, or user identifiers, can be intercepted or modified during transmission. MASVS-NETWORK-1 ensures that developers consider not only encryption but also how it is implemented and validated.

Key Practices to Fulfil

Android developers must follow a comprehensive set of network security best practices, which include:

- **Enforce HTTPS/TLS for All Communications:** All communication between the app and its backend must be conducted over HTTPS using TLS 1.2 or higher. Modern TLS ensures confidentiality, integrity, and authenticity of data in transit. Even metadata transmitted over insecure channels can be exploited by attackers for profiling or replay attacks. Developers should avoid hardcoding HTTP URLs and instead use build-time configuration or remote config for endpoint management.
- **Disable Cleartext Traffic in the Manifest:** Explicitly set android:usesCleartextTraffic="false" in the app's manifest to prevent accidental fallbacks to insecure HTTP. Starting from Android 9 (API level 28), this setting blocks cleartext connections unless explicitly allowed. Also, ensure the network_security_config.xml does not override this setting unintentionally for specific domains or subdomains unless there's a justified exception (e.g., development servers).
- **Use Strong TLS Configurations:** Configure the server to support only modern and secure cipher suites such as modern AEAD cipher suites like those in TLS 1.3's mandatory cipher suite list. Remove deprecated ciphers (like RC4 or 3DES) and disable older protocol versions including TLS 1.0 and 1.1. On the client side, developers can enforce stronger configurations using SSLSocketFactory or leverage hardened networking libraries like OkHttp, which follow best practices by default.

- **Enable Hostname Verification:** Hostname verification ensures that the certificate presented by the server matches the domain to which the app is connecting. Relying on Android's default HttpsURLConnection behaviour provides built-in hostname validation. Avoid overriding the HostnameVerifier to return true for all hostnames, a common but dangerous shortcut during development.
- **Implement Certificate Pinning:** Pinning restricts the app to trust only a specific certificate or public key rather than all those issued by any trusted CA. Developers can use Android's network_security_config.xml to define domain-specific pins or use third-party libraries like OkHttp's CertificatePinner. However, pinning requires careful lifecycle management to handle certificate rotations without breaking functionality. Prefer public key pinning with backup pins and plan for rotation to avoid service disruption.
- **Avoid Insecure Certificate Validation Practices:** Practices such as accepting all SSL certificates or using a TrustManager that blindly trusts the server are fundamentally insecure. These shortcuts completely undermine the security provided by TLS and enable MITM attacks. Audit your codebase for instances of insecure overrides, especially in utility or debugging classes often left in production accidentally.
- **Use the Network Security Configuration File:** Introduced in Android 7.0 (API level 24), network_security_config.xml allows fine-grained control over domain-level TLS settings, certificate pinning, and debug-only CA trust anchors. It decouples security policies from code and enables clear separation between production and debug builds. Policies such as trust-anchors, domain-config, and pin-set should be managed under source control to track changes.
- **Avoid Unprotected Open Ports and Local Sockets:** If your app exposes any ports for local use (e.g., IPC, WebView debugging, or ADB tools), ensure they are adequately protected through authentication or disabled in production builds. For example, content providers or bound services should implement proper permissions and exported flags to prevent unauthorized access. Use tools like adb shell netstat or ss to audit exposed ports during testing.
- **Protect Sensitive Data within Requests:** Never transmit sensitive data such as tokens, passwords, or account details in the URL query string, as these may be logged by intermediary systems. Instead, use HTTPS POST with parameters in the body and sanitize all outgoing logs. Developers should disable automatic logging of full request URLs or headers that may contain secrets, particularly when using third-party HTTP clients.
- **Prefer Proven and Well-maintained Networking Libraries:** Rather than writing custom networking stacks, adopt reliable libraries like OkHttp (used internally by Retrofit), Ktor, or Volley. These libraries implement secure defaults, connection pooling, TLS socket handling, and retry logic. Relying on well-tested libraries also improves maintainability and reduces the chances of introducing subtle bugs in TLS negotiation or connection management.
- **Secure Machine-to-machine (M2M) Communication:** For backend-to-backend or app-to-service communications, such as payment gateways, notification services, or internal APIs, ensure secure authentication via OAuth2, JWTs, or mutual TLS (mTLS). Avoid shared static API keys embedded in the app. Backend systems should validate the identity of the client and enforce access control based on specific scopes or service accounts.
- **Minimize Third-party Endpoint Exposure:** Each external API or service integrated into the app increases the attack surface. Use only trusted, vetted providers and assess their network security posture. For instance, if an analytics SDK transmits data to

external servers, confirm that it uses TLS and adheres to GDPR or local compliance standards. Prefer integrations that support end-to-end encryption or secure tunnelling.

- **Handle TLS Errors Gracefully but Securely:** Network failures should trigger user-facing error messages or controlled retries, not insecure fallbacks. Avoid automatically retrying with insecure HTTP or disabling certificate validation upon failure. Implement retry backoffs and provide clear user messaging, especially in critical apps like banking or healthcare, where trust and clarity matter.

Common Pitfalls

Despite following many best practices, developers often unknowingly introduce subtle misconfigurations or shortcuts that severely weaken network security. This section outlines common missteps observed in real-world Android applications that can undermine the protections required by MASVS-NETWORK-1.

- **Trusting All SSL Certificates During Development:** A frequent anti-pattern is overriding X509TrustManager or using insecure helper classes to accept all SSL certificates during development. While this can bypass errors during testing, if left in production builds, it allows attackers to present fraudulent certificates, making TLS meaningless. Such configurations are easily discovered via reverse engineering and automated scans.
- **Disabling Hostname Verification:** To suppress "Hostname mismatch" errors, some developers override the default HostnameVerifier to accept any hostname. This disables validation of the server's identity and enables man-in-the-middle attacks, even with valid SSL certificates. Hostname verification must never be bypassed outside of test builds and should use the system default behaviour for production endpoints.
- **Allowing Cleartext Traffic Unintentionally:** Some apps still allow cleartext (HTTP) traffic either due to legacy SDKs, embedded WebViews, or misconfigured network _security_config.xml. Failing to explicitly set android:usesCleartextTraffic="false" permits accidental fallback to insecure channels. Attackers on the same network can intercept or modify such traffic, exposing users to data theft and manipulation.
- **Using Deprecated TLS Versions and Weak Ciphers:** Supporting older protocols like SSL 3.0 or TLS 1.0 for compatibility with legacy systems introduces known cryptographic vulnerabilities. Similarly, weak ciphers like RC4 or 3DES are susceptible to attacks like BEAST and POODLE. Even if the app uses HTTPS, insecure protocol negotiation can be exploited unless strict TLS configurations are enforced on both the client and server.
- **Sending Sensitive Data via URL Parameters:** Embedding sensitive data such as session tokens, OTPs, or API keys in URL query strings can result in accidental exposure through logs, browser history, or intermediary systems like reverse proxies. Sensitive information should be sent in POST request bodies over HTTPS and never appear in URLs or headers unless properly encrypted and sanitized.
- **Leaving Debug Ports and Services Exposed:** Internal interfaces, like local web servers, debugging endpoints, or developer tools, may be unintentionally left open in production versions of the app. These components, if not disabled via build flags or configuration management, could expose backend functionality without authentication. Routine pentesting or dynamic analysis should be used to detect open ports and misconfigured services.
- **Hardcoding API Keys or Using Static Tokens for M2M Communication:** Machine-to-machine (M2M) interfaces often rely on API keys or tokens, but embedding them directly into the app source code makes them trivial to extract. Static tokens that never

expire or rotate can be exploited at scale. Instead, secure token exchange mechanisms (e.g., OAuth2 client credentials flow or mutual TLS) should be implemented, with periodic key rotation and backend-level validation.

- **Failing to Remove Debug CAs or Test Pinsets:** Developers sometimes configure debug-only certificate authorities (CAs) or pinsets to test against staging environments. If these are not stripped out during production release, attackers can exploit these alternative trust chains to perform MITM attacks. Maintain separate network_security _config.xml files for debug and release builds, and validate all trust anchors during build or CI/CD validation.

- **Overreliance on Custom Networking Implementations:** Writing low-level socket or TLS handling code without the support of hardened libraries (like OkHttp or Cronet) increases the risk of subtle bugs, insecure configurations, or lack of compatibility with newer Android security features. Using well-maintained, community-reviewed libraries provides security by default and ensures better support for evolving platform standards.

8.4.2 MASVS-NETWORK-2: Remote Endpoint Identity Pinning

Zero-trust Aarchitecture, Lock Down Connections

One of the core aspects of secure network communication in mobile applications is ensuring that the app connects only to trusted servers, especially those under the direct control of the developer or the organization. MASVS-NETWORK-2 emphasizes the necessity of identity pinning, which refers to binding the app's communication to a specific server identity. This helps mitigate the risk of man-in-the-middle (MITM) attacks, even in the event of a compromised certificate authority (CA) or a rogue network.

When apps perform identity pinning, they go beyond the traditional TLS validation performed by the operating system. Rather than trusting any valid certificate signed by a CA, the app explicitly trusts only a particular certificate or public key belonging to the intended server. This ensures that only a server with the correct identity, matching the pinned certificate or key, can successfully establish a secure connection.

Why Identity Pinning Matters

While TLS is designed to provide confidentiality, integrity, and authentication, it inherently trusts a large set of CAs maintained by the OS. If any of these CAs is compromised or if a fraudulent certificate is issued, an attacker could potentially intercept or modify the data in transit. For applications dealing with sensitive information, such as banking, healthcare, or enterprise systems, this is unacceptable.

By implementing identity pinning, developers enforce an additional layer of trust, reducing reliance on third-party CAs and significantly improving the resilience of the app's network security.

Common Methods for Identity Pinning

There are two primary methods for identity pinning in Android apps:

- **Certificate Pinning:** The app embeds the actual server certificate in the app bundle and validates it during each connection. If the certificate presented by the server does not match the pinned certificate, the connection is rejected.

- **Public Key Pinning:** Instead of pinning the entire certificate, the app pins the server's public key (or hash of the public key). This approach is more resilient to certificate renewals, as long as the key pair remains unchanged.

For example, the app may include a SHA-256 hash of the expected public key (e.g., sha256/abcdef...) and compare it against the server's key during the TLS handshake.

Scope of Pinning

It is important to note that MASVS-NETWORK-2 should apply only to remote endpoints that are under the developer's control. These are typically first-party APIs, backend systems, authentication endpoints, and cloud services directly managed by the organization. The app should not pin third-party services that are outside of the developer's operational scope, as those services may change their certificates or keys without notice, leading to broken functionality.

Best Practices for Iimplementing Identity Pinning

To properly implement and maintain identity pinning, developers should consider the following best practices:

- **Use Public Key Pinning Over Certificate Pinning** to reduce operational friction during certificate renewals. Public key pinning involves embedding the hash of the server's public key, often the SHA-256 hash of the Subject Public Key Info (SPKI), directly into the app, for example, sha256/47DEQpj8. This approach remains valid even when certificates expire or are reissued, as long as the key pair does not change. It also prevents reliance on a particular certificate's validity period, helping maintain connectivity without urgent app updates.
- **Store Pin Data Securely and Obfuscate It** to protect against static analysis and runtime tampering. Developers should avoid placing raw pin hashes or certificates in plaintext strings or resource files. Instead, they can encrypt pins using code obfuscators like ProGuard or R8 to rename and inline the pin validation logic, complicating reverse engineering attempts. Furthermore, runtime integrity checks, such as checksum verification of the app package, can detect tampering that might expose pinning details.
- **Plan for Pin Rotation** by embedding multiple pin hashes in the validation logic. For example, an app can check the server's presented certificate chain against both the current key pin and a backup pin to allow seamless migration. This multi-pin approach prevents sudden connection failures if a certificate or key is replaced. Typically, developers include at least two pins: the active one and a backup key's hash, updating the app with new pins well ahead of certificate expiry.
- **Implement Proper Fallback Mechanisms** to handle pin validation failures gracefully. Instead of immediately dropping the connection or crashing, the app might present user-friendly error messages indicating a security issue or switch to offline modes where feasible. This is especially useful if pin validation fails due to network proxies or captive portals. However, fallback must never disable pin enforcement silently; the app should maintain strict rejection of connections that fail pin validation.
- **Test Thoroughly Under Diverse Network and Device Conditions** Simulate scenarios like invalid or expired certificates, certificate chain tampering, MITM attempts using fraudulent certificates, and device clock misconfigurations that can affect TLS validation. Tools like Android Debug Bridge (ADB) combined with network interception

proxies (e.g., Burp Suite) can be used to test pin enforcement. Automated unit and integration tests should verify that pin validation fails appropriately when encountering unpinned or revoked keys.

- **Supplement traditional pinning with Certificate Transparency log monitoring** to detect unauthorized certificates issued for your domains. This provides early warning of potential certificate-based attacks without the operational overhead of strict pinning.

Common Pitfalls

While identity pinning significantly strengthens network security, improper implementation can introduce risks or operational issues:

- **Certificate or Key Mismanagement** is a leading cause of pinning failures. If developers pin to a certificate that is only valid in development or staging environments, the production app may reject legitimate server connections. Similarly, pinning to short-lived certificates or using weak hashing algorithms such as SHA-1 (which is deprecated due to collision vulnerabilities) can allow attackers to spoof server identities.
- **Hardcoding a Single Pin without Backups** risks catastrophic connectivity failures. If the pinned certificate or key is rotated on the server without updating the app, all clients will reject the connection until an app update is distributed, a process that may take weeks or months. This issue is often mitigated by using multi-pin validation with both current and future keys pinned simultaneously.
- **Applying Pinning Indiscriminately to Third-party Services** can break app functionality unexpectedly. Since third-party services control their own certificate management, they may update or rotate certificates without warning, invalidating pins hardcoded in the app. Best practice is to pin only endpoints fully controlled and managed by the developer's organization.
- **Insecure Implementation Details** can nullify pinning benefits. For instance, skipping pin checks under certain conditions, failing to validate the entire certificate chain, or logging sensitive pin hashes openly can expose the app to interception or downgrade attacks. Additionally, apps that do not enforce strict hostname verification alongside pinning leave gaps that attackers can exploit.
- **Lack of Monitoring and Alerting** on pin validation failures can delay detection of attacks or misconfigurations. Incorporating telemetry to capture failed pin validations (without logging sensitive details) helps developers respond rapidly to emerging threats or operational issues.

8.5 MASVS-PLATFORM

Platform Security Measures: Robust Protection Strategies

When you use apps on your phone, they often need to talk to the operating system (OS) of your device to function properly. This communication is essential for tasks like sharing data between apps or accessing features like web content within an app.

However, this interaction between apps and the OS can sometimes create opportunities for hackers or other apps to exploit vulnerabilities, potentially putting your app's security at risk. For instance, malicious actors might try to gain unauthorized access to your personal information or payment details by exploiting these connections.

Moreover, sensitive information like passwords or credit card numbers might be displayed on your screen while you are using the app. It is crucial to ensure that this sensitive data does not accidentally leak out, whether through features like auto-generated screenshots or by someone looking over your shoulder while you are using your phone in a public place.

So, this aspect of security focuses on ensuring that the communication between your app and the mobile platform is secure. This includes implementing safeguards to prevent unauthorized access to your data through these connections, as well as making sure that sensitive information is handled and displayed securely within the app.

8.5.1 MASVS-PLATFORM-1: Secure IPC Mechanisms

Data Sharing with Confidence

Inter-process Communication (IPC) is a fundamental mechanism in Android that enables interaction between different components of the same app or across different apps. While IPC is powerful, it also introduces significant security risks if not handled correctly. MASVS-PLATFORM-1 emphasizes the secure use of IPC mechanisms to prevent unauthorized access, privilege escalation, and potential leakage of sensitive data.

Android supports several IPC mechanisms such as Intents, Content Providers, AIDL (Android Interface Definition Language), Messengers, and Broadcast Receivers. Each of these can become a vector for attack if the app does not implement proper safeguards.

Secure IPC Design Practices

Developers should follow strict design practices when implementing IPC in Android apps:

- **Restrict Component Exposure:** Always ensure that app components such as Services, Activities, BroadcastReceivers, and ContentProviders are marked as non-exported unless there is a valid reason for inter-app communication. Setting android:exported="false" in the manifest explicitly prevents other apps from invoking them. Exported components should be considered potential entry points, and any exposure increases the attack surface. Even mistakenly exposed components can be discovered and exploited by malicious apps via static or dynamic analysis.
- **Use Permissions Judiciously:** When exposure is necessary, guard access using permissions, preferably custom and signature-level permissions. These permissions must be declared in the manifest and enforced via android:permission or programmatic checks. Signature-level permissions restrict access to apps signed with the same key, adding a strong layer of trust. Developers must also ensure that permission names do not conflict with system or third-party apps to avoid unintended elevation.
- **Validate Incoming IPC Data:** All data received from IPC interfaces, such as Intents, Messenger messages, or AIDL inputs, must be treated as untrusted. Proper validation includes checking for nulls, malformed input, unexpected types, and even logical anomalies like out-of-bound values or inconsistent flags. In high-risk components like financial apps or authentication flows, data should be further sanitized to prevent injection, spoofing, or privilege escalation attacks.
- **Apply Intent Filters Carefully:** Intent filters should be as specific as possible to avoid unintentionally accepting unwanted or malicious intents. Broad actions such as android.intent.action.VIEW or wildcards in data schemas increase the likelihood of external apps triggering the component. Where appropriate, include category and data

MIME types to narrow down the acceptable intent scope. Also, when using custom actions, ensure that they are not easily guessable or reused by other apps.

- **Use secure internal communication:** For intra-app messaging, use modern alternatives such as LiveData, WorkManager, or explicit callbacks. These methods ensure that messages remain within the app and cannot be intercepted or spoofed by third-party apps. LocalBroadcastManager is deprecated and should be avoided in new implementations.
- **Enforce Access Restrictions on Content Providers:** ContentProviders can expose structured data to external apps, and must be protected using permissions, grantUriPermission, or android:exported="false". Developers should avoid exporting ContentProviders unless required, and if shared, they must avoid exposing raw file paths or sensitive tables. Always use content:// URIs with read or write flags for temporary access, and revoke these when no longer needed. Additionally, exclude sensitive provider paths from backups to avoid unintended leaks.
- **Avoid Implicit Intents for Sensitive Actions:** Implicit intents can be intercepted, redirected, or manipulated by malicious apps if sensitive data or actions are involved. Always prefer explicit intents when launching critical components like user authentication, financial transactions, or internal tools. This reduces ambiguity and ensures the target component receives the intent directly, without passing through the OS's intent resolution process which may choose the wrong handler.
- **Apply Intent Verification for Incoming Intents:** Before accepting and processing any incoming intent, verify its authenticity by checking the sender's package name, digital signature, or UID. Use getCallingPackage() or getCallingUid() when available, and compare it against a whitelist. For intents received from AIDL, bound services, or deep links, ensure that the parameters align with expected formats and that only trusted apps can invoke them. This ensures that actions cannot be spoofed or forged by hostile actors.

Common Pitfalls

Despite best intentions, developers often overlook subtle implementation flaws. Below are some common mistakes that can weaken IPC security:

- **Assuming Defaults Are Secure:** Developers often assume that components are private by default, not realizing that once an intent-filter is added, the component may be implicitly exported (especially in pre-Android 12 apps). This can unintentionally expose internal functionality without any deliberate intent, leading to potential component hijacking or information leakage.
- **Trusting Intent Senders Blindly:** It's common to act on received intents, especially from deep links or other apps, without verifying their source. This opens the door to malicious apps injecting fake data, triggering actions inappropriately, or exploiting activities meant only for authenticated users.
- **Failing to Consider Component Lifecycle Behaviours:** Services and broadcast receivers may behave unexpectedly when triggered out-of-order or repeatedly by malicious apps. Developers often overlook how race conditions or unintended re-entry (e.g., from multiple malicious broadcasts) can affect logic execution, especially in services handling payment, login, or transactions.
- **Overexposing Data via Content Providers without Scoping:** Many apps mistakenly expose entire tables or databases through Content Providers when only a subset of data is needed. Without using projection, selection, or URI permission flags, this leads

to broader data exposure than intended, sometimes including credentials, logs, or user metadata.

- **Assuming That "Internal Use Only" Components Are Unreachable:** Even components intended strictly for internal use can be accessed if not explicitly secured. Developers might use internal naming conventions or app logic to indicate that a component "shouldn't" be accessed, but unless it is actively guarded (via permissions or android:exported="false"), other apps can still reach it.
- **Improper or Missing Cleanup of Granted Permissions:** Apps may use grantUriPermission() to share specific resources temporarily, but neglect to revoke them later with revokeUriPermission(). Over time, this can result in extended access to sensitive data, especially if granted to third-party apps or shared across activity lifecycles.
- **Overreliance on Implicit Security Through Obscurity:** Some apps rely on complex naming, undocumented actions, or hard-to-guess paths in deep links and custom actions, believing that "no one will find them". Attackers frequently reverse-engineer apps, and such hidden logic becomes a liability when not backed by actual enforcement mechanisms like signature checks or permission validation.

8.5.2 MASVS-PLATFORM-2: Secure WebView Usage

Securely Integrating Web Content

WebViews serve as powerful components in Android development, enabling apps to render web content directly within the app interface. While this offers functional flexibility and a seamless user experience, WebViews are also a well-known attack surface due to their ability to execute dynamic web content within the app's context. MASVS-PLATFORM-2 mandates that WebViews must be used in a secure manner to prevent exploitation such as JavaScript injection, phishing, or arbitrary code execution.

A secure WebView implementation ensures that the embedded browser is tightly controlled, trusted content is explicitly defined, and unnecessary capabilities are restricted. This helps to isolate the app's trusted execution environment from potentially malicious web-based behaviours.

Secure Usage Principles

Developers must adhere to several key principles while implementing WebViews:

- **Restrict JavaScript Execution:** JavaScript should be disabled using webView.getSettings().setJavaScriptEnabled(false) unless explicitly needed. Enabling JavaScript opens up risks of DOM-based XSS, especially if the content is not controlled. If required, JavaScript must only run in contexts loaded from hardcoded, trusted HTTPS URLs, never dynamically constructed or user-supplied sources.
- **Avoid Using addJavascriptInterface Unless Essential:** This method exposes Java methods to JavaScript code running within the WebView. If used, restrict its exposure to internal-only or tightly controlled web content, and ensure the target Android version is API level 17 or higher, where reflection-based access is mitigated. Never expose sensitive APIs or functionality through this interface in hybrid or externally facing WebViews.
- **Prevent JavaScript from Untrusted Sources:** JavaScript files loaded from unknown or third-party domains can be hijacked and modified. Avoid referencing external scripts unless served over HTTPS from trusted CDNs with subresource integrity (SRI). Inline

scripts should be used sparingly, and content security policies (CSP) should be considered when applicable in hybrid or embedded environments. For local HTML assets, use WebViewAssetLoader to serve content securely via https://appassets.androidplatform.net, preventing file:// access and mixed content issues.

- **Enforce HTTPS and Domain Whitelisting:** Always load content over HTTPS using webView.loadUrl("https://trusted.example.com"). Implement a strict allowlist of acceptable domains and use URL validation logic to enforce it. Avoid allowing redirections to open or wildcard-based domains, which could be abused to serve phishing or malicious payloads.

- **Avoid Loading Content from Untrusted or External Sources:** Avoid using loadData or loadDataWithBaseURL with user input or dynamic HTML fragments. These methods are particularly dangerous when JavaScript is enabled, as they allow full DOM manipulation and can bypass origin checks, potentially leading to universal XSS attacks or fake login overlays.

- **Validate URLs before Loading:** When passing URLs to loadUrl, ensure that they are strictly validated to match the intended scheme (HTTPS), domain, and path. URL parsing libraries or URI normalization can be used to prevent attackers from bypassing filters using encoded or malformed URLs. For example, http://trusted.com@evil.com should never be considered safe.

- **Override shouldOverrideUrlLoading:** Override this method in WebViewClient to intercept navigations and allow/disallow them based on security rules. This is critical for preventing navigation to unknown domains, deep links, or malicious redirection. Returning true gives you control, while returning false allows the WebView to proceed automatically, which may be undesirable.

- **Disable File Access When Not Required:** Set webView.getSettings().setAllowFileAccess(false) and setAllowContentAccess(false) unless explicitly required. Enabling file access can allow file-based XSS or leakage of app-internal content when combined with malicious local HTML files or exposed URIs. Additionally, avoid enabling access to file:// URLs entirely unless sandboxed properly.

- **Restrict Access to Internal App Resources:** If local file access is necessary (e.g., for embedded help content), ensure strict path validation and restrict access to a specific directory. Prevent traversal attacks (../) that could lead to unauthorized file access. Consider using WebViewAssetLoader to serve local assets safely and restrict origins via custom content providers.

- **Prevent Content Debugging in Production:** Disable debugging using WebView.setWebContentsDebuggingEnabled(false) in production builds. Leaving this enabled allows attackers or users with ADB access to inspect loaded HTML, intercept API keys, or modify JavaScript at runtime using Chrome DevTools or similar debugging interfaces. Conditional toggling based on build variant is strongly recommended.

- **Use Safe Browsing APIs:** Enable Safe Browsing using webView.getSettings().setSafeBrowsingEnabled(true) (on supported devices). This helps detect and block URLs flagged by Google for phishing, malware, or other threats. While it doesn't replace domain allowlisting, it adds a useful layer of runtime protection for unanticipated threats.

- **Disallow Third-party Cookies When Unnecessary:** Set CookieManager.getInstance().setAcceptThirdPartyCookies(webView, false) for WebViews rendering content from external domains. This prevents cross-site tracking and session leakage, which is especially important when the WebView is used in hybrid apps with embedded login or payments.

- **Avoid Loading User-generated or Dynamic HTML Content:** Never render raw user-submitted content using WebView methods like loadDataWithBaseURL. Even seemingly benign content can carry embedded JavaScript, iframes, or malformed HTML triggering layout-based attacks. Sanitize all inputs using an HTML sanitization library if rendering is absolutely necessary.

- **Handle WebResourceResponse Securely:** When overriding shouldInterceptRequest, validate incoming requests and avoid serving dynamically constructed responses without sanitization. Avoid passing raw query strings, parameters, or payloads directly into response bodies. Incorrect handling here could reintroduce XSS, directory traversal, or mixed content issues if external resources are involved.
- **Modern WebView Alternatives:** Consider using Chrome Custom Tabs or Trusted Web Activity for external content instead of embedded WebViews when possible. These provide better security isolation and automatic security updates.

Common Pitfalls

Despite available guidelines, certain patterns of misuse continue to surface during security assessments and in real-world breaches. Recognizing these pitfalls can help developers avoid subtle but impactful mistakes:

- **Assuming JavaScript Is Safe If Content "Looks" Static:** Developers sometimes enable JavaScript under the assumption that the HTML is benign because it's simple or server-rendered. However, even minimal content can be manipulated by attackers through redirected or tampered resources, leading to silent XSS or logic abuse.
- **Relying on Domain Names Alone for Trust Decisions:** A WebView may appear to load content from a trusted domain, but without validating the full URL, including subdomains, paths, and schemes, malicious actors can exploit open redirects, subdomain takeovers, or phishing subpaths. Domain whitelisting without strict validation is misleadingly fragile.
- **Forgetting to Update Security Settings Across Versions:** Developers might set security policies (like disabling debugging or JavaScript) for a specific WebView instance but forget to enforce them consistently across all instantiations, especially in larger apps or modular components. This leads to configuration drift where some WebViews remain exposed.
- **Trusting the Play Store Environment Too Much:** There's a common false sense of security that Play Store deployment means the app won't be tampered with. In reality, apps can be reverse-engineered, repackaged, or run in emulators. Leaving debugging or unguarded interfaces enabled assumes too much about the device's integrity.
- **Using WebViews for Login Screens without Safeguards:** Some developers build custom login UIs inside WebViews to mimic single sign-on or federated login flows. If not locked down tightly, this can be exploited for phishing. A WebView should never display login forms unless the content source and certificate pinning are both strictly enforced.
- **Assuming shouldOverrideUrlLoading Covers All Navigation Paths:** While this method intercepts standard link clicks, it doesn't always cover redirects triggered by JavaScript or form submissions. Relying on this alone for navigation control can give a false sense of security. Additional URL validation at every load point is necessary.
- **Misusing loadDataWithBaseURL without Null Base:** Developers often provide an empty or inappropriate base URL in loadDataWithBaseURL, assuming it's inert. However, if the base allows relative paths or inherits script access, it can open up access to local files or external scripts through relative references.

8.5.3 MASVS-PLATFORM-3: Secure User Interface Handling

Protecting Sensitive Information Through the UI

In mobile application security, the user interface (UI) is often seen as a layer responsible primarily for aesthetics and usability. However, it also represents a critical surface area for potential attacks if not designed and implemented with security in mind. MASVS-PLATFORM-3 addresses the need to use the UI securely, ensuring that sensitive interactions and data handled within the UI are properly protected from both active and passive threats.

Secure use of the UI entails ensuring that sensitive data is neither exposed unnecessarily on screen nor accessible through indirect means such as screen readers, screenshots, or overlay attacks. The goal is to minimize the risk of information leakage and to maintain the integrity and confidentiality of user interactions.

Design Considerations

UI security must begin at the design stage. Developers and UX designers should collaborate to define which screens require additional protection and what types of data warrant UI-level confidentiality controls. For example, in a mobile banking app:

- **Transaction PIN Input Screens** should disable screenshots and accessibility services.
- **Balance Display Areas** should be obscured when switching to multitasking or when inactivity is detected.
- **OTP Input Fields** should be read-only, non-copyable, and resistant to overlay capture.
- **Push Notifications** for sensitive events (like transaction alerts) should avoid displaying full account details or financial figures on the lock screen.

Key Secure UI Practices

Developers should adhere to the following secure UI design and implementation practices:

- **Preventing Tapjacking:** Tapjacking occurs when a malicious app overlays transparent elements to trick users into tapping sensitive buttons unintentionally. Android provides protection through the filterTouchesWhenObscured attribute, which should be enabled on views handling critical operations like fund transfers, approvals, or login. Additionally, runtime checks using onFilterTouchEventForSecurity() can help reject obscured touch events programmatically.
- **Protecting Against Cloak and Dagger Attacks:** Modern overlay attacks can capture sensitive interactions even when filterTouchesWhenObscured is enabled. Implement additional validation by checking for active accessibility services and display overlays using WindowManager and AccessibilityManager APIs before processing sensitive operations.
- **Disabling Screenshots on Sensitive Screens:** Screenshots and screen recordings can lead to passive data leaks when taken from sensitive views. By applying Window.setFlags (WindowManager.LayoutParams.FLAG_SECURE, WindowManager.LayoutParams. FLAG_SECURE) to critical activities, such as those displaying account details, passwords, or financial transactions, you can prevent these actions at the system level. This is especially important in shared device scenarios or in enterprise environments.
- **Masking Sensitive Information in Recent Apps View:** Android's task switcher can display a preview of the app's last active state. If the UI includes sensitive information,

such as a user's transaction history or personal details, these may be exposed in the snapshot. Developers should either enable FLAG_SECURE or replace the screen with a dummy/neutral layout (e.g., a logo or blurred screen) in the onPause() method to maintain privacy.

- **Avoiding Display of Sensitive Data in Toasts, Dialogs, and Notifications:** UI elements like Toasts and system dialogs are not inherently secure, they can be intercepted or logged by accessibility services or malicious overlays. Likewise, notifications are displayed outside the app context and should use non-sensitive, generic messaging. For instance, instead of showing "OTP: 123456", use "An OTP has been sent to your registered number. Open the app to continue". Use NotificationCompat.Builder.setVisibility(VISIBILITY_PRIVATE) to limit content on lock screens.

- **Protecting Accessibility Features:** While accessibility improves usability for users with impairments, it can also expose sensitive UI content to potentially malicious services. Input fields dealing with PINs, passwords, or financial values should explicitly set android:importantForAccessibility="no" or dynamically exclude views using ViewCompat.setImportantForAccessibility(view, ViewCompat.IMPORTANT_FOR_ACCESSIBILITY_NO) to prevent data harvesting by unauthorized accessibility tools.

- **Preventing Autofill of Sensitive Fields:** Android Autofill services can store and suggest user data, which may not be desirable for sensitive fields. Input elements like passwords, card numbers, and OTPs should use android:importantForAutofill="no" or android:autofillHints="none" to prevent the OS or third-party managers from saving or auto-filling data that should be entered manually during secure workflows.

- **Securing Input Validation at the UI Level:** Client-side input validation helps in reducing malformed data entering the app logic or UI-based injection attempts. For example, restricting the character set in user ID fields or enforcing length and format checks in email/password fields can stop many simple attacks early. Combine this with server-side validation to ensure layered security.

- **Obfuscating Sensitive Data in Logs or Errors:** Crashes or errors triggered from the UI should never expose sensitive input values. Avoid logging raw input from text fields like password or card number fields. Use logging sanitizers or manually strip values before logging. For example, logging "Transaction failed for account ending in 1234" is safer than logging the full account number or input value.

- **Avoiding Hardcoded UI Elements for Secrets:** In some cases, developers embed hardcoded tokens or secret values within UI labels or assets for convenience, especially during testing. This practice is dangerous, as reverse engineering can easily expose these secrets. Instead, all secrets should be retrieved securely at runtime, encrypted at rest, and never visible in any part of the UI or resource files.

- **Preventing UI Data Leakage:** UI elements displaying sensitive data should be treated as volatile and be cleared or hidden as soon as their relevance ends. For example, OTP fields should auto-clear after a timeout, and balance views should blur or hide automatically when the app is backgrounded. Consider using techniques like view masking, visibility toggling, or activity transitions to minimize accidental exposure.

- **Mitigating Task Affinity Abuse (StrandHogg Vulnerability):** StrandHogg exploits improperly configured task affinity and launch modes to hijack UI flows and impersonate screens. To counter this, explicitly set android:taskAffinity to a unique or empty value for sensitive activities, and restrict inter-task behaviour with launchMode="singleTask" or launchMode="singleTop" as applicable. This limits activity hijacking and improves control over app navigation. Note that Android 11+ has mitigations for known task hijacking exploits.

Common Pitfalls

Even with a solid understanding of secure UI practices, developers often fall into traps due to assumptions, convenience, or unawareness. The following are common oversights that weaken UI-level security in Android applications:

- **Assuming UI Security Is Handled by the OS**: Many developers incorrectly believe that Android automatically protects sensitive UI components. However, UI protections like FLAG_SECURE, accessibility filtering, and secure notification handling must be explicitly implemented, Android does not enforce these by default.
- **Using Placeholder or Demo Code in Production**: Temporary implementations such as hardcoded credentials, mock data, or test overlays often make their way into production builds unintentionally. These elements can expose sensitive information or create unexpected behaviour under attack scenarios.
- **Lack of Coordination Between Designers and Developers**: Security decisions at the UI layer are often left entirely to developers, with little input from UX or product teams. As a result, sensitive flows may be visually overexposed (e.g., balance displayed on the home screen), or security features (like blurring or hiding) may be stripped for "aesthetic" reasons.
- **Over-prioritizing Convenience Over Security**: Features such as Autofill, persistent notification previews, or saving form inputs are sometimes kept enabled for user convenience, even in areas where it introduces risk. This is particularly common in apps that prioritize speed-to-market without formal threat modelling.
- **Not Testing Against Real Attack Scenarios**: Many UI vulnerabilities, such as tapjacking, screen overlay attacks, and task hijacking, are not detected during traditional QA testing. Developers may skip manual tests or fail to use security tools/emulators that simulate overlay or multitasking-based exploits.
- **Assuming Input Validation Is a Backend Concern**: Client-side validation is often treated as optional or cosmetic. This assumption leads to unvalidated UI fields being abused for script injection, logic bypass, or other input manipulation, especially dangerous in hybrid apps or apps with embedded web views.
- **Relying on Device Trust for Sensitive UI Handling**: Developers sometimes assume that since the app runs on a trusted user's device, additional UI security layers are unnecessary. This overlooks common real-world risks such as stolen devices, malicious apps with overlay permissions, or user error (like sharing screens on unsecured networks).

8.6 MASVS-CODE

Secure Coding Practices: Fortifying Application Code

Imagine your mobile app as a bustling city with numerous entry points, each representing a different way data can flow: through the user interface, over the internet, or from files stored on the device. However, just like in any city, not everyone coming in can be trusted. There might be individuals with ill intentions trying to sneak in harmful substances.

To protect your city, or, in this case, your app, from these potential threats, you need to implement stringent security measures. Think of it as setting up checkpoints at every entrance, where each piece of incoming data is thoroughly inspected before being allowed further access. This process ensures that no malicious code slips through the cracks, preventing disastrous consequences such as data breaches or system crashes.

But security is not just about guarding against obvious threats like hackers trying to inject malicious code into your app. It is also about defending against more subtle dangers, such as vulnerabilities that can manipulate the inner workings of your app's memory. These vulnerabilities can be incredibly difficult to detect through standard testing methods but can be effectively mitigated through robust coding practices and adherence to established security standards.

To establish a formidable defence system for your app, it is essential to follow industry best practices outlined by organizations like OWASP (Open Web Application Security Project) and NIST (National Institute of Standards and Technology). These guidelines serve as a roadmap for developers, outlining the steps necessary to fortify their applications against a wide range of security threats.

Furthermore, the scope of security extends beyond just your app's code. It also encompasses the underlying operating system and any third-party software components your app relies on. Just as you diligently fortify your own code, you must also ensure that these external dependencies are kept up-to-date and thoroughly vetted for any vulnerabilities they may introduce.

In essence, building a secure app is akin to constructing a fortified stronghold in a constantly evolving digital landscape. By implementing robust security measures, staying vigilant against emerging threats, and adhering to established best practices, you can safeguard your users' data and provide them with peace of mind in an increasingly interconnected world.

8.6.1 MASVS-CODE-1: Platform Update Version Requirement

Data in Motion, Security in Place

Ensuring that an Android application runs on an up-to-date platform version is a foundational step toward establishing a secure mobile environment. MASVS-CODE-1 emphasizes the importance of aligning app compatibility with a platform version that is actively maintained and fortified with the latest security patches.

Older versions of the Android OS often contain publicly known vulnerabilities, which adversaries can easily exploit. Applications that continue to support outdated platform versions expose themselves, and by extension, their users, to a higher risk of compromise. This makes enforcing a minimum supported platform version not just a development choice but a security necessity.

Developers should define the minSdkVersion and targetSdkVersion (now replaced with targetSdk) wisely. The minSdkVersion determines the lowest Android version on which the app can be installed, while the targetSdkVersion declares the highest API level the app is designed to support and benefit from its security behaviour changes.

Essential Considerations

Developers should adhere to the following key best practices:

- **Set a Reasonably High Minsdkversion**, ideally one that excludes platform versions with critical and unpatched security issues. For instance, Android versions below API level 23 (Android 6.0) lack runtime permission prompts for sensitive actions, while versions below API level 26 (Android 8.0) lack background execution limits. Supporting very old versions may open the app to outdated WebView vulnerabilities, insecure SSL handling, and fragmented permission models. Raising the minSdkVersion enforces a baseline security posture across all devices using the app.

- **Always Target the Latest Stable SDK Version** to leverage security hardening improvements introduced in recent Android releases. By setting the targetSdkVersion (or targetSdk in Gradle Plugin 8.0+) to the latest API level, developers allow the app to adopt modern behaviours and benefit from security features like background activity restrictions, improved memory protections (e.g., hardened malloc), and changes in broadcast receiver behaviour. Not targeting the latest SDK causes the app to operate in legacy compatibility mode, weakening its security profile.

- **Ensure That the App Runs Reliably on Recent Platform Versions**, especially those actively supported by Google and OEMs. This includes testing compatibility with behavioural changes in new APIs, enforcing runtime permission dialogs correctly, handling scoped storage, and using JobScheduler or WorkManager for background tasks. A failure to test on recent versions could result in unexpected crashes, degraded UX, or broken security assumptions due to outdated implementation patterns.

- **Monitor Android Security Bulletins** to understand vulnerabilities in older versions and adjust the supported API levels accordingly. Google's monthly Android Security Bulletin outlines known vulnerabilities in various API levels, some of which are critical or remote-code execution (RCE) related. By aligning your minSdkVersion above vulnerable thresholds, you proactively eliminate exposure to those issues without needing to address each individually within the app codebase.

- **Avoid Supporting Deprecated Security Mechanisms** by staying aligned with current platform behaviour. This includes ensuring the app doesn't rely on outdated cryptographic providers (like MD5, SHA-1, or insecure random number generators), or protocols like TLS 1.0 and 1.1, which are disabled by default from Android 10 (API level 29) onward. Apps that rely on deprecated security APIs may silently fail or degrade the security of user data and network communication on modern devices.

Common Pitfalls

Despite understanding the importance of secure platform targeting, many developers unintentionally introduce risks due to oversight, convenience, or business pressures. Some of the most common pitfalls include:

- **Prioritizing Device Coverage Over Security** by setting an excessively low minSdkVersion. This often stems from a desire to support older devices, but it inadvertently includes users running OS versions with unpatched vulnerabilities and no modern security controls.

- **Delaying targetSdkVersion Updates** for fear of breaking existing functionality. This avoidance results in the app running in backward-compatibility modes, which preserve legacy behaviours and bypass newer security enforcements introduced in recent Android versions.

- **Assuming Passing Play Store Checks Means Secure Configuration:** Google Play's API targeting requirements set a minimum bar, not a security benchmark. Developers sometimes meet the bare minimum (e.g., targetSdkVersion required for publishing) without considering whether it's the most secure choice.

- **Neglecting to Test the App on Current Android Releases:** Without thorough testing on the latest platform versions, issues like permission handling changes, background process limitations, or scoped storage may go unnoticed, leading to crashes or degraded user experience.

- **Hardcoding Version-dependent Logic or Fallbacks Poorly:** Developers sometimes implement platform-specific workarounds in a way that breaks on newer OS versions or unintentionally disables security features, for example, defaulting to insecure storage or cryptography if a platform check fails.

8.6.2 MASVS-CODE-2: Enforce App Updates

Keeping your App Secure, One Update at a Time

In the dynamic world of mobile applications, updates are not just about adding features, they are a vital defence mechanism. MASVS-CODE-2 emphasizes the necessity of enforcing updates to keep all users on the most secure and compliant version. A solid update enforcement strategy not only reduces the attack surface but also enhances trust, usability, and regulatory alignment.

The Importance of Enforcing Updates

Mandatory updates help patch known vulnerabilities, implement advanced security controls, and ensure users benefit from the latest enhancements. Supporting older versions introduces risk, as adversaries often exploit outdated components. Enforcing updates maintains user safety, aligns with industry standards, and fosters long-term trust.

Tools and Techniques for Update Enforcement

Choosing the right update strategy requires balancing user experience with security needs. From built-in APIs to custom logic, developers have various options to implement secure and effective update flows.

- **Leveraging the In-app Update API:** Android's In-App Update API offers developers two modes: flexible and immediate updates. Flexible updates allow users to continue using the app while the update downloads in the background, suitable for minor bug fixes and feature rollouts. Immediate updates, in contrast, force the user to install the latest version before proceeding, which is ideal for fixing critical security flaws. Integration involves using AppUpdateManager to trigger update checks, while handling update states via listeners ensures a smooth experience. This API provides a native, streamlined approach to enforcing updates without relying on external services. Note that Google Play's In-App Update API has specific eligibility requirements and may not be available for all app distribution channels or enterprise apps.
- **Developing Custom Update Logic:** Custom update logic is essential when default APIs lack flexibility or are insufficient for nuanced workflows. Developers can build periodic or on-demand update checks during app startup, after login, or upon encountering sensitive actions. A REST API can be used to fetch the latest version metadata from the backend, and if the client version is outdated, the app can display a mandatory update dialog. Implementing conditions such as security event triggers or authentication failures can dynamically adjust enforcement policies. This method ensures tighter security control at the expense of slightly higher implementation complexity. Note that custom update mechanisms bypass Google Play's integrity verification and are strongly discouraged unless the app is distributed outside Google Play. They increase risk of sideloading and tampering.

- **Server-Side Version Enforcement:** A centralized version control system hosted on the backend allows fine-grained control over update policies. The server can maintain a "minimum supported version" and return that value during client handshake or version check APIs. If the client's version falls below the threshold, access can be restricted or certain features disabled using feature flags. This architecture supports region-specific compliance using IP-based geo-fencing and permits phased rollouts. Server-side enforcement also provides an opportunity to collect analytics on update adoption, crash rates by version, and security event tracking for legacy builds.

Designing for Compatibility and Integrity

Security should not come at the cost of usability. Ensuring that update enforcement does not break existing functionality, or leave users stranded, requires careful architectural planning.

- **Supporting Backward Compatibility:** While pushing users to update quickly, it is equally important to handle older versions gracefully. Implement version-aware APIs on the backend that tailor responses based on the client's app version, avoiding breakage for users who have not yet updated. Use version-specific feature toggles to hide or limit advanced functionalities not supported in older builds. Client apps should also handle deprecated endpoints or schema mismatches cleanly, falling back to safe defaults. Avoid hard blocks unless absolutely necessary, and provide contextually relevant prompts encouraging users to upgrade.
- **Ensuring Secure Update Channels:** All update-related communications, whether it's fetching version info, downloading updates, or accessing manifests, should be conducted over HTTPS with TLS 1.2+ to prevent interception. Certificate pinning can be used to protect against compromised CAs and man-in-the-middle attacks. Secure transport guarantees not only confidentiality but also authenticity, ensuring the update comes from a trusted source. For Android apps, using DownloadManager with enforced secure URLs ensures minimal attack surface during the delivery phase.
- **Validating Update Integrity:** Once an update is downloaded, it must be verified for integrity before installation. Use cryptographic signatures to sign update packages (e.g., .apk files), and verify them using public keys embedded in the app. Apply hash checks using SHA-256 or stronger algorithms to detect any alteration. Signed manifests, checksums, and validation steps during install-time or pre-launch (e.g., using SignatureVerifier) help ensure the code has not been tampered with. A mismatch should halt the installation and notify the user to prevent possible compromise.
- **Protecting Against Rollbacks and Tampering:** Rollback protection ensures that attackers cannot re-install vulnerable legacy versions of your app. On Android 9+ devices, rollback protection is integrated with Verified Boot, but apps can add additional checks. Store the highest installed version number in SharedPreferences or secure storage, and compare it during startup. If a lower version is detected, block usage and prompt for reinstallation. Pair this with anti-tampering checks like SafetyNet or Google's App Integrity API to validate the runtime environment and detect rooting or injection attempts.

Creating a User-centric Update Experience

A secure app is only as good as its adoption. Making updates intuitive and minimally disruptive improves user compliance and satisfaction.

- **Communicating the Value of Updates:** Users are more likely to update promptly when they understand the "why" behind it. Update dialogs should clearly explain the benefits, such as enhanced security, new features, or better performance. Where possible, provide a changelog or short bullet summary. Apps can use in-app banners, toast messages, or modal prompts styled consistently with the brand. Avoid overly technical jargon, and instead focus on real-world user value. Combining messaging with visuals (like icons or badges) improves engagement and perceived urgency.
- **Offering Graceful Update Timing:** Rather than forcing users to update immediately in all cases, offer context-sensitive grace periods. For example, give users 3–5 days to update unless a critical security flaw is discovered. Use countdown timers or soft-blocked UI to show the remaining time before enforcement. This allows users to finish active tasks or wait for Wi-Fi availability, improving the perceived fairness of the enforcement. Backend systems should store user-specific grace period expirations to maintain consistency across sessions.
- **Supporting Background Installation:** To minimize disruption, apps can support automatic background updates using native OS tools (e.g., Play Store Auto-Updates) or custom download managers. Once an update is downloaded silently, prompt the user only when a restart or minimal action is required. This approach is especially useful for low-priority updates or minor patches. Developers can use WorkManager or AlarmManager to schedule periodic update checks and manage battery-friendly downloads. This preserves a smooth user experience while maintaining update compliance.

8.6.3 MASVS-CODE-3: Avoid Vulnerable Components

Secure Components, Secure App

Third-party libraries and software components are indispensable in modern Android development, offering developers access to prebuilt functionalities and saving valuable time. However, incorporating external code into an app introduces risks that can compromise the overall security posture. MASVS-CODE-3 emphasizes the necessity of ensuring that all software components used are free from known vulnerabilities.

Importance of Secure Component Usage

Using components with known security flaws is akin to locking the front door while leaving the back door wide open. Attackers often exploit vulnerabilities in outdated or unpatched libraries, which may include flaws in data handling, cryptographic weaknesses, or even backdoors. This makes it essential to continuously monitor and manage the security status of all dependencies integrated into the app.

Best Practices for Compliance

Development teams should establish a reliable process to identify, assess, and remediate vulnerabilities in third-party components. Recommended practices include:

- **Use Dependency Scanners:** Tools like OWASP Dependency-Check, Gradle's dependencyCheck plugin, or JFrog Xray can automatically inspect your build artefacts and highlight components with known CVEs. These scanners parse metadata such as group ID, artefact ID, and version to cross-reference public vulnerability databases, helping you avoid insecure libraries early in development.

- **Prefer Actively Maintained Libraries:** Choose libraries with frequent commits, recent releases, and visible issue tracking activity. A regularly updated changelog and active response to pull requests are good indicators. These libraries typically receive security patches faster, reducing your window of exposure to newly discovered flaws.
- **Avoid Abandoned Projects:** Refrain from using libraries that have not seen updates in over a year, especially for critical functionalities like networking or cryptography. Lack of maintenance may indicate unpatched security issues or incompatibility with newer Android versions and security APIs.
- **Enforce Strict Version Control:** Use tools like Gradle's resolutionStrategy to control dependency versions explicitly and prevent automatic upgrades that may pull in unstable or insecure versions. Applying dependency locks (via dependencies.lock) ensures the same version is used across builds, preventing inconsistencies.
- **Monitor CVE Databases Regularly:** Incorporate feeds from the National Vulnerability Database (NVD) or GitHub's Advisory Database into your CI/CD pipeline using plugins or webhooks. Automated alerts can notify your team when a library used in your project is tagged with a new vulnerability.
- **Minimize Dependencies:** Avoid bloated libraries that provide more functionality than needed. Instead, favour modular solutions or native Android APIs when feasible. Fewer dependencies reduce the attack surface and ease the task of ongoing vulnerability management.
- **Isolate Critical Functionality:** When third-party libraries are used for sensitive operations such as authentication, data storage, or cryptography, place them in isolated modules or wrapper classes. This limits their access and allows you to swap them out quickly if a vulnerability arises.
- **Use Software Composition Analysis (SCA):** Integrate tools like Snyk, Black Duck, or Sonatype into your CI/CD to gain a comprehensive view of your entire dependency tree, including transitive dependencies. These tools offer remediation advice and direct links to patched versions, streamlining your security workflow.
- **Verify Transitive Dependencies:** Tools like Gradle's dependencies task or SCA dashboards help trace indirect dependencies introduced by top-level libraries. Review and audit these thoroughly, as they are often overlooked yet can introduce serious vulnerabilities.
- **Adopt a Component Lifecycle Policy:** Develop internal governance rules that define acceptable licenses, patch timelines, review processes, and sunset policies for outdated dependencies. This ensures consistent risk management practices across teams and releases.

Leveraging Compiler-level Protections

While selecting secure components is essential, developers must also ensure that the build and compilation processes do not undermine these efforts. Android's build toolchain provides several mechanisms to harden apps at compile time:

- **Enable ProGuard or R8 with Proper Configuration:** These tools perform code shrinking and obfuscation, making it difficult for attackers to reverse-engineer proprietary or vulnerable logic. A well-maintained proguard-rules.pro file should exclude only necessary classes from obfuscation, ensuring maximum protection for internal methods and logic paths.
- **Use Lint Checks for Dependency Analysis:** Android Lint provides static analysis capabilities, which can detect insecure or deprecated APIs in your codebase or third-party

libraries. Custom Lint rules can be created to enforce organizational policies, such as disallowing outdated networking libraries (e.g., Apache HTTP client).

- **Enable Warnings and Strict Compilation Flags:** Configure your build process to treat all warnings as errors (-W error flag) to avoid ignoring potentially dangerous code paths. Using Java or Kotlin compiler options like -Xlint:all helps enforce stricter compile-time safety checks.
- **Leverage Build-Time Security Flags:** Ensure that debug symbols are stripped in production builds (debuggable false in the release buildType) and enable minifyEnabled to remove unused code. Use shrinkResources true to eliminate unused assets, minimizing the risk of exposing test artefacts or dead code paths.
- **Adopt Secure Signing and Build Configurations:** Store keystores securely using Android's Keystore system or CI/CD secrets management tools. Avoid using test keys or signing configurations with weak algorithms (e.g., SHA-1). Always enforce V2 or V3 signature schemes for APK signing to prevent tampering.
- **Monitor Build Artefacts for Hardcoded Secrets:** Use static analysis tools or Gradle tasks to scan APKs and AABs for API keys, credentials, or other sensitive information accidentally included during build. Ensure secrets are injected securely using environment variables or secure keystore access.

8.6.4 MASVS-CODE-4: Validate Untrusted Inputs

Data Integrity Starts at the Entry Point

Handling untrusted input securely is fundamental to mobile app development. MASVS-CODE-4 emphasizes the necessity of validating and sanitizing all external input received by the app, whether from users, inter-process communication (IPC), network responses, or even device sensors.

Untrusted inputs represent potential entry points for a wide array of security vulnerabilities, including injection attacks, logic bypasses, insecure deserialization, and crashes. Android apps often interact with diverse input sources, making it crucial to establish strict boundaries and checks to ensure that malicious or malformed data does not propagate through the application logic or persist in sensitive components like databases, shared preferences, or backups.

Why Input Validation and Sanitization Matter

Failing to validate inputs can lead to:

- **SQL Injection** where malformed inputs manipulate database queries. Even with parameterized queries, improperly handled user input in raw queries or filters can introduce severe data access and integrity risks.
- **Command Injection** in cases where inputs are used to call system-level functionality. If user-supplied values are concatenated into shell commands or external process arguments, attackers can execute arbitrary code.
- **Data Corruption** when inputs carry unexpected data types or encodings. This can result in broken application logic, faulty business rules, or irreversible data pollution in storage systems.
- **Crashes and Denial of Service** due to unhandled input formats or lengths. Overly long strings, malformed JSON, or unsupported data types can crash apps, especially on memory-constrained devices.

- **Insecure Parsing and Escaping** leading to logic manipulation or injection. Inputs not correctly escaped or parsed can exploit differences in interpretation between components like parsers, renderers, or loggers.
- **Insecure Object Deserialization** where unsafe conversion of untrusted data to objects may allow arbitrary code execution or state tampering. Attackers can manipulate class mappings or field values to break encapsulation.

Practical Strategies for Handling Inputs

Developers should consider the following best practices:

- **Implement Whitelisting Over Blacklisting:** Rather than blocking a list of known bad characters (which is often incomplete), allow only specific formats that meet business needs. For example, constrain usernames to [a-zA-Z0-9_] using regular expressions and reject everything else. Whitelisting minimizes the attack surface and prevents bypasses using alternate encodings, homoglyphs, or non-printable characters that blacklists may miss.
- **Validate Data at the Point of Entry:** Input should be validated immediately upon receipt, before being stored or passed to other modules. For instance, an Intent extra received from another app should be checked for type, length, and content before being used. Avoid trusting UI input fields, even with client-side checks, malicious users can bypass them using custom keyboards, accessibility services, or adb commands.
- **Use Platform-provided Input Filters and Constraints:** Android provides built-in input control mechanisms like InputFilter, setInputType(), and android:digits for EditText fields. For modern apps, consider using TextInputLayout with validation and Compose TextField with input validation. These tools restrict user input at the UI level, reducing risk early.
- **Normalize Data Before Processing:** Input data should be normalized to avoid inconsistencies in encoding and format. Normalize strings using Unicode Normalization Form (e.g., NFC) to prevent canonicalization issues. Apply consistent case (e.g., .toLowerCase(Locale.US)) when storing or comparing strings, and trim whitespace to prevent accidental logic bypasses or database query errors due to unexpected padding.
- **Sanitize Content Displayed in WebViews or Logs:** Always escape HTML or JavaScript code when rendering dynamic content in WebViews using functions like Html. escapeHtml(). Avoid rendering raw user input without encoding, and disable JavaScript in WebViews unless absolutely necessary. Logs must also be sanitized, avoid logging raw input, especially from untrusted sources, as it may lead to log injection or sensitive data leakage.
- **Reject Data That Does Not Conform to Expected Types or Structures:** Use strict parsing for data types, e.g., prefer SimpleDateFormat.parse() with clearly defined formats over lenient parsers. Validate JSON keys and values against a schema rather than relying on automatic deserialization. If using libraries like Gson or Jackson, avoid auto-binding untrusted input directly to POJOs without explicit field validation, to prevent over-posting or unsafe object population.
- **Limit Input Size Where Possible:** Apply length and size restrictions on all user inputs, file uploads, and network responses. For instance, restrict string input fields to a maximum character count (e.g., 256 characters) and enforce size limits on images or documents (e.g., 5 MB max). This helps avoid memory exhaustion, buffer overflows, or performance degradation due to maliciously large payloads.

- **Handle Nulls and Unexpected Formats Defensively:** Assume every input can be missing, null, or malformed. Use safe accessors and null checks (e.g., Kotlin's ?. operator or Java's Optional) to handle absent data gracefully. For number fields, catch NumberFormatException explicitly and avoid fallback logic that may conceal bugs. Defensive programming prevents crashes and stops flawed data from cascading through the app.
- **Never Trust Data from IPC, Backups, or Shared Local Storage:** IPC mechanisms like Intents, bound services, or content providers may receive tampered data from malicious apps. Always validate data from these sources with the same rigor as user inputs. For data restored from backups (e.g., via SharedPreferences, Room, or file storage), re-validate on app launch or migration to avoid loading outdated or manipulated content.
- **Avoid Unsafe Dynamic Code Loading Based on Unverified Input:** Never use input-driven logic to load classes dynamically (e.g., using Class.forName(), DexClassLoader, or reflection APIs) unless the source is fully controlled and verified. If dynamic features are necessary, validate input against a strict list of known-safe module identifiers or hashes. Arbitrary code loading opens the door to code injection, privilege escalation, and remote execution attacks.

Common Pitfalls

Despite awareness of input-related risks, developers often fall into subtle traps that undermine security. Below are some commonly overlooked or misunderstood practices that can lead to violations:

- **Assuming UI-level Constraints Are Sufficient:** Developers often rely solely on input restrictions at the interface level, such as keyboard types or input masks. However, these can be easily bypassed using external input methods like adb, custom keyboards, or accessibility services. Input constraints at the UI layer must be treated as advisory, not authoritative.
- **Trusting IPC Data as Internal:** Treating data passed via Intents, bound services, or broadcast receivers as safe because it "comes from another component of the app" is risky. Many Android components can be exported inadvertently, allowing untrusted apps to inject data. Even within your own app, use signature checks or validation logic to enforce trust boundaries.
- **Using Auto-deserialization without Safeguards:** Object mapping libraries like Gson or Jackson are often used to deserialize JSON input into objects. Without schema enforcement or post-deserialization validation, these mechanisms may create partially formed or malicious objects, leading to unexpected behaviour, logic bypass, or worse, security bugs tied to type confusion or over-posting.
- **Sanitizing only for Display, Not for Storage or Logic:** Developers sometimes focus on escaping user input for display in WebViews or logs, but neglect to sanitize it before processing or storing. This can result in injection attacks at the database level (e.g., SQLite injection), or manipulation of business logic through malformed content.
- **Overlooking Encoding Inconsistencies:** Text inputs from different sources (e.g., network vs. local files) may use inconsistent character encodings or normalization forms. Failing to standardize these before validation can allow adversaries to exploit encoding quirks to bypass security filters. For example, visually identical but bytewise different characters may slip through regex checks.
- **Accepting Oversized Payloads as Benign:** Some developers do not impose strict size limits on file uploads, text fields, or blob data, assuming the device or server will handle

them. In practice, this can lead to memory exhaustion, unhandled OutOfMemoryError, or denial-of-service conditions, especially if input is streamed from external sources.

- **Restoring Unvalidated Data from Backups:** When using Android's auto-backup features or manual import/export mechanisms, apps may blindly reload settings, preferences, or local databases without re-validation. This assumes that backed-up data is inherently trusted, which may not be true, especially if backups were tampered with or came from older versions with different validation rules.

8.7 MASVS-RESILIENCE

Robust App Integrity: Thwarting Reverse Engineering

Imagine your app as a grand fortress, standing tall and proud amidst a digital landscape. Just like a fortress, your app holds valuable treasures within its walls; secrets, sensitive data, and intellectual property. Now, picture hackers as cunning thieves, constantly seeking ways to breach your fortress and plunder its riches.

To safeguard your fortress, you do not just rely on a single barrier. Instead, you employ a sophisticated system of defence-in-depth measures; multiple layers of security controls that fortify your app against various forms of attack.

First and foremost, these measures ensure that your fortress stands on solid ground; a trusted platform free from vulnerabilities and weaknesses. It is like building your fortress on a foundation of rock, resistant to the shifting sands of cyber threats.

But the defence does not end there. Just as a fortress is surrounded by vigilant guards and fortified walls, your app is equipped with alarms and barriers to prevent tampering while it is running. These safeguards create a virtual moat around your app, deterring would-be intruders from attempting to breach its defences.

Moreover, the defence-in-depth measures make it exceptionally challenging for hackers to decipher the inner workings of your app. It is akin to concealing the architectural plans of your fortress, making it a formidable puzzle for anyone attempting to unravel its secrets. This complexity deters attackers from conducting static analysis, trying to understand your app's structure without running it, and prevents dynamic analysis, which involves manipulating the app's code while it is running.

However, it is important to note that while these additional layers of protection bolster your app's resilience, they are not the sole determinants of its security. Rather, they complement other essential security controls, forming a comprehensive defence strategy tailored to your app's unique threat landscape.

By implementing these defence-in-depth measures, you are not just fortifying your fortress; you are erecting an impregnable stronghold that repels even the most determined adversaries, ensuring the safety and integrity of your valuable assets in the digital realm.

8.7.1 MASVS-RESILIENCE-1: Platform Integrity Validation

Data on Trust: Running on a Secure Platform

Platform integrity validation is a cornerstone of mobile application resilience. MASVS-RESILIENCE-1 emphasizes the importance of ensuring that the Android application runs on a device with an unmodified, trustworthy operating system. This control is crucial for mitigating threats from rooted or otherwise tampered environments, which can compromise sensitive app data, alter app behaviour, or bypass security mechanisms entirely.

At its core, this requirement ensures the app is aware of its execution context and actively verifies the integrity of the underlying platform before proceeding with sensitive operations. By detecting compromised environments early, the app can enforce defensive actions such as terminating execution, alerting the user, or degrading functionality to reduce risk.

Platform Integrity Validation Techniques

To ensure the app is not running in a compromised environment, developers must implement robust techniques that assess the integrity of the device. This section explores various detection mechanisms that help identify risks like rooting, emulation, and tampered system states.

- **Root Detection:** Rooting removes Android's built-in security boundaries, giving malicious apps or users elevated privileges. Effective root detection goes beyond checking for the su binary; it involves scanning for writable /system partitions, checking for the existence of busybox, presence of SuperSU or Magisk Manager apps, and monitoring system properties like ro.debuggable. Additionally, native code checks may be used to inspect process UIDs and kernel symbols for abnormalities.
- **Custom ROM Detection:** Custom or unofficial ROMs can introduce unpredictable behaviour or insecure system configurations. These ROMs may bypass security patches or use permissive SELinux policies. Apps can detect such environments by comparing the device fingerprint (ro.build.fingerprint) and brand/manufacturer tags against known production values. Inconsistencies in ro.build.tags, ro.bootimage.build .fingerprint, or altered build numbers may also signal an unofficial or modified firmware environment.
- **Bootloader Status Check:** An unlocked bootloader allows the installation of custom images and can be used to inject malicious code or disable verified boot. Detection can be done by inspecting values such as ro.boot.verifiedbootstate, which may return "orange" or "unlocked", indicating a compromised boot chain. Checking whether dm-verity (device-mapper-verity) is active and ensuring that Verified Boot status is "green" helps validate a secure boot process.
- **Emulator Detection:** Emulators are typically used for testing or malicious analysis, and running an app within one can expose its internal logic. Apps can check properties like ro.kernel.qemu=1, hardware strings like "goldfish" or "ranchu", and look for QEmu-related files such as /init.goldfish.rc. Other heuristics include generic device names (e.g., "Android SDK built for x86"), invalid IMEI numbers, or default Android IDs. Timing analysis (e.g., slow rendering or suspicious system uptime) can also hint at emulation.
- **Device Virtualization Environment Detection:** Virtual spaces or app-cloning platforms (such as Parallel Space or VMOS) are used to run apps in sandboxed or manipulated environments. These can interfere with instrumentation detection and user session management. Detection involves searching for duplicate app packages, monitoring process name anomalies, or checking for suspicious app containers and secondary user profiles. Heuristics may also include identifying overlapping package names or unusual memory maps.
- **Device Attestation (e.g., Play Integrity API):** Google's Play Integrity API has replaced the deprecated SafetyNet Attestation API. The Play Integrity API provides device integrity, app integrity, and account integrity verdicts. Attestation responses should be validated on the backend, include nonce verification to prevent replay attacks, and be tied to the current session or user state.

- **SELinux Status Check:** SELinux enforces mandatory access control, preventing unauthorized access between apps and system components. Apps can confirm if SELinux is running in "enforcing" mode by querying the getenforce command output or reading /sys/fs/selinux/enforce. Devices running in "permissive" mode are at higher risk, as security policies may be ignored. Checking for changes in file contexts, audit logs, or kernel security modules may also provide insight into SELinux status.
- **Secure Lock Screen Verification:** The absence of a secure lock screen weakens the device's local security posture and increases risk in scenarios involving theft or loss. Using the KeyguardManager API, apps can call isDeviceSecure() to verify whether the user has set up PIN, pattern, password, or biometric authentication. This is especially critical for apps handling confidential data or offering transaction approval. Some implementations may also require re-authentication before critical actions.

Practical Integration Strategies

Detection alone is ineffective without thoughtful integration into the app's lifecycle. This section highlights how and when to apply platform validation checks to maximize their impact while minimizing disruption to legitimate users.

- Perform platform integrity validation at app startup or before initializing critical features like login, transaction processing, or secure data handling. Early execution ensures threats are mitigated before they can exploit any logic.
- Use a layered approach, combining root, emulator, attestation, and lock screen checks, to reduce evasion chances. Relying on a single signal may result in bypasses or false negatives.
- Obfuscate and encrypt your detection logic and avoid exposing plain strings, method names, or known detection heuristics in the app package. Consider using native libraries or dynamic loading for sensitive checks.
- Log platform validation failures to a secure backend (with proper privacy considerations) for behavioural analysis and forensic insight. This allows organizations to correlate integrity failures with potential threats or attack campaigns.

Common Pitfalls

While implementing platform integrity controls, developers often make avoidable mistakes that weaken their effectiveness. This section outlines common errors and oversights that should be addressed to build truly resilient Android apps.

- **Relying on Superficial or Static Checks:** Many developers use outdated or simplistic checks, such as searching for the su binary in only one location, which can be easily bypassed by sophisticated attackers. Rooted environments often mask their traces using tools that hide such artefacts.
- **Hardcoding Detection Logic:** Embedding fixed package names, file paths, or property values makes it easy for attackers to reverse engineer and patch or bypass the detection routines. Dynamic, context-aware detection is more robust than rigid, static logic.
- **Assuming SafetyNet or Play Integrity Alone Is Sufficient:** These APIs can be useful, but they are not foolproof. Relying solely on them creates a false sense of security, especially if the response is not properly validated on a secure backend or is implemented without replay protection.

- **Ignoring Emulator and Virtualization Detection:** Some teams skip emulator or virtualization checks assuming their app won't be a target. In reality, attackers and automated fraud systems frequently operate in virtual environments where platform integrity validation is essential to detection and response.
- **Failing to Monitor Detection Failures in Production:** Detection without observability is a missed opportunity. Many apps do not log or report failed integrity checks, leading to blind spots in threat visibility and response planning. Silent failures leave the app vulnerable and hinder forensic analysis.
- **Inconsistent Enforcement of Detected Risk States:** Apps sometimes detect integrity violations but don't respond consistently, e.g., allowing the app to continue with full functionality. Weak or unclear enforcement diminishes the value of detection and invites abuse.
- **Performing Checks Too Late in the Lifecycle:** Platform validation is occasionally performed after sensitive operations are already in progress, which reduces its effectiveness. Delayed checks can leave critical paths exposed before mitigations are in place.

8.7.2 MASVS-RESILIENCE-2: Anti-tampering Mechanisms

Data Integrity Under Attack: Protecting Your App from Tampering

Tampering is one of the most common threats faced by Android applications post-deployment. Attackers often reverse engineer, modify, or repackage applications to inject malicious behaviour, remove security checks, or bypass licensing mechanisms. MASVS-RESILIENCE-2 focuses on the implementation of robust anti-tampering strategies that increase the difficulty of unauthorized code manipulation and ensure the integrity of the app's runtime environment.

Anti-tampering mechanisms are not foolproof, but they significantly elevate the skill, time, and resources required by attackers. These mechanisms serve as deterrents and delay tactics, buying critical time for organizations to detect, respond, and remediate threats.

Common Tampering Techniques

Understanding the common methods used by attackers helps in designing effective countermeasures. These include:

- **Repackaging the App:** Attackers extract the APK, modify its contents, often injecting malicious code or removing license checks, and then recompile and re-sign it with their own keys. This altered version can then be redistributed through unofficial channels to target unsuspecting users. Repackaging is one of the simplest yet most effective ways to compromise app security and trust.
- **Modifying Bytecode:** By decompiling the app's Dalvik bytecode (DEX files), attackers can alter the logic of key functions, such as authentication routines, in-app purchase verifications, or security checks. This modification allows bypassing restrictions or unlocking premium features without authorization. Tools like JADX or smali/baksmali facilitate such reverse engineering and patching.
- **Injecting Dynamic Hooks:** Using frameworks like Frida, Xposed, or Substrate, attackers can attach to the app's process at runtime and intercept or modify function calls and data flows without altering the APK itself. This technique enables live manipulation and can evade static defences, making detection and prevention more challenging.

- **Replacing or Patching Native Libraries:** Many apps include native code libraries written in C or C++ for performance or specialized functions. Attackers may extract these libraries and patch or replace them with altered versions that bypass security checks or introduce vulnerabilities. Since native libraries operate outside the managed environment, this can be a stealthy attack vector.
- **Manipulating App Resources:** Beyond code, attackers often tamper with app resources such as XML layout files, images, or configuration files. For example, removing security-related UI elements or changing resource strings to disable warnings can undermine app security. Since resources are loosely protected, verifying their integrity is essential to prevent these subtle tampering methods.

Core Anti-tampering Strategies

Developers should integrate multiple layers of defence. The following are widely adopted and effective techniques:

- **Checksum and Hash Validation:** This involves computing cryptographic hashes (e.g., SHA-256) of critical app components such as the DEX files, native libraries, or resource archives at runtime. The app compares these against known, trusted values hardcoded or securely stored within the app. Any mismatch signals potential tampering. This approach helps detect unauthorized modifications to the app's static content before or during execution.
- **Signature Verification:** The app should verify its own signing certificate to ensure it matches the original developer key. This check can be performed by reading the package signature information from the Android Package Manager and comparing it with an expected hash or certificate fingerprint. Repackaged apps signed with different keys will fail this validation, helping to detect unauthorized redistribution.
- **Detection of Debugging Tools:** Apps can detect the presence of debuggers or dynamic instrumentation frameworks by checking system properties, scanning loaded processes, or using Android Debug Bridge (ADB) detection techniques. For example, detecting the presence of the ptrace system call or monitoring the TracerPid in the /proc/self/status file can indicate active debugging. Early detection prevents attackers from stepping through code or modifying behaviour during runtime.
- **Integrity Checks of Critical Files:** Apart from code, it is important to verify the integrity of native shared libraries (.so files) and resource files. Developers can check file sizes, timestamps, or perform hash comparisons at runtime to detect unexpected changes. For native code, runtime verification might include confirming that loaded libraries' memory addresses and content are unaltered, as native components are often targeted for injection or patching.
- **Runtime Self-verification:** The app can implement internal consistency checks that periodically or randomly verify whether key methods or classes in memory have been altered or replaced. Techniques include validating method bytecode signatures, checking class loader integrity, or comparing function pointers to known safe values. This dynamic self-assessment helps detect runtime hooking or method replacement attempts.
- **Code Obfuscation of Tamper-checking Logic:** Since anti-tampering mechanisms themselves can become targets, obfuscating their code, through renaming, control flow flattening, or string encryption, makes reverse engineering and neutralization significantly harder. Combining obfuscation with dynamic loading or integrity verification of tamper detection code increases its resilience against bypass attempts.

- **Verification of App Resource Integrity:** Resources such as layouts, images, and configuration files must be validated to ensure they haven't been altered or replaced. Runtime checks can hash resource files or verify resource IDs against known values, preventing attackers from tampering with the UI or app behaviour by modifying assets.
- **Validation of Official Distribution:** To prevent tampered versions distributed outside trusted stores, the app should verify its installation source. Techniques include querying the package installer to confirm installation via Google Play Store or other official channels, or integrating Play Integrity APIs to ensure authenticity. This helps restrict the app's functionality or alert users if it's running in an untrusted context.
- **App-wide Integrity Enforcement:** Implement a centralized mechanism that combines all the above checks to enforce holistic app integrity. This can involve a dedicated security manager module responsible for monitoring code, resources, signatures, and environment status. Upon detecting tampering, the module can initiate appropriate countermeasures such as alerting, disabling features, or terminating the app.
- **Triggering Appropriate Responses Upon Detection:** When tampering is detected, the app should respond decisively to mitigate damage. Responses may include shutting down gracefully, wiping sensitive data, logging the event securely, or silently reporting the incident to a backend monitoring system. This ensures compromised instances are quickly identified and contained.

Common Pitfalls

While anti-tampering defences are crucial, many apps fall short in their practical implementation due to common pitfalls that undermine security or user experience:

- **Relying on a Single Protection Mechanism:** Many developers implement just one check, such as signature verification or simple hash comparisons, and assume it's enough. This leaves the app vulnerable because attackers only need to bypass one weak point to compromise the entire system. Defence in depth is essential.
- **Static-only Verification without Runtime Checks:** Verifying integrity only at startup misses sophisticated attacks that patch or hook code dynamically after launch. Without continuous or randomized runtime validation, in-memory tampering goes undetected.
- **Hardcoding Sensitive Values in Plain Text:** Storing expected hashes, signature fingerprints, or secret keys as clear constants inside the app makes them easy to extract and manipulate. Attackers can modify these values to bypass checks unless they are obfuscated or securely derived at runtime.
- **Neglecting Resource and Environment Integrity:** Many protections focus solely on code integrity while ignoring resource files (UI layouts, config files) and runtime environment checks. Tampering with resources or running on rooted/emulated devices can bypass protections or facilitate attacks if not monitored.
- **Overly Aggressive Detection Leading to False Positives:** Strict or frequent integrity checks without proper tuning can disrupt legitimate users, especially on customized or older devices, and generate noise that desensitizes response teams. Balancing sensitivity and user experience is key.
- **Failing to Protect the Anti-tampering Code Itself:** If the detection logic is easy to locate, analyse, and disable, attackers will quickly neutralize it. Lack of code obfuscation, dynamic loading, or self-checks for the anti-tampering routines leaves these defences fragile.
- **Ignoring App Distribution Channels:** Without verifying the installation source or leveraging platform integrity APIs, apps remain exposed to tampered versions distributed

outside official stores. This is a common oversight that allows attackers to bypass protections easily.
- **Lack of Incident Monitoring and Response:** Detecting tampering without logging or reporting leaves developers blind to attacks. Without a process to analyse, respond, and update defences based on real-world data, the app's security posture weakens over time.

8.7.3 MASVS-RESILIENCE-3: Anti-static Analysis

Making Static Analysis a Hard Nut to Crack

Static analysis is a fundamental technique used by attackers and security researchers alike to examine an Android app's code and resources without executing it. By inspecting the compiled APK or its bytecode, adversaries can discover sensitive information, reverse engineer business logic, or identify vulnerabilities. MASVS-RESILIENCE-3 emphasizes the need for apps to incorporate anti-static analysis defences that make it more difficult for unauthorized parties to analyse the app statically.

Anti-static analysis mechanisms are designed to hinder, confuse, or slow down the static inspection process. These countermeasures don't aim for absolute prevention, since a determined attacker with enough time and skill can eventually bypass them, but rather to raise the bar significantly and protect critical app assets and logic.

Key Defensive Mechanisms

To effectively protect an app against static inspection, developers must implement a range of carefully designed techniques. These strategies work together to obscure the app's inner workings, protect sensitive assets, and complicate reverse engineering efforts. Common approaches to implementing anti-static analysis include:

- **Code Obfuscation:** This involves transforming the app's code to make it difficult to understand when decompiled. Techniques include renaming classes, methods, and variables to meaningless names, making the control flow non-linear by adding opaque predicates or dummy code, and encrypting or encoding string literals so they aren't stored in plain text. By complicating the code structure, obfuscation tools like ProGuard, R8, or DexGuard increase the effort required to analyse and reverse engineer the app.
- **Anti-deobfuscation Techniques:** Beyond basic obfuscation, some apps implement methods that detect when the code is being analysed or decompiled and respond by corrupting the analysis output or crashing the app. This can include inserting confusing or invalid bytecode patterns, using self-modifying code that changes at runtime, or employing reflection to dynamically load or execute code segments. Such techniques actively interfere with automated deobfuscation tools and manual reverse engineering.
- **Removal of Debugging Information:** Debug symbols, stack traces, and other debugging metadata provide valuable context to an attacker trying to reverse engineer an app. A robust build process removes these from release versions, typically by disabling debug flags and stripping symbol files. Additionally, minimizing or encrypting log outputs helps prevent leakage of internal app state through static analysis of log strings or resources.
- **Elimination of Non-Production Code and Resources:** Apps often contain code or assets used for testing, staging, or debugging that should never be present in the production

build. Leaving such resources can expose backdoors, weaken security checks, or provide insights into app logic. Best practices include using build configurations and continuous integration pipelines to strip out any test-specific endpoints, feature flags, or sample data before publishing the app.

- **Prevention of Security Control Disabling Code:** Sometimes, developers include switches or methods that disable security mechanisms (like certificate pinning or root detection) during testing. Failing to remove or disable these controls in production builds can allow attackers to bypass protections by triggering these code paths. Rigorous code reviews and automated scans can ensure that such disabling code does not make it into the final app.
- **Packing and Encryption:** Wrapping the app or sensitive modules inside encrypted containers forces attackers to deal with runtime decryption, complicating static extraction. At runtime, the app decrypts and loads the code into memory, limiting the amount of plaintext code visible in the APK file. Tools like custom loaders or packers can be used, but developers must carefully manage performance and compatibility trade-offs.
- **Integrity Checks:** To detect tampering or unauthorized modification, apps may calculate cryptographic hashes or checksums over their code and resources at startup or at specific intervals. If these integrity checks fail, the app can refuse to run or trigger defensive actions. This approach discourages static modification or repackaging, as attackers must also bypass or mimic these checks to maintain app functionality.
- **Anti-decompilation Tricks:** Employing native libraries or complex runtime behaviours such as dynamic code loading (using DexClassLoader or similar mechanisms) can make static analysis less effective. By pushing critical logic into native code or loading encrypted code fragments dynamically, the app reduces the amount of analysable bytecode present in the APK, raising the difficulty for static analysis tools.
- **Ensuring Data Confidentiality:** Even if data is transmitted over encrypted channels (like HTTPS), sensitive information embedded within the app's resources or code should never be stored or sent in plaintext. This includes API keys, tokens, or cryptographic secrets. Proper key management, secure storage solutions (e.g., Android Keystore), and encryption of sensitive strings in the app help prevent leakage through static analysis.

Common Pitfalls

While deploying anti-static analysis defences, developers often encounter common pitfalls that can undermine security or impact app performance. Understanding these risks is essential to building robust protections that are both effective and maintainable.

- **Relying Solely on Obfuscation:** Treating obfuscation as a silver bullet can backfire; over-obfuscating without complementary defences often leads to brittle builds, poor performance, and frustrated developers, yet still leaves native libraries or resources exposed.
- **Misconfigured or Outdated Tools:** Failing to keep ProGuard, R8, DexGuard, or similar tooling up to date, or using default settings, can leave debugging symbols or resource names intact, negating many anti-analysis benefits.
- **Neglecting Native and Dynamically Loaded Code:** Concentrating defences only on your Java/Kotlin bytecode while ignoring native libraries (.so files) or dex files loaded at runtime allows attackers to bypass protections by targeting less-protected code paths.

- **Skipping Integrity Checks in CI/CD:** Forgetting to integrate tamper-detection into automated build pipelines means compromised or repackaged APKs can slip through unnoticed, undermining trust in distributed binaries.
- **Over-Encrypting Critical Assets:** Encrypting every string or resource indiscriminately may degrade app startup time and user experience; a targeted approach, focusing on keys, tokens, or business-critical logic, balances security with performance.
- **Leaving Test and Debug Backdoors:** Failing to strip feature flags, test endpoints, or "turn-off" switches for security controls from release builds hands attackers ready-made shortcuts to disable protections.
- **Underestimating Tool-Bypass Techniques:** Assuming that inserting opaque predicates or dummy code will thwart all decompilers ignores the existence of advanced deobfuscators; always combine multiple defences and validate them against real-world tools.

8.7.4 MASVS-RESILIENCE-4: Anti-dynamic Analysis

Preventing Runtime Manipulation and Analysis

Dynamic analysis poses a significant threat to mobile applications, especially when attackers use tools like Frida, Xposed, or dynamic debuggers to observe, modify, or hijack the runtime behaviour of an app. MASVS-RESILIENCE-4 addresses the need to harden applications against such runtime manipulations. It emphasizes the importance of incorporating anti-dynamic analysis techniques to resist attempts at reverse engineering, runtime tampering, or behaviour manipulation.

Dynamic analysis tools typically work by injecting code into the app's memory, attaching a debugger, or using instrumentation frameworks. Attackers use these methods to alter security mechanisms, intercept sensitive data, or bypass authentication flows. Anti-dynamic analysis techniques aim to recognize these intrusions and take preventive or defensive actions such as termination or function obfuscation.

Objectives of Anti-dynamic Analysis

This section outlines what anti-dynamic analysis techniques aim to achieve in a secure Android environment.

- **Prevent Attackers from Hooking or Intercepting Methods at Runtime:** Hooking frameworks like Frida and Xposed allow attackers to override method logic, alter function returns, or inject malicious behaviour. The objective is to disrupt these attempts by validating method integrity and monitoring runtime class structures.
- **Detect and Block Debugger Attachments During Execution:** Debuggers let attackers pause execution, inspect memory, or modify variables. Anti-debugging measures aim to recognize debugger presence via system flags and process inspection, thereby invalidating or aborting execution under suspicious conditions.
- **Recognize and Neutralize Popular Instrumentation Frameworks:** Tools such as Frida or objection use dynamic instrumentation to manipulate apps on the fly. The goal is to scan for signatures like loaded libraries, known memory regions, or suspicious Java classes that indicate their presence.
- **Maintain Application Integrity by Restricting Unauthorized Runtime Changes:** Runtime integrity can be compromised by patching memory, injecting code, or modifying loaded classes. By enforcing self-verification, runtime validation, and controlled error handling, apps can protect their execution path from unauthorized manipulation.

- **Minimize Runtime Attack Surface by Enforcing Strict App Configurations:** Disabling debug mode, removing test hooks, and ensuring clean release builds reduce the opportunities for attackers to attach tools or exploit insecure development artefacts during runtime.

Key Techniques to Implement

This section discusses specific strategies and technical approaches developers can apply to resist dynamic analysis threats.

- **Verification of Runtime Code Integrity:** Beyond static verification, apps should continuously validate that the code loaded in memory matches the expected bytecode or machine instructions. This guards against runtime patching, method hooking, or hot-patching frameworks that modify behaviour while the app runs. Methods include comparing in-memory code sections against precomputed hashes or using anti-hooking libraries.
- **Debugger Detection:** Actively monitor for debugger attachment by checking system properties and flags like Debug.isDebuggerConnected() and android.os.Debug.waitingForDebugger(). Additionally, parse /proc/self/status and inspect the TracerPid field, if this value is greater than zero, the app is likely being debugged. Incorporating these checks at both app startup and during runtime can disrupt or mislead analysts using debuggers to trace execution.
- **Anti-hooking Checks:** Hooking frameworks like Frida and Xposed often replace or wrap native and Java methods. To detect this, monitor method references and reflectively inspect whether critical methods have been altered, e.g., detecting discrepancies in method implementation addresses or checking for unexpected native symbols such as frida_agent_main. Suspicious shared libraries loaded into memory, such as libsubstrate.so, also indicate potential tampering.
- **Detection of Dynamic Analysis Frameworks:** Tools like Frida, objection, or Xposed leave runtime fingerprints, such as specific class names (com.frida, io.chaos.view) or loaded files (/system/framework/XposedBridge.jar). Scanning for such artefacts using reflection, file system checks, or inspecting /proc/self/maps helps in flagging an active instrumentation environment. Apps can terminate execution, disable features, or trigger decoys upon detection.
- **Disable Android: debuggable in Release Builds:** Leaving the android:debuggable="true" flag in production APKs allows adversaries to attach debuggers without needing to repackage the app. This flag should be explicitly disabled in the manifest for release builds, and its value validated during CI/CD pipeline checks. Android's BuildConfig. DEBUG flag can also be misused, so ensure proper build variant separation to prevent leakage of debug-only code.
- **Self-integrity Verification:** Protecting against method or class tampering requires computing hashes or checksums of critical bytecode segments (DEX files) or native binaries at runtime and comparing them against known-good values. This technique can be extended to verify the integrity of security-critical logic, ensuring it hasn't been altered by hooking tools or injected code. Runtime code introspection (e.g., via reflection or ClassLoader) helps in validating class consistency.
- **Runtime Application Self-protection (RASP) Strategies:** RASP enables the app to respond to threats in real-time by embedding threat detection and mitigation directly into its runtime logic. Common strategies include detecting unsafe OS conditions (e.g., presence of root, debugger, modified SELinux policies), monitoring for abnormal API

behaviour, or enforcing context-aware security decisions such as disabling payment modules when tampering is detected. RASP often integrates threat intelligence updates dynamically.

- **Tamper-aware Exception Handling:** Use controlled and misleading exception handling to confuse attackers, e.g., trigger app crashes, misdirect flows, or simulate benign-looking behaviours when certain attack patterns are detected. For example, if an illegal method replacement or illegal memory page access occurs, the app can handle it silently and either terminate or move into a decoy mode. This technique increases the effort required for dynamic analysis.
- **Obfuscation of Sensitive Logic:** Obfuscate security-relevant functions such as authentication, cryptographic flows, or license checks to make static and dynamic analysis more difficult. This can involve flattening control flows, renaming classes and methods, splitting logic into multiple layers, and using runtime-generated code. Although obfuscation doesn't prevent analysis, it significantly raises the bar for understanding and modifying the app.
- **Delayed Loading and Runtime Code Generation:** Deferring the loading of critical logic until after environment validation is a common resilience tactic. For example, security-sensitive classes or native libraries can be dynamically loaded only after anti-analysis checks pass. Apps may also generate or decrypt parts of their logic in memory during runtime, making it nearly invisible to static and early-stage dynamic analysis tools.
- **Debugger Trap Instructions:** Insert special instruction patterns or invalid operations (such as SIGTRAP or illegal syscalls) that trigger breakpoints or unexpected crashes when a debugger is active. These traps can be disguised within non-critical branches or exception flows and may also be encrypted or conditionally executed based on anti-analysis checks. This leads to confusion and instability for the analyst.
- **Certificate Pinning with Environment Checks:** Although primarily a network protection mechanism, certificate pinning becomes more resilient when combined with runtime environment validation. Before enabling SSL communication, the app can verify it's not being run on an emulator, proxy, or instrumented environment. This prevents MITM attacks where hooking frameworks attempt to bypass or replace SSL implementations.

Common Pitfalls

This section warns against mistakes and misconceptions developers often encounter when implementing anti-dynamic analysis techniques.

- **Relying Solely on One Anti-debug or Anti-hooking Method:** Developers often implement a single debugger check or Frida detection and consider the app secure. However, advanced attackers can bypass static or isolated checks. Security should be layered, combining several detection strategies and deploying them across multiple runtime phases.
- **Hardcoding Tool Signatures or Library Names:** While scanning for known tool artefacts (e.g., libfrida-gadget.so) is useful, relying exclusively on hardcoded names is brittle. Tool developers frequently obfuscate or rename components, rendering these detections ineffective unless regularly updated or combined with behavioural analysis.
- **Inadvertently Breaking App Functionality on Custom or Rooted Environments:** Aggressive anti-analysis mechanisms can lead to app crashes or blocked access for

legitimate users running custom ROMs or rooted devices for non-malicious reasons. Striking a balance between security and user inclusivity is often overlooked.

- **Neglecting Performance Impact and Crash Resilience:** Repeated file system scans, memory inspections, or intensive integrity checks, especially on the main thread, can degrade app performance or cause unhandled exceptions. Anti-analysis logic must be efficient, unobtrusive, and crash-safe under all runtime conditions.
- **Failing to Secure Fallback or Debug Logic in Release Builds:** Developers may disable main protections for the production build but leave behind backup or conditional debug logic, such as alternative authentication paths or verbose error messages, that become attack vectors. Secure development means treating all code paths as potentially exposed.
- **Over-trusting Obfuscation as a Security Measure:** Obfuscation adds complexity but doesn't stop dynamic analysis. It should not be seen as a replacement for active detection, runtime checks, or proper app hardening. Attackers can still dynamically trace obfuscated logic with the right tools.

8.8 MASVS-PRIVACY

Privacy by Design: Safeguarding User Data

MASVS-PRIVACY serves as a foundational framework for developers to uphold user privacy within mobile applications. Imagine it as a comprehensive manual that guides developers in constructing apps that respect and protect your personal information. However, it is crucial to recognize that MASVS-PRIVACY does not cover every intricate detail of privacy protection. There are already established standards and regulations, such as ENISA or the GDPR, which handle more extensive aspects of privacy regulation.

When developers adhere to MASVS-PRIVACY, they are primarily focusing on what they can directly examine within the app itself. This might involve scrutinizing the app's code, behaviour patterns during usage, or how it interacts with your data. Some tests can be automated, meaning they are executed by software, while others require human intervention due to the nuanced and complex nature of privacy considerations.

For instance, consider an app that claims to only collect basic information like your name and email address. However, upon closer inspection, it might be surreptitiously gathering additional data without your consent. This is where manual scrutiny becomes indispensable, a human eye is needed to meticulously analyse the app's data practices.

However, MASVS-PRIVACY should not be viewed in isolation. It functions as a vital piece of the larger privacy protection puzzle. In addition to MASVS-PRIVACY, developers and stakeholders must also consider broader assessments and legal frameworks, such as the General Data Protection Regulation (GDPR). These may require in-depth evaluations conducted by privacy experts who possess specialized knowledge in navigating intricate privacy laws and regulations.

In essence, while MASVS-PRIVACY offers invaluable guidance, it should be integrated into a holistic approach towards privacy protection. It serves as a fundamental component alongside other legal and regulatory frameworks to ensure comprehensive data protection compliance and safeguard user privacy effectively in the realm of mobile applications.

8.8.1 MASVS-PRIVACY-1: Minimize Sensitive Data Access

Data Minimization and Informed Consent

Modern Android applications often require access to user data or device capabilities to function effectively. However, excessive or unjustified access to sensitive resources can expose users to privacy risks, increase the app's attack surface, and potentially violate platform policies or regulatory requirements. MASVS-PRIVACY-1 advocates for the principle of least privilege: an app should request and use only the minimum data and permissions necessary for its core functionality.

This principle aligns security with user trust, reduces the potential for misuse, and supports compliance with privacy regulations such as GDPR and CCPA.

Essential Guidelines for Privacy-centric Design

Developers must adopt privacy-aware design choices that balance app functionality with responsible data access. The following considerations highlight core principles and technical practices to minimize exposure to sensitive data and resources.

- **Request Only Essential Permissions**: Start by mapping each app feature to the specific permission it requires, and question whether it truly needs that access. For example, instead of requesting ACCESS_FINE_LOCATION, consider if ACCESS_COARSE_LOCATION could suffice. Periodically audit declared permissions to detect remnants from deprecated features or legacy SDKs, as these often lead to inadequate permission management. This practice helps to reduce unnecessary prompts and strengthens user confidence in your app.
- **Defer Permission Requests Until Needed**: Avoid asking for permissions at install or app launch unless absolutely necessary. For example, request access to contacts only when a user attempts to share content or invite others. This not only increases permission grant rates but also aligns with Android's runtime permission model. Use clear, context-aware justifications in permission dialogs to increase user trust and ensure transparency.
- **Utilize Safer Alternatives When Possible**: Android provides indirect, less intrusive APIs that often eliminate the need for broad permissions. For instance, use the MediaStore or Storage Access Framework (SAF) instead of READ_EXTERNAL_STORAGE, or query content providers like ContactsContract through implicit intents where feasible. These mechanisms allow access to data through controlled user interaction and system prompts, limiting exposure and reducing risks of misuse.
- **Avoid Persisting Sensitive Data Unnecessarily**: If you must store user data, use the Android Keystore system for cryptographic keys and EncryptedSharedPreferences or EncryptedFile for secure storage. Do not store session tokens, passwords, or PII in plain text, even in private storage. Additionally, apply expiration and cleanup policies, such as deleting cached data upon logout, to minimize data retention and reduce impact in case of compromise.
- **Protect Data in Transit**: Always use HTTPS with TLS 1.2 or above for network communications, and enforce secure configurations using networkSecurityConfig.xml to restrict trust to known certificate authorities. Implement certificate pinning where feasible to guard against MITM attacks. Additionally, avoid sending sensitive data like access tokens or account identifiers via query parameters, as they may be logged in browser history or intercepted in proxies.

- **Review Third-party SDKs:** Integrate only trusted SDKs after evaluating their privacy policies, permission footprint, and data handling practices. Use tools like Exodus Privacy or perform static code analysis to identify embedded trackers and permission declarations. Some SDKs may collect device identifiers or behavioural data without clear disclosure, leading to unintentional privacy violations and even app bans from stores. Note that Google is phasing out the Android Advertising ID for new users who have not opted into ads personalization.

- **Implement Access Scoping:** Limit data exposure by applying fine-grained scoping to permissions and API usage. For example, instead of requesting broad access to all images, allow users to select specific files via system file pickers. When using background location, consider switching to foreground location with an active UI component unless continuous tracking is truly required. This minimizes unnecessary background access and aligns with Play Store policies.

- **Follow Android's Permission Best Practices:** Categorize permissions by functionality using permission groups, and handle permission denial gracefully by disabling or hiding dependent features. Use the shouldShowRequestPermissionRationale() method to explain denied requests and respect user choices. Avoid repeatedly prompting users once a permission is denied with "Don't ask again", as it leads to poor user experience and can increase uninstalls.

- **Dynamic Feature Modules and On-Demand Permissions:** Android App Bundles allow splitting features into installable modules. Sensitive permissions (e.g., CAMERA, MICROPHONE) can be declared in feature manifests rather than the base app, ensuring they're only requested when the user activates the relevant feature. This approach eliminates upfront permission requests during installation and aligns with the principle of deferred permission requests.

- **Android 13+ Restricted APIs:** Newer Android versions introduce granular controls over previously broad permissions. The NEARBY_WIFI_DEVICES permission replaces ACCESS_FINE_LOCATION for Wi-Fi scanning, while POST_NOTIFICATIONS requires explicit user opt-in. Developers should use the maxSdkVersion attribute for deprecated permissions and test permission workflows on all supported OS versions.

- **Photo Picker and Limited Media Access:** Android's new photo picker (available via MediaStore.ACTION_PICK_IMAGES) provides secure, user-mediated access to media without requiring READ_EXTERNAL_STORAGE permission. For apps targeting Android 10+, consider using the Storage Access Framework (SAF) for file operations instead of broad storage permissions.

Common Pitfalls

Even well-intentioned development teams can inadvertently compromise privacy due to overlooked details or outdated assumptions. This section outlines typical mistakes done, helping you avoid them early in the development lifecycle.

- **Assuming All Permissions Are Harmless:** Developers sometimes add permissions without fully understanding their implications, believing that if an app "might" use a feature, it's safe to prepare for it. For instance, including access to location or contacts "just in case" can lead to unnecessary scrutiny during app reviews or rejections from app stores.

- **Failing to Monitor Permission Creep:** Over the lifecycle of an app, especially in large teams or legacy codebases, permissions tend to accumulate. New features may introduce new permissions, but deprecated features rarely result in their removal. This silent permission creep increases the privacy attack surface and can go unnoticed for long periods.

- **Overreliance on Third-party SDKs Without Inspection:** Many developers trust SDKs to manage permissions ethically, but some libraries request sensitive permissions for internal analytics or ad tracking. Without auditing or sandboxing third-party components, apps can unintentionally inherit poor privacy practices.
- **Using Broad-scope Permissions When Narrower Alternatives Exist:** For convenience or faster development, teams often opt for broad access such as READ_EXTERNAL_STORAGE when access to a single image via SAF would suffice. These shortcuts may save time initially but expose the app to higher risk and potential non-compliance.
- **Encrypting Data at Rest But Neglecting In-Transit Protection:** Developers may focus on securing local storage through encryption but overlook how data moves through the network. This often results in sensitive information being sent over unencrypted channels or logged by intermediaries, which defeats the broader goal of privacy preservation.
- **Misunderstanding User Trust Dynamics:** Requesting multiple sensitive permissions at once, especially on first launch, can overwhelm users and reduce trust. Even if permissions are genuinely needed, poor timing and lack of context can lead to high denial rates and app uninstalls.

8.8.2 MASVS-PRIVACY-2: Prevent User Identification

Protecting Anonymity

Preventing user identification is a foundational pillar in privacy-centric app development. MASVS-PRIVACY-2 sets forth the expectation that an application should not expose, collect, or transmit information that could directly or indirectly lead to the identification of an individual user, unless it is explicitly required for the core functionality of the app and done with proper user consent.

This principle is especially relevant in applications dealing with sensitive contexts, such as healthcare, finance, or social services, where the mere association of activity with a specific individual can pose significant privacy risks. A secure-by-design Android application must minimize any opportunity for the app, third-party SDKs, or backend services to link app usage data back to a specific user identity.

Key Privacy-Protective Design Considerations

This section outlines foundational strategies and technical patterns that help developers minimize user identifiability, enforce data minimization, and implement privacy by design.

- **Avoid Collecting Personally Identifiable Information (PII) Unnecessarily:** Many apps request sensitive details, such as full names, birthdates, or email addresses, by default, even when not essential to functionality. Developers should critically assess each data field and eliminate PII collection unless it is strictly required. For example, a weather app should not request the user's name or contact number when location-based weather data alone suffices. In cases where PII is necessary, always implement secure data storage (e.g., encrypted SharedPreferences or secure backend communication via TLS).
- **Use Pseudonymous or Anonymous Identifiers:** Persistent identifiers like Settings. Secure.ANDROID_ID or TelephonyManager.getDeviceId() can uniquely identify users across apps and devices, posing a privacy risk. Instead, consider using app-scoped

UUIDs stored locally and regenerated upon reinstallation. For analytics, implement session-bound random tokens that expire or rotate, ensuring limited traceability over time. Anonymous identifiers should never be reused across multiple services or external systems without explicit user opt-in.

- **Refrain from Persistent User Tracking Mechanisms:** The use of device-level identifiers (e.g., IMEI, SIM serial, or MAC address) allows for long-term tracking even after app uninstall and reinstall. To prevent this, avoid accessing hardware identifiers unless mandated by the app's core functionality (such as for carrier apps). For attribution purposes, Google Play provides scoped identifiers like the Google Advertising ID, but even this should respect user reset actions and the "Limit Ad Tracking" flag. Implement checks to dynamically disable tracking when the user opts out.

- **Apply Robust Anonymization or Pseudonymization Measures:** Data that must be retained for telemetry or usage analysis should be processed in a privacy-preserving manner. Anonymization may involve techniques like one-way hashing of usernames with a salt, redacting sensitive fields before logging, or using differential privacy methods to inject statistical noise. Pseudonymization, by replacing identifiers with reversible tokens, is suitable where data correlation is required across sessions. Ensure that mapping keys are securely stored and access-controlled to prevent re-identification.

- **Disable Logging of Sensitive User Data:** Logging APIs like Log.d() or Log.e() should never be used to record data such as user credentials, tokens, location coordinates, or form entries. Developers should implement centralized logging wrappers that sanitize inputs before logging and ensure that logs are excluded from release builds via ProGuard rules or custom build configurations. Log retention should be limited in duration and scope, and remote crash reporting services must be vetted for data handling practices.

- **Prevent Device Fingerprinting:** Combining device properties such as Build.MODEL, Build.VERSION.RELEASE, screen size, and list of installed packages to generate a unique device profile is a form of fingerprinting. While some SDKs use this method for fraud prevention, developers should avoid or restrict its use. Any fingerprinting mechanism must be documented, justified by legitimate interest, and supported by user opt-in consent. Google Play policies explicitly prohibit the misuse of fingerprinting data without disclosure.

- **Implement Strict Data Minimization:** Every data point collected should be justifiable under the principle of necessity. For example, if the app features location-based recommendations, consider using coarse location via ACCESS_COARSE_LOCATION instead of ACCESS_FINE_LOCATION, or derive approximate location using network signals. Minimize retention by purging outdated records and storing transient data in-memory where persistent storage is not required. Adopting a "least privilege" access strategy helps reduce both risk and compliance burden.

- **Manage Third-party SDKs Carefully:** Many SDKs (analytics, ads, social integrations) embed background services that automatically collect data, often outside of the app's direct control. Developers should evaluate SDK documentation and privacy policies, restrict data access via ProGuard or network controls, and disable auto-collection features through SDK configuration options. Where possible, prefer open-source SDKs with transparency around data handling, and isolate third-party logic from sensitive app flows through modular design.

- **Respect Contextual Privacy:** Apps operating in sensitive domains (e.g., LGBTQ+ support, addiction recovery, or domestic violence help) must avoid creating metadata that can indirectly identify users. For example, using randomized session durations, obfuscating push notification content, and anonymizing interaction logs can help protect users from being profiled based on app behaviour. Developers should perform contextual privacy reviews for high-risk features and offer stealth modes or decoy UI when appropriate.

- **Explicit User Consent and Clear Privacy Policies:** If the app collects any information that could identify users, directly or indirectly, it must do so transparently. Integrate runtime permission prompts with contextual explanations, offer granular opt-in options (e.g., allow analytics but not personalized ads), and ensure that users can revoke consent at any time via in-app settings. The privacy policy should clearly list what data is collected, its purpose, retention duration, and any third parties with whom it is shared.

- **Privacy Sandbox and Advertising ID Deprecation:** With Google deprecating the Android Advertising ID (AAID), developers should migrate to privacy-preserving alternatives like the Topics API or Attribution Reporting API. Always check AdvertisingIdClient.Info.isLimitAdTrackingEnabled() and respect user opt-out preferences. For analytics, consider device-generated, app-scoped identifiers that reset on reinstall.

- **Differential Privacy Implementations:** When collecting usage metrics, apply differential privacy techniques to aggregate data with statistical noise. The AndroidX Security library provides utilities for implementing epsilon-differential privacy for float and integer values, helping prevent re-identification from large datasets.

- **Anonymous Authentication Patterns:** For apps requiring temporary sessions, Firebase Anonymous Authentication generates unique UIDs without personal data. OAuth 2.0 with PKCE (Proof Key for Code Exchange) enables stateless authentication suitable for privacy-sensitive applications. These methods allow functionality while minimizing identifiable data collection.

Common Pitfalls

Even well-intentioned apps can unintentionally expose user identities due to overlooked implementation flaws. This section highlights common mistakes and blind spots that often undermine privacy efforts.

- **Assuming Hashed Data Is Anonymous by Default:** Developers often believe that hashing usernames or emails makes the data anonymous. However, without a salt or if predictable inputs are used, these hashes can be reversed through dictionary attacks. Proper pseudonymization must go beyond basic hashing techniques.

- **Relying on "device ID" Abstraction Without Knowing Its Behaviour:** Using APIs like Settings.Secure.ANDROID_ID under the impression that it's privacy-safe can be misleading. On devices running Android versions prior to Oreo, this ID is shared across apps and persists post-uninstall, which can facilitate cross-app tracking without user knowledge.

- **Embedding Analytics SDKs with Default Configurations:** Many third-party analytics tools auto-collect user data, such as precise location, IP address, and app usage patterns, immediately upon initialization. Developers frequently forget to audit or configure these SDKs to disable unwanted tracking features, especially in privacy-sensitive apps.

- **Storing Identifiers in SharedPreferences Without Encryption:** Even if pseudonymous, storing user or session tokens in plain text within SharedPreferences exposes them to extraction on rooted devices or via backup utilities. Without using encrypted storage or Android Keystore integration, this becomes a weak link in otherwise sound privacy protections.

- **Misusing Crash Reporting Tools:** Tools like Firebase Crashlytics or third-party logging frameworks may capture detailed runtime traces, including stack data, memory state, and custom user annotations. If these traces contain identifiers or user-generated content, they can unintentionally reveal user identity during diagnostics.
- **Ignoring Metadata in App Logs and Network Traffic:** Even if user data is anonymized, logs or telemetry streams can leak indirect identifiers, such as timestamped activity, battery level patterns, or installed package lists, that allow for behavioural fingerprinting when aggregated over time.
- **Treating 'Anonymous Mode' as Feature-complete Without Audit:** Offering an "anonymous browsing" mode is not sufficient if underlying services (e.g., analytics, ad frameworks, or cloud sync) are still active in the background. Developers often overlook disabling background data collectors during anonymous sessions.

8.8.3 MASVS-PRIVACY-3: Transparent Data Usage

Building Trust Through Clear Data Practices

Transparency around data collection and usage is a cornerstone of building trust with users and maintaining compliance with global privacy regulations such as GDPR, CCPA, and others. MASVS-PRIVACY-3 emphasizes the importance of clearly informing users about what data is collected, why it is collected, how it is used, and with whom it is shared.

An Android application should not operate in obscurity when it comes to personal or sensitive user data. Developers must ensure that users are empowered with the knowledge necessary to make informed decisions. This not only protects users but also shields organizations from legal and reputational consequences.

Designing for Data Transparency

To ensure transparency in data handling, developers must adopt specific design and implementation practices that clearly communicate what data is collected, why it's needed, and how it's used, right from the first user interaction.

- **Clear and Accessible Privacy Policy:** The privacy policy should be readily accessible within the app, typically from the settings or the onboarding screen, and linked in the app store listing. It must clearly define what data is collected, how it is processed, and who it is shared with. Avoid using overly broad phrases like "we may collect information" without context. Instead, state specifics such as "The app collects your device model and OS version for crash analytics using Firebase Crashlytics". Additionally, update the policy to reflect any changes in data handling or third-party service providers.
- **Explicit Data Collection Declarations:** Each permission or data request should be accompanied by a contextual explanation. Android's runtime permissions provide an opportunity to present a rationale using the shouldShowRequestPermissionRationale() method. For example, if requesting SMS access, the app should explain this is required to auto-fill OTPs during login. Generalized or delayed explanations fail to meet the data transparency, as users must understand what is being collected before consenting.
- **Purpose-driven Collection Justification:** The principle of data minimization should guide developers to collect only what is strictly necessary. If location data is needed, the app should specify whether it's for real-time features like delivery tracking or one-time location-based personalization. This can be done by adding explanatory prompts

before permission dialogs or embedding justifications within UI flows. Avoid backend-driven silent data harvesting, as it bypasses informed consent and violates both privacy regulations and MASVS expectations.

- **Informed and Granular Consent:** Instead of bundling permissions under a single toggle, provide granular choices. For example, allow users to disable analytics tracking while keeping crash reporting enabled. This can be implemented via toggle switches in a privacy settings section, and the choices must persist across sessions. Avoid pre-selecting options or requiring users to opt out through obscure menus. Also, use Android's Data Safety Section in the Play Console to accurately reflect these granular controls in your app listing.

- **Transparent Third-party Sharing:** If user data is shared with third parties, the privacy policy must identify these entities and the purpose of sharing. For instance, "Usage data is shared with Mixpanel to analyse user engagement and optimize app features". Developers should also evaluate third-party SDKs to understand their data practices. Tools like Exodus Privacy can help audit embedded trackers. Failure to disclose these integrations results in an incomplete privacy declaration and may be considered deceptive.

- **Onboarding Disclosures and Contextual Prompts:** The onboarding flow should include brief, visually clear notices explaining what data the app will collect and why. For example, a screen saying "We use your camera to let you scan QR codes for quick payments" provides meaningful context. These disclosures must align with actual app behaviour and backend logging. Technical implementations can use shared preferences to flag whether a user has acknowledged each data-specific explanation.

- **Timely and Proactive Updates:** Privacy disclosures should not be static. Any time a new permission is introduced, a backend data flow changes, or a third-party SDK is updated to include new tracking capabilities, users must be informed. This includes updating both the in-app privacy summary and Play Store data safety declarations. Consider versioning your privacy policy and showing a changelog or update notice after app upgrades, particularly if the change affects how data is handled or stored.

- **Avoiding Obscure or Manipulative Interfaces:** Dark patterns such as hiding the "Deny" button, using confusing toggles, or misleading copy like "Enhance experience (recommended)" must be avoided. Transparency requires that choices are clear, reversible, and not influenced through manipulation. Use clear UI elements with proper labelling (e.g., "No, don't share my data") and ensure the design honours the user's selection across sessions. UX clarity is just as important as backend integrity in privacy-focused applications.

- **Google Play Data Safety Section:** Mandatory for all Play Store submissions, this declaration must accurately reflect data collection and sharing practices. Common pitfalls include under-reporting SDK data collection or misclassifying data types. Regularly audit your declaration against actual app behaviour, especially after adding new SDKs or features.

- **Just-in-Time Disclosure Patterns:** Implement micro-interactions that explain data access in context. Before accessing clipboard content, show a brief explanation ("Pasting from clipboard to autofill your input. We won't store this data".). Use Clipb oardManager.addPrimaryClipChangedListener() to trigger these disclosures only when needed. For location access, consider layered explanations that detail why precision level is required.

- **Privacy Nutrition Labels:** Inspired by iOS but applicable cross-platform, these visual summaries highlight data practices in standardized formats. Include an easy-to-scan matrix in your app's privacy policy showing what data is collected, its purpose, retention period, and whether it's shared with third parties.

Common Pitfalls

Even with good intentions, developers often fall short of data transparency due to over-looked details or assumptions. The following pitfalls are commonly observed in Android apps and can undermine transparency efforts, regardless of how robust other security measures may be:

- **Using Generic or Template-based Privacy Policies:** Many apps publish default or copy-pasted privacy policies that fail to reflect actual data handling practices. These documents often include outdated clauses, irrelevant third-party references, or fail to mention crucial details like data retention or cloud storage providers. This misalignment creates a false sense of transparency and can result in non-compliance during audits.
- **Requesting Permissions Without Context:** Some apps request sensitive permissions (e.g., location, SMS, contacts) without ever explaining their necessity in the app interface. Even if technically legal, this breaks user trust. Developers might rely solely on the OS-level permission prompt, which offers no real insight into why the data is needed or how it will be used.
- **Delaying Privacy Disclosures Until After Data Collection:** It's not uncommon for apps to collect data on first launch or during onboarding, before any meaningful consent is obtained or privacy disclosures are shown. This reactive approach contradicts the principle of informed consent and may render any subsequent explanation irrelevant in the eyes of the user.
- **Overloading Onboarding with Legal Jargon:** Trying to "front-load" all privacy information in the first launch can backfire. Users often skip or misunderstand legal-heavy onboarding screens. Instead of true transparency, this creates confusion and detachment. Effective apps strike a balance between initial clarity and ongoing, contextual privacy cues throughout the user experience.
- **Failing to Track and Communicate Changes:** Developers may update SDKs, change hosting providers, or start new data flows without informing users or updating documentation. Even subtle backend changes, like switching from on-device storage to cloud sync, can have major implications for privacy. A failure to disclose these changes makes the app appear opaque, even if no additional permissions are requested.
- **Assuming SDKs Handle Consent Automatically:** Some developers rely on third-party SDKs (especially analytics and ad platforms) without fully understanding their behaviour. They may assume these libraries manage their own consent logic, but this is often not the case. Without proper integration, these SDKs can begin tracking before the user has granted consent, exposing the app to privacy violations.

8.8.4 MASVS-PRIVACY-4: User Data Control

Empowering Users Through Transparent Data Management

Empowering users with control over their data is not only a privacy-centric best practice, but also a reflection of regulatory compliance and user trust. The MASVS-PRIVACY-4 requirement emphasizes that mobile applications must allow users to make meaningful decisions about their personal data, from viewing and managing to deleting it.

User control over personal data is a cornerstone of privacy-by-design principles. When users know what data is being collected, how it is being used, and can act upon it, they are more likely to trust the application. This principle aligns with data protection laws such as the GDPR, CCPA, and others, which require clear data management mechanisms for end-users.

Key Aspects of User Data Control

This section explores the fundamental components required for empowering users with full control over their personal data, detailing practical features and technical considerations essential for secure and privacy-compliant app development.

- **Data Access Transparency:** Applications should provide a centralized location, often within account settings or a dedicated privacy centre, where users can easily view the categories of personal data collected, such as name, email, geolocation, app usage patterns, and device identifiers. This transparency is essential for meeting compliance requirements like Article 15 of the GDPR. It also helps prevent issues stemming from inadequate data visibility controls, such as users being unaware that certain data types are being tracked or stored in the background.
- **Consent Management:** A robust consent system should support dynamic and granular preferences, allowing users to opt in or out of specific data operations like tracking, data sharing with third parties, or personalized recommendations. Instead of a one-time "Accept All" prompt, consent screens should include toggles with explanations, ideally integrated into onboarding or shown contextually when certain features are triggered. Backend systems must store and honour these preferences with proper time-stamps, using consent tokens or similar identifiers to enforce choices.
- **Data Modification:** Users should be able to update personal details such as email addresses, names, billing information, or preferences directly through the UI without submitting support tickets. For instance, profile editing forms should validate input in real time and ensure changes are securely propagated to the backend via authenticated API calls. Ensuring updates are reflected across all dependent services, like billing or notifications, avoids inconsistencies that could lead to privacy violations or degraded user experience.
- **Data Export:** To support portability, the app must offer downloadable archives of user data in machine-readable formats like JSON, XML, or CSV. These exports should include all user-generated content, metadata (e.g., timestamps, device info), and associated account settings. For security, the export process must require user re-authentication, possibly through multi-factor authentication, and the download link should be time-limited and encrypted.
- **Data Deletion:** Full or partial deletion options must be available to users, ranging from deleting search history or cached media to fully purging an account and associated data. Implementing this requires secure endpoint handling, soft-deletion safeguards (e.g., grace periods), and audit logs to track deletion events. Additionally, backend services should clean up dependencies such as logs, backups, or analytics data linked to the user identity to avoid shadow data persistence.
- **Account Deletion:** The application should allow users to delete their entire account in a few intuitive steps, with warnings about irreversible consequences. Technically, this involves token revocation, data cascade deletion, and possibly notification to integrated third-party services to remove shared data. Legal and compliance teams may

need to build in exceptions (e.g., for financial records), but users should be informed of what will remain and why.

- **Granular Permissions:** Within the app, users should be able to toggle access to permissions like GPS, camera, contacts, and background activity without navigating system-level settings manually. While Android enforces permission models at the OS level, apps can include additional logic (e.g., conditional UI displays) based on granted permissions. Educating users about why each permission is required and what features it impacts reduces resistance and supports informed decision-making.

- **Informed Choices:** User controls must be accompanied by plain-language descriptions and contextual help, such as tooltips, modals, or FAQs, that clarify how enabling or disabling an option affects privacy and functionality. For instance, disabling location access might reduce personalization in a navigation app. Providing meaningful explanations here avoids ambiguous consent and supports user agency while reducing friction.

- **Cross-device Synchronization:** For multi-platform apps, ensure privacy choices sync across devices via encrypted user preferences. When a user revokes location access on Android, this preference should automatically reflect in their web account and vice versa. Use end-to-end encrypted storage for sync tokens to prevent privacy leaks through preference data.

Practical Examples

This section explores real-world scenarios showcasing how various apps manage user data control, demonstrating best practices and practical strategies to enhance transparency and empower users.

- **Fitness App (e.g., step counters, health monitors):** The app offers a privacy dashboard where users can review stored workout sessions, heart rate history, GPS-tracked routes, and sleep data. A "Download My Health Data" button provides all metrics in CSV format. Users can delete selected entries, revoke location permissions, or disable sharing data with third-party wellness platforms via OAuth tokens, all directly within the app.

- **Social Media Platform:** Users can navigate to a "Privacy & Security" section to manage tagged photos, facial recognition data, or user-generated posts. A granular data control interface allows deleting chat histories or untagging photos in bulk. The platform provides a real-time preview of data export size and completion time. Consent settings include ad personalization toggles, cookie preferences, and friend recommendation visibility.

- **Messaging App:** The app allows users to clear chat histories, delete specific media files, or fully remove conversations. A "Delete My Account" feature securely removes user identity and associated messages from all servers, with a 30-day reactivation window. It supports end-to-end encrypted backups with user-managed keys, ensuring deleted messages cannot be retrieved from cloud storage.

- **E-Commerce App:** Users can manage stored delivery addresses, payment methods, and order history. A secure "Permanently Remove Account" option ensures that sensitive data, including loyalty points and transaction logs, are irreversibly deleted (except legally mandated invoices, which are pseudonymized). Consent preferences allow toggling product recommendation engines and email tracking pixels.

- **Travel/Navigation App:** The app displays a clear log of stored location history and recently searched destinations. Users can disable real-time tracking, clear location history, or export visited coordinates as KML files for reuse in other services. Consent to share anonymized location data with third-party analytics tools can be changed any time, with an audit trail shown to users for transparency.

Common Pitfalls

Despite the clear benefits and regulatory demands, many apps fall short of delivering effective user control due to several common pitfalls:

- **Opaque Data Practices:** Many applications fail to clearly communicate what data is collected or how it is used, leaving users confused or unaware. This lack of transparency erodes trust and violates core privacy principles. Simply providing dense privacy policies without actionable, user-friendly data access interfaces leads to poor data visibility.
- **One-Size-Fits-All Consent Models:** Overly simplistic consent flows, such as a single "Accept All" button or generic opt-out options, ignore the need for granular user choices. This results in ambiguous or uninformed consent, where users are not truly aware of what they agree to, exposing apps to compliance risks and backlash.
- **Buried or Difficult-to-Find Controls:** Privacy and data management features often reside deep within complex menu structures or require multiple steps to access. This poor discoverability discourages users from exercising their rights and undermines the app's commitment to user empowerment.
- **Incomplete Data Deletion:** Some apps implement deletion superficially, only removing data from visible user interfaces but failing to purge backups, logs, or third-party repositories. This hidden data persistence violates user expectations and data protection laws, exposing apps to regulatory penalties.
- **Ignoring Permission Contexts:** Merely requesting permissions without explaining their purpose or linking them to specific app features leads to user suspicion or denial. Worse, apps sometimes continue to collect data despite revoked permissions due to inadequate checks in backend systems.
- **Lack of Audit Trails and Confirmation:** When users make changes to their data or consent preferences, failing to provide clear confirmation or maintain an audit log diminishes accountability. Users are left uncertain if their requests were honoured, which can cause dissatisfaction or disputes.
- **Neglecting Cross-Platform Consistency:** Users expect data controls to be consistent whether they access the app on Android, iOS, or the web. Inconsistent options across platforms cause confusion and may lead users to unknowingly expose or lose control over their data on one platform.

Looking Ahead

In conclusion, the OWASP Mobile Application Security Verification Standard (MASVS) provides a robust framework for assessing the security of mobile applications. By adhering to the principles outlined in this standard, developers can ensure that their applications meet the highest security benchmarks, thereby protecting user data and enhancing overall app reliability. The insights gained from understanding and implementing MASVS are instrumental in navigating the complex landscape of mobile security threats.

Moving forward, it is essential for developers to remain vigilant and continuously update their security practices in line with evolving standards and emerging threats. Embracing a proactive approach to security not only mitigates risks but also fosters user trust and confidence. Integrating the MASVS framework into the development lifecycle empowers developers to build secure, resilient applications that stand the test of time.

Moreover, anticipating future trends and challenges in the mobile security landscape is crucial. The rapidly evolving nature of technology and cyber threats demands that developers stay ahead of potential vulnerabilities. By prioritizing security from the outset and incorporating the lessons learned from MASVS, the foundation is laid for a more secure mobile ecosystem. The next chapter explores these emerging trends and challenges, offering strategies to stay ahead in an ever-changing environment. Committing to the adoption and advocacy of best security practices in all projects is key to driving continuous improvement.

Chapter 9

Anticipating Future Trends and Challenges

> The future influences the present just as much as the past.
>
> – Friedrich Nietzsche

Friedrich Nietzsche, the German philosopher, challenges the conventional view of time as a linear progression from past to present to future. His perspective suggests that our expectations, aspirations, and concerns about what lies ahead can profoundly shape our actions and decisions today.

In the context of emerging Future Trends and Challenges, this quote underscores the dynamic and interconnected nature of security. The future trajectory of Android application security is shaped not only by past security incidents and practices but also by the trends and threats we anticipate. To effectively address these emerging challenges, developers and security professionals must consider how future technological advancements, shifts in user behaviour, and evolving threat landscapes will impact security.

By recognizing that the future can influence present actions as much as the past, we can take a forward-thinking approach to Android application security, staying ahead of potential threats and ensuring robust protection for users.

DOI: 10.1201/9781003640332-12

A LAYMAN'S PERSPECTIVE

Stay Ahead of the Curve in Android Security

In the ever-evolving landscape of Android application security, staying ahead of emerging threats and challenges is not just advisable; it is essential. Imagine navigating a ship through turbulent waters: without a vigilant eye on the horizon and the ability to adapt, the vessel risks running aground. This metaphor aptly captures the current state of Android security, where rapid technological advancements demand constant vigilance and proactive measures.

With mobile technology integrating into nearly every aspect of our daily lives, billions of users rely on Android applications for communication, commerce, entertainment, and critical services. Each app acts as a gateway to personal information, financial data, and sensitive communications, making them prime targets for cybercriminals. Developers and security professionals must proactively address these evolving threats to safeguard user trust and data integrity.

The cybersecurity landscape is set to undergo significant transformations driven by advancements in artificial intelligence, changes in user behaviour, and the emergence of novel attack vectors. Without proactive measures, these developments could leave applications vulnerable to sophisticated cyberattacks. In this chapter, we will explore critical aspects of Android application security, emphasizing the importance of anticipating and preparing for future trends.

This chapter explores the emerging threats such as the proliferation of IoT (Internet of Things) devices, AI-driven cyberattacks, and the growing sophistication of social engineering tactics. Understanding these challenges is the first step toward building robust security measures. Furthermore, it covers strategies to fortify defences through proactive security practices, fostering collaboration within the cybersecurity community, and implementing state-of-the-art security frameworks.

By embracing a culture of continuous learning, adaptation, and collective responsibility, developers and security practitioners can create a resilient Android ecosystem. The future of Android security depends on our ability to anticipate threats, integrate cutting-edge security measures, and maintain a steadfast commitment to protecting user data and application integrity.

9.1 Devsecops and Continuous Security Integration

In the rapidly evolving landscape of mobile app development, speed and agility are critical, but so is security. This section explores how the integration of security into every phase of the development pipeline is becoming the new norm. As DevOps practices accelerate release cycles, incorporating security through automated tools, testing, and compliant coding practices ensures that security does not fall behind. These sections examine how development teams can shift security left, streamline secure coding, and maintain compliance in high-velocity environments.

9.1.1 Speed of DevOps

Trend:

The advent of DevOps practices and Continuous Integration/Continuous Deployment (CI/CD) pipelines has revolutionized the speed at which application development teams can release new apps and updates. This acceleration is largely driven by market demand for rapid deployment and frequent iteration cycles to maintain competitiveness and meet user expectations.

Challenges:

The accelerated pace of DevOps introduces significant security challenges:

- **Incompatibility with Traditional Security Measures:** Manual and siloed security tools are increasingly incompatible with modern DevOps cycles. Without integration into CI/CD, security becomes a bottleneck or is bypassed entirely. As a result, vulnerabilities and security gaps may be inadvertently introduced into released Android applications, increasing the risk of exploitation.
- **Conflicting Objectives:** There is an inherent conflict between the objectives of developers and security teams within a DevOps environment. Developers prioritize speed and efficiency to push applications through the pipeline as quickly as possible. In contrast, security teams focus on thorough testing and the elimination of potential flaws. This discord can lead to situations where security is compromised in favour of speed, resulting in misconfigurations, unresolved vulnerabilities, and other flaws that leave applications susceptible to breaches and malfunctions.
- **AI-Accelerated Development:** The integration of AI coding assistants and automated code generation tools is further accelerating development cycles while potentially introducing new classes of security vulnerabilities through AI-generated code.

Action Items:

- **Adopt DevSecOps:** The integration of security into every phase of the development lifecycle, DevSecOps, emerges as the critical solution. By embedding security considerations and practices into the DevOps process, teams can ensure that security is not an afterthought but a fundamental component of the development cycle.

- **Automation Is Essential:** To cope with the fast pace of DevOps, security processes must be automated wherever feasible. This automation includes:
  - **Security Testing:** Automated security testing tools can continuously scan code for vulnerabilities throughout the development pipeline, providing immediate feedback to developers.
  - **Code Analysis:** Implementing both static and dynamic code analysis can identify security issues early in the development process, allowing teams to address potential threats before they reach production.
  - **Vulnerability Monitoring:** Continuous monitoring systems can track new and emerging vulnerabilities, ensuring that applications remain secure even after deployment.
  - **Infrastructure as Code (IaC) Security:** Automating infrastructure provisioning while ensuring security policies are enforced reduces risks associated with misconfigurations and human errors.

- **Foster a Security Culture:** Building a security-conscious culture is paramount in a DevSecOps environment. Developers must be educated on security best practices and encouraged to take ownership of security within their code. Promoting a mindset where "everyone is responsible for security" helps to align the goals of development and security teams, reducing friction and enhancing overall application security.

By embracing these strategies, organizations can navigate the challenges posed by the rapid pace of DevOps while maintaining robust security standards. The shift towards a

DevSecOps approach ensures that speed does not come at the cost of security, enabling the development of secure, reliable, and high-performing Android applications.

9.1.2 Adoption of Security Tools in CI/CD

Trend:

The adoption of modern Application Security (AppSec) tools (like Snyk, SonarQube, and GitHub's Dependabot), which integrate seamlessly into Continuous Integration/Continuous Deployment (CI/CD) pipelines, is rapidly increasing. This trend is driven by a growing recognition of the need for security within the application delivery process, especially as the speed and frequency of software releases continue to accelerate. Traditional application security teams often struggle to keep pace with these rapid cycles, necessitating automated solutions that can scale with the development workflow.

Challenges:

While the integration of security tools into CI/CD pipelines offers substantial benefits, it also introduces several challenges:

- **Complexity and Integration Overhead:** Incorporating security tools into CI/CD pipelines can add a layer of complexity that may be daunting for some teams, particularly those with limited security expertise or resources. The process requires careful planning and configuration to ensure that security tools complement, rather than disrupt, existing workflows.
- **Alert Fatigue:** One of the most significant challenges is managing the high volume of alerts generated by these tools. While these alerts are crucial for identifying potential security issues, they can overwhelm developers if not managed effectively. This phenomenon, known as alert fatigue, degrades the signal-to-noise ratio, making it difficult for developers to distinguish critical vulnerabilities from low-priority findings or false positives. As a result, essential alerts are often ignored, allowing security risks to go unaddressed.
- **Tool Compatibility and Performance Impact:** Security tools must seamlessly integrate with existing CI/CD tools without significantly slowing down the deployment pipeline. Poorly optimized tools can introduce performance bottlenecks, leading to delays that conflict with the fast-paced nature of CI/CD.

Action Items:

- **Optimize Alerting Mechanisms:** To combat alert fatigue and enhance the effectiveness of security tools, it is crucial to refine how alerts are generated and managed:
  - **Fine-tune Tools:** Adjust security tools to reduce false positives by honing in on genuine security risks. This requires regular updates and configurations tailored to the specific needs and context of the development environment.
  - **Provide Actionable Insights:** Alerts should not only notify but also guide developers with clear, actionable information. This helps developers quickly understand the nature of the issue and take appropriate steps to remediate it, minimizing the time spent on addressing non-critical alerts.
  - **Prioritize Alerts:** Implement risk-based alerting where critical vulnerabilities take precedence over low-risk findings to prevent distractions and inefficiencies.

- **Shift Left Security:** Moving security checks earlier in the development lifecycle, often referred to as "shifting left", ensures that vulnerabilities are caught and addressed as early as possible:
  - **Implement Security Gates:** Integrate security checkpoints within the CI/CD pipeline that can automatically halt the process if critical security issues are detected. This proactive approach prevents insecure code from progressing further down the pipeline, ensuring that security is maintained without compromising speed.
  - **Facilitate Early Remediation:** By identifying and resolving security issues early in the development process, teams can avoid the costly and time-consuming task of fixing vulnerabilities post-deployment. Early remediation not only enhances security but also supports more efficient development cycles.

By adopting these strategies, organizations can effectively integrate security tools into their CI/CD pipelines without overwhelming developers or sacrificing development speed. The key lies in balancing security and efficiency, ensuring that robust security measures are in place while maintaining the agility that DevOps practices demand.

9.1.3 Automated Security Testing

Trend:

Automated security testing is gaining significant traction in the field of Android Application Security, largely fuelled by the advancement of AI-driven security testing tools. These tools encompass capabilities such as vulnerability scanning, code analysis, and threat modelling, all aimed at identifying potential security vulnerabilities in Android applications. The primary objective is to enhance the efficiency, accuracy, and speed of security testing, making it a critical component of modern development practices.

Challenges:

Despite the promising benefits of automated security testing, there are notable challenges that must be addressed to ensure its effectiveness:

- **Minimizing False Positives:** A significant challenge is the prevalence of false positives, where security tools incorrectly flag a piece of code or behaviour as a vulnerability. These false alarms can lead to unnecessary work for developers, diverting attention away from genuine security issues and potentially causing delays in the development process.
- **Detecting Nuanced Security Issues:** Another challenge lies in the limitations of AI models in detecting complex or nuanced security issues. The effectiveness of these models depends heavily on the quality of the training data and the sophistication of the algorithms used. If the models are not adequately trained or the data lacks diversity, they may fail to accurately identify certain types of vulnerabilities, especially those that require a deeper contextual understanding.

Action Items:

- **Human-in-the-Loop Approach:** To overcome these challenges, it is essential to complement automated testing with manual reviews by security experts:
  - **Validate Findings:** Security professionals should verify the results generated by automated tools to ensure their accuracy. This step is crucial for distinguishing between false positives and legitimate security concerns.

- **Contextualize Results:** Experts can provide valuable insights and context that automated tools may lack, helping to interpret the findings and determine the appropriate response.

- **Shift Left Security:** Integrating security testing tools throughout the development lifecycle, commonly referred to as "shifting left", is a proactive strategy that enhances security:
  - **Early Detection:** By embedding security checks into the continuous integration (CI) process, vulnerabilities can be identified early in the development cycle when they are easier and less costly to fix.
  - **Faster Remediation:** Addressing vulnerabilities before they reach production not only reduces security risks but also helps maintain the pace of development by preventing the need for extensive post-release fixes.

- **Leverage Machine Learning:** Utilizing AI-powered tools that incorporate transformer-based models and advanced ML algorithms offers several advantages:
  - **Improved Detection Accuracy:** ML algorithms can be trained on extensive datasets of known security vulnerabilities, enhancing their ability to accurately detect a wide range of issues. As these algorithms are exposed to more data, their detection capabilities continue to improve.
  - **Continuous Adaptation:** ML-driven tools are capable of learning and adapting over time, allowing them to stay up-to-date with emerging security threats. This continuous learning process ensures that security testing remains effective even as new types of vulnerabilities are discovered.

By implementing these strategies, organizations can maximize the benefits of automated security testing while mitigating its challenges. The combination of advanced AI tools and human expertise provides a balanced approach that ensures robust security without compromising development efficiency.

9.1.4 Continuous Compliance

Trend:

Continuous compliance is increasingly becoming a crucial aspect of Android application security. This trend reflects the ongoing necessity for organizations to ensure that their practices, procedures, and applications consistently adhere to relevant security standards, regulations, and industry best practices throughout their lifecycle. For Android applications, this means maintaining compliance not only at the point of initial deployment but also through all subsequent updates, changes, and enhancements.

Challenges:

While continuous compliance offers substantial benefits in maintaining security and regulatory adherence, it presents several challenges:

- **Maintaining Compliance Throughout the Application Lifecycle:** One of the main challenges is ensuring that Android applications adhere to compliance requirements across their entire lifecycle, including after updates and changes are made. This necessitates continuous monitoring and validation of compliance controls to ensure that every change, whether in code, functionality, or third-party dependencies, does not introduce new compliance risks or violations.

- **Resource Constraints and Operational Overhead:** Continuously monitoring and validating compliance can be resource-intensive and may introduce significant operational overhead. Manual processes for compliance checking are time-consuming and prone to errors, making it difficult to maintain a consistent and comprehensive compliance posture.

Action Items:

- **Leverage Automation for Continuous Compliance:** Implement automated compliance monitoring tools and processes to streamline compliance management:
  - **Continuous Assessment:** Use automated tools to continuously assess applications against relevant regulations, security standards, and industry best practices. Automated tools can provide real-time insights and alerts, helping to quickly identify and address compliance issues.
  - **Reduced Manual Work:** Automating compliance checks reduces the need for manual intervention, freeing up development and security resources to focus on higher-priority tasks. This efficiency helps maintain a high level of compliance without overwhelming the team.

- **Utilize Mechanisms to Demonstrate Ongoing Compliance:** Establish clear mechanisms to document and demonstrate compliance:
  - **Policy Enforcement:** Enforce security policies and compliance requirements throughout the development process. Automated policy enforcement ensures that all changes adhere to predefined compliance standards, reducing the risk of accidental violations.
  - **Audit Trails:** Maintain automated audit trails that document all compliance checks and actions taken. These trails provide a detailed record of compliance activities, making it easier to demonstrate adherence during audits or in response to regulatory inquiries.
  - **Compliance Reporting:** Generate regular compliance reports that summarize adherence to regulations and standards. These reports can be used for internal reviews and audits and to demonstrate compliance with external stakeholders.

- **Integrate Compliance Checks into CI/CD Pipelines:** Integrate compliance checks into Continuous Integration and Continuous Deployment (CI/CD) pipelines to ensure early detection and resolution of compliance issues:
  - **Early Detection:** Incorporate automated compliance checks into the CI/CD process to identify and address compliance issues early in the development cycle, before they reach production. Early detection helps prevent non-compliant code from being deployed, reducing the risk of regulatory breaches and associated penalties.
  - **Faster Remediation:** Resolve compliance problems quickly through automated remediation processes or guided manual interventions. This minimizes disruptions and delays, ensuring that applications remain compliant without compromising development velocity.

By implementing these action items, organizations can maintain continuous compliance with security standards and regulations, enhancing the security and reliability of their Android applications. The key to success lies in leveraging automation, maintaining clear documentation, and integrating compliance checks throughout the development process.

9.2 Advanced Security Mechanisms and Intelligence

As cyber threats grow in complexity and sophistication, reactive defences are no longer sufficient. This section focuses on proactive and intelligent security mechanisms that operate at runtime and beyond. By leveraging techniques like real-time application protection, AI-driven threat detection, and continuous authentication, organizations can dynamically adapt to threats as they occur. These trends mark a shift toward self-defending apps and predictive security intelligence as core components of a resilient mobile strategy.

9.2.1 Runtime Application Self-Protection (RASP)

Trend:

Runtime application self-protection (RASP) solutions are becoming increasingly popular in the realm of Android application security. RASP operates by monitoring and analysing the behaviour of an application in real-time, detecting and mitigating security threats as they occur. This proactive defence mechanism is gaining traction as a vital component of mobile application security, offering the ability to respond dynamically to emerging threats.

Challenges:

While RASP solutions offer significant benefits, several challenges need to be addressed to ensure their effectiveness:

- **Balancing Security and Performance:** One of the primary challenges with RASP solutions is managing the trade-off between security and performance. Because RASP tools need to monitor application behaviour continuously during runtime, they can be resource-intensive, potentially degrading app performance and negatively impacting user experience. Achieving a balance where security is enhanced without compromising app speed and responsiveness is crucial.
- **Platform Diversity:** The diverse range of mobile platforms and operating systems poses another challenge for RASP solutions. Ensuring consistent protection across all platforms requires RASP tools to be adaptable and versatile, capable of handling the unique characteristics and constraints of each environment.
- **Limited Control Over Mobile Environments:** The mobile environment often limits RASP's ability to access essential runtime data and monitor app behaviour effectively. These constraints can hinder the ability of RASP solutions to provide comprehensive protection, particularly in environments where access to critical system resources or data is restricted.
- **Encrypted Data Challenges:** Inspecting encrypted data is another significant hurdle for RASP solutions. Encrypted data can obscure malicious activities, making it difficult for RASP tools to detect and respond to attacks targeting data in transit or stored in encrypted form. This limitation necessitates advanced strategies to monitor and protect encrypted data without compromising its integrity.

Action Items:

- **Implement Lightweight RASP Solutions:** To minimize the performance impact, organizations should choose lightweight RASP tools that offer robust protection without heavily taxing system resources. Selecting solutions that are optimized for mobile environments ensures that security measures do not degrade user experience.

- **Deploy Adaptable Controls:** Utilizing adaptable RASP controls that can dynamically adjust based on the application environment is essential:
  - **Targeted Monitoring:** Focus monitoring efforts on areas with the highest security risk, allowing for precise detection and response without overwhelming the system.
  - **Reduced Overhead:** By limiting monitoring to critical components and adjusting the intensity of monitoring based on current conditions, the impact on app performance can be minimized.

- **Adopt Risk-based Prioritization:** Prioritizing security controls based on a thorough risk assessment allows organizations to:
  - **Focus on Critical Threats:** By identifying and addressing the most severe security risks first, resources can be allocated more effectively, enhancing protection where it is most needed.
  - **Optimize Performance:** Efficient resource allocation ensures that security measures provide maximum protection without unnecessarily hindering application performance, maintaining a balance between security and user experience.

By embracing these strategies, organizations can effectively implement RASP solutions that enhance security while maintaining application performance and user satisfaction. The key lies in selecting appropriate tools, adjusting controls dynamically, and prioritising efforts based on risk, ensuring that security is robust, responsive, and efficient.

9.2.2 Mobile Threat Defence (MTD)

Trend:

Android devices are prime targets for increasingly sophisticated cyber threats, such as advanced malware, phishing, and network attacks. Mobile threat defence (MTD) represents an emerging class of security solutions designed to protect Android devices and applications against these advanced threats. Unlike traditional security measures, MTD solutions offer a comprehensive approach to threat detection, prevention, and remediation, targeting a business's mobile fleet and the applications running on these devices. MTD solutions are crucial in today's environment, where mobile devices are integral to business operations and often contain sensitive information.

Challenges:

While Mobile Threat Defence offers substantial benefits in enhancing mobile security, several challenges must be addressed to ensure its effective implementation:

- **Balancing Security with Performance and Usability:** One of the primary challenges is finding the right balance between robust security measures and the performance and usability of resource-constrained mobile devices. Implementing comprehensive security can be resource-intensive, potentially slowing down devices and negatively impacting the user experience. It is essential to ensure that security solutions do not compromise device functionality or deter user productivity.
- **Evolving Nature of Mobile Threats:** Another significant challenge is the continuously evolving threat landscape. New vulnerabilities and attack vectors are regularly discovered and exploited, requiring organizations to stay updated on the latest security threats and best practices for mobile threat defence. Keeping pace with these changes demands ongoing vigilance and adaptability, as well as access to real-time threat intelligence.

Action Items:

- **Adopt a Layered Defence Approach:** A layered approach to mobile threat defence provides the most comprehensive protection, addressing multiple potential attack vectors:
  - **Endpoint Protection:** Implement endpoint protection solutions that safeguard devices from malware, viruses, and other types of malicious software. This includes real-time scanning, application monitoring, and automated threat removal to protect devices from both known and emerging threats.
  - **Network Security:** Secure network connections to prevent unauthorized access and protect data in transit. This can involve using VPNs, encrypted communications, and network monitoring tools to detect and block suspicious activity.
  - **Behavioural Analysis:** Utilize behavioural analysis tools that monitor device behaviour to identify unusual patterns indicative of potential threats. By analysing behaviour in real time, these tools can detect and respond to attacks that traditional signature-based methods might miss.

- **Leverage Threat Intelligence:**
  - **MTD Feeds:** Utilize real-time mobile threat intelligence feeds to stay updated on the latest threats and vulnerabilities. These feeds provide valuable insights into emerging threats, helping organizations to anticipate and defend against new attack vectors.
  - **Machine Learning:** Leverage machine learning algorithms to enhance threat detection capabilities. Machine learning can analyse vast amounts of data to identify patterns and anomalies that may indicate a threat, enabling real-time responses to evolving threats.

- **Integrate with Mobile Device Management (MDM):** Integrating MTD solutions with Mobile Device Management (MDM) platforms can enhance security and streamline management:
  - **Enforce Policies:** Use MDM to enforce organization-wide security policies on Android devices, ensuring consistent protection across all devices in the fleet.
  - **Compliance Management:** Ensure that all devices comply with security requirements by using MDM to monitor compliance and enforce necessary configurations.
  - **Remote Management:** Enable remote management and configuration of security settings on devices, allowing for quick responses to emerging threats and minimizing potential security risks.

By implementing these action items, organizations can effectively deploy MTD solutions that protect Android devices without compromising performance or user experience. The key is to adopt a comprehensive, layered approach to security that leverages the latest threat intelligence and integrates seamlessly with existing management platforms.

9.2.3 Threat Intelligence Integration

Trend:

Threat intelligence involves the systematic collection and analysis of information regarding potential or ongoing attacks that pose a threat to an organization. By integrating threat intelligence feeds into the Continuous Integration/Continuous Deployment (CI/CD) pipeline, organizations can significantly enhance their threat detection and response capabilities. This integration enables them to identify and respond to security threats more swiftly and effectively, providing a proactive defence against a rapidly evolving threat landscape.

Challenges:

While the integration of threat intelligence offers substantial benefits, effectively leveraging this information to prioritize security efforts and mitigate emerging threats in real-time presents several challenges:

- **Threat Intelligence Data:** One of the primary challenges is obtaining threat intelligence data that is both accurate and up-to-date. For threat intelligence to be effective, it must provide real-time insights into emerging threats. However, collecting, analysing, and maintaining this data can be resource-intensive and time-consuming. Additionally, the fast-paced nature of the threat landscape can make it challenging to keep threat intelligence data current, potentially leading to outdated or irrelevant information.
- **Resource Constraints:** The process of integrating threat intelligence into security operations requires substantial resources, including skilled personnel, advanced tools, and adequate infrastructure. This can be a barrier for organizations that may not have the necessary capabilities to effectively manage and utilize threat intelligence data.

Action Items:

- **Focus on Integration:** Integrate threat intelligence feeds from reputable sources into existing security workflows to enhance threat detection and response:
  - **Security Monitoring:** Use threat intelligence feeds to enrich security monitoring data, enabling more accurate identification of potential threats based on real-world threat patterns. This enhanced monitoring helps to detect unusual or suspicious activities that may indicate an impending attack.
  - **Incident Response:** Inform incident response procedures with detailed threat intelligence, providing information about relevant attack vectors and mitigation strategies. This intelligence enables security teams to respond more quickly and effectively to incidents, minimizing the potential impact of threats.

- **Utilize Threat Intelligence Platforms:** Leverage threat intelligence platforms and security analytics tools to maximize the value of threat data:
  - **Data Aggregation:** Aggregate threat data from various sources, including internal security tools, external feeds, and open-source intelligence. This comprehensive approach ensures that security teams have access to a wide range of information, providing a complete picture of the threat landscape.
  - **Correlation and Analysis:** Use advanced analytics to correlate and analyse threat data, identifying patterns and emerging threats that may not be immediately apparent. This analysis helps to uncover new attack techniques and trends, enabling proactive defence measures.
  - **Actionable Insights:** Extract actionable insights from threat intelligence to guide developers and security teams in prioritizing vulnerabilities and focusing security efforts where they are most needed. These insights can help to allocate resources more efficiently, ensuring that the most significant threats are addressed promptly.

- **Emphasize Collaboration:** Collaborate with industry peers and Information Sharing and Analysis Centers (ISACs) to enhance threat intelligence efforts:
  - **Threat Exchange:** Participate in threat intelligence exchanges to share data and insights with other organizations, gaining a broader understanding of the threat landscape. This collaborative approach helps to identify emerging threats and develop coordinated responses.

- **Collective Defence:** Work together with other organizations to develop collective defence strategies against emerging threats targeting the Android ecosystem. By pooling resources and knowledge, organizations can enhance their defensive capabilities and create a more resilient security posture.

By implementing these action items, organizations can effectively integrate threat intelligence into their security operations, enhancing their ability to detect, respond to, and mitigate emerging threats. The key to success lies in leveraging accurate and timely intelligence, utilizing advanced analytics, and fostering collaboration across the security community.

9.2.4 AI-driven Threat Detection

Trend:

Artificial Intelligence (AI) and Machine Learning (ML), including deep learning techniques like convolutional and recurrent neural networks, are increasingly used to identify threats on Android devices. These technologies enable real-time detection and mitigation of emerging threats by analysing patterns and behaviours that indicate malicious activity. The effectiveness of this approach relies on the creation of comprehensive labelled datasets, which contain samples classified into distinct categories based on threat types. AI methods have demonstrated impressive performance in detecting Android malware, offering a proactive defence against a wide range of threats. However, many AI-based methods operate in a "black-box" manner, making predictions without transparency about the model's decision-making process, which can be a drawback when understanding and validating model outputs.

Challenges:

While AI-driven threat detection offers significant advantages, several challenges must be addressed to ensure its effectiveness:

- **Data Collection, Labelling, and Model Training:** One of the main challenges is the need for robust processes to collect, label, and train AI models on diverse datasets. This involves gathering large volumes of data on various security incidents, accurately labelling this data to ensure it reflects the nature of the threats, and training AI models to recognize these patterns. The quality of the data and the accuracy of labelling are critical to the model's ability to detect known and unknown threats effectively.
- **Rapidly Evolving Threat Landscape:** The threat landscape for mobile applications is continuously evolving, with new attack vectors and techniques emerging regularly. This dynamic environment requires AI models to be continuously updated with the latest threat intelligence and adapted to recognize new patterns of malicious behaviour. Keeping models current and effective in the face of rapidly changing threats is a significant challenge for developers and security professionals.
- **Adversarial AI Attacks:** AI-driven security systems themselves are becoming targets for adversarial attacks, where malicious actors attempt to fool AI models through carefully crafted inputs or model poisoning techniques.

Action Items:

- **Develop Robust AI Models for Threat Detection:** Focus on building and training AI models that can effectively identify security threats:

- **Security Incident Data:** Train AI models using historical data on security incidents, including malware samples, phishing attempts, and device vulnerabilities. This historical data provides a foundation for the model to learn from past threats and identify similar patterns in new data.
- **Threat Intelligence Feeds:** Integrate real-time threat intelligence feeds to keep the AI model updated on the latest threats. Continuous integration of threat intelligence ensures that the model remains aware of emerging threats and can adapt to new attack strategies.

- **Utilize Appropriate Learning Algorithms:** Employ suitable learning techniques to maximize the effectiveness of AI models:
  - **Supervised Learning:** Train models with labelled data to identify known threats, such as specific malware signatures or phishing techniques. Supervised learning helps the model learn to recognize patterns associated with these threats based on examples provided during training.
  - **Unsupervised Learning:** Use unsupervised learning to detect anomalies in user behaviour or application activity that might indicate unknown threats. Unsupervised learning enables the model to identify deviations from normal patterns, which can suggest new or evolving threats not previously encountered.

- **Continuously Improve the AI Model:** Regularly refine the AI model to enhance its performance and accuracy:
  - **Model Updates:** Regularly update the AI model with new threat data to improve its ability to detect evolving threats. Frequent updates help the model stay current with the latest threat landscape and maintain its effectiveness over time.
  - **False Positive Reduction:** Fine-tune the model to reduce false positives, which occur when the model incorrectly identifies harmless activity as a threat. Reducing false positives is crucial for minimizing unnecessary alerts and ensuring that security teams can focus on genuine threats.

- **Collaborate with Security Experts:** Work closely with experts to develop advanced AI models and enhance threat detection capabilities:
  - **AI Researchers:** Collaborate with AI and security researchers to develop advanced AI models specifically designed for Android security. Partnering with experts helps in leveraging the latest research and methodologies to build more robust and effective models.
  - **Security Community:** Share threat data and best practices with the broader security community to collectively improve AI-driven threat detection for all Android applications. Collaboration fosters a more resilient security ecosystem where shared knowledge and resources contribute to better protection against threats.

By implementing these action items, organizations can effectively leverage AI-driven threat detection to enhance the security of Android applications. The key to success lies in developing robust models, utilizing appropriate learning algorithms, continuously improving model performance, and collaborating with experts to stay ahead of emerging threats.

9.2.5 Continuous Authentication

Trend:

Continuous authentication is an emerging trend in Android application security that involves the implementation of adaptive authentication mechanisms. These mechanisms continuously evaluate user behaviour and device context to ensure secure access while maintaining a seamless user experience. By constantly verifying the identity of a user through a combination of behavioural and contextual factors, continuous authentication enhances security beyond the initial login, providing ongoing assurance that the legitimate user is still in control of the device.

Challenges:

Despite its potential benefits, implementing continuous authentication solutions poses several challenges, particularly in balancing security requirements with user convenience and privacy concerns:

- **Careful Design and Implementation:** One of the main challenges is designing continuous authentication systems that are both secure and user-friendly. This involves creating intuitive user interfaces that provide clear instructions and do not disrupt the user experience. Ensuring that the authentication process is smooth and minimally invasive is crucial to maintaining user satisfaction and trust.
- **Balancing Security with Privacy:** Another challenge is finding the right balance between security and privacy. Continuous authentication often requires the collection of sensitive data, such as location, behaviour patterns, and biometric information. Organizations must ensure that this data is handled responsibly, transparently, and in compliance with privacy regulations to avoid user pushback and potential legal issues.

Action Items:

- **Utilize Contextual Factors for Dynamic Authentication:** Leverage contextual data to enhance continuous authentication by dynamically adjusting security measures based on user behaviour and device context:
  - **Location-based Authentication:** Implement additional authentication prompts when sensitive information is accessed from unusual or unexpected locations. This helps ensure that only authorized users can access sensitive data, even if their device is compromised.
  - **Device Posture:** Analyse device orientation, movement patterns, and other sensor data to detect potential anomalies that may indicate unauthorized access. For example, a device being used in a different manner than usual could trigger additional verification steps.
  - **User Behaviour Analysis:** Continuously monitor user behaviour patterns, such as typing speed, app usage, and interaction patterns, to detect deviations from typical behaviour that might suggest a compromised account. This real-time analysis helps identify and respond to potential threats quickly.

- **Implement Multi-factor Authentication (MFA):** Enhance security by layering multiple authentication factors to verify user identity:
  - **Biometric Authentication:** Utilize biometric methods such as fingerprint, facial recognition, or iris scans for continuous verification. These methods provide strong security while minimizing user effort, as they can often be performed passively.
  - **Behavioural Biometrics:** Analyse user behaviour patterns, such as keystroke dynamics or touch gestures, to provide continuous identity verification. Behavioural biometrics adds an additional layer of security by monitoring how users interact with their devices.
  - **Contextual Factors:** Combine biometric and behavioural factors with contextual data, such as location and device posture, to create a more robust and adaptive

authentication approach. This comprehensive strategy helps ensure that authentication is both secure and user-friendly.

- **Adopt Risk-based Authentication:** Adjust security measures dynamically based on the perceived risk level to provide a balanced approach:
  - **Risk Assessment Engines:** Develop or integrate risk assessment engines that analyse user activity and context to determine the appropriate level of authentication required. These engines help balance security and convenience by adjusting authentication requirements based on the specific risk associated with each action.
  - **Adaptive Authentication:** Dynamically adjust authentication requirements based on the assessed risk level. For high-risk actions, such as accessing sensitive data or making significant changes to account settings, require stronger authentication, while low-risk tasks may require minimal intervention. This adaptive approach helps maintain security without unnecessarily burdening the user.

- **Build User Trust and Transparency:** Foster user trust by being transparent about continuous authentication processes and giving users control over their data:
  - **User Feedback Mechanisms:** Provide users with feedback and explanations for triggered authentication requests, helping them understand why additional verification is needed and reinforcing trust in the system.
  - **Transparency:** Be transparent about the data collected and how it is used for continuous authentication. Clearly communicate privacy policies and ensure that users are aware of how their information is being handled.
  - **User Control:** Offer users some control over the level of continuous authentication implemented for their accounts, allowing them to adjust settings based on their preferences and comfort level. Providing this control helps users feel more secure and involved in their own protection.

By implementing these action items, organizations can effectively deploy continuous authentication mechanisms that enhance security while maintaining a seamless user experience. The key to success lies in leveraging contextual and behavioural data, adopting a risk-based approach, and maintaining transparency and user control to build trust and ensure privacy.

9.3 Infrastructure and Architectural Shifts

The foundation on which apps are built and deployed is undergoing a dramatic transformation. This section covers the architectural shifts, such as microservices, containerization, zero trust models, and edge computing, that require rethinking traditional security approaches. These emerging models bring both opportunities and challenges, from improved scalability and resilience to increased complexity and new threat vectors. Addressing these demands a security architecture that is distributed, adaptive, and deeply integrated into the infrastructure.

9.3.1 Containerization and Microservices Architectures

Trend:

The adoption of containerization and microservices architectures is transforming how applications are developed, deployed, and maintained. Containerization encapsulates an application and all its dependencies into a portable, lightweight container, allowing it to be easily deployed across various computing environments. Microservices architecture further enhances this flexibility by breaking down an application into smaller, modular services that operate independently. Together, these two technologies enable the creation of scalable, distributed systems that are both flexible and fault-tolerant, allowing for easier updates and maintenance.

Challenges:

While containerization and microservices offer significant advantages, they also introduce several security challenges that must be addressed to ensure a secure deployment:

- **Insecure Container Images:** One of the primary security challenges in a containerized environment is the use of insecure container images. Containers are built from images, which serve as blueprints. If these images are not properly secured or contain vulnerabilities, they can become easy targets for attackers, potentially compromising the entire application environment.
- **Misconfigurations:** Misconfigurations are another common issue that can arise in containerized environments. These can occur due to a lack of proper knowledge, human error, or accidental oversight. Misconfigurations can expose containers to security breaches, open the door to privilege escalation attacks, or allow unauthorized access to sensitive resources.
- **Shared Kernel Vulnerabilities:** Containers typically share the same underlying Linux kernel, which can lead to security vulnerabilities if one container is compromised. This shared environment means that a vulnerability in one container could potentially impact others running on the same host, posing a significant security risk.

Action Items:

- **Implement Security Best Practices:** Adopting established security best practices for containerization is essential to minimize risks:
  - **Image Scanning:** Regularly scan container images for vulnerabilities before deploying them. Ensuring that images are secure and free of known vulnerabilities is a critical step in protecting the overall application environment.
  - **Vulnerability Management:** Proactively manage and address vulnerabilities identified in container images and the underlying system. This involves keeping images and systems up-to-date with the latest security patches and updates.
  - **Access Control:** Implement granular access controls to restrict access to containerized resources. Limiting access based on roles and responsibilities helps prevent unauthorized access and potential security breaches.

- **Adopt Advanced Container Security:** Implement rootless containers, distroless images, and consider sandboxed container runtimes like gVisor for enhanced isolation while maintaining performance.
- **Utilize Security-focused Infrastructure:**Use container orchestration platforms like Kubernetes, enhanced by tools such as Falco and Aqua Security for real-time threat detection and monitoring. Additionally, ensure that container images come from trusted sources that prioritize security during development.
- **Continuous Monitoring:** Continuously monitor containerised applications and their interactions for suspicious activity, often leveraging service mesh technology to enforce security policies on inter-service communication. Early detection of potential threats is crucial for maintaining a secure environment and preventing security incidents from escalating.

- **Implement Runtime Security Controls:** Deploy runtime security controls to detect and respond to security threats in real-time:
  - **Intrusion Detection:** Implement intrusion detection systems (IDS) that can identify and stop unauthorized attempts to access containerized resources, providing an additional layer of security.
  - **Anomaly Detection:** Utilize anomaly detection systems to monitor containers for unusual activity that might indicate a security breach. These systems can help identify potential threats before they cause significant damage.

By following these action items, organizations can effectively secure their containerized and microservices-based architectures, ensuring that they can leverage the benefits of these technologies without compromising security. The key is to maintain a proactive approach to security, incorporating best practices, continuous monitoring, and real-time response capabilities to address potential threats as they arise.

9.3.2 Zero Trust Architecture (ZTA)

Trend:

The zero trust architecture (ZTA) model is rapidly gaining traction in cybersecurity. At its core, the principle of Zero Trust is "never trust, always verify", meaning no user or device, regardless of whether they are inside or outside the organization's network, should be automatically trusted. Instead, every access request must be authenticated, authorized, and validated before being granted access to network resources. This shift from traditional perimeter-based security models to a more granular, identity-centric approach is becoming increasingly popular as organizations recognize the limitations of conventional security paradigms in today's dynamic threat landscape.

Challenges:

Implementing zero trust principles in diverse Android app environments presents several challenges:

- **Robust Identity and Access Management (IAM):** A major challenge is the need for comprehensive IAM capabilities. This involves managing digital identities, controlling access to resources, and ensuring proper user authentication and authorization. Implementing robust IAM systems that can effectively manage these aspects across a wide range of devices and user contexts is crucial but can be complex and resource-intensive.
- **Continuous Monitoring and Authentication:** Zero Trust requires continuous monitoring and real-time authentication mechanisms to ensure that only authorized users and devices can access network resources. While essential for maintaining security, these mechanisms can introduce additional complexity and operational overhead. Managing multiple security configurations, encryption protocols, and access control lists (ACLs) can be daunting, and the increased scrutiny may lead to user friction, impacting the overall user experience.

Action Items:

- **Adopt a Zero Trust Mindset:** Embracing a Zero Trust mindset is fundamental to successfully implementing ZTA. This involves:

- **Never Trust, Always Verify:** Operate under the assumption that no user or device is inherently trustworthy. Every access request must be rigorously verified, regardless of its source or origin.
- **Dynamic Access Control:** Implement access controls that adjust in real-time based on context, such as user roles, device security posture, and the sensitivity of the application or data being accessed. This dynamic approach ensures that access permissions are always aligned with current security policies and risk assessments.

- **Leverage ZTA Technologies:** Utilize technologies and practices that support the principles of zero trust architecture:
  - **Identity and Access Management (IAM):** Deploy centralized IAM systems to efficiently manage user identities and access privileges. These systems should be capable of integrating with various applications and services, providing a unified platform for enforcing access policies.
  - **Micro-segmentation:** Implement micro-segmentation techniques to divide the network into smaller, isolated zones. This approach limits the blast radius of a potential security breach, preventing attackers from moving laterally within the network and accessing sensitive resources.
  - **Continuous Authentication:** Introduce continuous authentication mechanisms that verify user identity throughout the duration of an access session. This ongoing validation helps to detect and respond to potential security threats in real time, ensuring that only legitimate users maintain access to critical resources.

By adopting these strategies, organizations can effectively implement zero trust architecture in their Android app environments, enhancing security without compromising user experience. The key to success lies in balancing rigorous security measures with operational efficiency, ensuring that security policies are both robust and adaptable to evolving threats.

9.3.3 Supply Chain Security

Trend:

Supply chain security has become a critical focus in Android application development, as the software supply chain includes all components that go into an application, such as third-party libraries, dependencies, and vendor relationships. Organizations are increasingly recognizing the importance of verifying the integrity and security of these components, as vulnerabilities in any part of the supply chain can compromise the entire application. Ensuring a secure supply chain is essential to prevent attackers from exploiting weaknesses that could be introduced through these external components.

Challenges:

Mitigating supply chain risks in the context of Android applications presents several significant challenges:

- **Comprehensive Visibility and Control:** One of the main challenges is achieving comprehensive visibility and control over the software supply chain. This involves understanding all the components that make up an application, knowing their origins, and assessing their security postures. The complexity and scale of modern applications, combined with the diverse sources of third-party components, make it difficult to maintain this level of oversight.

- **Insecure Third-party Components:** Another challenge is the potential for vulnerabilities to be introduced into the application through insecure third-party libraries and dependencies. These components, if not properly vetted and monitored, can serve as vectors for attackers to exploit, leading to potential breaches and compromises of the application.
- **Complexity of the Android Ecosystem:** The Android ecosystem's complexity, with its numerous device manufacturers, operating system versions, and app distribution channels, adds another layer of difficulty to supply chain security. This diversity requires developers to be vigilant in managing and securing all parts of the supply chain to protect against vulnerabilities that may arise from any component.

Action Items:

- **Implement Supply Chain Security Measures:** Establish a robust set of security measures to manage the software supply chain effectively:
  - **Dependency Tracking:** Maintain a comprehensive record of all third-party libraries and dependencies used in your application. This tracking should include version numbers, source locations, and any known vulnerabilities.
  - **Software Bill of Materials (SBOM):** Create and maintain an SBOM, a detailed inventory of all components used in your application. An SBOM helps ensure transparency and accountability, making it easier to identify and address security issues as they arise.
  - **Vulnerability Management:** Proactively identify and address vulnerabilities within your application and its third-party components. Regularly update dependencies to the latest secure versions and apply patches promptly to mitigate risks.

- **Establish Vendor Risk Management:** Develop a process for assessing and continuously monitoring the security posture of third-party vendors. This process should include security assessments, regular audits, and contractual agreements that specify security expectations and requirements.

- **Utilize Automated Tools:** Leverage automated tools and services to enhance supply chain security:
  - **Continuous Monitoring:** Continuously monitor the software supply chain for vulnerabilities and suspicious activity. Automated monitoring tools can provide real-time alerts and insights, helping to detect and respond to potential threats quickly.
  - **Regular Auditing:** Conduct regular audits of the supply chain to identify and address potential security risks. Audits help ensure that all components meet security standards and that any changes or updates do not introduce new vulnerabilities.
  - **Incident Response Planning:** Develop and maintain an incident response plan to effectively address security incidents and supply chain attacks. This plan should outline clear procedures for identifying, containing, and mitigating threats, as well as communication protocols for notifying stakeholders.

By implementing these action items, organizations can enhance the security of their software supply chains, reducing the risk of vulnerabilities and protecting their Android applications from potential attacks. The key to success lies in maintaining comprehensive oversight, continuously monitoring for threats, and fostering strong vendor relationships based on security best practices.

9.3.4 Edge Computing Security

Trend:

Edge computing is a paradigm that shifts data processing closer to where data is generated at the network's edge. This architecture offers benefits such as faster processing, reduced latency, and improved efficiency. In the context of Android application security, securing communication between Android devices and edge nodes is becoming increasingly important. Ensuring the integrity and confidentiality of data processed at the edge is critical to maintaining security in distributed edge computing environments. As more data processing occurs on edge devices, robust security measures are essential to protect against potential vulnerabilities and attacks.

Challenges:

Implementing effective security measures in resource-constrained edge environments presents several challenges:

- **Balancing Security and Performance:** One of the main challenges is designing and implementing security controls that can withstand the computational power of edge devices without compromising performance and scalability. Edge devices often have limited processing power, memory, and battery life, which makes it difficult to deploy traditional security measures that are typically resource-intensive. Achieving a balance between robust security and optimal performance requires careful architectural design and the use of lightweight security protocols.
- **Diversity of Domain-Specific Knowledge:** Another significant challenge is the fragmented nature of security research in edge computing. Security researchers tend to focus on specific domains or aspects of edge computing, often without considering the broader system. This isolated approach can overlook security challenges that arise at the interaction boundaries between different domains, leading to incompatibility and redundancy issues. Integrating domain-specific security measures into the overall edge computing pipeline requires a holistic view that considers the unique requirements and constraints of each domain.

Action Items:

- **Implement Secure Communication Channels:** Protect data transmission between Android devices and edge nodes using robust security measures:
  - **Encryption Protocols:** Encrypt data in transit using strong encryption algorithms such as TLS (Transport Layer Security) to ensure confidentiality and integrity. Encryption protects sensitive information from being intercepted or tampered with during transmission.
  - **Secure Tunnelling:** Utilize secure tunnelling protocols, such as VPNs (Virtual Private Networks), to create encrypted connections between devices and edge resources. Secure tunnelling adds an additional layer of protection by encapsulating data packets within a secure channel.

- **Establish Strong Access Control and Authentication:** Implement comprehensive access control mechanisms to ensure that only authorized devices and users can access edge resources:
  - **Authentication Protocols:** Deploy robust authentication protocols to verify the identity of devices and users attempting to access edge resources. Multi-factor

authentication (MFA) can enhance security by requiring multiple forms of verification before granting access.

- **Authorization Controls:** Enforce strict authorization rules based on user roles and permissions to restrict access to sensitive data and functions. Role-based access control (RBAC) can help manage permissions and prevent unauthorized access.

- **Utilize Edge Security Tools:** Deploy security tools specifically designed for edge environments to protect against potential threats:
  - **Edge Security Gateways:** Deploy edge security gateways to monitor network traffic, filter malicious activity, and enforce security policies. These gateways act as a barrier between the edge network and external threats, providing a first line of defence against attacks.
  - **Intrusion Detection Systems (IDS):** Implement IDS to detect suspicious activity and potential security threats targeting the edge network. IDS can monitor network traffic for signs of intrusion or abnormal behaviour, enabling rapid response to potential attacks.

- **Adhere to Security Frameworks and Standards:** Follow industry best practices and standards to ensure robust security in edge computing environments:
  - **Edge Security Frameworks:** Leverage existing edge security frameworks, such as the OpenFog Consortium's reference architecture, the Cloud Security Alliance (CSA) and ETSI MEC Security Recommendations, to guide the development and implementation of security measures. These frameworks provide valuable insights and guidelines for securing edge computing environments.
  - **Industry Standards:** Follow industry standards for secure communication protocols and data encryption, such as TLS for secure communication and AES (Advanced Encryption Standard) for data encryption. Adhering to these standards helps ensure that security measures are aligned with best practices and are capable of protecting against known threats.

By implementing these action items, organizations can effectively secure their edge computing environments, ensuring that data processed at the edge remains protected from potential threats. The key to success lies in balancing security and performance, utilizing specialized security tools, and adhering to industry standards and frameworks to create a comprehensive and resilient security posture.

9.4 Privacy, Trust, and Human Factors

Security is not just about code and infrastructure. It is also about people, trust, and ethical responsibility. This section explores the growing emphasis on user-centric security approaches, including privacy by design, biometric authentication, and combating misinformation threats like deepfakes. It also recognizes the critical role users play in the security posture of apps. Building trust through transparency, education, and responsible design is essential as regulations tighten and user expectations rise.

9.4.1 Privacy by Design

Trend:

The concept of Privacy by Design is gaining significant traction, primarily driven by stringent privacy regulations such as the General Data Protection Regulation (GDPR) in the European Union (EU) and the California Consumer Privacy Act (CCPA) in the United States.

These regulations emphasize the importance of integrating privacy considerations into the design and development phases of Android applications. By mandating robust guidelines for the collection, usage, and protection of personal data, these regulations aim to safeguard user privacy and foster greater transparency and accountability in data handling practices.

Challenges:

While Privacy by Design offers substantial benefits in protecting user data, implementing it effectively presents several challenges:

- **Balancing Privacy with User Experience and Functionality:** One of the primary challenges is maintaining a seamless user experience and app functionality while ensuring stringent privacy protections. This balance can be particularly difficult in data-intensive applications, where large volumes of data are processed and stored. Developers must carefully design apps to protect user privacy without compromising usability or performance, a task that often requires innovative solutions and careful consideration of user needs.
- **Navigating Technological and Regulatory Constraints:** Another significant challenge lies in the constraints imposed by existing technologies and platform rules. These include device hardware and operating systems, software development kits (SDKs), ad libraries, and app store review policies. These layers of complexity can create a substantial compliance burden as developers must navigate and adhere to a multitude of requirements and guidelines that may not always align with privacy-centric design principles.

Action Items:

- **Adopt a Privacy-first Design Approach:** Integrate privacy considerations from the outset of the development process to ensure that privacy is a core component of the application's architecture:
    - **Conduct Privacy Impact Assessments (PIAs):** Performing PIAs early in the development process helps identify and mitigate potential privacy risks before they become ingrained in the application's design. This proactive approach allows developers to address privacy concerns from the start rather than retrofitting solutions after issues have been identified.

- **Implement Privacy-enhancing Features:** Develop and incorporate features that prioritize and protect user privacy:
    - **Data Encryption:** Encrypt sensitive user data to protect it from unauthorized access or breaches. Encryption ensures that even if data is intercepted or accessed by unauthorized parties, it remains unreadable and secure.
    - **Data Anonymization:** Whenever possible, anonymize user data to reduce privacy risks. Anonymization involves removing or obfuscating personal identifiers, making it difficult to trace data back to individual users.
    - **User Consent Mechanisms:** Implement clear and informed consent mechanisms for data collection and use. Ensuring that users are fully aware of what data is being collected and how it will be used is crucial for maintaining transparency and building trust.

- **Adhere to Privacy by Design Principles:** Follow core privacy by design principles to guide the development process:

- **Data Minimization:** Collect only the data that is essential for the application's functionality. Limiting data collection reduces the risk of unnecessary exposure and simplifies compliance efforts.
- **Purpose Limitation:** Clearly define the purpose for which user data is being collected and ensure that it is only used for that specific purpose. This principle helps prevent the misuse of personal data and aligns with regulatory requirements.

By adopting these strategies, developers can effectively integrate Privacy by Design into their Android applications, ensuring compliance with privacy regulations while maintaining high standards of user experience and functionality. The key lies in embedding privacy as a fundamental component of the development process rather than treating it as an afterthought or secondary concern.

9.4.2 Biometric Authentication Mechanisms

Trend:

Biometric authentication, enhanced by advancements like 3D facial recognition and in-display fingerprint sensors, verifies identity using unique physical characteristics. With Android supporting a variety of biometric authentication mechanisms, particularly fingerprint and face recognition, the use of biometrics is becoming increasingly prevalent in mobile security. As these methods gain traction, it is crucial to safeguard user privacy while implementing biometric authentication mechanisms, given the sensitive nature of biometric data. Secure storage and transmission of this data are paramount to protecting users from potential privacy breaches.

Challenges:

Implementing biometric authentication features requires balancing security, usability, and privacy considerations, which presents several challenges:

- **Robust Security:** One of the main challenges is ensuring that biometric authentication mechanisms are robust and secure. This involves employing strong encryption methods to protect biometric data and implementing secure protocols for biometric data verification. Ensuring that biometric systems are resistant to spoofing and other attacks is also essential for maintaining security.
- **Usability:** Another challenge is ensuring that biometric authentication mechanisms are user-friendly. This involves designing intuitive user interfaces and providing clear instructions for users to ensure a smooth and seamless authentication experience. Balancing security with ease of use is critical, as overly complex systems can deter users and reduce overall adoption.
- **User Privacy:** Protecting user privacy is a significant challenge when implementing biometric authentication. This requires ensuring that biometric data is solely used for authentication purposes and is not shared with third parties. Additionally, organizations must comply with data protection regulations and implement privacy-preserving techniques to protect users' biometric information.

Action Items:

- **Implement Strong Authentication Methods:** Choose secure biometric methods that prioritize data protection and integrity:

- **Encryption:** Utilize Android's Keystore System to encrypt biometric data both at rest and in transit. Encryption ensures that biometric data remains confidential and secure, even if intercepted or accessed by unauthorized parties. Use APIs like Cipher and KeyGenerator, along with Android's new Identity Credential API and Privacy Sandbox technologies, to implement strong encryption protocols tailored for Android devices.
- **Hardware Security:** Leverage Android's trusted execution environment (TEE) or StrongBox Keymaster to isolate and protect biometric data. These hardware-backed security modules ensure that biometric information is stored and processed in a secure environment, reducing the risk of unauthorized access or tampering. Use Android's BiometricPrompt API to securely interact with biometric hardware while keeping data protected.

- **Apply Privacy-preserving Techniques:** Implement privacy-preserving protocols to protect users' biometric data:
  - **Data Anonymization:** Store biometric data in a non-identifiable format, such as a mathematical representation (e.g., cryptographic hashing), that cannot be easily linked back to a specific user. On Android, use the Keystore System to manage these anonymized representations, minimizing the risk of data misuse or privacy breaches.
  - **Trusted Execution Environment (TEE):** Process biometric data within Android's TEE, a dedicated, isolated environment that ensures sensitive information is handled securely. The TEE provides hardware-level isolation, preventing unauthorized access or tampering with biometric data during processing.

- **Conduct Comprehensive Security Testing:** Proactively identify and address vulnerabilities in biometric authentication systems:
  - **Security Assessments:** Conduct regular security assessments using tools like Android Lint and Google Play Protect, and evaluate the overall security posture of the biometric authentication system. These assessments help identify potential weaknesses and ensure compliance with Android's security best practices and standards.
  - **Penetration Testing:** Perform penetration testing to simulate real-world attacks and identify potential exploits in the biometric authentication implementation. This testing helps to uncover vulnerabilities that could be exploited by attackers, enabling developers to strengthen security defences.

- **Collaborate with Experts:** Engage with experts to enhance the security and privacy of biometric authentication mechanisms:
  - **Biometrics Experts:** Partner with biometrics experts to ensure that the chosen methods are secure, reliable, and resistant to attacks. Expert guidance helps in selecting and implementing the most effective biometric technologies for specific use cases.
  - **Privacy Advocates:** Collaborate with privacy advocates to develop solutions that comply with data protection regulations and respect user privacy. Working with privacy experts ensures that biometric authentication systems are designed with privacy in mind, minimizing the risk of data breaches and legal issues.

By implementing these action items, organizations can develop robust biometric authentication mechanisms specifically for Android applications. These mechanisms will provide secure, user-friendly, and privacy-respecting solutions by combining Android's strong technical safeguards (e.g., Keystore System, TEE, BiometricPrompt API) with comprehensive security testing and expert collaboration. The key is to adopt a balanced approach to biometric security while adhering to Android's unique architecture and security frameworks.

9.4.3 Deepfakes

Trend:

The rapid advancement of deepfake technology, fuelled by significant developments in artificial intelligence (AI) and machine learning (ML), has led to a rising prevalence of deepfake content across various digital platforms, including Android applications. Deepfakes are AI-generated media, such as images, videos, and audio recordings, that convincingly depict events or scenarios that never occurred. With the increasing availability of sophisticated AI algorithms and accessible tools, malicious actors can easily create deepfake content, posing a substantial threat to the integrity and trustworthiness of multimedia assets within Android applications.

Challenges:

Detecting and mitigating deepfake content in Android applications presents several complex challenges:

- **Increasing Sophistication of Deepfake Algorithms:** Deepfake algorithms are continuously evolving and improving in sophistication, making it progressively more challenging to distinguish between genuine and manipulated media. As these algorithms become more advanced, even high-quality detection systems can struggle to identify subtle manipulations.
- **Volume and Variety of Multimedia Content:** Another significant challenge is the sheer volume and diversity of multimedia content generated and consumed on Android devices. With millions of images, videos, and audio files being shared daily, effectively monitoring and analysing all content for deepfakes becomes a daunting task, requiring substantial computational resources and advanced detection techniques.
- **Potential Consequences of Undetected Deepfakes:** The potential consequences of failing to detect deepfakes, such as misinformation, identity theft, and reputational damage, underscore the critical importance of addressing this emerging threat. Undetected deepfakes can erode public trust, cause financial losses, and harm individuals and organizations, making robust detection and prevention measures essential.

Action Items:

- **Adopt a Multi-layered Approach:** A comprehensive strategy is required to effectively address deepfakes in Android security:
  - **Content Verification:** Use blockchain, digital watermarking, and cryptographic hashing to verify media origin and integrity. These techniques can help ensure that media content has not been tampered with and can serve as a first line of defence against deepfakes.
  - **AI-based Detection:** Deploy next-generation detection algorithms that utilize transformer models, multi-modal analysis (combining visual, audio, and temporal features), and real-time detection capabilities to identify sophisticated deepfake manipulation. These algorithms can analyse media content for signs of tampering, such as inconsistencies in lighting, facial expressions, or audio-visual synchronization, which are common in deepfake content.

- **User Education:** Educate users on critical media consumption habits and how to spot potential deepfakes. Providing guidance on recognizing deepfakes, such as looking for unnatural movements, inconsistencies, or artefacts, can empower users to be more discerning and reduce the impact of malicious content.

- **Foster Collaboration with Security Experts:** Collaboration is essential to staying ahead of the evolving deepfake threat landscape:
  - **Advancing Detection Techniques:** Work with researchers, security experts, and developers to continuously improve deepfake detection algorithms. Regularly updating detection models with new data and techniques helps keep pace with advancements in deepfake technology and improves the accuracy and reliability of detection efforts.
  - **Establishing Standards:** Collaborate with industry partners to develop industry-wide standards and best practices for deepfake detection and prevention in Android apps. Establishing standardized approaches ensures consistency and reliability across different platforms and helps build a unified front against deepfake threats.

By implementing these action items, organizations can enhance their ability to detect and mitigate deepfake content, protecting the integrity of multimedia assets and maintaining user trust in Android applications. The key to success lies in adopting a multi-layered approach that combines advanced detection techniques, user education, and collaboration with experts to effectively counter the evolving threat of deepfakes.

9.5 Disruptive and Frontier Technologies

Looking ahead, disruptive technologies are poised to redefine the security landscape. This section dives into frontier areas such as quantum computing, extended reality (XR), and blockchain, where each presenting new paradigms, capabilities, and threat models. While these innovations offer immense potential, they also demand a forward-thinking approach to security. Anticipating their impact today is crucial for developing resilient, future-ready Android applications.

9.5.1 Quantum Computing Threats

Trend:

The emergence of quantum computing presents a substantial threat to traditional cryptographic algorithms and security protocols currently used in Android application security. Quantum computers possess extraordinary capabilities in solving complex problems, such as factorizing large numbers and computing discrete logarithms, tasks that underpin the security of many widely used encryption techniques. As quantum computing technology advances in power and capacity, it poses a significant risk to the digital infrastructure and cloud-based systems that rely on these traditional cryptographic methods. The potential of quantum computers to undermine well-established encryption techniques necessitates a proactive approach to developing quantum-resistant security measures.

Challenges:

Adapting cryptographic algorithms and protocols to withstand the computational power of quantum computers while maintaining compatibility and efficiency with existing systems poses several challenges:

- **Compatibility and Efficiency:** Transitioning to quantum-resistant cryptographic (QRC) algorithms involves more than just developing new mathematical techniques. It requires ensuring that these new algorithms are compatible with current systems and can be implemented without significantly impacting performance or requiring extensive changes to existing infrastructure. Balancing security, compatibility, and efficiency is a complex task that requires careful planning and coordination.
- **Uncertainty of Quantum Advancements:** While quantum supremacy has been demonstrated in specific computational tasks, cryptographically relevant quantum computers (CRQCs) capable of breaking current encryption remain years away, though the timeline continues to accelerate with recent advances. This makes it challenging for organizations to know when to implement quantum-resistant measures. Preparing too early might lead to unnecessary costs while waiting too long could leave systems vulnerable to quantum attacks.

Action Items:

- **Invest in Quantum-resistant Cryptography (QRC) Research:** Organizations should proactively invest in the research and development of QRC solutions to prepare for the quantum era:
  - **Supporting Research Institutions:** Provide funding and resources to academic and research institutions working on developing QRC algorithms. Supporting this research can accelerate the discovery of effective quantum-resistant techniques that can be implemented across various platforms, including Android.
  - **Collaboration with Industry Partners:** Collaborate with industry partners and standards organisations, such as the U.S. National Institute of Standards and Technology (NIST) during its Post-Quantum Cryptography (PQC) standardization process, to develop and implement QRC solutions. This collective effort ensures a cohesive, forward-looking approach to addressing quantum threats.

- **Explore and Implement Post-Quantum Cryptography:** Adopt post-quantum cryptographic primitives, such as those being standardized by NIST, to resist quantum attacks. Some promising approaches include:
  - **Lattice-based Cryptography:** This approach utilizes mathematical structures called lattices for secure key generation and encryption. Lattice-based algorithms are considered strong candidates for post-quantum cryptography due to their resistance to quantum attacks and their versatility in supporting various cryptographic functions.
  - **Hash-based Cryptography:** Relying on cryptographic hash functions to build secure algorithms, hash-based cryptography offers a simple yet effective method for creating quantum-resistant digital signatures.
  - **Multivariate Cryptography:** This method employs complex mathematical problems with multiple variables to create secure encryption schemes. Multivariate cryptography is another potential avenue for developing quantum-resistant algorithms that can be used in Android applications.

- **Stay Informed on Quantum Advancements:** Continuously monitor developments in quantum computing and cryptographic research to stay ahead of emerging threats:
  - **Proactive Approach:** By staying informed about the latest advancements in quantum computing, organizations can identify potential threats early and implement mitigation strategies before quantum computers become capable of breaking current cryptographic algorithms.

- **Adaptation as Needed:** Be prepared to adapt security protocols and algorithms as new information about quantum computing capabilities emerges. This flexibility ensures that security measures remain effective against evolving threats and can be updated or replaced as needed.

By taking these steps, organizations can prepare for the potential impact of quantum computing on Android application security. The key is to proactively invest in research, explore and implement quantum-resistant cryptographic techniques, and maintain awareness of advancements in quantum technology to stay ahead of potential threats.

9.5.2 Extended Reality (XR) Security

Trend:

As extended reality (XR) technologies, including virtual reality (VR), augmented reality (AR), and mixed reality (MR), become more integrated into the Android ecosystem, ensuring the security and privacy of these immersive experiences is increasingly critical. XR offers highly interactive and engaging experiences that merge the digital and physical worlds. With the growing adoption of AR and VR applications on Android devices, the need to secure these experiences against potential threats is becoming more urgent.

Challenges:

Addressing security vulnerabilities unique to XR environments presents several challenges:

- **Protection of Spatial Tracking Data and Immersive Content:** One of the primary challenges in securing XR environments is the need for specialized security measures to protect spatial tracking data and immersive content delivery. Spatial tracking data, which captures a user's movements and interactions in the physical world, is sensitive information that can be exploited if not properly secured. Additionally, the delivery of 3D visuals and immersive experiences involves transmitting substantial amounts of data that could be targeted by attackers aiming to intercept or manipulate content.
- **Integration with Existing Network Infrastructures:** Another significant challenge is the integration of XR technologies with existing network infrastructures. This process can be complex and costly, requiring extensive modifications to ensure that XR applications function securely and efficiently. Furthermore, the immersive nature of XR introduces new types of cyber threats, such as spoofing or manipulating virtual environments, which need to be anticipated and mitigated.
- **AI-Enhanced Attacks:** The integration of AI in XR environments creates new attack surfaces including malicious AI models, compromised spatial computing algorithms, and AI-powered social engineering within immersive environments.

Action Items:

- **Implement Spatial Computing Security:** Deploy specialized security measures for spatial mapping data, eye-tracking information, and neural interface data that are increasingly collected by modern XR systems.
- **Implement Strong Data Transmission Security:** To protect sensitive data within XR environments, robust security measures must be adopted:
  - **Access Controls:** Utilize granular access controls to restrict unauthorized access to user data collected in XR environments. This includes implementing role-based

access controls and ensuring that only authorized users and devices can access sensitive information.

- **Encryption:** Encrypt data transmitted between XR devices and servers to protect sensitive information in transit. Strong encryption protocols, such as TLS (Transport Layer Security), should be used to ensure that data is secure from interception or tampering.

- **Utilize Privacy-enhancing Technologies:** Incorporate privacy-preserving techniques to protect user data in XR environments:
  - **Differential Privacy:** Implement differential privacy by adding statistical noise to user data, thereby protecting individual privacy while preserving the data's usefulness for analytics and insights.
  - **Federated Learning:** Use federated learning to train machine learning models on user devices without sharing raw data with a central server. This approach minimizes privacy risks by keeping sensitive data on the device, reducing the potential for exposure or misuse.

- **Foster Collaboration with Industry Partners:** Work closely with industry partners to enhance XR security:
  - **XR Platform Vendors:** Collaborate with XR platform vendors to ensure a secure development environment for XR applications. This partnership can help establish standardized security practices and provide developers with the tools and resources needed to build secure applications.
  - **Security Researchers:** Engage with security researchers to stay updated on emerging threats and develop best practices for XR security. Collaborating with the broader security community can provide valuable insights into new attack vectors and effective mitigation strategies.

By implementing these action items, organizations can enhance the security and privacy of XR experiences, protecting users from potential threats while fostering trust in these innovative technologies. The key is to combine strong technical safeguards with proactive security testing and collaboration, ensuring a comprehensive approach to XR security.

9.5.3 Blockchain Integration

Trend:

Blockchain technology, a distributed ledger system that records transactions across multiple computers, has revolutionized various industries and is increasingly being integrated into mobile app development. Blockchain holds significant potential to improve data security and reliability due to its decentralized nature and use of cryptographic techniques, making it extremely challenging for hackers to alter or corrupt data. Traditional apps often store data on centralized servers, making them more susceptible to attacks. In contrast, blockchain-based apps distribute data across a network of nodes, reducing the risk of a single point of failure and enhancing overall security.

Challenges:

While blockchain technology offers numerous security benefits, it also introduces specific challenges that must be addressed to ensure safe and effective integration:

- **Smart Contract Vulnerabilities:** One of the main challenges associated with block-chain integration is the potential for vulnerabilities within smart contracts. Smart contracts are self-executing agreements with the terms directly written into code, auto-mating processes and reducing the need for intermediaries. However, bugs or flaws in smart contracts can lead to serious security issues, such as funds being locked or stolen. Ensuring the security of smart contracts is crucial to prevent these types of vulnerabilities.
- **Weaknesses in Consensus Algorithms:** Another challenge lies in the weaknesses of consensus algorithms, which are used in blockchain networks to validate transactions and maintain the integrity of the ledger. Some consensus mechanisms can be vulner-able to specific types of attacks, such as the 51% attack, where an entity gains control of the majority of the network's mining power, potentially disrupting the network's operation and compromising security.
- **Layer 2 and Cross-Chain Vulnerabilities:** The growing adoption of Layer 2 scaling solutions and cross-chain bridges introduces new attack vectors including bridge exploits, rollup vulnerabilities, and interoperability security risks.

Action Items:

- **Conduct Thorough Security Audits:** Before integrating blockchain features, it is essen-tial to perform comprehensive security assessments to identify and address potential vulnerabilities:
  - **Smart Contracts:** Use formal verification and rigorous audits to ensure smart con-tracts are bug-free and secure before deployment. Regular audits can help identify vulnerabilities early and prevent exploitation.
  - **Decentralized Applications (DApps):** Perform security assessments of DApps that interact with blockchains to ensure they function as intended without exposing security risks. This includes evaluating the security of both the blockchain interac-tions and the application's broader ecosystem.
  - **Consensus Mechanisms:** Understand the security implications of the chosen block-chain platform's consensus mechanism. Assessing the strengths and weaknesses of different consensus algorithms helps in selecting the most secure option for the specific application use case.

- **Utilize Monitoring and Auditing Tools:** Implement blockchain monitoring and audit-ing tools to enhance security and quickly respond to potential threats:
  - **Anomaly Detection:** Use tools to identify unusual activity or suspicious transac-tions within the blockchain network. Early detection of anomalies helps prevent potential security breaches and ensures the integrity of the blockchain.
  - **Security Incident Response:** Develop and maintain robust security incident response protocols to proactively detect and respond to potential security inci-dents in decentralized ecosystems. This preparedness is crucial for minimising the impact of any security breaches that do occur.

- **Foster Collaboration with Security Experts:** Partnering with security experts is essen-tial for staying ahead of emerging threats and ensuring the secure integration of block-chain technology:
  - **Blockchain Experts:** Collaborate with blockchain developers and security profes-sionals to gain insights into best practices for secure blockchain integration. This collaboration helps in identifying potential risks and implementing effective miti-gation strategies.

- **Security Community:** Stay informed about emerging threats and vulnerabilities in the blockchain landscape by engaging with the security community, following security advisories, and adhering to industry best practices. Continuous learning and adaptation are key to maintaining a strong security posture in the rapidly evolving field of blockchain technology.

By implementing these action items, organizations can effectively integrate blockchain technology into their Android applications, leveraging its security benefits while mitigating potential risks. The key is to combine thorough security assessments, secure coding practices, proactive monitoring, and collaboration with experts to ensure a robust and secure blockchain implementation.

Looking Ahead

As the landscape of Android security continues to evolve, developers must remain proactive in adopting emerging technologies and methodologies. The rapid pace of DevOps, the integration of security tools in CI/CD pipelines, and the rise of automated security testing highlight the industry's shift toward a more resilient development process. At the same time, sophisticated security paradigms such as zero trust architecture, runtime application self-protection, and mobile threat defence are becoming essential in mitigating risks posed by increasingly complex attack vectors. The adoption of containerization, microservices, and edge computing further emphasizes the need for security to be embedded at every stage of application development and deployment.

Looking ahead, the convergence of artificial intelligence, quantum computing, and extended reality will present both opportunities and challenges for securing Android applications. AI-driven threat detection, continuous authentication, and deepfake countermeasures will play crucial roles in combating evolving threats. Meanwhile, privacy-by-design principles, supply chain security, and blockchain integration will help establish greater trust and transparency in mobile ecosystems. As these advancements take shape, developers must not only embrace new security frameworks but also foster a culture of continuous learning, collaboration, and user awareness. By staying ahead of emerging threats and proactively integrating security best practices, the Android development community can build more secure, privacy-focused, and resilient applications for the future.

For Product Safety Concerns and Information please contact our EU
representative GPSR@taylorandfrancis.com
Taylor & Francis Verlag GmbH, Kaufingerstraße 24, 80331 München, Germany

www.ingramcontent.com/pod-product-compliance
Lightning Source LLC
Chambersburg PA
CBHW080902220326
41598CB00034B/5454